Russian Theoretical Thought
in Music

Russian Music Studies, No. 10

Malcolm Hamrick Brown, Series Editor

Professor of Music
Indiana University

Other Titles in This Series

Russian Theoretical Thought in Music

Edited by
Gordon D. McQuere

UNIVERSITY OF ROCHESTER PRESS

First published 1983 by UMI Research Press
an imprint of University Microfilms International
Ann Arbor, Michigan 48106

Transferred to digital printing 2009 by the University of Rochester Press

University of Rochester Press
668 Mt. Hope Avenue, Rochester, NY 14620, USA
www.urpress.com
and Boydell & Brewer Limited
PO Box 9, Woodbridge, Suffolk IP12 3DF, UK
www.boydellandbrewer.com

Cloth ISBN-10: 0-8357-1457-8
Paperback ISBN-13: 978-1-58046-319-5
Paperback ISBN-10: 1-58046-319-3

Library of Congress Cataloging-in-Publication Data

Russian theoretical thought in music / edited by Gordon D. McQuere.
        p. cm. — (Russian music studies; no. 10)
    Includes bibliographical references and index.
    ISBN: 0-8357-1457-8 (hardcover: alk. paper)
        1. Music—Soviet Union—Theory—History. I. McQuere, Gordon
    D. II. Series.

    ML300 .R77 1983
    781'.0947—dc19
                                                            83009097

A catalogue record for this title is available from the British Library.

This publication is printed on acid-free paper.
Printed in the United States of America.

Contents

Introduction

To those whose knowledge of Russian music theory is limited by lack of Russian language skill to the few works that have been made available in English in recent years, perhaps only the names of Joseph Yasser, Joseph Schillinger, Sergei Taneev, and (more recently) Boris Asafiev are familiar. The present volume, which consists of essays by American scholars who are conversant with the Russian tongue and who are knowledgeable about music theory, will change that circumstance radically. In this brief introduction I will first say a few words about each of the six articles and then offer a general observation on the collection and its subject matter.

Nicolas Schidlovsky's essay, "Sources of Russian Chant Theory," traces the history of Russian research on Russian Orthodox chant from the earliest times to the present, providing an authoritative critique which will be of special interest to scholars of various other branches of ecclesiastical song, in particular to students of the Byzantine Greek repertory from which the Russian chant originated. In the course of the essay, the author addresses certain issues which are—as is the case with other essays in the collection—peculiarly Russian, such as the deleterious Western influences which began with the reign of Peter the Great. At the conclusion of his detailed consideration of musical practice and theory, in which paleographic studies naturally play a central role, the author suggests new ways in which further research might be pursued to fruitful ends.

In his study, "Varvara Dernova's System of Analysis of the Music of Skryabin," Roy J. Guenther provides a comprehensive view of that theorist's approach, first locating it correctly with respect to other theoretical approaches to Skryabin's music (for example, the quartal harmony explanation and the acoustic basis so prominent among Russian theorists during the early Soviet period). As a student of Tiulin and as a recipient of Yavorsky's influence, Dernova stands squarely in the middle of a line of theoretical activity (one hesitates to say tradition) that seems to be uniquely Russian. To the present-day reader Dernova's model of musical structure will be of considerable interest, particularly as framed by Professor Guenther, who in the final section of his essay presents his own very informative analyses of Skryabin's music based upon the ideas and terminology of Dernova. Here as in the other articles, the glossary of terms is very useful to the neophyte.

A major figure in modern Russian music theory receives very thorough consideration in Gordon D. McQuere's "The Theories of Boleslav Yavorsky." Yavorsky developed a complicated system of modes employing tritone resolutions and semitone voice leading, certain ideas relating pitch and rhythmic structures, and a concept called intonation, which was the predecessor of Asafiev's more general concept by the same name discussed by Professor McQuere in his article on that theorist in this collection.

The author's expertise is evident throughout the article as he leads the reader through the complexities of Yavorsky's thought as represented in the 1908 publication, *The Structure of Musical Speech,* and extending to his later work in speculative music theory, the goal of which was the development of a universal theory of music. Although Yavorsky was a student of Taneev it appears that he was influenced to a greater extent by the early nineteenth-century Belgian theorist, F.J. Fétis, by the twentieth-century Austrian-Swiss theorist Ernst Kurth, and, as might be expected, by the nineteenth and early twentieth-century writer, Hugo Riemann, whose impact upon Russian music theory was extensive.

Ellon Carpenter's large-scale survey, "Russian Music Theory: A Conspectus," which covers the period from about 1800 to 1950 will be of special interest to contemporary music theorists, documenting as it does the considerable vitality of music-theoretic impulses despite all the obstacles, among them language, isolation from the West, wars, internal political developments following the October Revolution, and the repressive effect of the Union of Soviet Composers after its founding in 1932.

The survey is divided into specific periods, of which the pre-revolutionary span from 1900 to 1917 is particularly interesting. The post-revolutionary developments within the academies and especially within the extraordinary Institutes is documented with authority, and the reader will find intriguing some of the notions that proliferated, for example, "metrotechtonic analysis." The material on the development of theoretical ideas, cross fertilization, and influences from the West is very informative. Readers familiar with Western music theory will perhaps be startled to learn that Richter and Prout were highly influential in Russia, while the name of Heinrich Schenker appears to be totally absent from the Russian literature.

Professor Carpenter's second contribution to the collection, "The Theories of Taneev, Catoire, Conus, Garbuzov, Mazel, and Tiulin," first takes up the work of each of these early twentieth-century theorists separately and then puts their work and the work of persons associated with them into focus with respect to subsequent Soviet music theory. Of the six men, Taneev is presented as the seminal figure, the first to carry music-theoretic thought beyond the immediate pedagogical concerns that characterize work in previous eras. The discussion of Taneev contains an extensive and valuable commentary on the generative algorithms in *Convertible Counterpoint,* the single published work by that author, then extends the discussion of his ideas by drawing upon material from correspondence and other sources. Here, as in the other articles, the interaction with Western European writings is of considerable interest. For example, Taneev's notion of unifying tonality more than hints at Schenker's global concept, which, of course, was not fully developed during Taneev's lifetime. (The mediating factor would appear to be the eighteenth-century treatise of Kirnberger.) Similarly, in the discussion of the theoretical work of Catoire the pervasive influence of Bussler's work on form is apparent, a book that was highly regarded in Germany and Austria by, among others, Alban Berg.

The comments on Conus's theory of metrotechtonicism (1924) are of interest, not only because the idea is hierarchical, suggesting the influence of Hauptmann and perhaps others, but also because by including the criticism of Conus's ideas by the musical figures Taneev and Arensky they demonstrate the seriousness with which eminent figures of the time considered theoretical ideas.

Of the remaining theorists, Tiulin seems to have had the greatest influence on subsequent music theory, and this is chronicled in detail, consistent with the definitive and comprehensive view presented by the author.

In the essay "Boris Asafiev and *Musical Form as a Process,*" Gordon D. McQuere presents a finely detailed study of the only published book on music theory by the man who is regarded as the father of Soviet musicology. The central portion of the article is a chapter-by-chapter abstract of *Musical Form as a Process* and *Intonation,* supported by very careful explanations of Asafiev's neologisms and focussing upon a clarification of Asafiev's notion of intonation, a rather difficult and elusive abstract concept. As do the authors of the other articles, Professor McQuere expends considerable effort to assure that Asafiev's work is correctly placed in its Russian setting with respect to significant and relevant historical events and to the music which the theoretical ideas are intended to illuminate, with the result that the essay is a significant contribution to our understanding of Russian culture in general.

The present volume is certain to become a standard reference work in the field of music theory, offering a panorama of the development of music-theoretic thought in Russia from early times up to the present. It is authoritative, informative, and incisive and should be of interest to all who are concerned with theoretical ideas about music and who are sufficiently open-minded to evaluate critically the work described by the four highly qualified contributors.

—Allen Forte

Russian Music Theory: A Conspectus

Ellon D. Carpenter

In comparison with Western music theory, a Russian theory of music emerged relatively recently. Apart from the theory of Russian chant, the first written sources of which date from the fifteenth century, a distinctly Russian theory of music cannot be said to have existed until the latter half of the nineteenth century. Until that time music theory in Russia was dominated by foreigners and foreign works. Moreover, Russian music theory attained significant levels of achievement only in the twentieth century, particularly in the years 1900 to 1950. Whereas in the late eighteenth and nineteenth centuries theorists in Russia, both foreign and Russian, emphasized primarily the practical, pedagogical aspects of music theory, in the early twentieth century they shifted the emphasis towards speculative, explanatory, and philosophical theory. The theories developed during this time provided the foundation for subsequent Soviet music theory; an understanding of their basic approaches and principles proves essential for the full understanding and appreciation of present-day musical theoretical thought in the Soviet Union. For these reasons, the theories of the first half of the twentieth century arouse great interest among musical scholars, both Russian and Western.

In the same way, though, that a study of this period increases our appreciation of contemporary Soviet music theory, so too does a study of the previous periods, which encompass the general development of a Russian theory of music, deepen our comprehension of the great strides made subsequently. Thus, part one of this article traces the development of music theory in Russia from its beginnings up to 1900; part two examines the events and developments in the years 1900 to 1950.

Part I: 1680–1900

1680–1800: Origins

Russia's first written music theory, the theory of chant (*znamennyi raspev* or "chanting by signs"), dates from the fifteenth century, the time when Russia finally emerged from its "dark ages," the nearly century and a half of Mongol rule. Chant was the primary form of professional, written music in Russia until the seventeenth century, when information about the new musical devices and styles of the West, namely the five-line staff, square notation, and polyphony, began to penetrate into Russia from Poland through the Ukraine. Polyphony and the new notational methods were eventually adopted for use in the church, thus ending the long tradition of chant and beginning a new era of Western-style polyphony.

The main source of information about this new style of polyphony, called *partesnoe penie* [part singing], was a Polish-trained composer and theorist from Kiev, Nikolai Diletsky (c. 1630–1690), who brought it to Russia in the 1670s and whose treatise, *Musikiskaya grammatika* [Musical grammar], translated into Russian in Moscow in 1681, provided Russians with a primer on how to compose part-song.[1] With this work commenced the development of a music theory based not on monophonic Russian chant, which already had its own tradition of theory, but on imported Western-style, multi-voiced (both polyphonic and homophonic) music.[2]

Yet Diletsky's *Grammar* remained the only written theoretical text on multi-voiced music in Russian for nearly a century. Although it provided aspiring Russian composers of church music a written means for learning about the techniques of composition, it did not create a theoretical tradition or lead to the appearance of additional treatises or, more specifically, compositional manuals of church music in Russia.[3]

In the latter seventeenth century, not only Western forms of sacred music but also Western secular music began to gain popularity in Russia as a result of the growing interest among Russians in the foreign musical entertainments brought into Moscow by the many diplomats, merchants, craftsmen, engineers, and the like, who settled there. Peter the Great (reigned 1682[9]-1725) in particular encouraged such interest. Although his personal involvement in music was limited to singing in church and a taste for Western military bands, his societal and educational reforms and innovations and his open espousal of Western practices and traditions in all areas set in motion a turning to the West that in music scarcely abated for a century or more after his reign.

It was not Peter, though, but his niece and eventual successor Anna Ivanovna (reigned 1730-1740) who began to import secular Western music— namely Italian opera—on a grand scale beginning in 1731.[4] After the establishment in 1736 of an imperial theater in St. Petersburg, performances of opera, as well as of ballet, chamber music, and orchestral music, became regular features in the capital.

The influx of foreign musicians needed for these performances continued throughout the eighteenth century. Most of the orchestral musicians, solo instrumentalists, singers, conductors, directors, and composers came from Italy. Anna had appointed Francesco Araja as her first maestro di capella, and her successors Elizabeth (reigned 1741-1762) and Catherine (reigned 1762-1796) continued the practice of appointing to this and similar posts prominent Italian composers such as Vincenzo Manfredini (maestro di capella, 1758-69 and 1798-99), Baldasarre Galuppi (maestro di capella, 1765-68), Tommaso Traetta (maestro di capella, 1768-75), Giovanni Paisiello (court composer, 1776-84), Giuseppi Sarti (maestro di capella, 1784-86 and 1790-1801), and Domenico Cimarosa (composer, 1787-90). The Spaniard Martin y Soler, in Russia from 1788 to 1806, was also court composer and maestro di capella, 1790-94.

Increasingly, though, Russian performers began to fill the ranks of orchestras, choruses, and other groups, reflecting greater educational opportunities for native musicians in Russia. Aspiring musicians could learn their craft at the St. Petersburg Theatrical School (founded 1738, formally opened in 1779), the Academy of Arts in St. Petersburg (founded 1757, music classes initiated in 1764), and the school of the Imperial Court Capella [Impereticheskaia Pridvornaia Pevcheskaia Kapella] (founded in 1738). Led by the Corps de Cadet (founded in 1732), which was the first secular school to offer a course in music, most educational institutions for Russian youth, such as gymnasiums, academies, institutes, and even Moscow University (founded in 1755) offered some sort of musical training. Such opportunities for nonprofessional study led to larger and more appreciative musical audiences and to growing numbers of musical amateurs, who performed and sometimes composed music for their own amusement.

Courses in thorough bass and composition were offered in some of these institutions. Most aspiring Russian composers, however, either went abroad to study in Italy or studied privately at home with foreign tutors. Three of Russia's first composers studied in Italy with Padre Martini: Dmitri Stepanovich Bortniansky in 1769-79, Maxim Sozontovich Berezovsky in 1765-73, and Yevstignei Ipatovich Fomin in 1782-86. Some Russian students of composition took lessons from visiting Italian composers. Before traveling to Italy, for example, Bortniansky studied with Galuppi. Martin y Soler and the Italian composer Antonio Sapienza (maestro di capella of the Imperial theaters, 1783-85) both taught at the St. Petersburg Theatrical School and the Smolnyi Institute (for nobelwomen) and gave private lessons as well. Sarti in particular had a number of Russian pupils, among them Artemy Lukianovich Vedel, Lev Stepanovich Gurilev, Stepan Ivanovich Davydov, Stepan Anikievich Degtiarev, and Daniil Nikitich Kashin.

During the reign of Catherine the Great, artistic development in Russia in the eighteenth century reached its peak. A native school of musical composition began to emerge, and the first publications on music appeared. Books by the German Jakob Staelin von Storcksburg (1712-1785), Russia's first music chronicler, the first collections of folk songs (by Vasily Fedorovich Trutovsky), and the first published theory books all date from the early years of her reign.[5] Russia's first commercial music publisher, Christian-Ludwig Weber, published translations of two foreign theory books in 1773, Georg Simon Löhlein's *Klavier-Schule,* and the anonymous *Essai méthodique.*[6] The *Essai méthodique,* which presents the bare rudiments of music, was directed to the young reader learning to read music. Löhlein's *Klavier-Schule,* though, constitutes the first important theory book on secular music available to Russian readers in their own language, and probably proved equally useful to amateurs, students of composition, and keyboard players.

These works represent two basic types of theory book in Russia up to 1830—books on thorough bass (Löhlein) and books on the rudiments of music or of elementary harmony *(Essai).* Of the three other theory books published in Russia in the eighteenth century, two, texts on thorough bass by Giovanni Paisiello and David Kellner, fall into the former category, and one, Demian Petrunkevich's *Manual for Young Males Studying Sight-Singing,* into the latter.[7] Because Petrunkevich was probably a Russian, his *Manual,* in addition to being the first manual of sightsinging published in Russia, achieves the distinction of being the first theory book of any sort written by a Russian.[8] It typifies nearly all the theory books written by Russians for the next seventy-eight years in that it is a short brochure containing only rudimentary information about music.

Thus by the end of the eighteenth century, the first steps towards the development of a Russian theory of music had been taken. A need for music theory caused by increasing numbers of performers, aspiring composers, and musical amateurs led to the publication of the first music theory books in Russian. An opportunity for music education was provided, although Russia did not yet have an institution of higher musical education where instruction in all areas, including theory and composition, could be obtained. In the 1780s, Potemkin, a powerful ally of Catherine's, officially established a Russian Music Academy with Giuseppi Sarti as its head, but unfortunately the Academy never actually came into existence. The founding of such an institution finally took place nearly eighty years later.

1800–1860: Foreign Influence

For the first sixty years of the nineteenth century, Russia remained without an institution of higher musical education. Lacking local means, Russians continued to look to foreign schools, teachers, and textbooks. In the field of theory and composition, if a student was not able to travel abroad (an option available to only a few, such as Glinka and the Rubinstein brothers, all of whom studied with the Berlin theorist Siegfried Dehn), he could turn to foreign instructors living in Russia. If instructors were not available or if he could not afford lessons, he could turn to translated foreign theory books or other works written by foreigners "in Russian for Russians," as one author stated,[9] which were generally designed for self-instruction. The great majority of theory books appearing during this period in Russia were published with this goal. Consequently, the foreign works chosen for translation and publication and those written in Russia by both foreigners and natives continued in the practical and pedagogical tradition established earlier.

The most significant of these works were written by foreign pedagogues in St. Petersburg or in Moscow, a number of whom had made their way to Russia in the late eighteenth and early nineteenth centuries.[10] The German theorists Johann-Heinrich Miller (1780-1827) and Johann Leopold Fuchs (1785-1853), the Czech theorist Joseph Hunke (1802-1883), plus Heinrich Bollet, Franz Xavier Gebel (1787-1843), Karl Arnold (1794-1873), Yury Arnold (1811-1898), Vikenti Lemokh, and others provided virtually the only means for serious theoretical study in Russia, either through private lessons or their public lectures. As is obvious from the names, a change took place in the source of pedagogical influence. The eighteenth-century Italian influence in theory pedagogy shifted in the nineteenth century to a German influence. The students of these theorists included many notables. Among Miller's pupils, for example, were the dramatist and poet Alexander Sergeevich Griboedov, the philosopher Prince Vladimir Fedorovich Odoevsky, the composer Alexander Alexandrovich Aliabev, the composer Alexei Nikolaevich Verstovsky, and the composer Matvei Wielhorsky (who also studied with Martin y Soler in St. Petersburg and Cherubini in Paris). Fuchs's many pupils included the music lexicographer Modeste Dmitrievich Rezvyi, the teacher and lecturer Yury Arnold, and for a few unsuccessful lessons, Glinka.

Although a growing number of Russians studied theory or composition, relatively few taught the subjects, and even fewer produced theory textbooks. Of the twenty-two theory books published in Russia between 1800 and 1860— eight between 1800 and 1829 and fourteen between 1830 and 1860—only three were written by Russian authors. All three fit the description of earlier theory books by Russians; they are brief works devoted to either the rudiments of theory or elementary harmony. Ivan Komendatov's *Basic Principles of Harmony* discusses chords, intervals, enharmonism, scales, and cadences; Fedor Drobish's *Beginning Knowledge in Practical Music* provides information about notation, keys, scales, ornaments, and rhythm; and Ivan Gabertsettel's *Tables of All the Chords* provides reference tables for thorough bass figurations.[11]

The remaining works, by non-Russians, are divided among books on thorough bass (six), composition (seven), harmony (two), music fundamentals (two), and general books that include theory as only one of several topics (two). Of these, eight are translations, among which Fétis's *La Musique mise à la portée de tout le monde* is the only familiar work by a well-known Western theorist.[12] Eleven books were written by foreigners in Russia: Vincenzo Manfredini (1737-99), the Hungarian Gustav Gustavovich Hess de Calvé

(1784-?), Fuchs, Gebel, K. Arnold, the Italian Nicolas Giulini, Lemokh, and Hunke. Given the lack of substantive Russian theory books from this period, these theorists provide the best information concerning music theory in Russia from 1800 to 1860. Also, with the exception of Manfredini and Fuchs, who published theory works in their respective native countries as well, these theorists wrote and published only in Russia, where they spent most of their lives. They have not been adequately recognized in other historical studies of theory.

Manfredini, Hess de Calvé, Fuchs, and Hunke provided the best of these Russian works.[13] Because Manfredini's *Regole armoniche* contained the most complete theoretical information yet available in Russian, it quite possibly served as a basic textbook for Russian students of theory and composition.[14] In addition to information on music fundamentals, elementary harmony, and figured bass covered in previous works, Manfredini included more detailed information on advanced harmony such as derived chords and modulation and, most importantly, on counterpoint and fugue, including part-writing rules, and simple, figurative, and double counterpoint. He also added segments on singing, vocal ornamentation, and various musical styles. Such a wide scope of theoretical topics (including counterpoint, a subject not treated since Diletsky's book in 1681) had not before been available in Russian.

Even though Manfredini wrote *Regole armoniche* while in Russia, he published it only in Italy. It is not known whether he intended ever to publish it in Russia, for it was translated and published there only after his death. Therefore the distinction of writing the first original theory book in Russian by a foreigner goes to Gustav Hess de Calvé. Although born a Hungarian, he accepted Russian citizenship in 1814, when he was thirty, a step he may have taken for reasons related to his professional work in Kharkov as a factory director and expert on mineralogy. His avocation, however, was music. He performed as a pianist, organized numerous concerts in Kharkov, composed music, and wrote critical reviews on music and the theater. His major work, *The Theory of Music,* encompasses both the aesthetic and theoretical elements of music as well as instruments, style, form, and the history and ethnography of music. His goal was "to give to the amateurs of music in Russia the means to the best understanding of their art."[15] Through his book he hoped to promote a greater appreciation of music, towards which, he said, Russia had a natural disposition, to foster an awareness among Russians of the need for better opportunities for music education, and to provide the necessary information for musical composition, which too many young virtuosos arrogantly attempted without proper theoretical knowledge.

Hess de Calvé placed great importance on the need for instruction in theory for composers, and devoted two hundred pages, or one-third of the length of the book, to a detailed presentation of the rules of composition as they were found in professional Western music. He consulted the works of numerous Western theorists ranging from Guido d'Arezzo to Albrechtsberger and most often mentioned the ideas of Kirnberger and Rameau. But rather than putting together a compendium of past theoretical thought or creating a new theory based on that legacy, Hess de Calvé derived his theory of harmony in large part from Kirnberger's writings, most notably *Die Kunst des reinen Satzes in der Musik.*[16] This places Hess de Calvé well within the mainstream of Western theoretical thought of the late eighteenth century. He adopted Kirnberger's theories of basic or essential chords, of essential and nonessential dissonances, of the consonant and dissonant properties of the six-four chord, and of the fundamental bass. He also adopted Kirnberger's biases against many of Rameau's theories, although, like Kirnberger, Hess de Calvé accepted Rameau's theory of chord inversion and the idea of fundamental bass.

Unfortunately, instead of following Kirnberger's logical sequential development of topics, Hess de Calvé's manner of presentation reverts to that used by theorists of the figured bass school. As did Heinichen, Mattheson, Löhlein, and others before him, Hess de Calvé classified all chords according to their intervallic construction. Like Mattheson, he discussed them in the numerical order of the lowest or most characteristic interval of the chords. Thus he began with what he called the second chord, or the 4/2 chord, and continued with the three-four chord, the four-six chord, the five-six chord, six chord, and seventh chord. However, this superimposition of Kirnberger's harmonic theories over an antiquated figured-bass approach resulted in a presentation that is incomplete and frequently illogical, placing, for example, the discussion of the basic seventh chord only after the discussions of all its inversions and those of the triad. Despite this and other drawbacks, Hess de Calvé's *Theory of Music* constituted a noteworthy achievement. No other theorist or writer about music in Russia had attempted to undertake such a large project solely for the benefit of his fellow countrymen. As he stated in the introduction, "We Russians still do not have one systematic work, adapted to current music."[17]

His efforts to enlighten Russians about music were not limited to Western professional music but extended to the folk music of their own country. Throughout the work, Hess de Calvé displays a predisposition towards the melody of native folk song, which indicates that he adopted not only Russian nationality, but its musical biases as well. In fact, he is remembered today more for his views on Russian music than for his derivative theoretical ideas.[18] His faith in the continuity and future of Russian music places him in the forefront of propagandists of Russian national music. He praised the oral tradition of folk song, called for the collection of folk songs and dances, and believed fervently in the future of Russian music. Yet his work must be counted as an important contribution to Russian theoretical literature as well, since it included the first and most exhaustive treatment of the subject written especially for Russians in their own language. *The Theory of Music,* a transitional work, helped to bridge the gaps between thorough bass, which was still popular in Russia in the early nineteenth century, and newer methods of harmony, and between the foreign tradition of professional music and the native tradition of folk music.

The 1830s brought several significant changes in Russian musical life, most importantly the appearance of Mikhail Glinka as Russia's foremost composer. His first opera, *Zhizn' za tsaria* [A Life for the Tsar], premiered in St. Petersburg in 1836. Another notable trend, begun already in the 1820s, involved a quickening pace of intellectual musical life in Russia. The new generation of intellectuals, literary men knowledgeable about music and able to write about it, included Prince Vladimir Odoevsky, Dmitri Yurevich Struisky, Osip Ivanovich Senkovsky, Alexander Dmitrievich Ulybyshev, Count Mikhail Yurevich Wielhorsky, Alexei Nikolaevich Verstovsky, and Feofil Matveevich Tolstoi. Through their writings, concerts, and other supportive activities, these men did much to encourage the continuing growth of musical life. An important scholarly undertaking from this decade, in which Prince Odoevsky took part, was the compilation and publication of the first Russian encyclopedia, *Entsiklopedicheskii leksikon* [The Encyclopedic Dictionary], begun in 1835. Unfortunately, only seventeen volumes—through the letter *d*—were published, the last in 1839; yet in those seventeen volumes were contained over one hundred articles on musical topics, including at least fifteen on theoretical topics alone.[19]

Pedagogical activity in music increased. Music classes in the various institutions and private lessons continued, while the theatrical schools in Moscow and St. Petersburg and also the Imperial Court Capella became centers for a higher level of musical education. In the late 1830s, the school of the Capella began offering classes in orchestral instruments, and soon added classes in piano and composition. At the same time, some instructors, among them Karl Domanevsky, Yury Arnold, Joseph Guillou, and Heinrich Bollet, began to give public lectures and courses in music theory and history. Thorough bass and counterpoint, the two subjects deemed necessary for composition, constituted the most frequently offered topics. Hoping to entice a wide audience, Domanevsky, for example, offered his lectures in three different languages—Russian, German, and French. But according to newspaper accounts, only a few dedicated and earnest pupils attended these courses, which continued throughout the 1840s, but apparently ceased during the 1850s.[20] In 1859, the newly formed Russian Musical Society began to sponsor similar classes, thus providing a foundation for the St. Petersburg Conservatory in 1861.

While the emphasis in subject matter in the public courses and lectures focused on thorough bass and counterpoint, the emphasis in the theory books was shifting towards harmony or general composition (a subject covering form or counterpoint in addition to harmony). From 1773 to 1830, six works on thorough bass and two works on composition were published; from 1830 to 1870, five works on thorough bass, seven works on composition, and two works on harmony were published. The most significant of these are two works by Johann Leopold Fuchs, which fall under the category of general composition, although the emphasis in both is predominantly on harmony, and two works, one on composition and one on harmony, by Joseph Hunke. Through their writings and pedagogical activities, these two theorists in particular exerted great influence on the development of music theory in Russia in the pre-Conservatory era.

Fuchs, who came to Russia from his native Germany probably shortly after the turn of the century, wrote his first work *A Practical Guide to the Composition of Music,* at the urging of his students and friends, who considered his method of teaching superior.[21] Like Hess de Calvé, Fuchs wrote this book specifically for Russians. His translator and former pupil Modeste Dmitrievich Rezvyi (1807-53) testified:

> Having spent a large part of his life in Russia, he wished out of gratitude to it to be useful primarily to *Russian Artists;* thus he conceived the idea of publishing this work in the Russian language.... If the proferred guide, by a superlative and perfectly new system of presentation, by its brevity and clarity, proves useful to foreigners, then all the more it deserves the gratitude of Russian Artists, so deprived in theoretical works on the musical art. Knowing that classes in choir singing are numerous in Russia, Fuchs also wished to disseminate his work among them and so added a special article on Russian Church Song; this all the more compels us to recognize his book as our native work.[22]

Since Fuchs intended his book mainly for independent study in composition, he provided the most systematic, comprehensive, and advanced survey of harmonic principles yet available in Russian. The main topics include intervals, basic chords, the principles of part-writing and voice-leading, figured bass, the formation and use of chords (triad, seventh chord, ninth chord, diminished-seventh chord, augmented-sixth chord, augmented triad, and six-four chord), nonharmonic tones, related modes, modulation, cadences, rhythm, and form. Underlining his practical approach, Fuchs placed chapters devoted to exercises periodically throughout the text, but separated both the actual exercises and many of the examples from the main text into two separate notebooks, the first containing examples and problems, the second the solutions.

Except for the chapter on Russian church music, his ideas are derived from Western European theoretical thought. Fuchs was especially influenced by the theories of Gottfried Weber, whose idea of fundamental harmonies *(Grundharmonie),* first presented by Weber in *Theorie der Tonsetzkunst,* he adopted.[23] According to Fuchs (and Weber), the fundamental chords *(Grund-Akkord)* include three forms of the triad (major, minor, and diminished) and four types of seventh chord (those naturally occurring on G, A, B, and C). In essence no difference exists between this idea and the Kirnberger-Hess de Calvé idea of essential chords, for the subcategories are exactly the same. In Fuchs-Weber, all other harmonies are derived from these fundamental chords. This clear method of chord classification based on the most common and most representative types of chords "facilitated and simplified a study, which was once a boundless ocean."[24]

Other than Fuchs's detailed discussions of such topics as augmented-sixth chords and modulation, which had not been adequately presented by either Manfredini or Hess de Calvé, and his logical presentation, perhaps the most useful and ultimately influential section of his *Guide* was the four-page Russian-German dictionary of seventy-two musical terms compiled by his translator Rezvyi. Since Rezvyi had no Russian model for the text (he did not mention any other translations he might have consulted), he had to invent many Russian expressions for previously untranslated terms. His choices turned out to be so appropriate that most of his inventions or adaptations came to be standard in Russian musical vocabulary. As a result of this and other lexicographical works, Rezvyi is recognized today as the chief codifier of Russian musical terminology, especially of that pertaining to theory.[25]

Fuchs's *Practical Guide* became the first theory book to receive substantial reviews in the Russian press rather than just the publication announcement or cursory review accorded Manfredini's or Hess de Calvé's works. No doubt this was due in part to the stature and reputation of the author as a composer and pedagogue, and also to the growing numbers of journalists and writers knowledgeable about and interested in music theory. The paucity of such works in the Russian language up to that point also contributed to the heralding in the press of its arrival. The critic Alexander Ulybyshev, in fact, blamed the neglect of musical composition in Russia directly on the lack of any suitable textbooks on this subject in Russian, and praised Fuchs for having "the fantastic idea to state the fundamentals of music Science in a form understandable to our fellow countrymen."[26]

Another critic, Dmitri Struisky, a self-styled musical amateur, related why he, rather than a professional musician, reviewed the book, which he described as "the best of all published music theories in the Russian language": "Russian Artists to this day have not studied music Theory; nothing is expected from them. Foreign guest artists in large part are ignorant of the Russian language and they are poor prospects."[27] Struisky's reasons for the insufficiencies of Russian musicians in theory—the lack of adequate educational opportunities and the naturally quick but lazy Russian disposition—echoed Hess de Calvé's complaints of twelve years earlier. Concerning Fuchs's *Guide,* Struisky criticized mainly its order of presentation and choice of examples. He felt that the discussion of seventh chords, for example, was placed prematurely in the early discussion of fundamental chords, and belonged more properly in the later discussion of modulation; and he pointed to the use of examples technically incompatible with the level of subject matter being presented, resulting in the reader's exposure to a particular practice before it had been introduced and explained in the text.

Fuchs tacitly acknowledged the validity of such criticisms by the alterations he made in the second edition of his work, *A New Method Containing the Main Rules of Musical Composition.*[28] Changes in the format and content make this edition essentially a new work. Fuchs tightened the organization by grouping the material more logically into eleven chapters and by integrating the examples, which are greatly increased in number, into a clearer and more detailed text. In the most significant change regarding content, Fuchs replaced the supplement on Russian church song with a supplement on counterpoint, from which it may be inferred that Russian composition students were more interested in learning Western contrapuntal methods. Another striking difference between the two editions concerns Weber's fundamental harmonies, which Fuchs deemphasized in the later work (perhaps as the result of Struisky's suggestion). He separated the discussion of the seventh chord from that of the triad and made fewer references to "basic" or "essential" chords in discussions of such derived chords as the augmented-sixth chord.

Fuchs's *New Method* can be considered the first truly "modern" Russian harmony textbook of the nineteenth century, based on its subject matter and its logical, organized presentation. Fuchs's emphasis on a detailed yet simplified and practical approach also characterized all subsequent harmony textbooks—both foreign and Russian—that were well received in Russia. Fuchs was the first to write a successful and popular harmony textbook specifically for use by Russian theory students.

Eight years after the appearance of Fuchs's *New Method,* Joseph Hunke published his *Guide to the Study of Harmony,* which, like Fuchs's works, is a practical textbook containing many problems and questions with the solutions in a supplement.[29] To the list of topics covered by Fuchs, Hunke added only a discussion of scale and deleted any discussion of counterpoint, which he covered in a later volume. Although in format Hunke's *Guide* differs little from Fuchs's later work, in content Hunke departed significantly from Fuchs's approach. He expanded the idea of "essential" chords and developed a theory of chord connection and progression. In addition to the triad and seventh chord—the "essential" or "fundamental" chords of previous theorists—Hunke identified a third "basic" chord, the ninth chord. But Hunke's concept of basic chordal forms embraces not just those few fundamental chords such as the triad or seventh chord which may be altered to form other chords, but also essential and altered forms of the three basic chords. Therefore his list of basic chords includes five types of triad, six types of seventh chord, nine types of ninth chord, and eight additional types of seventh chord formed from dropping the root of the ninth chord (called "imaginary"). In a supplement he included two eleven chords. Hunke further grouped these chords into two classifications: "similar" chords are formed from notes within the tonality, and include the previous essential chords plus two dominant ninth chords and two imaginary seventh chords; "dissimilar" chords are formed from notes outside the tonality, and resemble the altered chords. In his classification the augmented triad is considered a dissimilar chord, even though it occurs naturally on III in both the melodic (ascending) and harmonic minor modes.

Hunke formulated a theory of chord connection and progression from the treatment of dissonances and leading tones, which resolve to the nearest half step in the scale. Hunke considered any note a half step above or below a scale note as a leading tone and stated, "The most natural progression of chords is that which follows the direction of the leading tone."[30] Hunke's unique approach to chord classification and connection presaged future developments in Russian music theory towards the end of the century: the overemphasis on the classification of chords or progressions or both in attempts to develop a more thorough yet systematic understanding of the complexities of late romantic harmonic language.

Hunke's other theoretical work was a composition textbook, *A Guide to the Composition of Music,* in three volumes, each devoted to a different topic—melody, counterpoint, and form.[31] Hunke therefore became the first theorist in Russia to write extensively on these subjects, melody in particular, which had previously received much less attention than the other two subjects. In the volume on counterpoint, Hunke discussed all types of conterpoint and numerous varieties of fugue and canon, and included many examples from the literature. In the volume on form, Hunke discussed briefly all types of instrumental and vocal music from the simplest to the most complex forms. All were amply illustrated with examples, including entire works, such as an analysis of Beethoven's String Quartet op. 18 no. 1.

Hunke's approach to melody encompassed its formal and compositional aspects and also its aesthetic and expressive qualities. He discussed the formal, hierarchic, and rhythmic structures of melody in a manner similar to Reicha in his *Traité de mélodie.*[32] Since his foremost aim in this volume, though, was to present the information necessary for melodic composition, he devoted much of the text to methods of melodic and motivic variation.

Such detailed treatments of melody, counterpoint, and form, although more common in the West, were unique in Russian theoretical literature. Obviously Hunke was acquainted with the theoretical works on form and melody by Reicha, A.B. Marx, and J.C. Lobe. Similar works on form by Russians did not appear until the 1890s, and translations of works by well-known Western theorists such as Marx and Bussler in form and counterpoint did not appear in Russia until the 1870s and 1880s.[33] Both of Hunke's works were reprinted in 1887, testifying to a continuing need for them years after their original publication.

Hunke was the last in the distinguished line of foreign theory writers and pedagogues who dominated music theory and its literature in Russia. Whereas in the eighteenth century these theorists were Italians and were composers first and theorists second, in the nineteenth century the theorists came from northern countries such as Germany, Hungary, and Czechoslovakia, and are remembered more as theorists than as composers. During this period the general focus of theoretical works shifted from books on thorough bass to general works covering several aspects of composition, and finally to more specific works on harmony or other separate elements. This last trend continued throughout the nineteenth century and into the twentieth century. In harmonic theory specifically, the general course of development moved from thorough bass and the intervallic identification of chords towards a means of simplification and organization, namely, the theory of "essential" or "fundamental" chords, which was prevalent in Russian theory for thirty years or more, through the works of Hess de Calvé and Fuchs. Towards the end of this period, the new developments of Hunke, such as the classification of basic chords and the theory of chord progressions through the half-step resolution, ended the use of the theory of essential chords and presaged new developments. Thus the period of foreign-dominated music theory in Russia was ending at about the same time that a new, more sophisticated theory of harmony was developing. These changes coincided with the founding of the St. Petersburg Conservatory, which probably more than any other event caused the rapid growth of a native Russian theory of music after 1860.

For Russia in general and the musical world in particular, the late 1850s had been years of great change. Russia's defeat in the Crimean War, the accession to the throne of the new tsar Alexander II in 1855, and the subsequent push toward modernization which resulted in the abolition of serfdom all contributed to a more liberal atmosphere and helped to create conditions favorable to new developments in the musical world, such as the founding of the Russian Musical Society in St. Petersburg in 1859. This organization two years later provided the basis for Russia's first music conservatory. Also, Glinka died in 1857, just as a new generation of composers—the Five or the "Mighty Handful"—was rising to take his place. Thus from a musical viewpoint, an era ended with the 1850s. While in some respects the 1860s may be seen as the inevitable culmination of the previous thirty years, in many more respects it is the beginning of a new age, an age in which Russian musicians, composers, educators, writers, and others came to excel in areas previously dominated by foreigners.

1860-1900: Russian Pedagogical Theory

Developments of the greatest significance for Russian musical life and education took place in this period, resulting in a Russian musical culture of worldwide recognition. Perhaps the most far-reaching of these involved Russian musical education and specifically the founding of the conservatories in St. Petersburg in 1861 and in Moscow in 1865. With this vital step, the founders—Anton and Nikolai Rubinstein, with the help of the Grand Duchess Elena and others such as Prince Odoevsky—provided Russian musicians with a professional musical education in their own language and with a legal and social standing—the rank of Free Artist—commensurate with that of professionals in the other arts.

The presence of the conservatories had an immediate effect on musical life in St. Petersburg and Moscow, increasing the number of concerts and also the number of disputes between the two musical factions. One faction, the conservative, European-trained musicians, grouped themselves around Anton Rubinstein in support of the conservatories. The more liberal, self-trained "Slavophiles," who grouped themselves around Mili Balakirev, included Alexander Serov and the composers of the Five; they disdained the conservatories. The strong antagonism of these groups resulted as much from personal animosity between Rubinstein and Balakirev and between Rubinstein and Serov as from ideological or musical goals, i.e., the Slavophiles versus the Westerners.[34] Nationalism did play a part in this dispute inasmuch as, once again, Russia had to depend on educational methods and professors brought in from the West. Such musical autodidacts as Serov, Vladimir Stasov, and Balakirev objected to the European conservatory model that Rubinstein used in the St. Petersburg Conservatory and to the continued influx of European musicians to promulgate their "scholastic, pedantic" methods in Russia. For example, the first theory professor at the Conservatory was a Pole, Nicholas Zaremba, who, having studied with A.B. Marx in Berlin, followed Marx's methods in his own classes, with the exception of counterpoint, for which he used a textbook of Heinrich Bellerman.[35] Serov and the others believed that such an approach to music education, particularly for composers, was unwarranted and would stifle inherent creativity. It would be better, they thought, to ignore lengthy and detailed work in such areas as counterpoint—especially the strict style—and harmony and to concentrate solely on the reading and playing of full scores by the great masters.

In a published attempt to promote support for the conservatories, though, Rubinstein called all Russian musicians "amateurs" and stressed particularly the need for theory education, which most such amateurs ignored.[36] In so doing, unfortunately, Rubinstein offended some of those he had hoped to persuade. These new opponents retaliated in print, Serov, Stasov, and Cui each writing articles against the conservatory; and they also took action. Balakirev and Gavriil Ioakimovich Lomakin, a composer and singing teacher, for example, formed their own school, the Free Music School, which concentrated on teaching large numbers of nonprofessionals the rudiments of theory and singing, and on performances of great choral masterworks, especially those by

Russian composers. Serov devoted several articles and lectures to his preferred method of theory education—score-reading—and to other theoretical topics.[37]

In support of Rubinstein and the strict, European conservatory approach to music education, Hermann Larosh, a critic and 1866 graduate of the St. Petersburg Conservatory, advocated in print the benefits of studies in strict counterpoint, followed by free counterpoint and harmony. Larosh believed that Russian students of composition especially needed to master these subjects for two reasons. Russia had imported its present style of music during the Baroque era, after the era of strict counterpoint had passed. Therefore, Russian composers needed to compensate for their lack of counterpoint background through concentrated study. Also, because Russia had not yet produced any great musical masters with the exception of Glinka (whom Larosh appears to have considered an anomaly), and lacked the means for music education, Russia needed to go through a period during which theoretical pedagogy and not composition predominated. This would repeat what Larosh interpreted in history as a period of theory—the medieval period—followed by a period of practice—the Renaissance. In order for Russian music to acquire the stature of European music, theory was a necessary prerequisite. He also argued that the study of strict counterpoint should precede the study of harmony, since harmony arose from a combination of voices in a contrapuntal setting, and not the reverse.[38] His argument fell on deaf ears for the most part, with the exception of Tchaikovsky and Taneev; at the conservatories, harmony, not counterpoint, continued to be the cornerstone of theory pedagogy for many years.[39]

The dispute continued through the 1860s and into the early 1870s. The conservatory opponents lost momentum in 1871 when one of their most eloquent spokesmen, Serov, died, and when one of the leading members of the Five, Nikolai Rimsky-Korsakov, became professor of composition at the conservatory. Two of the principals also removed themselves from the controversy: Rubinstein resigned as director of the St. Petersburg Conservatory in 1867, and Balakirev resigned his post at the Free Music School in 1874. In the end the conservatories were not damaged, but continued to flourish under the leadership of Mikhail Azanchevsky, who directed the St. Petersburg Conservatory from 1870 to 1876, and Nicholai Rubinstein in Moscow.[40] Indeed, all the prominent Russian theorists of this period—Tchaikovsky, Rimsky-Korsakov, Anton Arensky, Mikhail Ippolitov-Ivanov, Georgy Conus, and Sergei Taneev—were products of or were associated with one of the conservatories.

The founding of the conservatories in the 1860s marked a new era of Russian hegemony in music theory and composition. During this decade, though, developments in theory largely continued previous trends. While some significant foreign works were translated and published,[41] of far greater interest for the development of a native theory of music were the writings of

Prince Odoevsky and Alexander Serov. Although these two musicians possessed opposite sentiments regarding the value of a conservatory education, they nonetheless shared an interest in developing a theory of folk song and in theory in general, and both wrote numerous articles on the subject.

Odoevsky (1803-1869), a philosopher, litterateur, and musician with a special interest in Russian music, is generally considered one of the founders of Russian classical musicology. His own research in Russian folk song and chant aided his attempts to define the national character of Russian music, and to establish folk music and chant as subjects for scientific study. Odoevsky championed the original, unadulterated versions of folk song, instead of the "corrected," "Europeanized" versions by collectors knowledgeable in Western theory such as had been appearing since the 1770s.[42] He used them as source material for studying and developing a theory of this music. By concentrating on the original versions of both chant and folk song, Odoevsky was able to isolate the unique qualities of indigenous Russian music, qualities that distinguished it from Western music.

Odoevsky emphasized most strongly the difference between Western music and Russian song in tonal or modal construction. He found no concept of tonality such as in Western music, but rather modes [*glasy*] comparable to the Western medieval modes. He asserted that Russian melodic patterns are limited to narrow leaps—no tritones, sixths, or sevenths—and step-wise motion; harmony is limited to triads; and rhythm is capricious, asymmetrical, and irregular.[43]

Odoevsky eagerly studied Western theory, both from imported and Russian texts.[44] He became disenchanted, however, with certain restricting elements of pedagogical and practical theory such as the hegemony of the seventh chord and of four-part writing, neither of which he found in Russian folk song, and with other strictures concerning parallel intervals and cadences.[45] He felt that a recognition and use of modes by contemporary composers would enrich music and would advance the theory of music in general.[46] All the same, he believed strongly in the value of the study of music theory, including thorough bass and other Western approaches, despite his increasing displeasure with them, as part of a complete education for all musicians, not just theorists and composers.[47] He agreed with Rubinstein regarding the amateurish level of music knowledge among musicians and the inattention to theory prior to 1859.

Odoevsky's disappointment with the scholastic aspects of Western theory and his search for the natural laws of harmony led him to a study of acoustics. In his writings from the 1860s Odoevsky came to accept only acoustics, "the laws of musical phenomena," as the rational basis for musical science.[48] The appearance in 1862 of Helmholtz's book, *Die Lehre von den Tonempfindungen als physiologische Grundlage für die Theorie der Musik,* probably persuaded him finally to adopt this position. He repudiated the authority of all existing practical musical textbooks that did not embrace acoustics as the basis for theory, and limited himself to experiments in acoustics.[49]

The culmination of Odoevsky's research came in his 1868 publication, *Musical Grammar*.[50] Writing for the general reader who was interested in composing or in reading special research about it, but who was largely technically ignorant, Odoevsky discussed the fundamentals of music in terms of acoustics and of his theory of native Russian song, showing how the modes of the latter (and scales and modes of general Western music as well) are derived through the former. This progressive approach to music theory with its emphasis on acoustics and on modes of native Russian song unfortunately did not become established in Russian traditional theory pedagogy and was hardly even noticed by his contemporaries.[51] Yet in the twentieth century, theorists produced especially fruitful research in the areas of modes and acoustics, showing Odoevsky to be an originator of studies in these areas. Through his support of Russian music and musical life, the conservatories, and theory pedagogy, and his writings and criticism on theory and music in general, Odoevsky contributed greatly to the development of a native tradition in music and music theory.

Alexander Serov, as a composer, critic, theorist, and lecturer, was also an active participant in these developments. Despite his opposition to music education in the conservatories, and particularly to strict theoretical instruction, his writings on theory are part of the development of a native Russian music theory, both of professional and of secular Russian folk music. His theory of folk music, developed as part of an attempt to establish Russian folk music as a subject suitable for scientific research, identified its modal structure as being related, not to the medieval modes as in Odoevsky's theory, but to the modes of ancient Greek music.[52] Thus, while Odoevsky assumed the octave as the natural boundary for the folk modes, Serov identified a seven-degree scale, formed from two conjunct diatonic tetrachords. Octave-based scales, formed from two disjunct tetrachords, also occurred, but far less frequently. In addition, all three types of tetrachord, including the type 1/2-1-1, rare in Western-European music, share equal importance in Russian folk song. Other aspects of Serov's theory are similar to Odoevsky's.

Serov also dabbled in Western theory.[53] More importantly, though, in the course of his career as a critic, he developed a method for analyzing vocal-dramatic or other programmatic works that fused aesthetic and dramatic analysis with the analysis of thematic content, a method which foreshadowed the analytical techniques developed by some twentieth-century theorists such as Boris Asafiev and Lev Mazel.[54]

The studies of Russian folk song and chant of the 1860s were the culmination of many years of research by Serov, Odoevsky, and Dmitri Razumovsky, the first modern scholar of Russian chant.[55] But outside of Serov's and Odoevsky's contributions, which were not entirely reliable, the theory of Russian folk song did not receive serious attention from Russian theorists until the twentieth century.[56] The development of a Russian theory of music similar to that of Western theorists was a greater challenge. Therefore, the Russian theorists who were being trained in the new conservatories turned their attention to writing books modeled on Western practice, following the examples set by Hess de Calvé, Fuchs, and Hunke.

The first Russian to produce a full-length theory book of this sort was the conservatory-trained Tchaikovsky. His textbook, *A Guide to the Practical Study of Harmony,*[57] although in the Western theoretical tradition, is unique and based on his own practice and experience, not on theoretical statements of any other theorist, Russian or Western. Even so, Tchaikovsky's aim in writing this book was a purely practical one; he had no need or desire "to bring to musical science a new system, new views," to provide "food" for the curiosity of "lovers of theoretical research and musical philosophical reasoning," or "to add a single note to the treasure of music theory."[58] He even resolved not to call his "modest, specially pedagogical work by the fine-sounding name of theory."[59] He believed that some day musical science would "finally find the key to the theoretical explanation of harmonic mysteries," but considered theories of harmony existing in his time to be "constructed on sand.... Nothing so confuses the beginner, nothing so weakens his energy and zeal for the study of music, as verbose, specious, prolix, though perhaps also witty, lofty phrases about harmony, encountered in some textbooks and lavished by some teachers."[60] He realized

> that in the rich musical pedagogical literature [my guide] would pass as an undiscovered phenomenon. But in Russia, having scarcely one good translated work in this area (I speak about the *Textbook of Harmony* of Richter), I am bold to think that my work, pursuing serious practical goals in the matter of music, has some useful information; it is called for by the obvious need for textbooks.[61]

Therefore the student and the development of the student's abilities in composition became of paramount concern to Tchaikovsky. Rather than inventing a new and complex harmonic system or inundating the student with a myriad of rules, Tchaikovsky chose to develop a simple and systematic order for the principles of chord formation and voice-leading. Since theory can state these principles only in a general way, Tchaikovsky throughout the book encouraged the student to rely on his own musical instincts when "exceeding the limits of defined theory."[62] Thus Tchaikovsky advocated an empirical approach to the study of harmony.[63]

Tchaikovsky devoted much of the text, an entire section in fact, including a chapter on strict contrapuntal part-writing, to the principles of voice-leading, reflecting his belief—influenced by Larosh—that voice-leading is "the entire essence of harmonic technique."[64] For Tchaikovsky, rules were useful only up to a point. In a passage concerning the retention of the common tone between chords, for example, he stated: "The unconditional use of the rule is necessary in so far as it does not hinder us in achieving our main goal: a thorough development of the freedom of the voices."[65] And, "The true beauty of harmony requires the full independence of each voice."[66] At times, melodic necessities may override harmonic laws:

> Though deduced by way of experience and confirmed by musical feeling, harmonic laws are indisputable in their essence; but in a fully developed harmony, melodic requirements of voices are so strong, that they frequently justify decisive deviations from these laws. The predominance of the melodic element and the subordination of chord combinations to it are expressed particularly clearly by incorrect resolutions of dissonant chords.[67]

As a means of assuring the attainment of creative independence on the part of the student, Tchaikovsky included numerous examples of the harmonization of a given melody, as well as of figured bass. Unlike Richter, for example, whose exercises in melodic harmonization indicated the chord choices, Tchaikovsky left chord choice entirely up to the student. He did restrict the student at first to triads and certain dissonant chords, but later allowed the student full use of all available, justifiable harmonic combinations. This new emphasis on melodic harmonization was further encouraged by Rimsky-Korsakov in his textbook, and it soon became common practice in textbooks in Russia.

In further contrast to Richter, who at first concentrated only on the three principal triads, Tchaikovsky introduced all the triads of the major mode at once and allowed the student to use them all from the very first exercise. However, he gave the names only for the three principal triads—tonic, dominant, and subdominant—explaining that they constitute "the essence of the harmony of the major scale" because of their deep inner connections.[68] These connections exist as a result of the position in the circle of fifths of the keys that they represent as tonic triads. He considered the minor triads (which he did not name) to be less significant than the major triads because, even though they contain an equally close connection among themselves, they are weak and soft. But the minor triads are related to the major triads, just as the major and minor modes are related, and Tchaikovsky grouped them accordingly:

> Thus we may divide the entire mass of major and minor triads of the major mode into three groups, with two triads in each: the *tonic* from triads on the 1st and 6th degrees, the *dominant*, from triads on the 5th and 3rd, and the *subdominant*, from triads on the 4th and 2nd degrees.[69]

He did not include the diminished triad on the seventh degree. Tchaikovsky's groupings are not, however, to be considered functional; they merely represent the relationship between the triads and their connections through common tones.[70]

Tchaikovsky also grouped the seventh chords according to their inner construction, although in a different way. He considered the seventh and ninth chords to be dissonant because they contain dissonant intervals. The ninth chord is thus "doubly dissonant." These dissonant chords are not independent; they receive their support and justification only in the following chord, the chord of resolution. He considered the dominant seventh chord the most important one, and separated it from the other seventh chords. He called the remaining seventh chords "sequence chords," since they most frequently appear in sequences. Those in the major mode he placed in three groups based on intervallic structure: I^7 and IV^7 (major triad with major seventh); II^7, III^7, and VI^7 (minor triad with minor seventh); and VII^7 (diminished triad with minor seventh). He regarded the sequence chord on VII in both major and minor as a ninth chord without the lowest note, in order to determine its proper resolution.

Tchaikovsky introduced new interpretations of modulation and the augmented-sixth chord into Russian harmonic theory. He changed the nomenclature and definition of modulation, directing the emphasis more towards the means of modulation, i.e., how it is effected, and further refining the entire theoretical concept. Previous theorists had defined modulation in three ways; chord changes within a given key were called "modulation"; a temporary sojourn into a new key was called "deviation"; a definite change of key involving a lengthier process to move into and establish the new key was called "transfer."

Tchaikovsky distinguished between "direct" modulation and "passing" modulation. A "direct" modulation is completed by one chord, the dominant of the new key, that has the ability immediately to leave the previous key and move into a new key, to which it belongs exclusively. It therefore does not function as a common chord. A "passing" modulation is completed by one or more secondary keys. He declined to set down any limits for the passing modulation, either concerning the choice of key into which to modulate or the length or time to spend in any of the secondary keys, leaving such decisions up to the personal taste and musical instincts of the student. In Tchaikovsky's view, then, modulation is brought about either by a single chord, which is not a common chord, or a series of chords.

Theorists usually construct the augmented-sixth chord on the lowered sixth degree of the scale and resolve it either to the dominant or to the tonic six-four chord. Tchaikovsky constructed this chord on the lowered second degree and resolved it to the tonic in root position. An augmented-sixth chord that most theorists would consider to be in F major or F minor, for example, Tchaikovsky considered to be in C major. But when analyzed in C major, his augmented-sixth chords—Db-F-G-B, Db-F-B, and Db-F-Ab-B, equivalent in F major to the French, Italian, and German augmented-sixth chords—are in fact altered V or VII chords. The French sixth chord, for example, is the second inversion of the dominant-seventh chord in C major with a lowered fifth.[71] Tchaikovsky claimed the construction of these chords on the lowered sixth degree to be incorrect for this reason:

> The use of chords with the augmented sixth on the lowered sixth degree is no more than a modulatory deviation into the mode of the dominant, which, not being a conclusively expanded cadence, does not produce the impression of a full modulation. But one has only to combine one of these chords with a triad on the *dominant* of an extended cadence in order to feel the modulatory character of the chord with the augmented sixth on the lowered sixth degree.[72]

Thus Tchaikovsky considered the augmented-sixth chord on the lowered sixth degree to be endowed with a strong modulatory character. He did admit to one augmented-sixth chord constructed on the lowered sixth degree that resolved to a tonic six-four chord—the augmented-sixth chord with a doubly augmented fourth, A♭-C-D♯-F♯ in C.

Tchaikovsky's treatment of the augmented-sixth chord and its resolution, with the exception of the fourth version, did not become part of Russian harmonic theory.[73] Several other of his pedagogical ideas, though, continued to be used at the Moscow Conservatory. The introduction of all the triads at an early stage, the harmonization of melody, the changed views towards modulation, and the study of "accidental" chords after the study of diatonic chords and modulation helped to establish the "Moscow tradition" in the teaching of harmony, with its source the *Guide to the Practical Study of Harmony* by Tchaikovsky.[74]

Tchaikovsky's textbook significantly aided the development of a Russian theory of music. It provided a needed Russian model for a practical, pedagogical textbook, a type of theory book that continued to dominate. Following Tchaikovsky's example, Russian theorists began writing theory books in greater and greater numbers. Of the eight-three theory books published in Russia during this period, fifty-eight, or nearly 70 percent, were by Russians. Nearly half of this number, twenty-seven, appeared in just one decade, the 1890s.

Many Russian theorists continued the tradition established by Petrunkevich and Komendatov and wrote textbooks on elementary theory. Beginning with Odoevsky's *Grammar*, twenty-nine works of this sort were published during this forty-year period. Nicholai Kashkin, one of the first theory instructors at the Moscow Conservatory, wrote the first of these works to achieve regular use and a popularity comparable to that of Tchaikovsky's work in the field of harmony. The harmony textbook ranks next in number; eighteen such works by Russians, beginning with Tchaikovsky's, were published. These two types of books account for 81 percent of all Russian theory books published from 1860 to 1900; of the foreign works published in Russian, only about one-third were of these types.

Usually mentioned alongside Tchaikovsky's book as another innovative contribution to Russian music theory is Rimsky-Korsakov's *Practical Manual of Harmony*.[75] Rimsky-Korsakov conceived of writing a textbook of harmony after he began teaching the subject at the Imperial Court Capella in 1883 and after numerous discussions with his Conservatory colleague, Anatoly Lyadov to whom the textbook is dedicated.[76] To Rimsky-Korsakov, the major deficiencies of existing harmony textbooks consisted in their lack of "practical directions and gradual pedagogical methods for the harmonization of melodies and good choice of chords... [and for] modulation. Textbooks... avoid the main basis of modulation—the relatedness of keys and common chords."[77] He felt that his textbook, although perhaps deficient in other areas, at least succeeded "in stating the methods of melodic harmonization and of modulation rather completely and gradually as well, moving from simple means to the more complex."[78]

He described his unique approach in his autobiography:

> Four scales were taken as the foundation of harmony: major and minor natural, and major and minor harmonic. The first exercises consisted in harmonizing the upper melodies and basses with the aid of the principal triads alone: the tonic, the dominant, and the subdominant and their inversions. With so scant a stock of chords, the rules of part writing proved very accurate. Through exercises in harmonizing melodies, with the aid of only the principal steps, the pupil's sense of rhythmic and harmonic balance and tendency towards the tonic were developed. Later to the principal triads there were gradually added accessory tones, the dominant chord of the seventh and the other chords of the seventh. Figured bass was entirely done away with; on the other hand, to exercises in the harmonization of melodies and basses was added independent writing of half-periods from the same harmonic material. Later followed modulation, the science of which was based on the relationship of keys and the modulatory plan, and not on the external connection (through common tones) of chords foreign to one another. In this way modulation proved ever natural and logical.[79]

Thus his approach involves four elements: (1) a different scale system, (2) an initial restriction to the three principal triads, (3) an emphasis on melodic harmonization and independent writing with no figured bass, and (4) an innovative approach to modulation, based on key relationships and a modulatory plan. Rimsky-Korsakov's emphasis on melodic harmonization had already been foreshadowed by Richter and Tchaikovsky; but Rimsky-Korsakov's contribution concerned not only an increased stress on melody and his use of actual chorales as melodic material, but also a more systematic approach to chord choice and to modulation. In contrast to Tchaikovsky, who relied on an intuitive, empirical approach to harmonization and to composition generally, Rimsky-Korsakov did not hesitate to set forth additional rules and guidelines.

Rimsky-Korsakov's four modes included the newly introduced harmonic major mode, which has a lowered sixth degree: C D E F G A♭ B C.[80] Although he referred to the melodic minor mode occasionally in the text, he did not include it here. The use of the harmonic major mode in particular increases the melodic and harmonic possibilities usually available to the composer, introducing such chords as the minor triad on IV, the diminished triad and the half-diminished seventh chord on II, and the diminished seventh chord on VII. But Rimsky-Korsakov discounted the use of the augmented triad on VI and the seventh chords on IV and VI, which contain augmented triads.

He considered the principal chords to be the triads on I, IV, and V, and the dominant seventh chords of the major and minor modes. He called all the remaining triads and seventh chords "accessory chords." For the first fourteen lessons, Rimsky-Korsakov restricted the pupil to the three primary triads. In his subsequent discussions of the accessory chords, he presented the following groupings: to dominant harmony belong the diminished triad on VII (first inversion), the half-diminished- and diminished-seventh chords on VII, and the V^9 chord; to subdominant harmony belong the minor triad on II (both fundamental and first inversion), the minor subdominant triad, and the diminished triad on II (first inversion), the latter two from the harmonic major mode. These groupings carry a certain connotation of function, unlike Tchaikovsky's groups of related triads, especially in the uses of the diminished triad on VII and the minor triad on II, which Rimsky-Korsakov illustrated in the position of—and therefore as substitutions for—the dominant and the subdominant, respectively. Given his emphasis on the primary triads and on these groupings, it is not difficult to view Rimsky-Korsakov's approach to harmony as incipiently functional.

Rimsky-Korsakov changed the order and degree of key relatedness and used it as a basis for modulation. Since Fuchs, nearly all theorists in Russia had discussed this question, some more elaborately than others. Fuchs and Tchaikovsky, for example, merely distinguished between nearly related and remotely related tonalities; other theorists devised up to six degrees of relatedness, all determined generally through common tones and the similarity of key signatures.[81] Over the years, with one exception, the tonalities differing from the main tonality by three or fewer accidentals in their key signatures came to be recognized as related. Usually the major dominant and subdominant and the relative and parallel minor were considered as in the first degree of relatedness. The minor supertonic and mediant and the major supertonic and lowered supertonic were considered in the second degree. And the minor dominant and subdominant (the latter with a difference of four accidentals) and the major submediant and lowered mediant were considered in either the second or third degree of relatedness. These are illustrated in the top circle in figure 1. Rimsky-Korsakov broke with this tradition, stating that the six tonalities whose tonic triads are included in the given tonality are to be considered as nearly related or in the first degree of relatedness. These include the usually accepted dominant, subdominant, and relative minor, as well as the minor subdominant, mediant, and supertonic, which had heretofore been considered in the second or third degree of relatedness.[82] The minor subdominant is included as a result of the lowered sixth degree of the harmonic major scale. In the minor mode, a similar occurrence takes place with the inclusion of the major dominant as well as the major submediant and subtonic (in the tonality of A minor, that would mean E, F, and G major). The parallel minor, generally considered to be in the first degree of relatedness, is relegated by Rimsky-Korsakov to the second degree of relatedness, as are a host of other tonalities never before included in the second degree of relatedness, each one, however, sharing at least one common triad with the given tonality.

The two circles of fifths (fig. 1) clearly illustrate the difference. In the top circle, showing the traditional degrees of key-relatedness (indicated by the numbers next to the letter names), only twelve of the possible twenty-three tonalities are related to C major. In the bottom circle, representing Rimsky-Korsakov's system, six more tonalities have been added, two to the first degree and four to the second degree.[83]

The methods for modulating to tonalities in the first degree of relatedness revolve around the use of a common chord. For modulation involving tonalities in the second degree of relatedness, Rimsky-Korsakov introduced the idea of the modulatory plan. Devising a modulatory plan consists of determining which triads are common to the tonalities involved and then finding the most satisfactory choice and order of the intermediate key(s), based on these triads as tonic chords. The choice of intermediate key(s) is then determined by the intervallic distance between the modulatory and intermediary tonalities. A variety of intervallic distances is the most desirable combination.

Rimsky-Korsakov classified all the tonalities not in the first or second degrees of relatedness to a given tonality, all of which do not share any common triads with it, as remote tonalities (for example, in C major: G♭ and B major, E♭, G♯, C♯, and F♯ minor). A modulatory plan to arrive in these tonalities would use nearly related tonalities as intermediate tonalities. Rimsky-Korsakov gave some examples of good and bad modulatory plans involving remote tonalities. For example, in modulating from C major to E♭ minor, the plans C-f-D♭-e♭ and C-d-b♭-e♭ are good plans, since the intervallic distances between the tonalities vary; the plans C-F-B♭-e♭ and C-f-b♭-e♭ are poor, since the intervallic distances between each adjoining pair of tonalities are perfect fourths.

Rimsky-Korsakov divided modulation into two categories—gradual and sudden. A gradual modulation is the type just discussed; a sudden modulation involves false progressions and enharmonism. Key relatedness may also be used to effect a sudden modulation, but it is not the primary means. Rimsky-Korsakov also discussed nonchromatic and chromatic modulation as subdivisions of gradual modulation. A chromatic modulation involves a change of mode in the course of the modulation. He also discussed the previously accepted types, transition (transfer) and digression (deviation), as

Fig. 1   Top circle of fifths: traditional degrees of key relatedness.
          Bottom circle of fifths: Rimsky-Korsakov's system of key
          relatedness

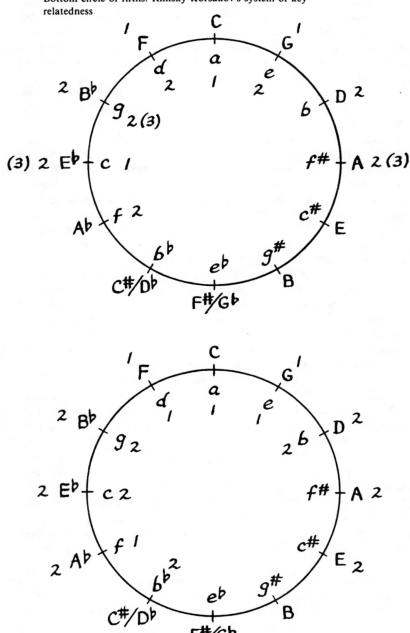

subdivisions of both gradual and sudden modulation. A false progression, used in a sudden modulation, is any pair of adjacent chords, which belong separately to different tonalities or modes. The two most useful are the deceptive cadence (resolving to ♭VI in major, ♯iv°⁷ in minor) and the false progression of a dominant-seventh chord. The latter includes triads and seventh chords a third apart, or seventh chords a fourth, fifth, or third apart. Although Rimsky-Korsakov stated that no special explanation of false progressions in sudden modulations is required, he did recommend that tonalities related no further than the second degree be used, leaving the more remotely related tonalities for gradual modulations.

The enharmonic means for a sudden modulation include augmented triads, augmented-sixth chords, and the diminished-seventh chord. The augmented chords constitute the second category of a group Rimsky-Korsakov called chromatically modified chords, which are independent chords formed from chromatic passing tones. In the first category he placed three chords, the first two of which he introduced into Russian theory. The false dominant-seventh chord on II of major and minor, similar to a secondary dominant, resolves either to I or V. The false diminished seventh chord on raised II of major, the same chord as the previous one but with a raised root, resolves to I. Only the third chord, the major triad on the lowered second degree of major and minor, commonly known as the Neapolitan-sixth chord, had been mentioned by previous theorists.

In addition to the usual augmented-sixth chords, Rimsky-Korsakov included a new variety, the doubly augmented six-five chord (A♭-C-E-F♯ in C major). He correctly resolved all the augmented-sixth chords either to the dominant or to the tonic six-four chord.

Rimsky-Korsakov's textbook was a valuable addition to the small but growing body of Russian theoretical literature, and continued to dominate other newer textbooks by virtue of its clear presentation of harmonic principles. The continued popularity of his teaching methods as presented in the textbook, aided no doubt by his thirty-seven-year tenure at the St. Petersburg Conservatory, helped to create the "St. Petersburg school" of harmony pedagogy. Later theorists, both in Moscow and in St. Petersburg, adopted and developed his ideas concerning the natural and harmonic modes, modulation based on the relatedness of tonalities and common chords, the modulatory plan, his emphasis on melodic harmonization, and particularly his theory that the harmony student progresses more smoothly if confined in the beginning to exercises using only the three principal triads, an approach that was reinforced later by the adoption of functional harmony.

His book has gone through numerous editions, has been translated into many other languages, and is still highly regarded in the Soviet Union. This is all the more remarkable when one considers that Rimsky-Korsakov taught himself nearly everything he knew about theory in general and harmony and counterpoint in particular only after he became a professor of theory and composition. He later wrote, "Thus having been undeservedly accepted at the Conservatory as a professor, I soon became one of its best and possibly its very best *pupil,* judging by the quantity and value of the information it gave me!"[84]

Despite the large number and variety of theory textbooks published in Russia during the next twenty years, none surpasses Tchaikovsky's or Rimsky-Korsakov's work in popularity or distinction. The next generation of theorists, including Georgy Eduardovich Conus (1862-1933), Nikolai Mikhailovich Ladukhin (1860-1918), and Anton Stepanovich Arensky (1861-1906), wrote harmony textbooks that generally reflected the influence of either Tchaikovsky or Rimsky-Korsakov. Others, such as Yury Vladimirovich Kurdiumov (1859-1936) and Mikhail Mikhailovich Ippolitov-Ivanov (1859-1935), wrote harmony books of a different sort that were novel but overly complex, and therefore far less useful than might have been expected.

Anton Arensky, in his harmony textbook, *A Short Guide to the Practical Study of Harmony,*[85] maintained in varying degrees the traditions of both Tchaikovsky, his predecessor at the Moscow Conservatory, and Rimsky-Korsakov, his teacher. Arensky followed Tchaikovsky's approach concerning the triads of the scale, which he introduced and grouped in a similar manner; but he derived certain other approaches such as the modulatory plan from Rimsky-Korsakov. He also used the principle of key relatedness in modulation, but refrained from adopting the harmonic major mode, thereby decreasing the number of tonalities related in the first degree by one, the minor subdominant. He continued to use the terms created by Tchaikovsky, direct and passing, to describe modulation, but defined them slightly differently. A passing modulation became the joining of several direct modulations (without cadences) into one whole that concluded with an expanded cadence. A direct modulation moves to nearly related tonalities, a passing modulation to remote tonalities. For the modulatory plan, Arensky cautioned the student to pay special attention to the intermediate tonalities, and gave as models five modulatory plans from C major to E♭ major and back again. He followed Rimsky-Korsakov in the construction of the augmented-sixth chord.

In a supplement Arensky discussed some of the chords introduced by Rimsky-Korsakov, such as the minor subdominant and the diminished-seventh chord on the raised second degree. He also explained five other relatively unusual harmonic practices not discussed by either Tchaikovsky or Rimsky-Korsakov. These include an unusual resolution of the dominant-seventh chord, rhythmically weak cadences, modulation without common tones or modulating chord (for example, C-F♯[6]-B), an organ point on some tone other than the dominant or the tonic, and the use of the added sixth in triads.

Until Arensky in 1893-94 published his textbook on form, the first such textbook written by a Russian, conservatory students had to rely on Hunke's

Guide and on translated works by Ludwig Bussler for the study of form.[86] Since no one book combined information on both polyphonic and homophonic forms, Arensky sought to correct this deficiency in his *Guide to the Study of the Forms of Instrumental and Vocal Music.*[87] In volume 1, he discussed polyphonic forms in strict and free styles; in volume 2 he discussed homophonic forms, beginning with the motive and ending with sonata allegro form and vocal forms. The influence of the German theorist Hugo Riemann, whose works began to be translated into Russian in the 1890s, is noticeable.[88] For instance, Arensky mentioned accent in his definition of motive: "The basis of each musical work, both homophonic and polyphonic, is the motive. By this term is implied a series of notes in a given work of which one has the greatest accent. The usual length of the motive is one or two bars."[89] Arensky's *Guide* remained the only such Russian form textbook until the 1930s. Taneev had planned such a work, but never wrote it. Translated works on form by Ebenezer Prout were apparently also used.[90]

The theoretical writings of Georgy Conus before 1900 consisted of pedagogical works written for use in his classes at the Moscow Conservatory, where he taught from 1891 to 1899. Conus was a 1890 graduate of the Conservatory; his teachers had been Arensky and Taneev. He again taught at the Conservatory from 1920 to 1933, and became well known during this time for his theory of "metrotechtonicism." From 1922 to 1929 he served as dean of the scientific compositional faculty.[91] In his first work, *A Synoptical Table of the Elementary Theory of Music,*[92] a huge (1 1/2 meters by 1 meter) list covering topics of elementary theory, Conus distinguished between mode and scale, a differentiation infrequently found in textbooks of this time, in spite of Odoevsky's efforts to separate the two concepts. Conus defined mode not in the context of a "church mode" but in a more general sense:

> The character of the music depends on the scale on which it is based. The scale, thus, has the significance of a model: it is some sort of musical type. Such a significance of scale is expressed by the word mode (mood) [*lad (naklonenie)*]. Modes differ as scale structures differ. In contemporary music two modes prevail: major and minor.[93]

To accompany this table, Conus devised an exercise book, filled with numerous problems on every aspect of elementary theory, a pedantic approach popular at the time.[94]

Such a pedantic approach also characterizes Conus's harmony textbook, *A Textbook for the Practical Study of Harmony.*[95] An over-emphasis on rules and pedantry, exemplified by "tables" such as "The Construction, Resolution, and Preparation of All Chords on the Same Note," "The Construction and Resolution of Chords with the Augmented Fifth and Augmented Sixth on the Same Note," and "The Table of Enharmonically Equal Chords" dominates the text. Such tables of chords, all constructed on the same pitch, become useless exercises unless the student is learning to play figured bass.[96] But they typify the attempt by Russian theorists of the 1890s to lend a "scientific" aura to the theory of harmony. In other respects, Conus's book remains in the mainstream of the tradition begun by Tchaikovsky and continued by Arensky.

Another Moscow theorist and composer, Nikolai Ladukhin, who after his graduation from the Moscow Conservatory in 1886 taught there until 1917, followed Arensky's practice by adopting elements from both Tchaikovsky and Rimsky-Korsakov for his own work, *A Guide to the Practical Study of Harmony.*[97] In general, Ladukhin simply expanded Arensky's 1891 textbook; but he was more receptive to the ideas of Rimsky-Korsakov. For example, while adopting Tchaikovsky's chord groups, he added the diminished triad on VII to the dominant chord and recognized the harmonic major scale, although he did not accord it the same level of significance as did Rimsky-Korsakov. His approach to modulation veered more towards that of Rimsky-Korsakov, as well. New to his book was a short exposition of the rudiments of form, such as the sentence and the period, which were intended to help pupils with the rhythmic aspect of modulation.

These three Moscow theorists, Conus, Arensky, and Ladukhin, provided the main contributions to practical Russian music theory in the 1890s. Through their adherence to the fundamental harmonic principles and approaches developed by Tchaikovsky and Rimsky-Korsakov in the 1870s and 1880s, they underscored the significance of the textbooks of those two great Russian theorist-composers. In the mid-1890s, two other theorists, Mikhail Ippolitov-Ivanov and Yury Kurdiumov, produced theory works that deviated from these established traditions of the Russian theory of harmony; but these works, probably because of their unorthodox approaches, were far less successful than the more traditional textbooks. Yet, while failing to achieve their intended purpose, these works signaled a new era in Russian music theory, for in their attempts to create a more comprehensive approach to the complexities of contemporary harmonic language, Ippolitov-Ivanov and Kurdiumov opened the way towards viewing music theory less as a pedagogical tool and more as a scientific discipline.

Both Ippolitov-Ivanov and Kurdiumov wrote books about chords. Ippolitov-Ivanov concentrated on the construction and resolution of chords, Kurdiumov on the classification of chords and chord progressions. In his work, *The Study of Chords, Their Construction and Resolution,* Ippolitov-Ivanov, a graduate of the St. Petersburg Conservatory who taught at the Moscow Conservatory (1893-1905) and later became its director (1905-1922), also classified chords, based partly on his own system of dissonance classification.[98] Dissonances within the key are the nonconsonant intervals formed between the notes of both the major and minor modes. For consonances, he adopted Helmholtz's classification: (a) absolute: doubled prime or unison, octave, duodetsima or doubled octave; (b) perfect: fifth and fourth; (c) middle: major sixth, major third; and (d) imperfect: minor third, minor sixth. "Artificial" dissonances are formed from the chromatic changes of one or both tones of an interval—consonant or dissonant—in the tonality; and "accidental" dissonances are formed from an accidental change of one or both of the tones of an interval in the tonality.

Ippolitov-Ivanov then classified chords, according to their intervallic structure, as "basic," "compound" or "derivative," "artificial," or "accidental." A basic chord is included within the limits of the octave and is made up from tones in the key. Basic chords include all triads and seventh chords naturally occurring in both the major and minor modes. A compound or derivative chord is formed from a compound interval such as a ninth or an eleventh, and is therefore dissonant. An artificial chord is formed from artificial dissonant intervals; among these are the augmented-sixth chord, and chords with a doubly augmented fourth or a doubly diminished fifth. Accidental chords are formed from chromatic changes in the inner voices, i.e., from chromatic nonharmonic tones such as passing tones or suspensions, in any of the basic or derivative chords in the tonality. For each of these categories, Ippolitov-Ivanov discussed and illustrated nearly all possible chordal formations and their resolutions as found in the harmonic practice of his day; this adds up to an excessively large number of chords.

Ippolitov-Ivanov also devoted chapters to other topics such as cadences, voice-leading, nonharmonic tones, modulation, organ point, and figured bass. Concerning modulation, he followed the tradition of Tchaikovsky in a broad sense, distinguishing between a "basic" modulation—similar but not identical to a "direct" modulation—and a passing modulation. A basic modulation is brought about by one of the chords belonging to the dominant group preceded by a common chord between the two tonalities, not just by the dominant chord as in Tchaikovsky's definition of a direct modulation. A passing modulation joins tonalities that share no common chord, by means of related tonalities that do. In Ippolitov-Ivanov's view, the dominant group, including the dominant triad and seventh chord, the diminished triad and seventh chord on VII, the rarely used minor seventh chord on VII, and the dominant ninth chord, defines the tonality. While this grouping resembles Rimsky-Korsakov's, Ippolitov-Ivanov also placed II and IV in the subdominant group and III and VI in the mediant group, the latter a new designation in Russian music theory. As in Rimsky-Korsakov's groupings, an incipient functionalism is evident.

Ippolitov-Ivanov's subject matter resembles that of a harmony textbook, but, as in Conus's work, his approach is far too complex and detailed to have been pedagogically useful. However, these works indicate an attempt by theorists to provide a firmer, more extensive foundation for studies in harmony with less emphasis on the empirical approach. Nevertheless, they failed to provide an adequate alternative; *The Study of Chords,* for example, resembles more a catalogue of late nineteenth-century harmonic practice with an

emphasis on chordal construction. Ippolitov-Ivanov's static approach, based
on superimposed thirds, intervallic construction, and figured bass, culminated
an era in Russian theory that was passing.[99]

Yury Kurdiumov, an 1887 graduate of the St. Petersburg Conservatory
who became a teacher, critic, and composer, took a more novel but still
unsuccessful approach to harmony in his major theoretical work, *The
Classification of Harmonic Combinations.*[100] Kurdiumov aimed in this work
primarily

> to establish general principles on which harmonic combinations may be founded, through
> what becomes clear from the classification of these combinations. The author attempts to
> show that the very order which is basic to the most usual harmonic progressions of the
> consonant triads of the key (ordinary progressions) is expressed in the mass of other unusual
> harmonic progressions, consisting not only of consonant chords but also of all kinds of
> dissonant chords and different tonal combinations.[101]

As a secondary goal, Kurdiumov invented a system of chord representation
through nonmusical means such as letters, numbers, and punctuation marks.
Such a system, he reasoned, could be useful for transmitting song harmonies,
for example, over the telegraph.[102]

The harmonic foundation of his classifications consists of the consonant
triads of the major and minor modes. Kurdiumov included both the harmonic
major and the natural major in his concept of the major mode. He treated the
relationship between major and minor as one of correspondence and not of
imitation.[103] Simultaneous combinations—called "linkages"—of these simple
triads result in complex, sometimes dissonant, harmonic tonal combinations
such as seventh chords; consecutive combinations of these triads result in
harmonic progressions, sequences, and modulations. Kurdiumov devoted
most of the text to the classification of these consecutive combinations, or
progressions. "Ordinary," "active" progressions, for example, are those
progressions most characteristic of a given tonality. "Tonal," "active"
progressions are those most characteristic of a combination of two tonalities.
"Modally active" progressions possess the capability to effect a modulation. He
classified this group according to which keys they may combine through
modulation.

Kurdiumov viewed these progressions as links in a harmonic chain. The
aspiration to a definite harmonic center of gravity (tonic) is what Kurdiumov
called an "active source." In correspondence with this active source, the links of
the harmonic chains are unified and connected. But in the opposite
phenomenon, a "passive source," these links are varied and isolated:

> The more narrow and unbroken the links of the harmonic chain, the more they, so to speak,
> lose their individual quality, being subordinated to the single aspiration to merge with tonic,
> then the more the element of activeness is present in harmony. But if the connection between

the links of the harmonic chain are weak, if each of them aspires to make itself a center of gravity, to establish its own tonic, then the more the harmony will carry a similar sporadic character, the more the element of passiveness will be present in it. This is defined by the general tonality of the harmony of a given work and not by the presence in it of one passive progression.[104]

Thus it is the "active" progressions that characterize either tonalities or their combinations, or effect modulations. But a harmony with a passive character does not necessarily mean the presence of something "sluggish or flaccid":

Frequently the reverse [is true]: a grandiose and fantastic harmonic content frequently directly requires the predominance in harmony of the passive source; an active harmony may not always obediently meander with all the twists of the fantasy of genius.... In a musical work [in which] the harmony is passive... the strict logic of the harmonic combinations obediently yields directly to different artistic requirements of a higher order.... In general, these artistic requirements of a higher order influence... not only harmony, but also melody, [and] finally, the general coloring (instrumentation, nuances).[105]

Although Kurdiumov's system contains many forward-looking ideas such as these, they are unfortunately obscured by his emphasis on classification and his new method of chord representation, neither of which found a place in Russian music theory. However, his approach undoubtedly influenced certain aspects of Russian music theory. He began to raise important questions about musical language, such as the nature and function of tonality, of harmonic progressions, and of higher tertian structures, questions to which Russian theorists soon turned their serious attention in the twentieth century. Also, some of his many new terms crept in Russian theoretical language largely through the work of Boleslav Yavorsky. Terms that Kurdiumov applied in a harmonic context, Yavorsky later applied in a modal-melodic context.[106] Kurdiumov also initiated the practice of identifying intervals through semitone content, a practice that Yavorsky continued.

Despite their deficiencies, the works of both Kurdiumov and Ippolitov-Ivanov point towards new directions, Kurdiumov's towards the emergence of a more speculative form of music theory, and Ippolitov-Ivanov's towards the expansion of the pedagogical theory of harmony beyond that embraced by Tchaikovsky and Rimsky-Korsakov. However, within the nineteenth-century practical, pedagogical tradition that prevailed in the conservatories, Tchaikovsky and Rimsky-Korsakov stand out as the most innovative and influential theorists of their time. The pedagogical foundations that they established were maintained and developed by succeeding generations of theorists. The progress made in the development of independent Russian theoretical thought, the decrease in foreign influence, the large numbers of conservatory-trained composers and theorists, and the many theory books produced in Russia from 1860 to 1900 all testify to the efficacies of the conservatories and of these pedagogical traditions. These traditions have been enriched by various new approaches of both practical and speculative origin throughout the twentieth century.

Part II: 1900-1950

The years 1900-1950 saw great progress in theoretical thought in Russia. During this time the ideas of such prominent Russian and Soviet theorists as Sergei Ivanovich Taneev, Boleslav Leopoldovich Yavorsky, Georgy Eduardovich Conus, and Georgy Lvovich Catoire, followed by Boris Vladimirovich Asafiev, Nikolai Alexandrovich Garbuzov, Yury Nikolaevich Tiulin, Lev Abramovich Mazel, and Varvara Pavlovna Dernova, came to fruition and had an enormous impact on the establishment of theory as a legitimate subject of scientific research. During the nineteenth century, music theory, both in its practical and pedagogical aspects, was most commonly referred to as the theory of composition. In the twentieth century, though, it acquired the additional connotation of speculative theory, or, as it was frequently called, the science of music; theorists attempted to answer questions that had been largely ignored by earlier Russian theorists, questions concerning the very foundation of music—its structure, its perception, its underlying laws. They turned their attention to such topics as mode, formal and harmonic analysis, acoustics, harmonic systems, musical energy, and harmonic function. Yet, although music theory gained respectability as a separate discipline, it was still considered a part of the field of musicology, as it was in Germany. Theoretical musicology, as it came to be called, gained acceptance primarily in the postrevolutionary period and was still growing in 1950.

1900-1917: Musical Science

The first two decades of the twentieth century provided many of the elements that brought about the transformation from pedagogy to science. Already practical music theory in Russia had reached a rather sophisticated level, particularly when compared to what it had been just forty years earlier. By 1900 a sizable body of practical theoretical literature existed, a number of conservatory-trained composers and theorists were working professionally or teaching in the same conservatories, and traditions of composition and theoretical study had been established. This contributed the necessary foundation for continued progress in the field. Also, certain individuals, both in Russia and abroad, were instrumental in stimulating new levels of theoretical thought in Russia. The Russian theorist and composer Sergei Taneev became so influential through his theoretical work and his pedagogical and organizational activities that he was later referred to as the founder of music theory in Russia.[107]

From abroad the theoretical and historical works of Hugo Riemann and the general scope of musicological activity being undertaken in Germany and Austria were also influential. The wide disparity between such activity in those countries, for instance, and similar activity in Russia was made clear to Russians in the article "The Science of Music" from the Russian translation of Riemann's *Musiklexikon,* published in Moscow in the years 1901-1904.[108] Concerning musical science in Germany and Austria, the article states:

> The science of music only recently is beginning to gain for itself an independent place side by side with the rest of the sciences. . . . The combining of the different spheres of mathematical, physical, physiological and psychological acoustics, musical aesthetics, musical archeology and paleography, in general of all special historical researches in music and of the different branches of the theory of music, the study of composition, instrumentation, etc., into one aggregate idea "the Science of music" (musical science) was accomplished in Germany particularly through the efforts of F. Chrysander and P. Spitta. . . . [In] 1902 lectures on certain segments of the science of music were given in all German and many Austrian universities.[109]

In contrast to this, the author (presumably Yuly Dmitrievich Engel, the editor of the Russian edition) described the situation in Russia:

> In Russia the science of music is in a very rudimentary state, and it is difficult even to foresee when it will come out of [this state]. We have no special journals or societies dedicated to the study of subjects of the science of music, and the few articles belonging here are huddled together in very different publications. There is not one music department attached to a Russian university, nor are there even private lectures speaking on segments of the science of music.[110]

This rather grim assessment was not altogether realistic, but even so, additional steps were soon taken to improve the situation.[111] Already in 1902 in Moscow a musical society was founded as a forum for the dissemination of new theoretical ideas. The "Musical Scientific Society," founded by a circle of Moscow musicians gathered around Taneev, sponsored lectures on contemporary research in music, particularly in music theory. At their monthly meetings for the years 1902-1904, the members, including Viacheslav Alexandrovich Bulychev, Alexander Tikhonovich Grechaninov, Mikhail Vladimirovich Ivanov-Boretsky, Mikhail Nikolaevich Kurbatov, Emili Karlovich Rozenov, D.S. Shor, Taneev, and others, heard lectures on such topics as acoustics, musical form, musical perception, and the theories of Reimann. Of all the lectures, the most interesting from the theoretical point of view are those on the application of the golden section to music by Rozenov, the lecture on formal analysis by Conus, and Engel's on the theories of Riemann.[112]

Unfortunately, the activities of the Musical Scientific Society ceased in 1905. The members considered themselves unprepared to carry out further scientific research in music because of the inadequacies of their own education in music theory. Yet, while attempting to supplement their theoretical knowledge, they were hindered by a paucity of source materials and literature in music theory: "Russian musical theoretical and historical literature, as is well known, is almost nonexistent; and Western European literature was inaccessible to us both by its remoteness and expense, and, particularly, by its language."[113] The remedy seemed obvious: to establish a library in which could be collected all the necessary scores and theoretical literature so that vital research could be carried out successfully. Thus a new society, the Musical Theoretical Library Society, was formed in 1908, with its main purpose the founding of a library. By 1911 this was accomplished with the opening of a free reading room attached to the collection, which by 1913 numbered 11,600 volumes.[114]

Corollary activities of the library society included the organization of scientific talks and lectures, performances of little-known works of classical music, the holding of ceremonial meetings dedicated to prominent musical figures (the first such meeting was dedicated to Nikolai Rubinstein, after whom the library was named), and the publication of scientific works. In 1912 the society was formally divided into three departments, a musical theoretical department, a musical historical department, and a musical pedagogical department. Within these departments, sections dedicated to research in some special branch of the department were established, the first being the piano pedagogy section of the pedagogical department. Bulychev, the chairman of the society, envisioned the following goals for the society:

> In a word, it is difficult to envisage all the varied activity necessary for the systematization of scientific musical activity, but three urgent problems now appear in outline as the basis of such activity: (1) the development of a national musical science, (2) the creation of periodical publications on various musical questions, and (3) also the establishment of musical scientific institutes, equivalent to the department of music in foreign universities, from which it would be possible to graduate our musical scholars.[115]

Not all these goals were fulfilled by the society itself, which formally ceased to exist after 1924 when its library was joined to the library of the Moscow Conservatory. But it must be noted that all of its goals were eventually accomplished. Already by 1915 three musical periodicals, two newer ones in addition to the *Russkaia muzykal'naia gazeta* [Russian musical newspaper] already in existence, were serving as the main forums for theoretical ideas.[116] As a result, the number of articles that appeared after 1910 far outweighed the number of books published during the same period. In large part these articles reflect the new trends in theoretical thought that were emerging in the first two decades of the twentieth century.

Still, numerous and varied books on theory, the majority of them textbooks modeled on nineteenth-century works, also appeared.[117] Several works, though, broke with previous trends, and established new directions in theoretical thought. The most significant of these were Boleslav Yavorsky's *Structure of Musical Speech,* and Sergei Taneev's *Moveable Counterpoint in the Strict Style.*[118] Both authors developed original ideas: Yavorsky directed his attention to the formation of mode as a temporal process based on his theory of "auditory gravity," and Taneev simplified and at the same time universalized the study of moveable counterpoint through the application of mathematics.

It is difficult to overestimate the importance of these two works, either as contributions to music theory in general, or in their value for the future development of theory in Russia. Although Yavorsky's work was published first—in 1908—Taneev's work was given the major credit for contributing to the founding of a new science in Russia, as Yavorsky explained in a congratulatory letter to his former teacher Taneev:

> I rejoice and celebrate. Finally what I always considered as one of the very outstanding events in our musical life was made general property. I attach such significance to your work, because in my opinion this is the first work that transfers musical art, that is, something unconscious, intangible for the human *intellect,* into the sphere of science. This is the first theoretical work based on precise laws, the logical application and development of which create a constructed edifice. Only since the appearance of this work is it possible to look at the cultural development of musical art in that part with which your work is concerned. All works on the history of music up to this time appear only as more or less successful biographical sketches, frequently illuminating the influence of the general culture only on the *direction* of the creation of composers, not at all explaining the process of creation in its most concealed secrets. Only when the sufficiently fantastical so-called theory of composition is turned into a musical science that examines the laws directed by musical thought and expressions, and on the basis of these laws constructs an edifice of musical creation, and also makes it possible to guess, to predict, and to explain the impossibility of phenomena, will there appear the history of musical art.[119]

In his letter Yavorsky mentioned a topic that became the subject of several articles and other writings around this time: the science of music. This term came to be used frequently in place of the theory of music, which had a practical, applied connotation closely connected with the theory of composition. Its adoption reflected the interest of theorists in applying to musical research methods and approaches borrowed from the natural sciences and from mathematics, and through their application discovering music's underlying laws, processes, structures, etc., as in the other sciences. Thus music came to be viewed for purposes of research either as a biological organism, as a purely physical occurrence, as a mathematical phenomenon, or, later, as a psychological or sociological phenomenon. Even though Odoevsky and Serov had advocated the development of a musical science in the last century, only at this time were theorists attempting to define it and to uncover its limits, methods, goals, and subject matter within the context of Russian musical studies.

One of the first efforts in this direction was made by Nadezhda Yakovlevna Briusova, a follower of Yavorsky's, in a small brochure, *The Science of Music, Its Historical Path and Contemporary State.*[120] Briusova defined the material and method of musical science:

> [The act of] sounding, which gives an auditory touch to temporal forms, of such is the world of musical embodiment. The science of music researches this world, its nature and its life. The results of scientific research should give exact knowledge about the laws that direct the sounding, temporal life of this world. The method of the science of music is the same as the method of all natural sciences that study the physical construction of whatever the world may be.[121]

For Briusova, Yavorsky had already revealed the true nature and essence of mode, thereby enriching the science of music. In this brochure, she traced the development of research into mode and expounded on the present state of knowledge about it, in language derived from Yavorsky's theories.

While Briusova obviously believed that the science of music had made great strides by 1910, other authors conceded that it was still in its infancy. In 1912 the composer and writer Leonid Leonidovich Sabaneev (1881-1968) wrote, "Essentially—musical science... really is just born."[122] Like Briusova, who considered that any previous science of music was encased in a "period of scholastic dogmatism," during which the essential questions of mode were ignored,[123] Sabaneev held a very low opinion of musical science before his time. "Everything that previously existed was one continuous uncultured misunderstanding, musical sorcery..., the writing of prescriptions, devoid of any hint of system as a basic sign of a 'scientific' discipline."[124] Theorists, he stated, "were untalented people, musical failures, who did not have the more visible career of performer or composer."[125] His goal for musical science was simple, to study musical organisms. His methods were to study the given facts and to evaluate those facts on the bases of taste, intuition, and musical understanding. Sabaneev likened the true musical scholar to a "fully armed researcher," with a full knowledge of music and physics, an ability to feel, an analytical mind, and the ability of generalize. In addition to ordering and reevaluating the past, the researcher must also discover new horizons, new possibilities. But Sabaneev saw little hope of progress for musical science, since in his view such a researcher did not exist.

A third, completely negative view of the value of the science of music was expressed by the composer and aesthetician Konstantin Romanovich Eiges, who stated that in Germany, "the living spirit of music has died away and in its place exists 'the science of music'; instead of composers, [there exist] musicologists, musical scholars, and bibliophiles."[126] He described the situation in Moscow as of 1913:

> Lately in Moscow lectures about music have become popular. There has appeared among us a completely new type of musician, who is interested not so much in music as in the theory of music, and not so much the theory of music (as a practical discipline) as the natural scientific basis of the musical system and theory, with the questions "why?" and "from what?", without the answers to which (in his opinion) it is impossible to proceed to the study of music as art. . . . The manifestation of such musicologists in Russia, where music and musical creation are found in blossoming strength, is completely inopportune and may be understood only as an imitation.[127]

Eiges's criticisms stemmed from his beliefs that musical creation was a supernatural process, scientifically unexplainable, and that the art of music—including music theory—should be kept separate from science. His view, fortunately for the future course of theoretical thought in Russia, was in the minority.

Each of these writers—Briusova, Sabaneev, and Eiges—discussed musical science from the viewpoint of their personal biases. None offered an objective appraisal of the state of musical science, nor did they attempt to solve any of its attendant problems. One who did, though, the theorist and ethnomusicologist Viktor Mikhailovich Beliaev (1888-1968), in a series of short articles called "sketches," discussed the interrelation between music theory and composition, the goals and methods of musical theoretical research, contemporary theorists, the relationships among theory, art, and science, and the scientific qualities of music theory.[128] Beliaev defined theory, which term he preferred to the nebulous "science of music," by its opposition to practice; in that sense it denotes the "objective observation" of musical creation. He also mentioned several other incorrect interpretations of theory: as a "game of imagination" that attempts to influence practice rather than be derived from it, as a "universally recognized law" (in contrast to "hypothesis"), and as "supposition" (in contrast to "experiment").[129]

The goal of musical theoretical research, according to Beliaev, is the elucidation and proof of the laws of musical creation; the order of research methods is observation, description, classification, construction of hypotheses or suppositions, confirmation with facts, and the establishment of laws. For the individual application of these methods, Beliaev used the term "methodological plan." As a model of the application in musical research of such a plan, Beliaev could point to none save the "mathematical" plan Taneev used in his *Moveable Counterpoint in the Strict Style*. He attributed the "lack in musical theoretical research of developed methods" to "the relative youth of music theory, which, in spite of the antiquity of its origins, is at present in the infantile period of observation, of description, and of classification."[130] As might be expected, he held Taneev in the highest regard as "a prominent representative of contemporary musical theoretical thought,"along with Prout and Riemann.[131] Prout he valued for his descriptive and detailed analyses, Riemann for his designation of tonal functions, and Taneev for his work in moveable counterpoint.[132]

Beliaev did not believe in the ability of the science of music to "forecast,"as did Briusova. That, in his view, was the task of musical creation, which grows from theory and is eventually justified by theory, thus establishing a circle of interactivity between theory and creativity. To Beliaev, theory and composition constitute two sides of the same coin. Music is an art, and its main element remains its spiritual nature. Consequently, theory is a part of art, not of science. Up to his time, the practice had been "to reject the scientific qualities of the theory of art and in particular of the theory of music and to be satisfied with theories having applied significance."[133] Yet he saw danger in the move to replace the theory of music with the science of music, out of the fear that science would ignore the spiritual aspects of art:

> Therefore it is necessary to consider harmful and, fortunately, even impossible the significant aspiration in our time to create a so-called "science of music" instead of the theory of music for our art, because, first of all, the limits of the "science of music," in the sense of science as such, are so narrow and artificial, and second, because scientific research has completely different problems than artistic theoretical [research]. Let no one think, however, that the above-stated rejects the participation of science in artistic theoretical research. Scientific discoveries and conclusions also have value for art, but their significance in this case is secondary—they are only the *material* that artistic creation uses.[134]

Beliaev thus embraced a more moderate and realistic interpretation of the relationship between science and art and of the application of science within art than did Eiges.

Apart from the attempts to define musical science and discover its methods, much of the theoretical interest in the immediate prerevolutionary years centered around methods of analyzing the later music of Skryabin. Unfortunately, the many efforts brought forth few fruitful results. The only theorist who seemed to understand the harmonic language in Skryabin's music was Yavorsky, but many years passed before anyone applied his theories properly to Skryabin's music.[135] In the meantime theorists attempted to explain his music by a variety of pseudoscientific means.

Of these means, an acoustical explanation, whereby the notes of the so-called mystic chord (C-F#-Bb-E-A-D) were said to be derived from the overtone series, specifically from partials 8, 9, 10, 11, 13, and 14, gained the most notoriety. Sabaneev, the main author and propagandist for this view, put forth this explanation as early as 1910.[136] His critics, though, quickly pointed out that just one of these tones was found in equal temperament (8), that three of them (11, 13, 14) could only be approximated in equal temperament, and that the piano, Skryabin's main instrument for composing, was tuned in equal temperament. Sabaneev evasively answered that this chord, and the harmony of Skryabin in general, was consonant, but "only for those people who understand it." Since for the time being it was impossible to play Skryabin music in the proper tuning, for lack of the proper instrument, one must listen to it while "correcting mentally the defects of intonation."[137] Thus, the burden fell on the listener, who had to make mental tuning corrections, and who, if he considered the music to be dissonant, obviously did not understand it.

In later articles, Sabaneev expanded his acoustical interpretation of Skryabin's harmony to include a chordal approach, in which a central chord served both as the sole foundation for a piece of music and as a symbol, an "astral body," of its psychological "secret look," which had to be comprehended before a full understanding of the musical work became possible.[138] He also advocated the harmonic development of music following the "'acoustical direction' of theoretical thought," i.e., the widening of the sphere of consonance through the inclusion of successive partial tones.[139] He pointed out other historical directions of harmonic development as well, including voice-leading, which caused accidental chords that eventually were considered consonant and independent, and mode, in which the harmony arose from an interaction of the tones of the mode. He did not give this latter, modal direction in theory—an oblique reference to the modal theories of Yavorsky—much scientific credence: "The acoustical direction still is more well-founded scientifically than the newer, modal direction."[140]

The final stage of Sabaneev's theories was "ultrachromaticism." Ultrachromatic music was music of the future; it lay outside the bounds of equal temperament, and necessitated its destruction. Ultrachromatic sounds, which required a new "polyphonic instrument" for their realization, so far existed only in the "creative imaginations of some people more progressive in this realization."[141] In the overtone series, which Sabaneev called "the basic consonant harmony," there could be no dissonances, only degrees of consonance. Sabaneev predicted that ultrachromatic music would use harmonies united with tone colors, called "harmony-timbres," which would exist in three orders, consisting of progressive combinations of overtone series. He foresaw the existence of a fifty-three-note octave, formed by the joining of the harmonic systems of the three orders.

Sabaneev believed that Skryabin in his music helped to pioneer ultrachromaticism. But Arseny Avraamov (1886-1944), who also embraced ultrachromatic music as the music of the future and proposed how to build an instrument for its realization, rejected the interpretation of Skryabin's music as ultrachromatic, preferring the term "omnitonality" as understood by Taneev.[142] Omnitonality, which accepts equal temperament, is the antithesis of ultrachromaticism, which destroys equal temperament. In defense of his position, Avraamov pointed out the various ways in which Skryabin's music is rooted in the equal-tempered system.[143]

In response to Avraamov, Sabaneev replied that "*all* music is ultrachromatic.... The intention of every composer (of this I am convinced) is always ultrachromatic,... [and] every *ear* is ultrachromatic."[144] He based his argument on the interpretation of ultrachromaticism as an aural-mental exercise founded only on one's intuition. He confessed that at this point he himself did not know the future path of ultrachromaticism, or even whether its tones would consist of the upper overtones. He did believe, however, that the first step towards the creation of a tonal language for ultrachromaticism was to be the creation of "natural ultrachromatic scales," which he imagined intuitively but not concretely:

> And so my path is not from harmony, but from scales, which embrace and include harmony. This question demands an intuitively analytical treatment, and I have to point out that a number of investigators (including that extremely profound and interesting theorist Yavorsky) altogether repudiate the priority of acoustic relations in the matter of the formation of scales.[145]

Ultimately, Sabaneev's theory of ultrachromaticism had no solid scientific or theoretical foundation. However, it was part of a growing interest in the invention of new tonal systems, an interest that reached its apogee in the 1920s. Not all musical scholars advocated such radical ideas, though. Nicholai Kashkin in 1917 came out against the modernistic tendencies in composition and theory, particularly against Sabaneev's ideas of ultrachromaticism and expanded tonal systems. As a counter-measure, he proposed the study and analysis of prominent musical works beginning with Wagner on a scientific theoretical basis, and the systematization of the results. The conclusions would then serve as guiding norms for further development, particularly of harmony. To accomplish this, he proposed the founding of a department of contemporary harmony. He further advocated research into the bases of musical science; this included, in addition to the study of the newest harmony, studies of melody, rhythm, and the criteria for the aesthetic evaluation of musical works. Being of Taneev's generation, Kashkin believed in the value of established practices and preferred to base future work on the tradition of the past, rather than breaking with those traditions. Ironically, his and Taneev's antimodernistic views eventually triumphed in Soviet music theory, but not before a period of further experimentation had already taken place.[146]

Thus during the prerevolutionnary period, 1900-1917, Russian music theorists began to expand their theoretical work to include the speculative, "scientific" aspects of music theory, creating a "science of music." Stimulated by Western scholars, Russian theorists took an active role in developing Russian theoretical thought by providing access to research materials, forums for lectures, and means of publication. Yet only a small number of scholarly studies were published—those by Taneev and Yavorsky—and these works resulted not so much from increased activity in music theory as from research begun previously and independently. Other theorists devoted much effort to exploring new "scientific" elements in theory. Having established the methods and guidelines for this new study, they were free to turn their attention to such areas as acoustics, new tonal systems, and formal analysis. However, the real fruition came not in this period but after the interruptions caused by the 1917 Revolution.

1917-1932: Exploration and Expansion

As a result of World War I and, more importantly, the October Revolution and the subsequent civil strife, scholarly work in music was temporarily suspended. In spite of hardship and privation, though, teaching and concert activities continued; but the publication of music journals and books ceased because of a lack of means. Those organizations that had promoted research in music were dissolved, leaving no forums for the dissemination and exchange of scholarly views.

Within a few years the situation improved. Scholarly research institutes were established; lectures were given and reports were made; and bulletins, journals, and books were published. All these labors were carried out with great enthusiasm by the scholars who joined these institutes.

These activities were made possible partly because of the organizational power and control over the arts of the new government. Already on the day after Lenin seized power in Petrograd, he appointed Anatol Lunacharsky as the head of the People's Commissariat of Public Education, or NARKOMPROS [Narodnyi komissariat prosveshcheniia], and placed all the arts under his control. Eventually, all the cultural institutions, including theaters, publishing firms, all music schools, and libraries, were nationalized. The conservatories were promoted to the status of an institution of higher learning, or VUZ [Vyshee uchebnoe zavedenie], and later reorganized.

During the early years of their existence, the various institutes underwent several reorganizations. For most of the 1920s the main institutes were GIMN and GAKhN in Moscow, and RIII in Leningrad. The first, however, was the AK MUZO. In Narkompros, each of the arts was given a special subdivision; the music division, MUZO [muzykal'nyi otdel], established control over all areas of musical activity. In 1919 in Leningrad an academic subdivision (AK MUZO) was formed.[147] A similar subdivison formed in Moscow in 1920 divided its activity into four areas of musical research—historical, theoretical, experimental, and ethnographic. In 1921 AK MUZO of the Moscow Narkompros absorbed the musical sections of a defunct Moscow organization devoted to the promotion of proletarian culture, PROLETKULT [Proletarskaia kul'tura], and formed three new subsections: scientific-theoretical (headed by E.K. Rozenov), scientific-experimental (Nikolai Garbuzov), and ethnographic (V.A. Fedorov). The scientific-theoretical subsection was further divided into two smaller sections—theoretical-methodological (Georgy Conus) and historical-aesthetic (L. Sabaneev).

Research was undertaken almost from the beginning. During the year 1920-1921, for example, the Scholarly Council heard approximately forty lectures, nine of which were later accepted for possible publication. Among these, six addressed theoretical subjects, four on the topic of new tonal systems.[148] None of these lectures were ever published under the sponsorship of AK MUZO, however, for it soon ceased to exist. By fall 1921, a new institute was being planned; the State Institute of Musical Science, or GIMN [Gosudarstvennyi institut muzykal'noi nauki], was formally opened November 1, 1921.

GIMN, according to its director Nikolai Garbuzov, was to be "a scholarly and scientific artistic institution, intended for the thorough development of musical scientific questions."[149] Although it was devoted to the study of all aspects of musical science, theoretical research took a prominent place. Garbuzov himself was a theorist and composer with training in the natural sciences. Many of the theorists who had been members of the Musical Scientific Society and later of the Musical Theoretical Library Society, such as Rozenov, Conus, P. Renchitsky, Eiges, Yavorsky, and Briusova, also joined the new institute; their research interests influenced the work of GIMN. Also, the extensive collection of the Musical Theoretical Library Society was placed at the disposal of GIMN until 1925, when it was transferred to the Moscow Conservatory where it remains. Within GIMN were four permanent associations, theoretical, historical, ethnographical, and philosophical. The theoretical association included a number of temporary commissions devoted to separate problems such as timbre, architectural acoustics, mind perception, vocal methodology, musical endowments, new musical systems, and the legacy of Skryabin. Separate laboratories and workshops were also established. In addition to an acoustical laboratory headed by Garbuzov, a laboratory of metrotechtonic analysis of musical works, headed by Conus, was founded.

Of particular interest was the work done by the commission on the development of new musical systems. Sparked by research from the last decade on this topic and by reports from Prague on the quarter-tone works of Alois Haba, theorists considered new systems an important current theoretical topic.[150] Several systems were demonstrated at GIMN:

1.   The natural overtone-undertone seventeen-degree modulatory system, presented by the chairman of the commission E.K. Rozenov, with a plan for a harmonium with three manuals and transpositional adaptations;

2.   A movable twenty-eight-degree, tertian-quintal modulatory system with a plan for a keyboard and a moveable roller for transposition;

3. A fifty-three-degree equal-tempered system with a plan for a harmonium and a four-manual keyboard, presented by L.L. Sabvaneev.[151]

Other topics at GIMN included new means of musical nomenclature and notation, Yavorsky's theory of modal rhythm, Conus's theory of metrotechtonicism, musical logic, and acoustics.[152] In proposals for further work, Sabaneev offered to begin a scientific study of musical style using the "biometrical methods" of natural science.[153] Thus, from the beginning, theoretical research at GIMN embraced a wide variety of topics.

Also in Moscow in 1921 a research institute devoted to all the arts was founded, the Russian (later State) Academy of Artistic Sciences, or GAKhN [Gosudarstvennaia akademiia khudozhestvennykh nauk]. Its music division opened January 1922, with Sabaneev as head. The theorists who joined the Academy, generally the same as those in GIMN, studied various areas of music theory and acoustics, as well as aesthetics, history, psychology and physiology of musical perception, and artistic technique. A commission for the study of new scales was also formed. During its first year, from February to December 1922, eight members of the music division gave eleven lectures; those by Conus and Briusova addressed questions of musical form and analysis, a topic singled out from other separate questions of music theory as meriting special consideration.[154]

In 1923, both GIMN and GAKhN underwent reorganization as a result of their attempted merger, which lasted nine months, and subsequent break up. GIMN's historical and philosophical associations were placed within GAKhN, leaving the theoretical and ethnographical associations; some theorists, including Yavorsky and his followers and Conus, chose to remain affiliated only with GAKhN. The secretary of GIMN described how this changed the Institute:

> Thus, the thorough and complete scope of musicology, which so advantageously distinguished GIMN from Western European music research institutes, was violated. But, having lost its universal scope, GIMN used this circumstance to concentrate work in natural scientific and experimental methods.[155]

GIMN retained unchanged the ethnographical section, and created four new sections from the remaining theoretical association—the physical-technical section (headed by Garbuzov, who was still GIMN's director), with commissions on acoustics and instrument studies; the physiological-psychological section, with commissions on perception, musical endowments, and experimental aesthetics; and two experimental pedagogical sections on vocal and piano methodology. Subsidiary establishments included various laboratories and workshops as before, minus Conus's metrotechtonic laboratory.

Much of the research in music theory was now concentrated in the commission on acoustics. Garbuzov, also head of this commission, was interested primarily in the acoustical foundations of music theory; he believed that through the application of acoustics music theory could be made more exact and more contemporary.[156] Besides Garbuzov's study, the acoustical commission continued to develop and evaluate new tonal systems. Work was carried out by Rozenov, Pavel Leiberg, Renchitsky, and Avraamov. Over twenty lectures on new musical systems, including newly devised instruments and notation systems for them, were read at GIMN meetings. Each researcher advocated a different system. Sabaneev continued to lecture on a fifty-three-degree equal-tempered system, which was obviously not the ultrachromatic system he had proposed earlier, since that system opposed equal temperament.[157] Rozenov, who had earlier devised a seventeen-degree system, developed a nine-degree "harmonic" mode, which is similar to the octatonic scale but with two half steps in place of one whole step (C D♭ D♮ E F G A♭ B♭ B♮ C).[158] Renchitsky investigated quarter-tones in addition to new methods of notation and nomenclature. Leiberg proposed a forty-one-degree tempered system and devised an instrument for it.[159] Avraamov invented what he called the "Universal System of Tones," which contained forty-eight tones to the octave, a number Avraamov considered sufficient to reproduce all folk-song modes and "the timbral-harmonic complexes... familiar to inhabitants of industrial centers of production [i.e., factories]."[160] Concerning the tuning of these new tonal systems, Garbuzov concluded:

> The work of A.M. Avraamov, P.B. Leiberg, and E.K. Rozenov has conclusively shown that it is possible to solve the problem of the expansion and transformation of the tonal system only with the aid of some form of equal temperament (24- 41- 48- and 53-degree), [and] that pure tuning is technically unrealizable.[161]

The first public demonstration and concert of quarter-tone music in Moscow was given in 1927 by Georgy Rimsky-Korsakov, a grandson of the composer, who was the chief exponent of this music in Leningrad.[162]

Garbuzov's research in acoustics, the preliminary results of which he published in numerous separate articles, culminated in the formulation of a new method for the analysis and derivation of modes and chords, published in his two-volume work, *The Theory of Multi-based Modes and Chords*.[163] He postulated the origin of modes and chords not just in one overtone series but in two or more related ones. His acoustically based approach to mode opposed Yavorsky's "psychologically" based approach and Garbuzov wrote several articles attempting to prove the fallibility of Yavorsky's theories from an acoustical point of view.[164]

The connection between acoustics and music theory continued to dominate research in the physical-technical section throughout the remaining years of GIMN's existence (until 1931), owing to Garbuzov's interest in the topic. Plans for the last year included research topics directly related to his work.[165] Topics related to music theory were also researched in the physiological-psychological section, where Ekaterina Alekseevna Maltseva and Sofia Nikolaevna Beliaeva-Ekzempliarskaia were influenced by the work on music psychology of Carl Stumpf, an honorary member of GIMN. They virtually initiated research on this topic in Russia.[166] Their studies included the perception of various musical elements such as form, melody and rhythm, and musical expression.[167] Rozenov continued research on the golden section in music, a topic he first took up in the early 1900s for the Musical Scientific Society. His results were published in 1925.[168]

In the music section of GAKhN, following its break with GIMN in 1923, music theory continued to be important, especially since Yavorsky and Conus had elected to remain there exclusively. One of the three new subsections of the music section was devoted entirely to music theory, and the other two subsections, music history and music psychology, gave attention to related aspects. Within the theory subsection three special commissions were created: music aesthetics (Rozenov), metrotechtonic analysis (Conus), and the biometrical method of research (Sabaneev). In the biometrical method of research, Sabaneev attempted to calculate scientifically the characteristics of a given musical style through the determination of the frequency of the "type-elements," such as individual chords, harmonic density, tonal changes, etc. Sabaneev's goal was to create a "Laboratory of the Exact Science of Music"; since "musical science is a type of natural science," the method of investigation should be similar: "the discovery and description of its laws."[169] However, this commission lasted only until 1926, when Sabaneev emigrated.

The theory subsection proposed the following research topics for the year 1925-1926: the structure of musical works, research into different musical systems, an explanation of the essence of revolutionary music, style, color hearing, and new currents in music. From 1925 to 1928, for example, lectures were presented on such topics as modal analysis, revolutionary music, contemporary music, Kastalsky and folk polyphony, metrotechtonic analysis, atonality, bases for harmony, rhythmic perception, motivic analysis, and musical theoretical categories.[170] In 1927-1928, Rozenov nearly dominated the theory lectures with the presentation of ten chapters from his unpublished work, *The Scientific Foundation of the Study of Harmony.*[171]

During this same period (1925-1928), the Commission of Metrotechtonic Analysis undertook a study of all the sonatas and symphonies of Beethoven. The Commission of Music Aesthetics turned its attention to questions of motivic variety and unity, the perception of musical symmetry, melodic and intervallic perception, rhythmic perception, and the emotional aspects in formal analysis.[172] The Group for the Research of Mode, formed in 1927, focused on aspects of Yavorsky's theory of modal rhythm, for example, the psychology of modal perception, and intonation (Yavorsky and Beliaeva-

Ekzempliarskaia); modal aspects of folk song (Sergei Vladimirovich Protopopov), acoustics (G. Rimsky-Korsakov), and complex modes (Zuckermann).[173]

The Music Psychology Subsection investigated connections between psychology and music theory. Rozenov, in conjunction with his work in the Commission on Musical Aesthetics, carried out research on the perception of musical symmetry and of unity, and Yavorsky and Beliaeva-Ekzempliarskaia worked on the perception of mode and the principles of melodic construction and motion, the results of which were eventually published.[174] In the Music History Subsection, music theory was studied as a historical phenomenon. Maria Medvedeva reported on the theories of Anton Reicha, and Beliaev prepared manuscripts of Taneev for publication.[175] A special commission for the editing of Taneev's *Doctrine of the Canon* was formed in 1926.[176]

GAKhN's music section occasionally undertook joint research with other sections. For instance, in 1927 the music section and the sociology department of GAKhN formed a joint plan to investigate problems of musical form, contemporary musical creation and sociological bases, metrotechtonic evidence of static elements in musical form, and the sociological basis of modal formation.[177] Reports indicate that most of the earlier musical sociological research was limited to music history, except for a lecture by Sabaneev given in 1924, "The Analysis of Sociological Elements of the Musical Phenomenon."[178] In GAKhN's theory subsection, the only topic directly influenced by Marxist philosophy was that of revolutionary music, suggested and researched by Briusova. With the exception of the joint research by the music and sociology sections, Marxist elements in theoretical research were rare during much of this period.[179]

In Leningrad, the Section on the Theory and History of Music, OTIM [Otdel teorii i istorii muzyki], of the Russian (State) Institute for the History of the Arts, RIII, later GIII [Russkii (Gosudarstvennyi) institut istorii iskusstv], which opened on February 19, 1920, emphasized the historical and sociological aspects of music more than the theoretical aspects.[180] Initially, RIII, which at first was little more than a central meeting place for musicians and scholars, lacked a unity of purpose and ideology. Despite Boris Asafiev's reconstruction of OTIM in 1921 after he was elected dean, the divisiveness between those scholars who wished to continue their prerevolutionary work and those who wished to create a new sociologically based approach continued.[181] In 1927 a second reorganization was undertaken and a new plan that crystallized the guidelines and goals of the institute was adopted. The new guidelines offered few compromises:

1. The work of MUZO [Music Section] should be fully joined with musical contemporaneity and its proposed problems, both in the area of theoretical thought on music, and also in living musical practice.

2. Music itself in its sounding and movement should be the material and foundation of all research work of MUZO.
3. MUZO... has no right... to delve into the past for its own sake.
4. The examination of music as a sociological phenomenon should be the basic point of view of MUZO. Therefore, however attractive and interesting may be the independent development of a discipline that analyzes music as a physical, biological, or some other phenomenon, it may not have a place in MUZO.
5. As far as music... is at the center of attention, no sectional sphere of musicology may conduct research in MUZO outside its connection with other research in MUZO. The complexity of the scientific approach must bring about a unity of objective.
6. Finally, the slogan of research practicality should be the basis of the work of MUZO, in order to have the possibility of concentrating on the urgent problems of contemporary musicology and musical society.[182]

GIII, in other words, was moving in the direction of a Marxist musicology, stressing the collective, all-embracing, sociological, and practical aspects of research, particularly of contemporary musical society. Point number four above specifically excluded many approaches already taken by Russian theorists such as Sabaneev, Yavorsky, and Conus. Partly as a result of these directives and partly as a result of the dearth of theoretical research in prerevolutionary St. Petersburg, less research on theoretical topics was carried out at GIII than in the Moscow institutes. Only in one of its three sections, the section on musical language headed by the theorist Anatoli Butskoi, was research conducted on such topics as microtonal music (in the acoustical laboratory headed by Lev Nemirovsky), new methods of notation, ultrachromaticism, and the harmonic and melodic language of the music of Russian composers such as Borodin and Rimsky-Korsakov. Also, a committee on Bach attached to the music section sponsored research on polyphony. G. Rimsky-Korsakov continued his research on quarter-tone music, directed an ensemble of quarter-tone music from 1925 to 1932, and investigated the acoustical properties of Yavorsky's theory of modal rhythm. Articles on these topics were published in *De Musica,* a collection edited by Asafiev that appeared between 1923 and 1927.[183] The guiding force at the institute and its most prominent theorist was its dean, Asafiev, who published his theoretical views in the first volume of his monumental work *Musical Form as a Process* in 1930.[184]

Thus three institutes, GIMN and GAKhN in Moscow and GIII in Leningrad, provided for the continuing growth and development of Russian thought in music theory. Coupled with the zealous enthusiasm of the musical scholars, this support of scholarly activity resulted in numerous innovative studies. Garbuzov credited the success and versatility of postrevolutionary musical science to its connection with the natural sciences and to the new conditions of collective work coupled with the application of laboratory methods.[185] The change in emphasis from practical music theory to scholarly musical science was accepted from the beginning, although the study and cultivation of "practical" aspects of music and music theory were still considered important parts of musicology. Accordingly, the conservatories also contributed to theoretical research through the teaching and publications of their professors, many of whom were also members of the institutes. In 1925 postgraduate departments of musicology were added to the conservatories as a result of the transfer of the teaching and training of musicologists from the institutes. The Moscow Conservatory began to publish its own journal, *Muzykal'noe obrazovanie* [Musical education], in 1925 (until 1930), in which appeared scholarly articles, including articles on the theories of Garbuzov, Yavorsky and Conus. Georgy Lvovich Catoire, a theory professor at the Moscow Conservatory who never took part in the activities of the institutes, published his harmony textbook, *A Theoretical Course of Harmony,* in 1925-1926.[186] His theories on functional harmony, based on those of Riemann and Gevaert, influenced the future development of harmonic theory in the Soviet Union. Yury Nikolaevich Tiulin of the Leningrad Conservatory wrote a textbook on harmonic analysis based on the Bach chorales in an effort to provide a more practical basis for theoretical work.[187] Many of the theories recently developed or researched at the institutes were also used as bases for various courses at the conservatories. For example, during one year at the Moscow Conservatory, Catoire's functional theories, Conus's theory of metrotechtonicism, and Yavorsky's theory of modal rhythm (taught by Briusova) each received a separate course.

Amid the proliferation of studies and approaches in music theory, by 1930 four main lines of theoretical thought, each very different from the others, had become prominent: those propounded by Yavorsky, Conus, Catoire, and Garbuzov. Yet in spite of their unique approaches, the authors were concerned with some of the same general topics. For example, Yavorsky and Garbuzov both examined the generation of mode and the resulting chords. Catoire, and to a lesser extent Garbuzov, concentrated on functional harmony. Catoire, Conus, and Yavorsky were all concerned with musical form, various types of formal symmetry, and metric groupings. A fifth line of thought came into prominence in 1930 with the publication of Asafiev's *Musical Form as a Process.* This important work, the culmination of Asafiev's distinguished and prolific musicological activity of the previous decade, greatly influenced Soviet theoretical thought, largely through the theory of "intonatsiia"[intonation].[188] Also in 1930 Yavorsky's theories received a more systematic explication with the appearance of Sergei Vladimirovich Protopopov's *Elements of the Structure of Musical Speech,* edited by Yavorsky.[189]

The years between 1929 and 1932 became critical ones for Soviet music theory and musicology in general. During this time the proletarian musical organization, The Russian Association of Proletarian Musicians, or RAPM [Rossiiskaia assotsiatsiia proletarskikh muzykantov], acquired almost total control over musical activities, resulting in the suppression of those not in agreement with their radical ideas. For example, no journals but those supervised by RAPM, such as *Proletarskii muzykant* [Proletarian musician], published 1929-1932, and *Za proletarskuiu muzyku* [For proletarian music], published 1930-1932, appeared. *Muzyka i revoliutsiia* [Music and revolution], begun in 1926, ceased publication in 1929 when its organization, an offshoot of RAPM, was dissolved; and *Muzykal'noe obrazovanie* [Musical education] stopped publication in 1930 as a direct result of the influence of the proletarian movement. *Sovremmenaia muzyka* [Contemporary music], the publication of the Moscow Association for Contemporary Music (ACM), begun in 1924, also stopped publication in 1929.[190] The institutes were also affected. In 1931, GIMN was liquidated. In 1929, GAKhN became GAIS, the State Academy of the Arts, which was then transferred to Leningrad in 1932. To fill in the void, a Scientific Research Institute was established in 1932 at the Moscow Conservatory, and an acoustical laboratory, where Garbuzov worked, was founded in 1933. GIII remained in existence in Leningrad. The RAPM policy, advocating a simplistic approach to music aimed at the masses, naturally alienated many of the composers and musicologists, who preferred the more advanced contemporary trends and chafed under this dogmatic, inflexible authority.

The RAPM movement also focused attention on the philosophical aspects of music theory. In 1932, Garbuzov, for instance, incorporated changes into his theory of multi-based modes and chords making it more compatible with Marxist-Leninist thought before publishing the second volume of his 1928 work. Yavorsky endured the scrutiny of a four-day conference devoted to his theory of modal rhythm in February 1930 to determine if his theory was compatible with Marxist philosophy. This conference was sponsored by Narkompros and chaired by Lunacharsky, who summarized the conclusions of the conference and its surrounding events:

> When proponents of the old, already stagnant musical theories, and the very young, who still did not have any baggage [ideas] in the majority of cases, and comrades who considered themselves as conformists strongly attacked Yavorsky, a conference, at which I presided, was created by Narkompros. After extensive discussions the opponents gave up their positions completely and accepted a resolution, which stated that Yavorsky's theory still was far from Marxist, but is in the process of being transformed into such, and represents an exceptionally valuable hypothesis, capable of enriching Marxist musical thought. However shortly after this a new attack on Yavorsky was made in GAIS under disgraceful and inequitable conditions, including the direct intimidation of students of Yavorsky, as a result of which several of the students faint-heartedly betrayed their teacher.... Unfortunately, this occurred far from the authority of the [Communist] Party, which would have stopped this unjust matter.[191]

This new attack in GAIS, which began after Yavorsky presented a report to GAIS on his latest research on mode, took the form of unannounced discussions of Yavorsky's theories over a period of six weeks in the spring of 1931, at the end of which Yavorsky saw no alternative but to resign his active membership in GAIS.[192]

The internal quarrels between the proletarian and the more modern factions of the musical world ended, though, in April 1932, when the resolution of the Communist Party's Central Committee "On the Reconstruction of Literary and Artistic Organizations" banned all proletarian organizations, including those in music.[193] A musicians' union, Soiuz sovetskikh kompozitorov [The Union of Soviet Composers], was formed, with the best composers and musicologists as its members. The following year the union began to publish a journal, *Sovetskaia muzyka* [Soviet music], the only journalistic forum for scholarly work in music both then and now.[194] While the main musicological task of the composers' union, as stated in the first issue of *Soviet Music*, was to develop a Marxist-Leninist musicology, it also vowed to remain moderate.[195] But the new directives turned out to be no less dogmatic than those of RAPM. "Socialist realism," adopted in 1934, became the watchword, and those who did not follow Marxist-Leninist philosophy were branded "formalists."[196] Thus ended an era of freedom and enthusiasm in musical activity.

The period of Soviet music theory from 1917 to 1932 has been called by one Soviet theorist "a time of search and revision, a period of formation."[197] This it was, but, more importantly, it was also a time of great flexibility and of individual creation. Initially, the topics of research in the institutes were chosen less on the basis of the development of ideology than on the basis of the diverse research interests of the members, most of which had been developed prior to the revolution. Although efforts were being made to develop a Marxist musicology, particularly in Leningrad under the guidance of Asafiev, this task was not yet accomplished.

1932-1950: Synthesis

A new generation of theorists in the 1930s undertook the task of establishing Marxist-Leninist guidelines in music theory. Before 1932 younger theorists such as Viktor Abramovich Zuckermann, Lev Abramovich Mazel, and Iosif Yakovlevich Ryzhkin, all of whom graduated from conservatories after the Revolution, concentrated their research on the theories of established theorists such as Garbuzov, Conus, and Yavorsky. About 1932, though, they came to consider much of the work of these older theorists too "one-sided": music could not be explained solely on the basis of its acoustical foundations (Garbuzov), its modal formations (Yavorsky), its functional properties (Catoire), or its symmetrical, architectural embodiment (Conus). They began to search for new approaches that would integrate theoretical analysis with the analysis of the historical, sociological, and philosophical aspects of music. Asafiev was already well along this path; consequently, his theories became one of the cornerstones of Soviet musical thought. This period has been called "a time of search and positive judgment, a period of affirmation,"[198] by which is meant the affirmation of a Marxist-Leninist approach to theoretical musicology, the coordination of music theory with the principles of historical and dialectical materialism.

Soviet theoretical thought after 1932 thus became less innovative than it had been previously, concentrating on the philosophical direction rather than the exploration of purely theoretical methods. Theorists avoided more radical theoretical ideas; instead they relied on proven and acceptable analytical techniques, expanding them if warranted, to aid in the formation of a Marxist theory of music. Yet some published works continued to reflect trends of the past decade. A book on musical form by Catoire, left unfinished at his death in 1926, was completed and published by his students Mazel and Kabalevsky.[199] Conus published two major works before his death in 1933; a third work was published posthumously.[200] Garbuzov remained active, teaching at the Moscow Conservatory and directing its acoustical laboratory. He also published a study of folk song that used his theory of modal formation and a textbook of musical acoustics.[201] Both Yavorsky and Asafiev continued their work but published no new studies during the 1930s.

At the conservatories, theorists began to develop new courses that took advantage of the by now rich Russian theoretical legacy and integrated it with Marxist philosophy. Mazel and Ryzhkin, both 1930 graduates of the Moscow Conservatory who began teaching there almost immediately, developed a course in the history of theoretical systems in music. They eventually published the material for this course, first in articles in *Soviet Music,* then in book form as *Essays on the History of Theoretical Musicology.*[202] The first volume was dedicated to pre-twentieth-century theory and contained articles by Ryzhkin on Rameau and on the traditional school (essentially, nineteenth-century theory up to Riemann), and by Mazel on the functional school; the second volume contained separate articles on the theories of Ernst Kurth (Mazel), Yavorsky (Ryzhkin), and Garbuzov (Ryzhkin). In the introduction to the second volume, Mazel discussed the theories of Conus and Catoire. These essays interpret the history of music theory from the viewpoint of Marxist-Leninist thought; in the author's words, they "attempt to examine the history of music theory not as an immanent process, but in connection with the general historical process, particularly in connection with the corresponding socially conditioned artistic, scientific, and philosophical directions."[203]

A number of theorists contributed to a new course in musical analysis, in which various existing analytical approaches were combined to form a type of analysis that would lead to conclusions about the expressive side of music. Zuckermann pioneered lectures on this topic at the Moscow Conservatory during the academic year 1931-1932, using the overture to *Alceste* by Gluck as the basis for his analysis. Beginning in 1933, theorists included the analysis of historical and stylistic elements as well. Other theorists who taught this course were Mazel and Ryzhkin in Moscow and Vladimir Vladimirovich Shcherbachev, Tiulin, and Boris Alexandrovich Arapov in Leningrad. This new integrated approach to analysis substituted for earlier unilateral approaches, which were no longer considered adequate.[204]

Although no textbook for this course was published, several published studies, primarily by the Moscow theorists and by Yuly Kremlev in Leningrad, developed this method of analysis. In his article on Rimsky-Korsakov's opera *Sadko*, Zuckermann analyzed the opera's subject and its music.[205] Through a detailed analysis of the orchestral intermezzo between the fifth and sixth scenes—the "underwater" music, as Zuckermann called it—which coordinated a description of the musical elements with the programmatic content, he concluded that the aspects of the music that were most important to Rimsky-Korsakov were "the coloring and graphic detail on the one hand, and a consideration of the formal musical logic on the other."[206] Zuckermann also examined the influence of folk music on the melodies and the modal harmonic language of *Sadko*, which, he determined, combines "the coloring of the old 'narodnosti' [national traits]" with the fantastic modal harmonic elements used by Rimsky-Korsakov logically and expressively in connection with the content.[207] Zuckermann's analysis used some of Yavorsky's terminology, such as "unstable modes (diminished and augmented)" and "tritonal juxtaposition of modal-tonalities," but the combination of expressive and philosophical analysis with musical analysis constitutes the study's most unusual feature.

Kremlev's analysis of the music of Debussy, "On the Impressionism of Claude Debussy," the first extended analysis of Debussy's music, or of impressionism in general, in the Soviet Union, is a far better work by Western standards.[208] But according to the editors of *Soviet Music* this article "still preserves in its analysis a significant portion of formalistic tendencies."[209] Kremlev's failing was that he did not relate the musical analysis in the second part of the article to philosophical statements made in the earlier part of the article, which was, as in Zuckermann's article, devoted to extra-musical elements. Unlike Zuckermann, though, who analyzed Rimsky-Korsakov's modal and harmonic language in a general manner, Kremlev analyzed Debussy's music chord by chord, pointing out the "afunctional" quality of impressionism, the tonal vagueness, and the transfer of function into color.

In a later article, "On the Musical Language of Musorgsky," Kremlev, taking heed of the earlier criticism, summarized the originality of Musorgsky's philosophical thought as embodied in the melodic and harmonic characteristics of his music.[210] Kremlev depicted Musorgsky as fighting against the traditional schemes of music and, after absorbing the folk and realistic styles of Glinka and Dargomyzhsky, forging them into a new melodic style, a synthesis of the best elements of his predecessors. Kremlev discovered in Musorgsky's harmonic innovations the manifestation of "a new understanding of musical logic, as the logic of the folk realistic style, bringing to the West an emancipation from the binding metaphysics of Wagnerism."[211] In Kremlev's opinion, Musorgsky was the first to write "with pure harmonic colorings based on the coloristic unity of tonalities. With this he marked a world-wide level in the development of musical thought."[212]

Lev Mazel, in his book, *The Fantasy in F minor by Chopin. An Experiment in Analysis,* carried out the most ambitious analytical undertaking.[213] Believing that "the problems of analysis of a musical work and of musical style are the central problems of our musicology," Mazel attempted, through the analysis of all the separate elements of the Fantasia, and through the application of various existing analytical methods, including those of Riemann, Catoire, Yavorsky, Conus, and Kurth, to synthesize the analyzed parts into a whole that would reflect its content and reveal its sociological basis.[214]

In addition to creating new courses, the creation of new harmony textbooks that reflected the new philosophical orientation also took priority. The first effort, a collective one, was carried out by a group of Moscow theorists, Iosif Ignatevich Dubovsky, Sergei Vasilevich Yevseev, Igor Vladimirovich Sposobin, and Vladimir Sokolov, all former students of Catoire's. Their work, *A Practical Course of Harmony,* studied "all harmonic phenomena . . . through the prism of dynamics. . . . The primacy of the theory of functionality . . . permeates our entire book."[215] The authors adopted Catoire's theory of functionality and his harmonic systems—diatonic, major-minor, and chromatic—but simplified his system of chord designation by making it more similar to the traditional Roman-numeral system but with allowance for harmonic function: T, D, and S for the principal triads; S_{II}, D_{III}, TS_{VI}, and D_{VII} for the secondary triads (lower-case letters for minors: s_{II}, etc.); D_D for secondary dominant; S_S for secondary subdominant. These symbols are still used today by many Soviet theorists. In another innovation, the authors relied nearly exclusively on examples from the musical literature. They still included specially written examples of voice-leading and chord illustration where necessary. Although the authors intended this book for practical use, they did not ignore the theoretical side; included were statements about the theories of Helmholtz, Riemann, Garbuzov, and Yavorsky. In the second edition of their book, *A Textbook of Harmony,* published three years later, they deleted these references and simplified the book still further.[216] The textbook as it exists today remains a totally practical one.[217]

Tiulin's *Study of Harmony* contrasts sharply with this collective work by the so-called brigade of Moscow theorists.[218] Tiulin's work, as scholarly as the brigade's textbook is practical, contains a major theoretical statement of one of the prominent theorists of this period. He believed that only through the "consideration of creative practice," through "a corresponding revision of all the positions of existing musical theoretical science," and through "the confirmation of these positions of theoretical conceptions as a whole," was it possible to uncover the artistic laws of theory, which he considered to be "the connecting link between the training disciplines and the creation of artists."[219] Essentially Tiulin did for harmony what Mazel had done for analysis: he developed a composite theory of harmony based on the fundamental principles that mode is the primary foundation of musical thought and that the basic melodic and harmonic connections within the mode are generated by their respective functions. He examined this modal-functional foundation of music in various manifestations—historical, acoustical, psychological, and practical—drawing, as did Mazel, from the works of other theorists such as Yavorsky, Garbuzov, Catoire, Riemann, and Kurth. Many of Tiulin's ideas almost immediately won permanent places in Soviet harmonic and modal theory. Thus through the works of Mazel and Tiulin are transmitted many of the most fruitful and useful ideas of previous theorists. The combination of these earlier ideas with their own unique perspectives and with the introduction into music theory of aspects of historical and dialectical materialism contributed to the development of a more unified Soviet music theory during the 1930s.

In 1940, Mazel published an article in *Soviet Music* in which he discussed the role of theoretical musicology in terms of its development, current state, and future path.[220] His views were not well received by some, including the editors of *Soviet Music*. They criticized Mazel for overemphasizing his own role and the roles of other Moscow theorists such as Zuckermann and Ryzhkin and underevaluating the importance of Yavorsky and Asafiev in the development of Soviet theoretical musicology.[221] They also reproved him for the distinctions he made between the separate roles of the critic and the musicologist. Mazel likened the critic to a judge who evaluates contemporary music according to his intuition and who attempts to influence the future development of musical creation based on his opinions. The musicologist, on the other hand, focuses mainly on "the legacy of musical art" and is "concerned ... with the givens of a formal analysis" made "on a scientific basis" and with the "knowledge of artistic phenomena, the intensification of its nature, and the enrichment ... of its objective value for contemporaries and following generations."[222] The editors of *Soviet Music* called Mazel's definition of musicology "impassive, isolated from life... [and] socially useless."[223] They advocated that theorists become more involved in contemporary issues, and in the development of Soviet musical culture.

Aleksei Stepanovich Ogolevets's *Foundations of Harmonic Language* appeared in 1941.[224] In this lengthy work (970 pp.), Ogolevets touched on nearly every topic connected with harmony; he devoted a large part of it, though, to expanded tonal systems, a topic that had not received much public attention in the previous decade. Accepting the twelve-tone chromatic scale as diatonic, he advocated seventeen- and twenty-two-degree systems, an idea derived from his studies of Arabian and Indian music. In his choice of topic, and scope and breadth of approach, Ogolevets recalled—and surpassed—the wide-ranging efforts in music theory of the 1920s. Based on the fundamental trends of this period, Ogolevets's work is an anomaly, a work that if accepted would have signaled broad changes in the Marxist theoretical approach.

Russia's entry into World War II brought with it a decrease in theoretical activity. Virtually no significant theoretical works were published during the war. Only in 1946 did theoretical works again begin to appear, and through 1948, several important works were published. However, none appeared in 1949 or 1950, a circumstance caused by the Resolution of the Central Committee of February 10, 1948 and the attacks on musicologists (including theorists) and critics at the conference of the musicological members of the Composers' Union a year later (February 18, 21, and 22, 1949).[225] Singled out among theorists for censure at the 1949 meeting were Ogolevets and Mazel above all, as well as Anatoli Konstantinovich Butskoi and Viktor Osipovich Berkov. The theorists Alexander Naumovich Dolzhansky, Ryzhkin, Zuckermann, and Vladimir Vasilevich Protopopov also received criticism.

Ogolevets endured the strongest criticism, not only from Tikhon Khrennikov, the head of the composers' union and the main speaker, but also from other musicologists. As examples of "formalistic," "anti-patriotic," "cosmopolitan," and "reactionary" musicology, Khrennikov quoted liberally from Ogolevets's recently published second work, *An Introduction to Contemporary Musical Thought.*[226] Ogolevets had divided world musical development into four cycles and placed contemporary musical thought between the third and fourth cycles; the fourth cycle was to be the adoption of Ogolevets's proposed seventeen- and twenty-two-degree systems. He also praised Stravinsky and rejected any politicization of music or musical thought. For these and other views, he was firmly denounced; he was ridiculed when he appeared at the conference in an attempt to explain himself.[227] Mazel's 1940 article on Soviet theoretical musicology brought many of the same criticisms earlier leveled against him by the editors of *Soviet Music;* he was also criticized for his remarks in a lecture comparing Shostakovich's Ninth Symphony to American popular culture.[228]

Butskoi and Berkov underwent criticism for their recently published books. Butskoi's work, *The Structure of a Musical Work,* was at the printer's on February 10, 1948. A professor of theory at the Leningrad Conservatory, he had already made changes in the work since writing it in 1941 as his doctoral dissertation, and, as he related in the foreword, was reluctant to delay the publication of the book in order to make further changes. Instead he hoped to mollify any unfavorable impression the book might make by stating that his analytical system contained only "preliminary conclusions and generalizations" that would be verified, expanded, or corrected by further collective research efforts of Soviet musicologists.[229] Butskoi investigated the aesthetic aspects of form and attempted to derive general laws of structure in such areas as meter, theme, and the form as a whole. Although in some respects his approach represents the antithesis of Conus's metrotechtonic analysis, both attempted to generalize about musical form and to discover its basic laws of structure. He was criticized, though, for overemphasizing Western theorists at the expense of Russian theorists, for quoting German modernistic music (Strauss) and neglecting Soviet music, for ignoring the content of musical works, and for quoting Marx and Engels only to cover up the "poverty" of his "formalistic" work.[230]

In *The Harmony of Glinka,* Berkov conducted a thorough study of the harmonic aspect of Glinka's music: its modal content, functional relations, chord choices, tonality, tonal plans, and methods of harmonic variations.[231] He pointed out the plagal (subdominant) element in Glinka's music, Glinka's fondness for the harmonic major scale and the minor subdominant, and the functional correlations of tonalities in his tonal plans. He identified three sources of Glinka's musical language—Russian folk song, music and musical life in Russia, and the world classical and romantic culture—but was criticized for emphasizing the cosmopolitan, romantic source of Glinka's music rather than the folk music source. Berkov, along with Ryzhkin, Zuckermann, and Vladimir Protopopov, was also reprimanded for not taking part in the work of the composers' union.

Thus, to sum up the official opinion, any theoretical work that was based on Western theoretical ideas (or even appeared to be so) was branded as "formalistic," and any work in which Russian folk music, Soviet music, or Russian theorists appeared to be neglected was labeled as "anti-patriotic" or "cosmopolitan." By the end of the Moscow conference and a similar conference held in Leningrad (March 5 and 6, 1949), thirty-five musicologists and critics had been censured or reprimanded.

Yet just as many theorists escaped criticism; among these were Sergei Sergeevich Skrebkov, Igor Sposobin, Garbuzov, Semen Semenovich Bogatyrev, and Andrei Fedorovich Mutli in Moscow, and Khristofor Stepanovich Kushnarev and Tiulin in Leningrad, most of whom also published works during this period. For example, Skrebkov and Sposobin, theory professors at the Moscow Conservatory, both published textbooks.[232] Garbuzov, in his work *The Zonal Nature of Pitch Audibility,* turned his attention to the explanation of his recently developed theory of "zone."[233] Bogatyrev, from 1949 dean of the theory and composition department of the Moscow Conservatory, in *Double Canon,* expanded Taneev's methods concerning moveable counterpoint and the canon to include double canon, a subject not fully developed by Taneev.[234] Mutli, a professor at the Moscow Conservatory, expanded Rimsky-Korsakov's idea of modulation based on the relatedness of tonalities in his work, *On Modulation.*[235] Other works published during this period include Yavorsky's *Bach's Suites for the Clavier* and the second volume of Asafiev's *Musical Form as a Process, Intonation.*[236]

Undoubtedly many works planned or written during this period went unpublished. For example, in 1948 one of Tiulin's graduate students, Varvara Dernova, a 1930 graduate of the Leningrad Conservatory in pedagogy, was working on a new way of analyzing Skryabin's music based on Yavorsky's theories. However, she did not publish the results of her research for twenty years; *The Harmony of Skryabin* finally appeared in 1968.[237]

In 1950 another musicological conference, the All-Soviet Scientific Session on Musicology, took place, attended by 262 delegates from all over the Soviet Union representing musical institutions of higher learning. Instead of the accusatory atmosphere of the 1949 meetings, the atmosphere for this conference was positive, constructive, even conciliatory. Plans for textbooks were submitted and reviewed, and broad guidelines for future musicological work were adopted.[238] Most of the textbooks discussed were in music history, but several theoretical works were also reviewed. In the meeting of the theoretical commission, a textbook for a special course of harmony, written by Tiulin and Nikolai Georgievich Privano (also of the Leningrad Conservatory) was approved; but plans for textbooks on polyphony, one by Skrebkov and Bogatyrev and another by Anatoly Nikodimovich Dmitriev, head of the theory department of the Leningrad Conservatory, were not so readily accepted.[239] The commission requested that Skrebkov and Bogatyrev include more information on polyphony in nonpolyphonic works, on nonimitative polyphony and on Russian polyphony, and asked Dmitriev to make substantial changes in the content and structure of his planned work.[240]

In the report of the session given in *Soviet Music,* Mikhail Blok pointed to several deficiencies of Soviet music theory, including the "weakness" of current analytical methods, the lack of serious study devoted to the "role of Russian folk music as the basic foundation of professional creation, history, and theory," and the lack of models of folk music in theoretical studies.[241] Blok summarized the future goals of Soviet musicology as determined at the session:

> To rebuild our musicological science on the basis of Marxist-Leninist methodology; to interpret the exhaustive directions given in the resolutions on ideological questions and in the appearance of comrade Zhdanov at the meeting of the agents of Soviet music; to eliminate formalistic and cosmopolitan tendencies and also other survivals of the influence of bourgeois ideology;... to reveal the deep interconnections of Russian musical culture with the musical cultures of fraternal peoples of the Soviet Union; to emphasize the world-wide significance of Russian and Soviet musical cultures.[242]

As restrictive as these guidelines were, focusing exclusively on Russian and Soviet culture as seen through Marxist-Leninist ideology, they nevertheless enabled musicologists and theorists to resume work. In 1951 and

1952, for example, a number of theory works were published, including several textbooks, additional works by Garbuzov on his theory of zone, and a work on melody by Mazel.[243] For most of the 1950s, Soviet theorists kept their work within the prescribed limits. Fewer and less innovative theoretical works were published, and most of these were practical textbooks. In the 1960s, though, as a result of a more tolerant official policy, the situation began to change. New trends in theoretical thought began to appear, and have continued to appear until the present time. It must be emphasized, though, that most recent research either is based on or in some way reflects the legacy of the period from 1900 to 1950. Rare is the work that does not recall to some degree ideas formulated by Asafiev, Yavorsky, Tiulin, Mazel, Taneev, Catoire, Conus, or Garbuzov, such as those concerning mode, function, or intonation. Thus an understanding of this rich history of Russian and Soviet music theory is essential to appreciate and understand contemporary Soviet music theory and thereby enrich our own fund of knowledge about music theory in general.

Notes

1. Some sources give the date of the Russian version as 1680. Diletsky wrote three earlier versions of this work, each in a different language: the original in Polish, *Toga zlota* (Vilnius, 1675); in Church Slavonic, *Grammatika musikijskovo penia* (Smolensk, 1677), and in Russian, *Idea grammatikii musikiiskoi* (Moscow, 1679). In 1723, Diletsky's work was translated into Ukrainian in St. Petersburg. Diletsky's *Grammar* was first published by Stepan Smolensky in 1910: *Musikiiskaia grammatika Nikolaia Diletskogo* [The musical grammar of Nikolai Diletsky] (St. Petersburg, 1910) is based on the 1681 manuscript. A facsimile edition of the Ukrainian manuscript from 1723 was published in Kiev in 1970: *Nikola Diletsky, Gramatika musikalna*. A new Soviet edition based on the 1679 manuscript was recently published: Nikolai Diletsky, *Idea grammatiki musikiiskoi* [The idea of musical grammar], Pamiatniki russkogo muzykal'nogo iskusstva [Monuments of Russian musical art], vol. 7, trans. and ed. Vladimir Protopopov (Moscow, 1979). This anniversary edition contains a description, history, facsimile, transcription, and translation (into modern Russian) of the 1679 manuscript, as well as excerpts and descriptions of other versions, and articles investigating nearly every aspect of Diletsky's life and work. Protopopov's work itself is a monument to fine scholarship. For a discussion of Diletsky's work in more detail, see my dissertation, *The Theory of Music in Russia and the Soviet Union from c. 1650 to 1950* (Ph.D. diss., University of Pennsylvania, in progress).

2. For a detailed investigation of Russian chant theory, see Maksim Viktorovich Brazhnikov, *Drevnerusskaia teoriia muzyki. Po rukopisnym materialam XV-XVIII vv.* [The old Russian theory of music. According to manuscript materials of the 15th-18th cc.] (Leningrad, 1972). See also Nicolas Schidlovsky, "Sources of Russian Chant Theory," in this volume.

3. Two foreign-language works on music theory were published in Russia during this time, both written by scholars at the Academy of Sciences: Leonhard Euler's *Tentamen novae Theoriae Musicae* (St. Petersburg, 1739) and Wolfgang Kraft's speech to the Academy on the

relationship between color and music, later translated into Russian (by G.N. Templov) and published as *Rech Volfganga Krafta o muzykal'nom soglasii* [The speech of Wolfgang Kraft about musical accords] (St. Petersburg, 1744). Neither work had any marked influence on the development of a Russian theory of music.

4.   The first performance was Giovanni Alberto Ristori's *commedia per musica, Calandro,* in the Kremlin in Moscow, on December 11, 1731.

5.   Jakob Staelin von Storcksburg, a German invited in 1735 to come to Russia as a member of the Academy of Sciences, became the editor of the *St. Petersburg vedomosti* [St. Petersburg Gazette]. His reports on Russian musical life appeared in that newspaper and later were compiled into a book, *Nachrichten von der Musik in Russland* (Leipzig, 1769-70), a primary source of information for Russian music of the eighteenth century. This work was translated into Russian and published in 1935 as *Muzyka i balet v Rossii XVIII veka* [Music and ballet in Russia of the 18th century].

     Vasily F. Trutovsky, *Sobranie russkikh prostykh pesen s notami* [A collection of simple Russian songs with music], 4 vols. (St. Petersburg, 1776-95).

6.   Georg Simon Löhlein, *Klavikordnaia shkola, ili kratkoe i osnovatel'noe pokazanie k soglasiu i melodii prakticheskimi primerami iziasnennoe* [Klavier-Schule, oder kurze und gründliche Anweisung zur Melodie und Harmonie, durchgehends mit praktischen Beispielen erkläret] (Moscow, 1973).

     Metodicheskii opyt, kakim obrazom mozhno vyuchit detei chitat muzyku, stol zhe legko, kaki obyknovennoie pis'mo [Essai méthodique sue la manière d'enseigner aux enfants à lire la musique aussi facilement que l'ecriture ordinaire], trans. Evgraf Smagin (Moscow, 1773). Smagin was a teacher in the French department of Moscow University during the 1760s. Only his initials (E.S.) are given in the book, but it is generally thought that he was the translator.

7.   Giovanni Paisiello, *Regole per bene accompagnare il Partimento; o sia il Basso Fondamentale sopra il Cembalo... Composte per Sua Altezza Imperiale La Gran Duchessa di tutte le Russie* (St. Petersburg, 1782). David Kellner, *Vernoe nastavlenie v sochinenii general-basa* [Treulicher Unterricht im General-bass], trans. I. Zubrilov (Moscow, 1791). Demian Petrunkevich, *Nastavlenie otrokam uchashchimsia Notnomu Peniu, c iasneishim pokazaniem Tonov vsemu notnomu pravilu prinadlezhashchikh* [A manual for young males studying sight-singing, with the clearest indication of tones belonging to all music rules] (St. Petersburg, 1793). While in Russia, Sarti began a *Trattato del basso generales,* but never finished it.

8.   Boris Lvovich Volman, *Russkie pechatnye noty XVIII veka* [Russian printed music of the 18th century] (Moscow, 1957). Petrunkevich's work—and later similar Russian works—has gone largely unnoticed by Soviet musicologists except Volman.

9.   Gustav Gustavovich Hess de Calvé, *Teoriia muzyki, ili Rassuzhdenie o sem iskusstve, zakliuchaiushchee v sebe istoriiu, tsel, deistvie muzyki, general-bas, pravila sochineniia (kompozitsii), opisanie instrumentov, raznye rody muzyki i vse, chto otnosiatsia k nei, v podrobnosti* [The theory of music, or a discourse about the seven arts, including history, purpose, effects of music, thorough bass, rules of composition, a description of instruments, different sorts of music, and all that belongs to it in detail], trans. R.T. Gonorsky (Kharkov, 1818), pt. 1, p. 4.

10.   A revealing—though fictional—portrait of such a foreign pedagogue is given by the great Russian writer Ivan Turgenev in his novel *Dvorianskoe gnezdo* [A nest of gentlefolk], published in 1869. He relates the story of the impoverished German Christopher Lemm, a once-promising composer who migrated to Russia at the age of twenty-eight but lost hope of leaving Russia to return home after twenty years because "he did not want to return home a

beggar from Russia, that great Russia, the El Dorado of the artist" (Moscow: Foreign Languages Publishing House, n.d., p. 221).

11. Ivan Komendatov, *Nachal'noe osnovanie o garmonii, ili Tochnoi poriadok proiskhozhdeniia vsekh postepenno dvadtsati dvukh glasov, prinadlezhashchikh dlia odnoi tol'ko oktavy* [The basic principles of harmony, or the exact order of the origin of all twenty-two glasy (modes), belonging to only one octave] (Moscow, 1801). Fedor Drobish, *Nachalnoe svedenie v prakticheskoi muzyki* [Beginning knowledge in practical music] (Moscow, 1836; 2nd ed., 1854). Ivan Gabertsettel, *Tablitsy vsekh akkordov, dlia oblegcheniia uchashchikhsia garmonii i sochineniia* [Tables of all the chords, for the facilitation of students of harmony and composition] (St. Petersburg, 1840).

12. Francois-Joseph Fétis, *Muzyka, poniatnaia dlia vsekh, ili kratkoe izlozhenie vsego nuzhnogo, chtob sudit' i govorit' ob iskusstve sem, ne uchivshis onomu* [Music, understandable to all, or a short statement of all that is needed to judge and speak about art for those who have not studied it], trans. P. Beliakov (St. Petersburg, 1833). Other foreign works were by Lud. Minelli, F. Tsykh, Jean-Baptiste-Louis Gresset, Bonifacio Asioli, and N. Finagini.

13. The other works are less satisfactory for a variety of reasons. Minelli's *General-bass* (Moscow, 1808) and *Udobnogo sposoba sochiniat proizvedeniia muzyki i akkompaniro-vaniia* [A pleasing method of composing musical works and of accompanying] (1808?) are on thorough bass and accompaniment; Gebel's *Rukovodstvo k sochineniiu muzyki* [A guide to the composition of music], trans. P. Artemov, vol. 1 (Moscow, 1842?) is incomplete; Karl Arnold's *Kratkoe rukovodstvo k izucheniiu pravil kompozitsii* [A short guide to the study of the rules of composition] (St. Petersburg, 1841) is disputed as to its authorship by Yury Arnold; and Lemokh's *Obshchee rukovodstvo k izucheniiu muzyki* [A general guide to the study of music] (Moscow, 1848) is nothing more than a poorly translated version of A.B. Marx's *Allgemeine Musiklehre* (Leipzig, 1839).

14. Vicenzo Manfredini, *Pravila garmonicheskie i melodicheskie dlia obucheniia vsei muzyki* [The harmonic and melodic rules for the study of all music], trans. Stepan Degtiarev (St. Petersburg, 1805). This translation is based on the second edition of Manfredini's work, published in 1797. He wrote the original version while in service to Catherine the Great, during the years 1762-69, thus becoming actually the first in Russia to write such a work: *Regole Armoniche o sieno Precetti regionati per apprendere i principj della Musica, il portamento della Mano, e l'accompagnamento del Basso sopra gli Strumenti da Testo, come l'Organo, il Cembalo ec. dedicate a Sua Altezza Imperiale Paul Petrovicz Gran Duca Di Tutti le Russie ec. ec. ec.* (Venice, 1775).

15. Hess de Calvé, *Teoriia muzyki*, p. 4.

16. Johann Philip Kirnberger, *Die Kunst des reinen Satzes in der Musik* (Berlin, 1771; 1776-79).

17. Hess de Calvé, *Teoriia muzyki*, p. 4.

18. See, for example, Y.A. Kremlev, *Russkaia mysl' o muzyke. Ocherki istorii russkoi muzykal'noi kritiki i estetiki v XIX veka* [Russian thought on music. Essays on the history of Russian musical criticism and aesthetics in the 18th century], vol. 1 (Leningrad, 1954), pp. 36-39, 62-66, 158.

19. These include harmony, chord, voice-leading, alteration, leading tone, scale, thorough bass, diatonic progressions of tones, diatonic mode, and dominant.

20. For his course on thorough bass and counterpoint given in 1832, Domanevsky hoped for one hundred pupils; the number who enrolled is not known. Bollet, for his courses on thorough

bass and counterpoint in 1839-40, had only twelve students, eight in thorough bass and four in composition ("Smes'. Kursy muzyki v St. Peterburge" [A mixture. Courses of music in St. Petersburg], *Severnaia pchela* [The northern bee], no. 218 [September 27, 1840]).

21.   Johann Leopold Fuchs, *Prakticheskoe rukovodstvo k sochineniiu muzyki, v pol'zu samouchashchikhsia, i v oblegchenie uchitelei s prilozheniem osobennykh pravil dlia sochinitelei russkogo tserkovnogo peniia i dvukh notnykh tetradei, iz kotorykh pervaia zakliuchaet v sebe primery i zadachi, a vtoraia reshenie zadach* [A practical guide to the composition of music, for independent study and for the facilitation of teachers, with a supplement of special rules for the composition of Russian church song, and two music notebooks, of which the first includes examples and problems, and the second the solutions to the problems], trans. Modeste Rezvyi (St. Petersburg, 1830). For a biography of Fuchs, see Boris Steinpress, "Der Petersburger Musiker Leopold Fuchs," trans. Ernst Stöckl, *Die Musikforschung* 15, no. 1 (1962): 39-44.

22.   Ibid., pp. iii-iv.

23.   Jacob Gottfried Weber, *Versuch einer geordneten Theorie der Tonsetzkunst*, 3 vols. (Mainz, 1817-1821).

24.   Alexander Dmitrievich Ulybyshev, Review, *Severnaia pchela*, no. 125 (October 18, 1830).

25.   In addition to serving as music editor for the first six volumes of the *Encyclopedic Dictionary*, to which he contributed several significant theoretical articles following the theories of Fuchs, Rezvyi was also the music editor of the *Slovar' tserkovno-slavianskogo i russkogo iazyka* [Dictionary of the Church Slavonic and the Russian language], published by the section of Russian language and literature of the Academy of Sciences in 1847. Concerning Rezvyi's efforts as Russia's first great music lexicographer, Prince Odoevsky stated:

> [Rezvyi is] not only a thorough musical expert and a talented composer, but, with his translation of Fuchs's "General-bass" [sic], he first established our technical musical language—not an easy task, successfully fulfilled and deserving of universal gratitude. This work required on the part of the translator not only the knowledge of both languages, but also a complete command of music, both as a *science* and as an *art*. If today the teaching of music in the Russian language is possible, if each of us may now write about music without concentrating on each step, for this we are obliged solely to the honorable works of Rezvyi. (V.F. Odoevsky, Letter to the editor of *Literaturnaia gazeta* [Literary newspaper], no. 10 [March 15, 1845], pp. 185-86.)

26.   Ulybyshev, Review.

27.   Dmitri Yurevich Struisky, "Bibliografiia. Russkie knigi" [Bibliography. Russian books], *Literaturnaia gazeta* [Literary newspaper] 2, no. 61 (October 28, 1830): 203.

28.   Johann Leopold Fuchs, *Novaia metoda, soderzhashchiia glavniia pravila muzykal'noi kompozitsii i rukovodstvo k prakticheskomu primeniiu ikh; s kratkim izlozheniem osnovanii dvoinogo kontrapunkta, kanon i fugi* [A new method, containing the main rules of musical composition and a guide to their practical application; with a short statement of the basis of double counterpoint, canon, and fugue], trans. G.K. Arnold (St. Petersburg, 1843).

29.   Joseph Karlovich Hunke, *Rukovodstvo k izucheniiu garmonii, prisposoblennoi k samoucheniiu* [A guide to the study of harmony, adapted for independent study] (Moscow, 1852).

30.   Ibid., p. 10.

31.   Joseph Karlovich Hunke, *Rukovodstvo k sochineniiu muzyki* [A guide to the composition of music], 3 vols. (St. Petersburg, 1859-63). The three volumes are entitled *Uchenie o melodii* [A

study of melody] (1859), *O kontrapunkte* [On counterpoint] (1861), and *O formakh muzykal'nykh proizvedenii* [The forms of musical works] (1863).

32. Anton Reicha, *Traité de mélodie* (Paris, 1814).

33. See below, note 86.

34. For a detailed treatment of this question, see Robert Ridenour, *Nationalism, Modernism and Personal Rivalry in Nineteenth-Century Russian Music* (Ann Arbor: UMI Research Press, 1981).

35. Hermann Larosh, testifying in Modeste Tchaikovsky, *The Life and Letters of Peter Ilich Tchaikovsky,* trans. Rosa Newmarch, 2 vols. (New York: Haskell House Publishers, Ltd., 1970), 1:46.

36. Anton Rubinstein, "O muzyke v Rossii" [On music in Russia], *Vek* [Century], no. 1 (January 4, 1861), reprinted in Boris Asafiev, *Anton Grigorevich Rubinshtein v ego muzykal'noi deiatel'nosti i otzyvakh sovremennikov* (1829-1929) [Anton Grigorevich Rubinstein and his musical activity and opinions of contemporaries (1829-1929)] (Moscow, 1929), pp. 87-92.

37. Alexander N. Serov, "O muzyke v Peterburge" [On music in Petersburg], *Biblioteka dlia chteniia* [A library for reading], no. 28 (February, 1861), pp. 17-28; "Zalogi istinnogo muzykal'nogo obrazovaniia v S.-Peterburge" [Pledges of true musical education in St. Petersburg], *Severnaia pchela* [The northern bee], no. 124 (1862); "Muzyka, muzykal'naia nauka, muzykal'naia pedagogika" [Music, musical science, musical pedagogy], *Epokha* [Epoch], nos. 6 and 12 (1864).

    Serov's lecture series took place in the years 1858-59, 1863, 1864, 1865, 1866, 1868, and 1870 (Y.V. Keldysh, "Serov," *Muzykal'naia entsiklopediia* [Musical encyclopedia], vol. 4 [Moscow, 1978], col. 946).

38. Hermann Larosh, "Mysli o muzykal'nom obrazovanii v Rossii" [Thoughts on musical education in Russia], *Russkii vestnik* [The Russian herald], no. 7 (July, 1869); "Mysli o sisteme garmonii i ee primenenii k muzykal'noi pedagogike" [Thoughts on the system of harmony and its application to musical pedagogy], *Muzykal'nyi sezon* [The musical season], no. 18 (1871); "Istoricheskii metod prepodavaniia teorii muzyki" [The historical method of teaching the theory of music], *Muzykal'nyi listok* [Musical leaflet], no. 2 (1873), pp. 17-22; no. 3 (1873), pp. 33-40; no. 4 (1873), pp. 47-53; no. 5 (1873), pp. 65-68.

39. This was so at the Moscow Conservatory, at least, until Sergei Taneev began teaching counterpoint there in 1886. Tchaikovsky had also stressed voice-leading and attention to individual melodic lines in his course on harmony.

40. It was Azanchevsky who thwarted attempts of the Grand Duchess Elena Pavlovna to change the direction of the St. Petersburg Conservatory and who persuaded Rimsky-Korsakov to take a position at the Conservatory. See Ridenour, 213-15.

41. Oskar Kolbe, *Kratkoe rukovodstvo k izucheniiu generalbasa* [A short guide to the study of thorough bass], trans. from German by Izdal K. Oppel (Warsaw, 1864); F.A. Gevaert, *Rukovodstvo k instrumentovke* [A guide to instrumentation], trans. P.I. Tchaikovsky (Moscow, 1866); Ernst Friedrich Richter, *Uchebnik garmonii. Prakticheskoe rukovodstvo k ee izucheniiu* [A textbook of harmony. A practical guide to its study], trans. A. Famintsyn (St. Petersburg, 1868).

42. Odoevsky mentioned collections by Trutovsky, Prach, Kashin, and Shprevich in his article, "Russkaia i tak nazyvaemaia obshchaia muzyka" [Russian and so-called general music], *Russkii* [Russian], lists 11 and 12 (April 24, 1867), pp. 170-77.

43. Vladimir Odoevsky, "Pis'mo kn. V.F. Odoevskogo k izdateliiu ob iskonnoi velikorusskoi muzyke" [A letter of Prince V.F. Odoevsky about true Great-Russian music], *Kaliki perekhozhie. Sbornik stikhov i issledovanie P. Bessonova* [Wandering minstrels. A collection of poetry and research of P. Bessonov], part 2, no. 5 (Moscow, 1863), pp. i-xi; "Mirskaia pesnia, napisannaia na vosem' glasov kriukami s kinovarnymi pometami" [Secular song, written in the eight glasy with neumes with cinnebar notes] *Trudy pervogo arkheologicheskogo s'ezdc v Moskve, 1869* [Works of the first archeological congress in Moscow, 1869], vol. 2 (Moscow, 1871), pp. 484-91; "Razlichie mezhdu ladami (Tonarten, tons) i glasami (Kirchen-tonarten, tons d'eglise)" [The difference between modes (Tonarten, tons) and glasy (Kirchen-tonarten, tons d'eglise)], ibid., pp. 481-84.

44. From his writings, it is clear that Odoevsky had read and studied the works of the theorists published in Russian such as Hess de Calvé and other prominent Western theorists such as Fétis.

45. See his articles "Mirskaia pesnia" [Secular song] and "Opyt muzykal'noi eresi" [An experiment in musical heresy], the latter unpublished until 1956 when it was included in a collection of Odoevsky's writings, *Muzykal'no-literaturnoe nasledie* [Musical literary heritage], ed. G. Bernandt (Moscow, 1956), pp. 448-51. Bernandt dates this article from the years 1850-56; it was probably written towards the end of that period.

46. Odoevsky, "Osmoglasie," *Nasledie,* pp. 451-52. This article dates from the 1860s.

47. Odoevsky, "Etiudi ob organicheskikh zakonakh muzykal'noi garmonii" [Studies in the organic laws of musical harmony], *Nasledie,* pp. 443-48. According to Bernandt, this article was originally written in French in 1854.

48. Odoevsky, "Zvukovye sovpadeniia; opyt primeneniia ikh zakona k teorii akkordov" [Sound coincidences; an experiment in the application of their law to a theory of chords], *Nasledie,* pp. 456-59.

49. For example, in 1863-64, he constructed a piano in which there were separate keys for each note in the enharmonic scale. (Dmitri Razumovsky, "Muzykal'naia deiatel'nost kniazia V.F. Odoevskogo" [The musical activity of V.F. Odoevsky], *V pamiat' o kniaze Vladimire Fedoroviche Odoevskom* [In memory of Prince Vladimir Fedorovich Odoevsky] [Moscow, 1869], p. 38.) Building this piano may have been part of an experiment to stretch his hearing facility to comprehend microtones, for at one point he wrote: "Music may be called all-sounding only when the sounds between D and E♭ become intelligible to us." (Odoevsky, "Osmoglasie," p. 452.)

50. Odoevsky, *Muzykal'naia gramota* [Musical grammar] (Moscow, 1868); rpt., *Nasledie,* pp. 346-69.

51. Only two comments concerning the book have been found in Odoevsky's papers, one a letter from Hunke dated June 10, 1868 (the book was published in March of that year), praising Odoevsky for the brevity and truth in his book and for his life-long devotion to music. (From the Manuscript Division of the Leningrad Public Library. Cited in Bernandt, *Nasledie,* pp. 635-36.)

52. Alexander Serov, "Russkaia narodnaia pesnia, kak predmet nauki" [Russian folk song, as a subject of science], *Muzykal'nyi sezon* [The musical season], no. 18 (1869), no. 6 (1870), no. 13 (1871); reprint Serov, *Izbrannye stat'i* [Collected articles], vol. 1 (Moscow, 1950), pp. 81-108.

53. Serov, "Muzyka, muzykal'naia nauka, muzykal'naia pedagogika"; "Razlichnye vzgliady na odin i tot zhe akkord" [Different views on one and the same chord], *Muzykal'nyi i teatral'nyi vestnik* [The musical and theatrical herald], no. 28 (July 15, 1856), pp. 495-97; "Ritm, kak spornoe slovo [Rhythm, as a disputed word], ibid., no. 25 (June 24, 1856), pp. 452-55; "Kurs

muzykal'noi tekhniki"[A course in musical technique], ibid., no. 16 (April 22, 1856), pp. 297-99; no. 19 (May 13, 1856), pp. 351-52; no. 20 (May 20, 1856), pp. 367-68; no. 21 (May 27, 1856), p. 383; no. 22 (June 3, 1856), pp. 395-96; no. 24 (June 17, 1856), pp. 431-33; no. 32 (August 12, 1856), pp. 563-65. These latter articles began what was to be a lengthy series on the technical aspects of music; Serov abruptly ended the series after just seven segments. The first article cited was to be part of another series serving as preparation for a complete musical textbook on musicology, but Serov never realized this project either. Noteworthy, though, is the first use by a Russian of the word *muzykoznanie* [musical knowledge], translated in this article as "musicology."

54. See for example Serov, "Tematizm uvertiury 'Leonora' (Etiud o Betkhovene)" [The thematicism of the "Leonora" overture (An etude on Beethoven)], *Izbrannye stat'i,* vol. 1 (Moscow, 1950), pp. 409-24; "Deviataia simfoniia Betkhovena, ee sklad i smysl'"[The Ninth Symphony of Beethoven, its constitution and thought], *Sovremennaia letopis'* [Contemporary chronicle], no. 16 (1868); "'Zhizn' za tsaria' i 'Ruslan i Liudmilla'"["A Life for the Tsar" and "Ruslan and Ludmilla"], *Russkii mir* [The Russian world], no. 67 (1860); "'Rusalka' Dargomyzhskogo" [Dargomyzhsky's "Rusalka"], *Muzykal'nyi i teatral'nyi vestnik* [The musical and theatrical herald], nos. 20, 24, 26, 28, 32-34, 36-38 (1856); "'Ruslan'i ruslanisty"["Ruslan" and the Ruslanists], *Muzyka i teatr* [Music and the theater], nos. 1, 2, 4, 5, 7, 8, 10 (1867-68).

55. Razumovsky's major work is *Tserkovnoe penie v Rossii (Opyt istoriko-tekhnicheskogo izlozheniia)* [Church song in Russia (An experimental historical technical presentation)], 3 vols. (Moscow, 1867-69).

56. See for example Alexander Kastalsky, *Osobennosti narodno-russkoi muzykal'noi sistemy* [Characteristics of the folk Russian musical system] (Moscow-Petrograd, 1923); Viktor Beliaev, *Belorusskaia narodnaia muzyka* [Byelorussian folk music] (Leningrad, 1941); and Khristofor Kushnarev, *Voprosy istorii i teorii armianskoi monodicheskoi muzyki*[Questions of the history and theory of Armenian monodic music] (Leningrad, 1958).

57. Petr Ilich Tchaikovsky, *Rukovodstvo k prakticheskomu izucheniiu garmonii* [A guide to the practical study of harmony] (Moscow, 1871). Tchaikovsky's textbook has been translated into English: *Guide to the Practical Study of Harmony,* trans. Emil Krall and James Leibling from the German version of P. Juon (Canoga Park, California: Summit Publishing Company, 1970).

58. Tchaikovsky, *Rukovodstvo,* in *Polnoe sobranie sochinenii* [The complete collected works], vol. 3-A, ed. Vladimir Protopopov (Moscow, 1957), pp. 3-4. All quotations are taken from this Russian edition, in my translation.

59. Ibid., p. 3.

60. Ibid.

61. Ibid., p. 4.

62. Ibid., p. 66.

63. Yuly Engel (1868-1927), who had studied with Taneev, later had this to say about the "empirical method" of theory pedagogy:

> Usually in former times, and frequently even now, the teaching of the theory of composition was reduced and is reduced to the practical mastery of the well-known series of norms of harmony, voice-leading, [and] musical form. These norms are mastered by students by an applied method, as something self-sufficient, irrespective of time and space. Do it this way, do not do it this way.... By such a purely empirical

method Taneev himself studied with Tchaikovsky, who in turn had studied the same with Zaremba, who in turn had studied the same with someone [A.B. Marx], etc., etc. ("S.I. Taneev, kak uchitel'" [S.I. Taneev, as a teacher], *Muzykal'nyi sovremennik* [Musical contemporary], no. 8 [1916], p. 40.)

64. Tchaikovsky, *Rukovodstvo,* p. 155.

65. Ibid., p. 19.

66. Ibid., p. 29.

67. Ibid., p. 160.

68. Ibid., p. 10.

69. Ibid., p. 11.

70. One Soviet theorist denies categorically that Tchaikovsky intended his grouping of triads in the major mode to be interpreted as functional; he emphasizes that this grouping is only "a factual recognition of the parallel major-minor system, and also of the variable-functional connections of harmonies.... It is difficult to recognize these joinings as particularly *functional.* The 'true role' of chords as representatives of some 'group' is not found in the textbook." (A.A. Stepanov, "Voprosy garmonicheskoi struktury i funktsional'nosti v 'Rukovodstve k prakticheskomu izucheniiu garmonii' P.I. Chaikovskogo" [Questions of harmonic structure and functionality in *The guide to the practical study of harmony* of P.I. Tchaikovsky], *Voprosy muzykovedeniia* [Questions of musicology], vol. 1 [Moscow, 1972], p. 165.) For a definition of "variable-functional connections of harmonies," see the section on Yury Tiulin in my article, "The Contributions of Taneev, Catoire, Conus, Garbuzov, Mazel, and Tiulin," in this volume.

71. Some theorists consider these chords special forms of the augmented-sixth chord. McHose, for example, calls them augmented-sixth chords of the first (dominant) class (Allen Irvine McHose, *The Contrapuntal Harmonic Technique of the 18th Century* [New York, 1947], p. 275). Piston cites the augmented-sixth chord on the lowered second degree as "a comparatively rare treatment of the augmented sixth as a dominant" (Walter Piston, *Harmony,* 4th ed., rev. and exp. Mark DeVoto [New York, 1978], p. 426).

72. Tchaikovsky, *Rukovodstvo,* p. 128.

73. According to Larosh, other theorists shared Tchaikovsky's views, but Larosh did not:

> Usually theorists consider the triad to which the augmented-sixth chord resolves as tonic. Among them is Tchaikovsky, who, in his recently published *Guide to the Practical Study of Harmony,* insists on such a view with particular energy. It is remarkable that no one with a view similar to Tchaikovsky's took the trouble to look at the works of Mozart, Gluck, or Haydn from the point of view of the use of the disputed chord; they would have made certain that in the classics this chord never precedes the tonic triad, and that is why to explain it as the position of the fifth in the dominant-seventh chord (as they do) has not the slightest foundation. The use of this chord as presented in their explanation begins in the history of music no earlier than Franz Schubert, and thus may not be considered basic; it is no more than a magical exception. (Herman Larosh, "Istoricheskii metod prepodavaniia teorii muzyki" [The historical method of teaching the theory of music], *Sobranie muzykal'no-kriticheskikh statei* [A collection of musical critical articles], vol. 1 [Moscow, 1913], p. 275.)

74. At the suggestion of the Society of Ancient Russian Art, Tchaikovsky wrote a second harmony textbook, *Kratkii uchebnik garmonii* [A short textbook of harmony] (Moscow,

1874), aimed at the musical amateur wishing to learn to write choral music. It is, as its title suggests, a shortened version of his *Guide.*

75. Nikolai Andreevich Rimsky-Korsakov, *Prakticheskii uchebnik garmonii* [A practical manual of harmony] (St. Petersburg, 1886). An English edition exists: *Practical Manual of Harmony,* trans. Joseph Achron (New York: Carl Fischer, Inc., 1930). This version was actually Rimsky-Korsakov's second version. The first volume of the first version, printed in a lithograph edition, appeared in 1884; the first and second volumes together appeared in 1885 as *Uchebnik garmonii* [A textbook of harmony]. The two versions differ in length and method, the second being much more concise. Differences in the theoretical content of the two versions are small, though, concerning mainly key relatedness and the modulatory plan. Tchaikovsky, to whom Rimsky-Korsakov had sent the first volume of the lithograph edition for his evaluation, had gently criticized the work for its verbosity and circumstantiality. See Tchaikovsky's letter of April 8, 1885, to Rimsky-Korsakov, published in *Sovetskaia muzyka* [Soviet music], 1945, no. 3, p. 134. Tchaikovsky's marginal notes in his personal copy of the lithograph edition have also been published: P.I. Tchaikovsky, "Zamechaniia na poliakh 'Uchebnika garmonii' N. Rimskogo-Korsakova" [Notes in the margins of *The textbook of harmony* of N. Rimsky-Korsakov], *Polnoe sobranie sochinenii* [The complete collected works], 3-A: 226-49.

76. Rimsky-Korsakov wrote:

> From constant talks with Anatoli [Liadov] regarding this subject, I came to know his system and methods of instruction, and conceived the idea of writing a new textbook of harmony, according to a wholly new system as regards pedagogic methods and sequences of exposition. Essentially, Liadov's system was an outgrowth of his professor Y.I. Johansen's system, and mine of Liadov's." (N.A. Rimsky-Korsakov, *My Musical Life,* trans. from 5th rev. ed. by Judah A. Joffe [1923; reprint London: Ernst Eulenberg Ltd., 1974], pp. 272-73.)

Although Rimsky-Korsakov gave credit to Liadov, nothing so far has been uncovered that clarifies the extent of Liadov's influence on Rimsky-Korsakov. No writings by Liadov on this subject exist, and his teacher Johansen wrote only a very basic work on counterpoint, *Dvukh, trekh i chertyrekh golosnyi prostoi, dvoinoi, troinoi i chetyrnoi strogii kontrapunkt* [Two-, three-, and four-voiced simple, duple, triple, and quadruple strict counterpoint], pt. 1, trans. I. Kazanli (Moscow, 1904).

77. N.A. Rimsky-Korsakov, *Prakticheskii uchebnik garmonii* [A practical textbook of harmony], vol. 4, *Polnoe sobranie sochinenii* [Complete collected works] (Moscow, 1960), p. 237.

78. Ibid., p. 238.

79. Rimsky-Korsakov, *My Musical Life,* p. 272.

80. Glinka used this mode frequently. (See Viktor Berkov, *Garmoniia Glinki* [The harmony of Glinka] [Moscow-Leningrad, 1948].) But although Rimsky-Korsakov, along with Glinka, Chopin, and Liszt, also used unusual modes in his music, he did not include them in his textbook. He occasionally referred to them in his autobiography, though: "The conclusion [of the third movement of *Antar*] is a diverging passage of chords on an ascending eight-step scale (tone, semitone, tone, semitone, etc.), which I had once used before in *Sadko*" (*My Musical Life,* p. 93). The Russian theorist Andrei Fedorovich Kazbiriuk, in his *Popularnoe izlozhenie osnovnykh nachal muzykal'noi teorii prisposoblennoe k samoucheniiu* [A popular statement of the basic principles of music theory adapted for independent study] (Kiev, 1885), had noted several unusual modes, such as the Hungarian mode (with an augmented fourth),

the black-key scale (the pentatonic Chinese or Scottish mode), and the whole-tone scale, which, he pointed out, was first used in Russian music by Glinka in the opera *Ruslan and Liudmilla.*

81. See *Teoriia diatonicheskikh gamm* [The theory of diatonic scales] by G. Aristov (Kazan, 1871), *Kratkaia muzykal'naia grammatika* [A short musical grammar] by A.I. Rubets (St. Petersburg, 1871), and *Prakticheskoe rukovodstvo k izucheniiu elementarnoi teorii muzyki* [A practical guide to the study of the elementary theory of music] by V.Y. Villuan (Nizhnii Novgorod, 1878).

82. One precedent exists: Fuchs in 1830 included the minor supertonic and the mediant as related keys.

83. The top circle represents the *maximum* number of related keys. Very often theorists restricted the first two or three degrees of relatedness to just six or eight keys, leaving out the more distantly related keys; this widened the gap between their systems and that of Rimsky-Korsakov even further. Previously, even though the minor subdominant was the most remote key from the given key according to the circle of fifths, it was always included in the second degree of relatedness, never the third degree.

84. Rimsky-Korsakov, *My Musical Life,* p. 119.

85. Anton Arensky, *Kratkoe rukovodstvo k prakticheskomu izucheniiu garmonii* [A short guide to the practical study of harmony] (Moscow, 1891). Arensky also wrote in 1890 a collection of exercises, *Sbornick zadach (1000) dlia prakticheskogo izucheniia garmonii* [A collection of exercises (1000) for the practical study of harmony] (Moscow, 1897).

86. Ludwig Bussler, *Uchebnik form instrumental'noi muzyki* [A textbook of the forms of instrumental music], trans. Nikolai Kashkin and Sergei Taneev (Moscow, 1884); *Uchebnik muzykal'nykh form v tridtsati zadachakh* [A textbook of musical forms in thirty problems], trans. Y.A. Pikhalskaia (St. Petersburg, 1883). Although both of these works are translations of Bussler's *Musikalische Formenlehre* (Berlin, 1878), the Kashkin and Taneev translation is the better of the two. Taneev introduced works of Russian composers in place of some of the examples of Western music. A translation of A.B. Marx's *Allgemeine Musiklehre* was also available: *Vseobshchii uchebnik muzyki,* trans. from 8th Germ. ed. by A.S. Famintsyn (St. Petersburg, 1872). Kashkin and Taneev also translated Bussler's counterpoint textbooks *Svobodnyi stil'* [Free style], trans. N.D. Kashkin (Moscow, 1885) and *Strogii stil'* [Strict style], trans. S.I. Taneev (Moscow, 1885).

87. Anton Arensky, *Rukovodstvo k izucheniiu form instrumental'noi i vokal'noi muzyki* [A guide to the study of forms of instrumental and vocal music], 2 vols. (Moscow, 1893-94).

88. Among Riemann's theory books translated and published were *Katekhizis muzykal'nogo diktanta* [A catechism of musical dictation], trans. A. Ladukhin (St. Petersburg-Moscow, 1894); *Uproshchennaia garmoniia, ili Uchenie o tonal'nykh funktsiiakh akkordov* [Vereinfachte Harmonielehre oder die Lehre von den tonalen Funktionen der Akkorde], trans. Y. Engel (Moscow, 1896); *Sistematicheskoe uchenie o moduliatsii, kak osnova ucheniia o muzykal'nykh formakh* [Systematische Modulationslehre als Grundlage der musikalischen Formenlehre], trans. Y. Engel (Moscow, 1898); *Akustika s tochki zreniia muzykal'noi nauki* [Katechismus der Akustik] (Moscow, 1898). A Russian pupil of Riemann's, Anna Ivanovna Charnova, published articles about his harmonic theories: "Gugo Riman, novator v oblasti teorii i garmonii" [Hugo Riemann, an innovator in theory and harmony], *Teatr* [Theater], nos. 284 and 287 (1897), and "Gugo Riman i ego novyi metod prepodavaniia teorii garmonii" [Hugo Riemann and his new method of teaching the theory of harmony], *Muzyka i penie* [Music and singing], no. 3 (1898).

89. Arensky, *Rukovodstvo k izucheniiu form,* 1:57.

90. Ebenezer Prout, *Muzykal'naia forma* [Musical form], trans. S.L. Tolstoi (Moscow, 1896); *Fuga* [Fugue], trans. A. Timitseva-Gering (Moscow, 1900); *Prikladnye formy* [Applied forms], trans. Y. Slavinsky (Moscow, 1910); and *Analiz fug* [Fugal analysis], trans. V. Beliaev (Moscow, 1915). A work by J.C. Lobe, *Rukovodstvo k sochineniiu muzyki; Opera* [A guide to the composition of music; Opera], trans. N. Kashkin, vol. 4 (Moscow, 1898), was also published.

91. On Conus's theory of metrotechtonicism, see my article, "The Contributions of Taneev, Catoire, Conus, Garbuzov, Mazel and Tiulin," in this volume.

92. Georgy Conus, *Sinopticheskaia tablitsa elementarnoi teorii muzyki* [A synoptic table of the elementary theory of music] (Moscow, 1893).

93. Georgy Conus, cited in Viktor Zuckermann, "Muzykal'no-pedagogicheskie trudy G.E. Koniusa" [The musical pedagogical works of G.E. Conus], *G.E. Konius. Stat'i, materialy, vospominaniia* [G.E. Conus. Articles, materials, reminiscences] (Moscow, 1965), p. 112.

94. Georgy Conus, *Sbornik zadach, uprazhnenii i voprosov (1001) dlia prakticheskogo izucheniia elementarnoi teorii muzyki* [A collection of problems, exercises and questions (1001) for the practical study of the elementary theory of music] (Moscow, 1892).

95. Georgy Conus, *Posobie k prakticheskomu izucheniiu garmonii* [A textbook for the practical study of harmony] (Moscow, 1894).

96. A similar approach had been taken over forty years earlier in a work by Gabertsettel; see note 11.

97. Nikolai Ladukhin, *Rukovodstvo k prakticheskomu izucheniiu garmonii* [A guide to the practical study of harmony] (Moscow, 1898). Ladukhin's other works include *Opyt prakticheskogo izucheniia intervalov, gamm,i ritma* [An experiment in the practical study of intervals, scales, and rhythm] (Moscow, 1894); *Kratkaia entsiklopediia teorii muzyki* [A short encyclopedia of the theory of music] (Moscow, 1897); *Kratkii kurs garmonii* [A short course of harmony] (Moscow, 1901); and *Kurs garmonii v zadachakh, obraztsakh i primerakh* [A course of harmony in problems, models, and examples] (Moscow, 1913).

98. Mikhail Ippolitov-Ivanov, *Uchenie ob akkordakh, ikh postroenie i razreshenie* [The study of chords, their construction and resolution] (Moscow, 1897). The first chapter was earlier published in lithographic form in 1895.

99. Ippolitov-Ivanov made no mention of this work in his autobiography, *50 let russkoi muzyki v moikh vospominaniiakh* [50 years of Russian music in my reminiscences] (Moscow, 1934).

100. Yury Kurdiumov, *Klassifikatsiia garmonicheskikh soedinenii* [The classification of harmonic combinations] (St. Petersburg, 1896).

101. Kurdiumov, pp. iv-v.

102. Over 60 years earlier, in 1833, Odoevsky had proposed the development of a musical telegraph in his work, *Opyt o muzykal'nom iazyke, ili telegrafe, mogushchem posredstvom muzykal'nykh zvukov vyrazhat vse to, chto vyrazhaetsia slovami, i sluzhit posobiem dlia razlichnykh signalov, upotrebliaemykh na more i na sukhom puti (s prilozh, tablitsy "Alfavity muzykal'nogo telegrafa")* [An experiment in musical language, or telegraph, capable by means of musical sounds to express all that is expressed by words, and to serve as a guide for different signals, used on sea and on land (with a supplementary table "An alphabet of the musical telegraph")] (St. Petersburg, 1833).

103.   Minor is not the imitation of major, but results only *by means of* this imitation. Kurdiumov referred the reader to A. von Oettingen, *Harmoniesystem in dualer Beziehung* [Entwickelung] (Dorpat, 1866).

104.   Kurdiumov, *Klassifikatsiia,* p. 21.

105.   Ibid., pp. 21-22.

106.   For example, the terms linkage, chain, and aspiration to the center of gravity. Both also employ the term *oborot,* which Kurdiumov uses in the sense of a progression. Yavorsky, however, uses it in a slightly different sense; see Gordon D. McQuere, "The Theories of Boleslav Yavorsky," in this volume.

107.   "If it is possible to consider any of the Russian theorists the source of the Russian science of music, then it is S.I. Taneev," stated Viktor Beliaev in "'Analiz moduliatsii v sonatakh Betkhovena' S.I. Taneev" ['The analysis of modulation in the sonatas of Beethoven' by S.I. Taneev], *Russkaia kniga o Betkhovene* [The Russian book on Beethoven] (Moscow, 1927), p. 191. For more about this article and about Taneev, see my article, "The Contributions of Taneev, Catoire, Conus, Garbuzov, Mazel, and Tiulin," in this volume.

108.   Hugo Riemann, *Musiklexikon,* 5th ed. (Berlin, 1900). "Nauka o muzyke" [Musikwissenschaft], *Muzyakl'nyi slovar'* [Musiklexikon], ed. Yuly Engel (Moscow, 1901-04).

109.   "Nauka o muzyke," pt. 12, p. 906.

110.   Ibid., pp. 906-07.

111.   In the fields of music history (historical musicology) and ethnomusicology, by 1900 there existed serious biographical and historical studies, first of European music and later of Russian music, collections and studies of folk music, scholarly investigations of Russian chant, a periodical, *Russkaia muzykal'naia gazeta* [The Russian musical newspaper], published 1893-1918 and dedicated to the study of various aspects of musical life in Russia, in which were published historical documents and materials pertaining to Russian music, and articles in various other publications. However, the unification of these areas with acoustics, aesthetics, and music theory had yet to be undertaken.

112.   E.K. Rozenov, "On the Golden Section in Its Application to the Temporal Arts (Poetry, Drama, Music)," read January 28, 1904. Rozenov defined the role of the golden section in music, and gave illustrations. In works by Bach, Beethoven, Mendelssohn, and Chopin, he showed that "almost all the main subdivisions and . . . the places of the culminating points (points of modulatory aspiration, high melodic points, the point of greatest strength) strictly observe the law of the golden section." (*Russkaia muzykal'naia gazeta* [The Russian musical newspaper], no. 25-26 [1904], p. 638). Rozenov (1861-1935) was an 1889 graduate of the Moscow Conservatory in theory and piano.

        Georgy Conus, "Musical Form and Its Analysis," read March 12, 1903. Yuly Engel gave two lectures on the theories of Riemann, collectively titled, "The Fundamentals of the System of Harmony of Riemann," read November 12 and December 17, 1903. In these lectures, Engel, who translated some of Riemann's works into Russian (see note 88) and edited the translation of his *Musiklexikon,* presented Riemann's views on chord function, on the characteristics and roles of the three principal triads (tonic, subdominant, and dominant), on tonality, on the acoustical bases of major and minor (undertones), and on metrical construction.

113.   V.A. Bulychev, *Obshchestvo muzykal'no-teoreticheskaia Biblioteka v Moske. Otchet obshchestva Muzykal'no-teoreticheskaia Biblioteka v Moskve za pervye 4 goda ego deiatel'nosti. 1909-1912* [The Musical Theoretical Library Society in Moscow. An account of

the Musical Theoretical Library Society in Moscow for the first 4 years of its activity. 1909-1912] (Moscow, 1913), p. 5.

114.   Ibid.

115.   Ibid., p. 21.

116.   *Muzyka* [Music], published from 1910 to 1916 in Moscow, and *Muzykal'nyi sovremennik* [The musical contemporary], published from 1915 to 1917 in St. Petersburg.

117.   Again, works on harmony (17) and elementary theory (11) were the most numerous, followed by works on counterpoint (5) and exercise books (5). Among the harmony textbooks were A.I. Puzyrevsky, *Muzykal'noe obrazovanie. Osnovy muzykal'no-teoreticheskikh znanii* [Musical education. The fundamentals of musical theoretical knowledge] (St. Petersburg, 1903), and N.F. Soloviev, *Polnyi kurs garmonii* [A complete course of harmony] (St. Petersburg, 1911). Several were special studies of modulation: V.P. Stepanov, *Postroenie moduliatsii na osnove rodstva stroev* [The construction of modulation on the basis of the relatedness of keys] (Moscow, 1909); V. Malichevsky (Maliszewski), *Uchenie o moduliatsiiakh* [A study of modulations] (Moscow, 1915); and K. Shvedov, *O moduliatsiiakh v blizkie stroi* [On modulation into near keys] (Moscow, 1916). Stepanov expanded Rimsky-Korsakov's approach to modulation through key-relatedness by applying the principle of chord substitution. Distantly related chords substitute for nearly related chords with which they have a quintal or tertian relationship. A short book on melody by M. Popov-Platonov, *Teoriia melodii* [A theory of melody] (St. Petersburg, 1913), was also published.

118.   Boleslav Yavorsky, *Stroenie muzykal'noi rechi* [The structure of musical speech] (Moscow, 1908); Sergei Taneev, *Podvizhnoi kontrapunkt strogogo pis'ma* [Moveable Counterpoint in the Strict Style] (Moscow, 1909). On Taneev, see "The Contributions of Taneev, Catoire, Conus, Garbuzov, Mazel, and Tiulin," in this volume.

119.   Letter from Yavorsky to Taneev, September 15, 1909, cited in F. Arzamanov, "Zavety S. Taneeva" [Testaments of S. Taneev], *Sovetskaia muzyka* [Soviet music], 1956, no. 11, p. 30.

120.   Nadezhda Briusova, *Nauka o muzyke, eia istoricheskie puti i sovremennoe sostoianie* [The science of music, its historical path and contemporary state] (Moscow, 1910).

121.   Ibid., p. 1. Briusova originally read this material as a lecture at the Society of Free Aesthetics on November 11, 1909. It was first published in the journal *Vesy* [Libra], no. 10-11 (1909). Another lecture, *Vremennoe i prostranstvennoe stroenie formy* [The temporal and spatial construction of form], read on February 1, 1911, was published in Moscow the same year. Briusova (1881-1951), a fellow student of Yavorsky's at the Moscow Conservatory from which she graduated in piano in 1904, directed her later writings towards the topics of musical education and folklore.

122.   Leonid Sabaneev, "Muzykal'niia besedy, III. Nauka o muzyke" [Musical discussions, III. The science of music], *Muzyka* [Music], no. 74 (1912), p. 375.

123.   Briusova, *Nauka o muzyka*, p. 3.

124.   Sabaneev, "Muzykal'niia besedy," p. 375.

125.   Ibid., p. 376.

126.   K. Eiges, "Nauka o muzyke" [The science of music], *Muzyka* [Music], no. 154 (1913), p. 725.

127.   Ibid., pp. 725-26.

128. Viktor Beliaev, "Muzykal'no-teoreticheskie eskizy [Musical theoretical sketches], *Muzyka* [Music], no. 215 (1915), pp. 187-90; no. 223 (1915), pp. 331, 333; no. 224 (1915), pp. 347-48.

129. Ibid., no. 215, pp. 187-88.

130. Ibid., p. 190.

131. Ibid., no. 223, p. 331.

132. Beliaev later edited Taneev's manuscript, *Uchenie o kanone* [The doctrine of the canon], for posthumous publication in 1929. The works of both Prout and Riemann were influential in Russia at this time.

133. Beliaev, "Eskizy," no. 224, p. 347.

134. Ibid.

135. The musicologist Varvara Dernova. See Roy J. Guenther, "Varvara Dernova's System of Analysis of the Music of Skryabin," in this volume.

136. Leonid Sabaneev, "Prometei" [Prometheus], *Muzyka* [Music], no. 1 (1910), pp. 6-10; and "Sovremennaia techeniia v muzykal'nom iskusstve" [Contemporary trends in musical art], *Muzyka* [Music], no. 2 (1910), pp. 38, 42, and no. 4-5 (1910), pp. 85-88.

137. Leonid Sabaneev, "Poslednii otvet"[The last answer], *Muzyka*[Music], no. 20 (1911), p. 457. This article constituted the last in a series of exchanges in the pages of *Muzyka* between Sabaneev and Pavel Karasev, a composer and author, who became the first to question Sabaneev's views in print.

138. This chord was not always the so-called mystic chord of *Prometheus,* but often a "deformation" of that "synthetic" chord, caused by the raising or lowering of one or more of the partial tones. See Sabaneev, "Sed'maia sonata Skriabina" [The Seventh Sonata of Skryabin], *Muzyka* [Music], no. 64 (1912), pp. 195-201. Later, Sabaneev derived these changes from the seventeenth and nineteenth partial tones.

139. Leonid Sabaneev, "Muzykal'nye besedy, XI. Istoricheskii khod razvitiia garmonii"[Musical discussions, XI. The historical path of development of harmony], *Muzyka* [Music], no. 117 (1913), p. 116.

140. Ibid.

141. Leonid Sabaneev, "Muzykal'nye besedy, XXI. Ul'trakhromaticheskaia orientirovka" [Musical discussions, XXI. Ultrachromatic understanding], *Muzyka*[Music], no. 121 (1913), p. 194.

142. Arseny Avraamov, "Smychkovyi polikhord" [The bowed polychord], *Muzykal'nyi sovremennik* [The musical contemporary], 1915, no. 3, pp. 44-52. Taneev, in the introduction to his *Moveable Counterpoint in the Strict Style,* discussed omnitonal harmony—the term derived from Fétis—as that based on chromaticism rather than diatonicism. He disapproved of it because it destroyed the logic of tonality and form and contributed to the decline of the art of composition.

143. Avraamov referred to Skryabin's careless enharmonic writing, his extensive composing for the tempered piano (over 90% of his output), and the incompatibility of his "mystic" chord with the upper overtones. See Arseny Avraamov, "'Ul'trakhromatizm' ili 'omnitonal'nost'" ['Ultrachromaticism' or 'omnitonality'], *Muzykal'nyi sovremennik* [The musical contemporary], 1916, no. 4-5, pp. 157-68.

144. Leonid Sabaneev, "Ul'trakhromaticheskaia polemika" [The ultrachromatic dispute], *Muzykal'nyi sovremennik* [The musical contemporary], 1916, no. 6, p. 104.

145. Ibid. This view reverses his earlier stance on the near-exclusive role of harmony in ultrachromaticism, as in the harmony timbres. In his earliest writings on Skryabin's music, Sabaneev derived scales from the higher overtones. Here, though, he stated: "It is my profound conviction, based on intuition, that the *scale,* as a scheme of tones on which the thought of the creator is projected, was not formed from overtones at all." (Ibid., pp. 107-08.)

146. Nikolai Dmitrievich Kashkin, "Muzyka i muzykal'naia nauka" [Music and musical science], *Russkaia volia* [Russian will], no. 10 (January 11, 1917). See also G. Glushchenko, *N.D. Kashkin* (Moscow, 1974).

147. In a "Draft of a Position about the Academic Division," published by the Leningrad AK MUZO in 1919, the author asserted that the field of music theory, unlike that of history, where everything was understood and nothing new was anticipated, was a virtually untouched area of research: "The methods of music history, in general, are established in sufficient measure.... The schematic, or theoretical, part of the science of music is in a different state. A theory of music still does not exist." (cited in T.I. Livanova, "Deiatelnost' AK MUZO NARKOMPROSA—Nachal'naia stranitsa sovetskogo muzykoznaniia" [The activity of AK MUZO NARKOMPROS—the first page of Soviet musicology], *Iz proshlogo sovetskoi muzykal'noi kul'tury* [From the past of Soviet musical culture], ed. and comp. T.I. Livanova, vol. 2 [Moscow, 1976], p. 279.)

148. These lectures included: E.K. Rozenov, "Osnovaniia dlia ustanovleniia novoi tonal'noi sistemy" [The basis for establishing a new tonal system] and "Proiavlenie zakona zolotogo secheniia v poezii i muzyki" [The manifestation of the law of the golden section in poetry and music]; N.V. Petrov, "Ob osnovaniiakh novoi tonal'noi sistemy" [On the basis for a new tonal system]; P.N. Renchitsky, "K voprosu o naimenovanii i izobrazhenii novykh intervalov pri rasshirenii zvukovoi sistemy" [On the question of designating and representing new intervals relative to the expansion of the sound system]; L. Sabaneev, "Ul'trakhromatizm" [Ultrachromaticism]; and K.R. Eiges, "Chto takoe nauka o muzyke?" [What is the science of music?]. Not accepted for publication was an article by Conus, "Plany metrikotek-tonicheskogo stroeniia 48 *Pesen bez slov* Mendelsona" [Plans of the metrotechtonic structure of the 48 *Songs without Words* of Mendelssohn] (Livanova, pp. 272-73).

149. Gosudarstvennyi tsentral'nyi muzei muzykal'noi kul'tura imeni M.I. Glinki [Glinka State Central Museum of Musical Culture], f. 321, no. 1328; cited in T.I. Livanova, "Iz proshlogo sovetskoi muzykal'noi nauki (GIMN v Moskve)" [From the past of Soviet musical science (GIMN in Moscow)], *Iz proshlogo sovetskoi muzykal'noi kul'tury* [From the past of Soviet musical culture], ed. and comp. T.N. Livanova, vol. 1 (Moscow, 1975), p. 272.

150. A translation of an article by Haba was published in 1923: "Garmonicheskaia osnova chetvertetonnoi sistemy" [The harmonic basis of the quarter-tone system], *K novym beregam muzykal'nogo iskusstva* [Toward new shores of musical art], no. 3 (1923), pp. 6-10. A translation of Milhaud's article on "Polytonality and Atonality" also appeared in this issue.

151. Mikhail Ivanov-Boretsky, *Piat' let nauchnoi raboty gosudarstvennogo instituta muzykal'noi nauki (GIMN'a) 1921-26* [Five years of scientific work of the State Institute of Musical Science (GIMN) 1921-26] (Moscow, 1926), p. 15.

152. A lecture by Yavorsky, "Ob osnovnykh elementakh muzyki" [On the basic elements of music], was published in *Iskusstvo* [Art], no. 1 (1923), pp. 185-94, the official bulletin of GAKhN. Briusova and Maria Medvedeva applied Yavorsky's theories to musical analysis, Beliaev gave a lecture on "The Logic of Musical Thought," and Pavel Leiberg and Alexander Samoilov researched acoustical topics (Ivanov-Boretsky, pp. 15-16).

153. Ivanov-Boretsky, *Piat' let,* p. 23.

154.   Briusova, "O znachenii taktovoi cherty" [On the significance of the bar line], "Konstruktsiia formy muzykal'nykh proizvedenii" [The construction of the form of musical works], and "Analiz preliudii Shopena" [The analysis of a prelude of Chopin]; Conus, "Metriko-arkhitektonicheskii metod zvukogo tvorchestva" [The metrical-architechtonic method of sound creation] (A.I. Kondratev, "Rossiiskaia akademiia khudozhestvennykh nauk: muzykal'naia sektsiia" [The Russian Academy of Artistic Science: the music section], *Iskusstvo* [Art], no. 1 [1923], pp. 428-29).

155.   Mikhail Ivanov-Boretsky, "Muzykal'naia nauka za desiat' let" [Musical science at ten years], *Muzyka i revoliutsiia* [Music and revolution], no. 27 (1927), p. 19.

156.   Nikolai Aleksandrovich Garbuzov, "Akustika i teorii muzyki" [Acoustics and the theory of music], *Muzyka i revoliutsiia* [Music and revolution], no. 3 (1926), pp. 18-21. Among other things, Garbuzov pointed out that the character of a chord depends not only on its structure, but also on the register in which it sounds. See "The Contributions of Taneev, Catoire, Conus, Garbuzov, Mazel, and Tiulin," in this volume.

157.   Sabaneev emigrated in 1926 and discontinued this research.

158.   See E.K. Rozenov, "Novoe v uchenie o garmonii" [New ideas in the study of harmony], *Muzyka i revoliutsiia* [Music and revolution], no. 9 (1927), pp. 26-31. Rozenov's other lectures (unpublished) for the acoustical commission include "Obzor rabot Komissii po razrabotki novykh tonal'nykh sistem" [A survey of the work of the commission on the development of new tonal systems], and "Analyz temperatsii ot 12 do 48 stupeni po sposobu Rimskogo-Korsakova" [An analysis of temperament from 12 to 48 degrees by the method of Rimsky-Korsakov] (Ivanov-Boretsky, *Piat' let*, p. 28).

159.   P.I. Renchitsky, "24-zvukovaia ravnomernaia muzykal'naia sistema, kak rasshirenie obshcheupotrebitel'noi temperatsii" [A 24-tone equal-tempered musical system, as an expansion of the usual temperament] and "Vozmozhnye akusticheskie istolkovaniia priemlemosti garmonii noveishei polutonovoi i chetvertitonovoi muzyki" [Possible acoustical interpretations of the acceptability of harmony in newest half-tone and quarter-tone music]; P.B. Leiberg, "O garmoniume 41-stupennoi temperatsii" [About a harmonium in 41-degree temperament] (Ivanov-Boretsky, *Piat' let*, p. 28).

160.   A.M. Avraamov, "'Universal'naia sistema tonov' (U.T.S.), ch. 3. Itogi i perspektivy" ['The universal system of tones (U.T.S.), part 3. Results and perspectives], *Zhizn' iskusstva* [The life of art], no. 12 (1926), p. 4. Avraamov wrote disparagingly of other tonal systems, such as those by Haba, A. Lourie, G. Rimsky-Korsakov, Busoni, Leiberg, and Rozenov. The "Universal System of Tones" was the subject of his dissertation. In 1934, he gave a course at the Moscow Conservatory entitled, "The History and Theory of Tone Systems." His other lectures at GIMN included "Detemperatsiia muzyki" [The detemperament of music], and "Ul'trakhomatism" [Ultrachromaticism] (Ivanov-Boretsky, *Piat' let*, p. 29).

161.   N.A. Garbuzov, "Novye techeniia v muzykal'noi nauke v period revoliutsii" [New trends in music science in the period of the revolution], *Muzyka i revoliutsiia* [Music and revolution], no. 1 (1926), p. 31.

162.   "V GIMNe" [In GIMN], *Muzyka i revoliutsiia* [Music and revolution], nos. 5-6 (1927), p. 39: "The demonstration attracted great interest and served as an occasion for a vital exchange of opinions." Rimsky-Korsakov and his group of performers presented music by Haba, N. Malakhovsky, A. Kenel, and himself. A concert by Avraamov in 1929, however, provoked a more negative response: "The attempt ... 'to revive' music on the basis of dogmatic assertions based on nothing, is doomed unconditionally to failure." (A.V. Rabinovich, "Kontsert-demonstratsiia A. Avraamova" [The concert demonstration of A. Avraamov], *Muzykal'noe obrazovanie* [Musical education], no. 3-4 [1929], p. 51.)

163.   N.A. Garbuzov, *Teoriia mnogoosnovnosti ladov i sozvuchii* [The theory of multi-based modes and chords], 2 vols. (Moscow, 1928-32).

164.   See, for example, N.A. Garbuzov, "K voprosu ob edinichnoi i dvoinoi sistemakh B. Iavorskogo"[On the question of the single and double systems of B. Yavorsky], *Muzykal'noe obrazovanie* [Musical education], no. 1 (1930), pp. 18-22; and "Zavisit li garmonicheskoe dvizhenie v muzyke ot neustoichivosti tritona"[Does harmonic motion in music depend on the instability of the tritone], *Muzykal'noe obrazovanie*[Musical education], no. 3 (1930), pp. 16-21.

165.   Included were: "Akusticheskoe srodstvo natural'nykh zvukoriadov, kak estestvennaia prichina ladovogo dvizheniia" [The acoustical relatedness of natural scales as the natural source of modal movement] and "Issledovanie zony vospriiatiia intervalov"[Research into the zone of the perception of intervals] (Livanova, vol. 1, p. 311).

166.   Probably the first had been Samuil Moiseevich Maikapar (1867-1938) in *Muzykal'nyi slukh. Ego znachenie, priroda, osobennosti i metod pravil'nogo razvitiia* [Musical hearing. Its significance, nature, characteristics, and method of correct development] (Moscow, 1900; 2nd ed., Petrograd, 1915). He also gave two lectures to the Musical Scientific Society: "Sub'ektivnye opredeleniia razmera chistykh konsoniruiushchikh intervalov" [The subjective determination of the size of pure consonant intervals] (reported in *Russkaia muzykal'naia gazeta* [The Russian musical newspaper], no. 25-26 [1904]) and "Siamskaia muzykal'naia sistema" [The Siamese musical system] (reported in *Russkaia muzykal'naia gazeta* [The Russian musical newspaper], no. 27-28 [1904]).

167.   Livanova, vol. 1, pp. 321-24.

168.   E.K. Rozenov, "Primenenie zakona 'zolotogo secheniia' v poetike i muzyke"[The application of the law of the "golden section" in poetry and music], *Sbornik rabot Fiziologo-psikhologicheskoi Sektsii (Trudy GIMNa)* [Collected works of the physiological psychological section (Works of GIMN)], vol. 1 (Moscow, 1925), pp. 96-136. According to Rozenov, this article was finished in 1921, when he presented the material in a lecture to AK MUZO (see note 148), and contained significant additions to his 1904 lecture on the same topic. Sabaneev and Lev Mazel followed Rozenov's example; Sabaneev wrote "Etiudy Shopena v osveshchenii zakona zolotogo secheniia. Opyt pozitivnogo obosnovaniia zakonov formy"[The etudes of Chopin in light of the law of the golden section. An experiment in the positive basis of the laws of form], *Iskusstvo* [Art], nos. 2 and 3 (1925); Mazel wrote "Opyt issledovaniia zolotogo secheniia v muzykal'nykh postroeniiakh v svete obshchego analiza form"[Experimental research in the golden section in musical constructions in the light of the general analysis of form], *Muzykal'noe obrazovanie* [Musical education], no. 2 (1930), pp. 24-33.

169.   Leonid Sabaneev, "The Biometrical Method in its Application to the Question of the Study of Style," trans. S.W. Pring, *Pro Musica Quarterly* 6, no. 11 (December 1927): 22.

170.   The titles for some of these lectures include: Briusova, "Moduliatsionno-ladovyi analiz 'Stseny u Il'men-ozera' iz 'Sadko' Rimskogo-Korsakova"[A modulatory modal analysis of "Scene at Il'men Lake" from *Sadko* of Rimsky-Korsakov] and "Revoliutsionnaia muzyka" [Revolutionary music], published in *Muzykal'noe obrazovanie* [Musical education], no. 1-2 (1926); Viktor Beliaev, "Sovremennaia muzyka v Evrope"[Contemporary music in Europe] and "A.D. Kastalsky i ego russkaia polifoniia [A.D. Kastalsky and his Russian polyphony]; Georgy Conus, "O nezyblemosti vremennykh osnov khudozhestvennoi muzykal'noi formy" [On the stability of temporal bases of artistic musical form], "Ob absoliutnom ravnovesii v muzykal'nom stroitel'stve i ob uklonenii ot nego" [On the absolute equality in musical organization and on deviation from it], and "Priroda muzykal'nogo sintaksisa" [The nature

of musical syntax]; Pavel Leiberg, "Ob atonal'nosti" [On atonality]; E.K. Rozenov, "Kriticheskii analiz osnov ucheniia o garmonii" [A critical analysis of the bases of the study of harmony] and "Muzykal'nyi ritm i svoistva ego vospriiatiia" [Musical rhythm and the characteristics of its perception]; Sergei Skrebkov, "Analiz finala sonaty Betkhovena op. 31 no. 2 d moll" [An analysis of the finale of the Sonata of Beethoven op. 31 no. 2 in d minor]; and A.F. Losev, "K voprosu o sistematike muzykal'no-teoreticheskikh kategorii" [On the question of the systematization of musical theoretical categories]. (Aleksei Sidorov, "Muzykal'naia Sektsiia" [The musical section], *Biulleteny GAKhN* [Bulletins of GAKhN], no. 4-5 [1926], pp. 48-53; no. 6-7 [1927], pp. 46-50; no. 8-9 [1927-28], pp. 45-48; no. 10 [1927-28], pp. 40-44; no. 11 [1928], pp. 48-51.)

171.   Sidorov, *Biulleteny GAKhN,* no. 10 (1927-28), pp. 40-41; and no. 11 (1928), p. 48. Rozenov never did publish this work, in which he advocated the adoption of a "harmonic" mode as a basis for contemporary music.

172.   Lectures included works by E.A. Maltseva, "Razlichnye tipy intervalov v melodii i osobennosti ikh vospriiatiia" [Various types of intervals in melody and particularities of their perception], "Ritmicheskoe oformlenie u Bakha, kak sredstvo muzykal'nogo vyrazheniia" [Rhythmic formation in Bach, as a means of musical expression], "Vyrazitel'nye formy melodicheskikh soedinenii u Bakha" [Expressive forms of melodic combinations in Bach], and "Vyrazitel'nye formy v instrumental'nom soprovozhdenii u Bakha" [Expressive forms in instrumental accompaniment in Bach]; by Rozenov, "O podkhode issledovaniia printsipa emotsional'nosti v muzykal'noi estetike" [On a research approach to the principle of emotionalism in musical aesthetics], "Analiz vyrazital'nykh i izobrazitel'nykh momentov v opere Rossini 'Moisei'" [The analysis of expressive and decorative moments in the opera 'Moses' of Rossini], and "Analiz vyrazitel'nykh priemov v opere Verdi 'Otello'" [The analysis of the expressive devices in the opera 'Otello' of Verdi]; and by Sergei Skrebkov, "O formakh raznoobraziia pri razrabotki motivov v 1-i fortepiannoi sonate Prokofiev" [On types of variety in the motivic development in the First Piano Sonata of Prokofiev]. (Sidorov, *Biulleteny GAKhN,* no. 6-7, p. 48; no. 8-9, p. 47; no. 10, p. 41; no. 11, p. 49.

173.   Sidorov, *Biulleteny GAKhN,* no. 8-9, p. 47; no. 10, pp. 43-44; no. 11, p. 51.

174.   Sofia Nikolaevna Beliaeva-Ekzempliarskaia and Boleslav Leopol'dovich Yavorsky, "Vospriiatie ladovykh melodicheskikh postroenii" [The perception of modal melodic structures], *Sbornik eksperimental'no-psykhologicheskikh issledovanii* [A collection of experimental psychological research], ed. V.M. Ekzempliarsky, vol. 1 (Moscow, 1926), pp. 3-35; Yavorsky, "Konstruktsiia melodicheskogo protsessa" [The construction of the melodic process], *Struktura melodii* [The structure of melody] (Moscow, 1929), pp. 7-36; and Beliaeva-Ekzempliarskaia, "Vospriiatie melodicheskogo dvizheniia" [The perception of melodic movement], ibid., pp. 37-93 (also in *Archiv fur die gesämte Psychologie,* vol. 92 [1934]).

175.   Maria Medvedeva, "Anton Reikha—opyt izucheniia ego teoreticheskikh rabot" [Anton Reicha—an experimental study of his theoretical work] and "Novaia sistema fugi A. Reikha" [A new system of fugue of A. Reicha] (Sidorov, *Biulleteny GAKhN,* no. 10, p. 42; no. 11, p. 49).

176.   Sidorov, *Biulleteny GAKhN,* no. 6-7, p. 48. *Uchenie o kanone* [The doctrine of the canon] by Taneev was published in 1929. In 1927 GAKhN also published *Russkaia kniga o Betkhovene* [The Russian book on Beethoven], which contains some previously unpublished analyses of Beethoven sonatas done by Taneev. In 1925 GIMN published a commemorative volume dedicated to Taneev, *Sergei Ivanovich Taneev. Lichnost', tvorchestvo i dokumenty ego zhizni* [Sergei Ivanovich Taneev. Personality, creativity and documents of his life].

177. Sidorov, *Biulleteny GAKhN,* no. 10, p. 40.

178. Leonid Sabaneev, "Analiz sotsiologicheskikh elementov muzykal'nogo iavleniia" [The analysis of the sociological elements in musical phenomenon], cited in D. Usov, "Muzykal'naia zhizn' v SSSR: Izuchenie muzyki v sotsiologicheskom otdelenii GAKhN" [Musical life in the USSR: The study of music in the sociology section of GAKhN], *Muzykal'noe obrazovanie* [Musical education], no. 1 (1928), p. 63.

179. Much interest did exist in topics related to revolution or political philosophy in the Association of Proletarian Musicians, later Russian Association or RAPM, which encouraged a proletarian ideology that today is considered by the Soviets as "vulgar." This group opposed the musicological factions dedicated to contemporary music and promoted a simplistic style of music that would appeal to the masses. For example, in an article entitled, "Atonal'naia muzyka" [Atonal music], published in *Muzykal'naia nov'* [Musical news], the first journal supervised by RAPM, the theorist G.L. Liubomirsky, the author of several theory textbooks, wrote that atonal music may be suitable for the specialists but not for the masses, who could not perceive atonal or alogical music. They required logical—hence tonal—music (no. 6-7 [1924], p. 12). Avraamov expressed similar sentiments: "Really 'healthy' logical music for workers should be written on the formula of the first problem in the harmony textbook of Rimsky-Korsakov (I-IV-V-I)" (Avraamov, "Atonal'naia muzyka [Atonal music], *Muzykal'naia nov'* [Musical news], no. 9 [1924], p. 13).

180. This Institute actually had a prerevolutionary origin, in the arts library of Count Zubov, who opened it to the public in 1912, with courses offered beginning in 1913. In 1916 it was given the status of an institution of higher learning, and after the revolution was nationalized and ultimately reorganized into the RIII. See Boris Schwarz, *Music and Musical Life in Soviet Russia 1917-1970* (New York: W.W. Norton & Co., 1972), for an excellent overview of Soviet musical life and pp. 88-105 for information on the institutes and conservatories.

181. S.L. Ginzburg, a member of the Institute, described the two lines of research: "A line of prerevolutionary 'scientific figurative' study of music (the predominance of biographists outside of sociological aspects, the idealistic speculative musical aesthetics, a complete isolation from living music, etc.) and a line of new, concrete, and actual musical science, connected with questions and ideology of contemporaneity." (S.L. Ginzburg, "Muzykal'naia nauka: Itogi i perspektivy muzykal'no-nauchnoi raboty v Leningrade" [Musical science: Results and perspectives of musical scientific work in Leningrad], *Muzyka i revoliutsiia* [Music and revolution], no. 11 [1928], p. 46.)

182. Ibid., p. 46. MUZO here refers to the Musical Section of GIII. The term "practicality" (in Russian *praktitsizm*) means, in Leninist political philosophy, an emphasis on practice as opposed to theory.

183. In the four volumes of *De Musica* are forty articles and reports. A fifth volume, entitled *Muzykoznanie* [Musicology], that appeared in 1928, contains nine articles. Also, an entire issue of *Melos* (no. 6 [1926]) was devoted to coverage of research done at OTIM; it contains four articles by Soviet musicologists. Rimsky-Korsakov's articles include "Obosnovanie chetvertitonovoi muzykal'noi sistemy" [The basis of a quarter-tone musical system], *De Musica* 1 (1925): 52-78; "O vysote kombinatsionnykh tonov" [On the pitch of combination tones], *De Musica* 3 (1927): 155-65; and "Akusticheskoe obosnovanie teorii ladovogo ritma" [The acoustical basis of the theory of modal rhythm], *Muzykoznanie* [Musicology] 4 (1928). (*Musicology* is technically volume 4 because the first volume of *De Musica* was not numbered.) Rimsky-Korsakov's dissertation at GIII (1929) was "Evoliutsiia muzykal'nykh zvukoriadov" [The evolution of musical scales].

184. Boris Asafiev, *Muzykal'naia forma kak protsess* [Musical form as a process] (Leningrad, 1930). See Gordon McQuere, "Boris Asafiev and *Musical Form as a Process,*" in this volume.

185. N.A. Garbuzov, "Novye techeniia" [New trends], pp. 31-33.

186. Georgy Catoire, *Teoreticheskii kurs garmonii* [A theoretical course of harmony] 2 vols. (Moscow, 1925-26). See "The Contributions of Taneev, Catoire, Conus, Garbuzov, Mazel, and Tiulin," in this volume.

187. Yury Tiulin, *Vvedenie v garmonicheskii analiz na osnove khoralov Bakha* [An introduction to harmonic analysis on the basis of Bach chorales] (Leningrad, 1927).

188. In some respects, Asafiev's ideas paralleled those of Ernst Kurth's whose book, *Grundlagen des linearen Kontrapunkte* (1917), was translated by Z. Evald and published under the editorship of Asafiev in 1931. Kurth's theories were the basis for several Soviet studies, such as P.V. Akimov's *Vvedenie v polifoniiu na osnove energeticheskikh uchenii (Ernst Kurt)* [An introduction to polyphony on the basis of the study of energy (Ernst Kurth)] (Leningrad, 1928).

189. Sergei Protopopov, *Elementy stroeniia muzykal'noi rechi* [Elements of the structure of musical speech], 2 vols. (Moscow, 1930).

190. See Schwarz, pp. 54-60.

191. Anatoly Lunacharsky, cited in *B. Iavorskii. Stat'i, vospominaniia, perepiska* [B. Yavorsky. Articles, reminiscences, correspondence], ed. I.S. Rabinovich, 2nd ed. (Moscow, 1972), pp. 666-67. See also "Konferentsiia po teorii ladovogo ritma" [The conference on the theory of modal rhythm], *Proletarskii muzykant* [Proletarian musician], no. 2 (1930), pp. 6-9; and A.N. Lunacharsky, "Neskol'ko zamechanii o teorii ladovogo ritma" [Some observations on the theory of modal rhythm], ibid., pp. 101-13.

192. *B. Yavorsky,* p. 667.

193. For the text (in English) of this resolution, see "Annex A" in Andrey Olkhovsky, *Music Under the Soviets: The Agony of an Art,* trans. Aaron Avshalomoff and Louis Jay Herman (New York: Frederick A. Praeger, 1955), pp. 278-79.

194. Today, scholarly articles on music and music theory are more likely to be published in collections of articles devoted to special topics. *Soviet Music* deals with musical activities in the Soviet Union.

195. Nikolai Cheliapov, "O zadachakh zhurnala 'Sovetskaia muzyka'" [On the tasks of the journal *Soviet Music*], *Sovetskaia muzyka,* 1933, no. 1, pp. 1-5.

196. See Viktor Gorodinsky, "K voprosu o sotsialisticheskom realizme v muzyke" [On the question of socialist realism in music], *Sovetskaia muzyka,* 1933, no. 1, pp. 6-18. For a discussion of the history and principles of this philosophy, see C. Vaughan James, *Soviet Socialist Realism: Origins and Theory* (New York: St. Martin's Press, 1973).

197. Iosif Yakovlevich Ryzhkin, "Sovetskoe teoreticheskoe muzykoznanie (1917-1941)" [Soviet theoretical musicology (1917-1941), *Voprosy teorii i estetiki muzyki* [Questions of the theory and aesthetics of music], vol. 6-7 (Leningrad, 1967), p. 152.

198. Ibid.

199. Georgy Catoire, *Muzykal'naia forma* [Musical form], 2 vols. (Moscow, 1934-36).

200. Georgy Conus, *Kritika traditsionnoi teorii v oblasti muzykal'noi formy* [Criticism of traditional theory in the sphere of musical form] (Moscow, 1932); *Metro-tektonicheskoe*

issledovanie muzykal'noi formy [A metrotechtonic investigation of musical form] (Moscow, 1933); and *Nauchnoe obosnovanie muzykal'nogo sintaksisa* [The scientific basis of musical syntax] (Moscow, 1935).

201. Nikolai Garbuzov, *O mnogogolosii russkoi narodnoi pesni* [On the multi-voicing of Russian folk song] (Moscow, 1939); and *Muzykal'naia akustika* [Musical acoustics] (Moscow, 1940).

202. Iosif Ryzhkin, "Traditsionnaia shkola teorii muzyki" [The traditional school of music theory], *Sovetskaia muzyka* [Soviet music], 1933, no. 3, pp. 74-98; "Nashi spory i Z.F. Ramo" [Our arguments and J.P. Rameau], ibid., 1933, no. 5, pp. 101-11; and Lev Mazel, "Funktsional'naia shkola v oblasti teoreticheskogo muzykoznaniia" [The functional school in the sphere of theoretical musicology], ibid., 1934, no. 4, pp. 76-90. Iosif Ryzhkin and Lev Mazel, *Ocherki po istorii teoreticheskogo muzykoznaniia* [Essays on the history of theoretical musicology], 2 vols. (Moscow, 1934-39). These essays constituted the Soviet response to Lucien Chevallier's "Les Theories Harmoniques" from Livignac and de la Laurencie's *Encyclopédie de la Musique et Dictionnaire du Conservatoire* (vol. 1, part 2 [Paris 1925]), which was translated into Russian and published in 1931-32: *Istoriia uchenii o garmonii* [The history of the study of harmony], trans. Z. Potagova and V. Taranushchenko, ed. I.V. Ivanov-Boretsky (Moscow, 1931-32). In his review of this work, Ryzhkin addressed the deficiencies of Chevallier's work from a Marxist point of view (*Proletarskii muzykant* [Proletarian musician], no. 8 [1931], pp. 39-43).

203. Ryzhkin and Mazel, *Ocherki,* 1:2.

204. Lev Mazel, "O sovetskom teoreticheskom muzykoznanii" [On Soviet theoretical musicology], *Sovetskaia muzyka* [Soviet music], 1940, no. 12, pp. 15-29.

205. Viktor Zuckermann, "O siuzhete i muzykal'nom iazyke opere-bylini 'Sadko' " [On the subject and musical language of the opera bylina *Sadko*], *Sovetskaia muzyka* [Sovet music], 1933, no. 3, pp. 46-73.

206. Ibid., p. 62.

207. Ibid., p. 64.

208. Yuly Kremlev, "Ob impressionizm Kloda Debiussi" [On the impressionism of Claude Debussy], *Sovetskaia muzyka,* 1934, no. 3, pp. 23-46.

209. Ibid., p. 23, editorial preface.

210. Yuly Kremlev, "O muzykal'nom iazyke Musorgskogo" [On the musical language of Musorgsky], *Sovetskaia muzyka,* 1939, no. 3, pp. 27-33.

211. Ibid., p. 33.

212. Ibid. Other analytical articles of this type include Iosif Ryzhkin, " 'Menuet' Taneeva (O khudozhestvennom obraze)" [The "Minuet" of Taneev (on the artistic form)], *Sovetskaia muzyka,* 1934, no. 4, pp. 62-75; Viktor Zuckermann, " 'Turkmeniia' B. Shekhtera" ["Turkmeniia" of B. Shekhter], ibid., 1936, no. 4, and "Neskol'ko myslei o sovetskoi opere" [Some thoughts on Soviet opera], ibid., 1940, no. 12; Vladimir Protopopov, "Muzykal'nyi iazyk 'Zolotogo petushka' " [The musical language of "The Golden Cockerel"], ibid, 1938, no. 6, pp. 20-31 and "Obraz Borisa v opere Musorgskogo" [The image of Boris in the opera of Musorgsky], ibid., 1939, no. 4, pp. 34-38.

213. Lev Mazel, *Fantaziia f-moll Shopena. Opyt analiza* [The F minor Fantasy of Chopin. An experiment in analysis] (Moscow, 1937). This work was written in 1934 and discussed in two meetings of the history theory section of the Scientific Research Institute of the Moscow Conservatory.

214. Mazel, *Fantaziia,* p. 7.

215. *Prakticheskii kurs garmonii* [A practical course of harmony], 2 vols. (Moscow, 1934-36), 1:6.

216. *Uchebnik garmonii* [A textbook of harmony] (Moscow, 1937-38).

217. 4th ed. (1955); latest available printing, 1973.

218. Yury Tiulin, *Uchenie o garmonii* [A Study of Harmony] (Leningrad, 1937); 2nd ed., 1939; 3rd corrected and augmented ed., 1966.

219. Tiulin, *Uchenie o garmonii,* pp. 10-13.

220. Mazel, "O sovetskom teoreticheskom muzykoznanii."

221. "K diskussii o sovetskom muzykoznanii" [Toward a discussion of Soviet musicology], *Sovetskaia muzyka,* 1941, no. 4, pp. 90-98.

222. Mazel, "O sovetskom teoreticheskom muzykoznanii," pp. 20-21.

223. "K diskussii," p. 95.

224. Aleksei Ogolevets, *Osnovy garmonicheskogo iazyka* [Foundations of harmonic language] (Moscow, 1941).

225. "Ob opere 'Velikaia Druzhba' Muradela" [On the opera "Great Friendship" by Muradeli], *Sovetskaia muzyka,* 1948, no. 1, pp. 3-8; "Vystupleniia na otkrytom partiinom sobranii v Soiuze sovetskikh kompozitorov SSSR, posviashchennom obsuzhedeniiu zadach muzykal'noi kritiki i nauki (18, 21, i 22 fevralia 1949 g.)" [Addresses at the open Party meeting in the Union of Soviet Composers of the USSR, dedicated to a discussion of problems of musical criticism and science (18, 21, and 22 February 1949)], *Sovetskaia muzyka,* 1949, no. 2, pp. 16-36.

226. Aleksei Ogolevets, *Vvedenie o sovremennom muzykal'nom myshlenii* [An introduction to contemporary musical thought] (Moscow, 1946). Khrennikov's criticisms were presented in his speech, "O neterpimom otstavanii muzykal'noi kritiki i muzykovedeniia" [On the intolerable lag of musical criticism and musicology], *Sovetskaia muzyka,* 1949, no. 2, pp. 12-13.

227. "Vystupleniia," pp. 28-29.

228. Ibid., pp. 16-17. Khrennikov, pp. 8-9.

229. Anatoli Konstantinovich Butskoi, *Struktura muzykal'nogo proizvedenii* [The structure of a musical work] (Leningrad-Moscow, 1948), p. 5.

230. "Vystupleniia," p. 30.

231. Viktor Berkov, *Garmonii Glinki* [The harmony of Glinka] (Moscow, 1948). This work was based on Berkov's 1942 dissertation of the same title.

232. Skrebkov's first published book was *Polifonicheskii analiz* [Polyphonic analysis] (Moscow, 1940). During this postwar period he wrote, together with O.L. Skrebkova, *Khrestomatiia po garmonicheskomu analizu* [Selections for harmonic analysis] (Moscow, 1948). Sposobin wrote *Muzykal'naia forma* [Musical form] (Moscow, 1947), in addition to being one of the writers of the collective *Uchebnick garmonii* [Textbook of harmony], the third edition of which was published in 1947.

233. Nikolai Garbuzov, *Zonnaia priroda zvukovysotnogo slukha* [The zonal nature of pitch audibility] (Moscow-Leningrad, 1948). Another work of this period was *Drevnerusskoi narodnoi mnogogolosie* [Ancient Russian folk polyphony] (Moscow-Leningrad, 1948).

Garbuzov's idea of zone concerns the relation between the physical and qualitative properties of sound as perceived by the human ear. He wrote five books on the topic. More recently, Soviet theorists have defined an aesthetic meaning to the idea of zone.

234. S.S. Bogatyrev, *Dvoinoi kanon* (Double canon) (Moscow-Leningrad, 1947). Bogatyrev completed this work in 1939, but made some corrections and additions in 1940 and again in 1946 after uncovering (in 1945 and 1946) several pages of writings by Taneev on the subject of double canon, apparently his only writings on the topic. Bogatyrev's work was accepted as his dissertation in 1947.

235. Andrei Mutli, *O moduliatsii, K voprosu o razvitii ucheniia N.A. Rimskogo-Korsakova o srodstve tonal'nostei* [On modulation. On the question of the development of the teaching of N.A. Rimsky-Korsakov on the relatedness of tonalities] (Moscow-Leningrad, 1948). Mutli's 1944 dissertation was entitled, "O melodicheskikh funktsiiakh garmonii" [On the melodic functions of harmony].

236. Boleslav Yavorsky, *Siuity Bakha dlia klaviera* [Bach's Suites for the clavier] (Moscow, 1947). This was a posthumous publication, edited by Sergei Protopopov; Yavorsky died in 1942. Boris Asafiev, *Muzykal'naia forma kak protsess. Intonatsiia* [Musical form as a process. Intonation], vol. 2 (Moscow-Leningrad, 1947). Asafiev died in January 1949; his role during the previous year was unclear.

237. Varvara Dernova, *Garmoniia Skriabina* [The harmony of Skryabin] (Leningrad, 1968). See Roy J. Guenther, "Varvara Dernova's System of Analysis of the Music of Skryabin," in this volume.

238. Mikhail Semenovich Blok, "Vazhnyi etap v razvitii sovetskogo muzykoznaniia (Vsesoiuznaia nauchnaia sessiia po muzykoznaniiu)" [An important phase in the development of Soviet musicology (The all-Soviet scientific session on musicology)], *Sovetskaia muzyka*, 1950, no. 4, pp. 48-54.

239. Two theory textbooks of Tiulin and Privano were eventually published: *Teoreticheskie osnovy garmonii* [The theoretical bases of harmony] (Leningrad, 1956), and *Uchebnik garmonii* [Textbook of harmony], 2 vols. (Moscow, 1957-59).

240. Blok, p. 53. Skrebkov alone wrote a textbook on polyphony, *Uchebnik polifonii* [Textbook of polyphony] (Moscow, 1951). Dmitriev later published *Polifoniia kak faktor formoobrazovanie* [Polyphony as a factor of form structure] (Leningrad, 1962).

241. Blok, p. 53. The deficient areas mentioned by Blok have received much attention over the last thirty years and now constitute major research spheres within Soviet music theory.

242. Blok, p. 54.

243. T.V. Popova, *Muzykal'nyi zhanry i formy* [Musical genres and forms] (Moscow, 1951); S.S. Skrebkov, *Prakticheskii kurs garmonii* [Practical course of harmony] (Moscow, 1952); I.V. Sposobin, *Elementarnaia teoriia muzyki* [The elementary theory of music] (Moscow, 1951); N.A. Garbuzov, *Zonnaia priroda tempa i ritma* [The zonal nature of tempo and rhythm] (Moscow, 1950) and *Vnutrizonnyi intonatsionnyi slukh i metody ego razvitiia* [Inner-zonal intonational hearing and methods of its development] (Moscow, 1951); and L.A. Mazel, *O melodii* [On melody] (Moscow, 1952).

Sources of Russian Chant Theory

Nicolas Schidlovsky

> I see the trampling of the true faith... and can no longer bear to
> hear the Latin singing in Moscow.
> —Germogen, Patriarch of Russia
> (early 17th century)

The investigation of Russian chant originates in nascent reformist tendencies of early nineteenth-century Russian Orthodox liturgical singing. The published work appearing since then is the first substantial literature that we have on the subject. Prior to this, writing on the chant was little cultivated, and throughout the centuries the traditional theoretical treatise used by the Russians was of minimal proportions: as a grammar on the neumatic notation, the musical *azbuka* is characteristic for its brevity and forthright practicality; it addresses only the form of old unison chanting and is unrelated to the growth of polyphony.

But, important as it is for our understanding of the music, the literature on the Russian chant offers a number of difficulties. It is extensive, scattered, and often unavailable in the libraries. It is, of course, written mostly in the Russian language, and to steer one's way through the material requires a sense of the history behind its development. Finally, the Western student soon discovers that what might be called a "theory" of the music has to do primarily with questions of notation: speculative ideas of the type known in medieval and Renaissance Europe are conspicuously absent. The present essay takes into consideration all of these difficulties. Its main purpose is to provide a compact introduction to a largely unknown subject, moreover, a subject of particular import in view of trends in current theory and musicology.

In all branches of seventeenth- and eighteenth-century Russian Orthodox religious art, the imitation of European ideals left a devastating imprint—traditional procedures and indigenous aesthetic codes acquired a new profile. By the beginning of the nineteenth century, it was the reaction to fashionable innovation, or "Italianization" as it was known, that triggered research in the domain of liturgical music.

Along with the adoption of church singing in the concerto style of the baroque and rococo, Russia of the eighteenth century saw the evolution of the so-called *obikhodny* chant that was later collected and edited by Aleksei Lvov (1798-1870) and Nikolai Bakhmetev (1807-1891). This style of majestic, harmonized singing, always a cappella in the Orthodox practice, flourished at the Imperial Court in St. Petersburg. Even if its origin and derivation are still little understood, the impact it had on the future is overwhelmingly clear: it set a standard that dominates Russian church music to this day. The appeal of the singing lies primarily in its simple triadic progressions suitable for long phrases of recitative to be performed either by modest ensembles or large choral groups. Under favorable conditions, the amplification of harmonies by octave doubling results in the characteristic sonority known as the "Synodal" choral style.

Unfortunately, however, the singing scarcely resembles the ancient unaccompanied melodic singing of the Russians, the so-called *znamenny* chant rooted in the practice of Byzantium. Thus, to the knowledgeable associates of Lvov and Bakhmetev it was clear that, effective as it was, the harmonized music they heard only tenuously reflected tradition, and that a legitimate practice was to be restored only through the recovery of the original chant, both its history and sources. During the half-century or so preceding the Revolution in 1917, an emerging scholarship went in quest of reform. This quest, part of a broad cultural movement in Russia of the time, involved a fundamental revaluation of Western paradigms in search of their proper place within the life of a rapidly advancing nation.

After slow and uncertain beginnings, the work on the chant made gradual progress: it became increasingly specialized, with appreciable results both in the practical and scientific realms. A useful starting place for a survey of the research is the *Bibliography* of Anton Preobrazhensky (1870-1929) published in 1897.[1] While incomplete, it contains over two hundred entries and gives a good picture of the nature of the literature. In his *Dictionary,* which appeared during the same year, Preobrazhensky made special mention of the late Metropolitan Evgeny of Kiev (1767-1837), the eminent founder of the field.[2] Exactly a century earlier, the honorable hierarch had laid the cornerstone in a speech delivered while still a professor at the seminary in Voronezh. First published in 1799 in that city, the speech had a second printing in 1804 in St. Petersburg; later editions appeared in Moscow in 1817 and, finally, in 1897.[3] The following passage illustrates the views expressed in this widely acclaimed document:

> Besides this famous Russian choral director (i.e. Bortniansky), the works of many foreign kapellmeisters have in our time been adopted as compositions of the Greek-Russian Church, for example, Galuppi (teacher of Bortniansky), Kerzelli, Dimmler, and the eminent Sarti. But even so, the truth must be stated that either because of their unawareness of the power and expressiveness of many moments in our church poetry, or because of a prejudice only

for the laws of their music, they have often disregarded the sanctity of the place and subject of their compositions, so that generally speaking, it is not the music which is adapted to the sacred words, but instead, the words are merely added to the music and often in a contrived manner. Apparently, they wanted more to impress their audience with concert-like euphony than to touch their hearts with pious melody, and often during such compositions the church resembles more an Italian opera than the house of worthy prayer to the Almighty.[4]

In the preceding paragraphs the author outlines the history leading up to the existing deplorable state. Although he is quite objective in recognizing the achievements of the Italianate musicians and is far from vindictive, interestingly enough, he focuses on Dimitri Bortniansky (1751-1825), the most famous of all the foreign-trained composers; refined, sensitive, and highly respected for his many sacred and secular works, Bortniansky was soon to become a favorite target of criticism.

During the first half of the nineteenth century, the authors who undertook to write on the subject represented different degrees of competence. Their writing is often diffuse and lacks qualified evidence. But it is, nonetheless, the stimulus for the better, critical work of the later specialists. Among the early authors, Vukol Undolsky (1815-1864) stands out as a discerning scholar. His work published in 1846 was acclaimed by the well-known Russian theorist and critic, Vladimir Odoevsky (1803-1869), who credited the author with opening "a new and hitherto unknown side in the history of our old singing."[5] According to Odoevsky, Undolsky had demonstrated an interpretation other than that of the majority of musicians "for whom ancient Russian singing began with Bortniansky." By mid-century, the new historical inquiry could boast of considerable accomplishments. Most importantly, it was beginning to gain support and recognition of its own ideals. This is evident in the first comprehensive textbook to appear on the subject, the monumental three-volume history of Russian church singing by Dimitri Razumovsky (1818-1889).[6] Just one year before the publication of the first volume, Razumovsky was granted the chair in church music at the newly opened conservatory in Moscow.

At the end of the century, a sizeable literature was available on many topics concerning church singing. But it is indicative of the basic orientation of this work that hardly any of the publications deal with analyses of the znamenny repertory. Among the entries in Preobrazhensky's *Bibliography* the largest number are writings of a pedagogical, aesthetic, and theological bent; four of the seven categories dividing the catalogue can be identified as materials of this type.[7] In much the same way, the entries classified as "theory" reveal a leaning towards questions of contemporary church practice; they are mostly concerned with harmonized singing and sometimes with the use of traditional melodies in harmonized form. At the center of such discourse is the model provided in the *obikhody* of Lvov and Bakhmetev, with the major point of contention being other experimental approaches, especially that of the controversial Nikolai Potulov (1810-1873).[8] In all of this, the authority of the old music is commonly recognized, but practically no attention is given to the possibility of reestablishing the authentic tradition of unison singing. At best, it seems, most of the authors were seriously misguided. In their struggle to justify new polyphonic composition, they attempted to implement alien concepts of modal theory which, as in some of the writings of the European Renaissance, occasionally resulted in unfortunate fabrications of bizarre and invalid thought.[9]

Although rare figures such as Odoevsky and Razumovsky were conversant with the old neumes and were able to transcribe them, throughout this period the main source of the chant was an official publication by the Holy Synod. This provided the traditional melodies in the diastematic "Kievan" or "square" notation (see plates 1 and 2).[10] In the early eighteenth century, Peter I removed the ecclesiastical presses from Moscow to the new northern capital, St. Petersburg, only to reinstall them soon after, in 1727, in the original location under the auspices of the Synod. Not until 1741 did other accessories return, and a few decades later, sometime between 1770 and 1772, the first edition of the chant appeared, guided chiefly by Stepan Byshkovsky, director of the Synodal Press. Little is known about the efforts surrounding this publication except that a small but competent group of clergy and singers was responsible for its redaction.[11] With the arrival of reformist sentiments, the books became the banners of tradition; they led the way to significant developments benefiting the interests of composers and scholars alike. However, that they continued to be published throughout the century and up to the Revolution is somewhat strange given the limited use they must have had in the actual church practice. Exactly how they were used in the services is uncertain, and it appears that the singers who did perform from them were trained to improvise a harmony to accompany the bare chant.[12] In the decades before the Revolution there emerged a number of publications collecting regional recensions of the music. These tended to follow the format of the Synodal editions; they gave the melodies in simple, unharmonized form, but sometimes rejected the square notation in favor of the modern system.[13]

Among the many authors listed by Preobrazhensky, three deserve special attention: Ivan Voznesensky (1837-1916), Stepan Smolensky (1846-1909), and Vasilii Metallov (1862-1926). Along with Preobrazhensky himself, these scholars represent the mainstream of thought from what might be called the second generation of research on the chant. As we shall see, Smolensky and Metallov, in particular, were unusually prolific and talented writers.

As the first extensive efforts devoted to the analysis of the monophonic repertory, Preobrazhensky listed two works by Voznesensky in both the "history" and "theory" categories of his catalogue.[14] In these books Voznesensky gave a detailed study of the main branches of the Russian chant found in the publications of the Synod; he was completely systematic in examining the central tradition of both the "large" *(bol'shoi)* and "small" *(malyi)* znamenny chants as well as the "Kievan," "Bulgarian," and "Greek" families. In spite of the author's insistence on a disagreeable modal terminology, these volumes must be recognized for their overall thoroughness. The works listed for Metallov are his two texts on the history and teaching of church singing; these were designated for seminary and public school use and were modeled on Razumovsky's work of thirty years earlier.[15] The more prominent works of this author, however, were yet to come; these began to appear shortly thereafter with his *Azbuka* and *Osmoglasie.*[16]

Despite the efforts of Razumovsky and others, a resourceful scientific study of the old chant begins with Stepan Smolensky, who embarked on a close examination of archival materials and, by the end of the century, published a handful of unprecedented works. When Razumovsky died in 1889, the choice fell naturally on Smolensky to take the professorship at the conservatory. Thus, Smolensky, already an established writer at the time, assumed a leadership among scholars not only by virtue of merit, but in rank. It was his activity that later brought European-wide recognition to the neighboring Moscow Synodal School as an outstanding center for the development of choral singing. His earliest writing focused on the large collection of manuscripts from the Solovetsky Monastery; together with preparing an atlas of specimens, he devoted a short article to explaining the importance of the material.[17] He wrote:

> The comparative study and assessment of the contents of the znamenny manuscripts afford the opportunity to make some conclusions and deductions of interest both for the history of church singing in Russia and for liturgics. This area is still completely untouched and is replete, on the one hand, with positions established through convention and without foundation, and on the other hand, with new and unsuspected [ideas] which have much to correct and to shed unexpected light on the issues of doubt.[18]

In a word, Smolensky introduced a source-critical standard unknown at the time. In the same article he describes the famous seventeenth-century *Azbuka* by Alexander Mezenets, a copy of which he published during the following year in a landmark edition.[19] As he states, the treatise is of some relevance to research. Historically, written in 1668, it is evidently the work of a consummate master. Moreover, it belongs to a time of rapid decline in the chant and stands as an urgent appeal in defense of the old practice. In particular, it aims to clarify the neumatic system whose subtleties the square notes completely overlook. In an appendix to the edition, Smolensky included an extensive chart of the notation where he arrived at a remarkably clear portrayal of the chant's development. Thus, other lasting results of his work were to recognize the history of musical writing as a locus of immediate concern and to affirm an essential continuity of the melodic tradition dating back to the earliest times. As his later publications show, however, Smolensky sensed that the problems

Plate 1.   The Russian Neumatic (Znamenny) Notation
            (19th-century manuscript from the author's collection)

Plate 2.   The Kievan ("Square") Notation
         (Early 19th-century print from the author's collection)

of research inevitably extend beyond the confines of the azbuka and the elementary questions of transcription.

The development of the square notation used in the Synodal edition of the chant coincides with a turbulent period in Russian history. In the mid-seventeenth century, the councils precipitated by the textual and liturgical revisions of Patriarch Nikon resulted in a vehement turn against enforced changes in the churches. This is the origin of the so-called Old Believers, a popular movement which by the turn of the century took upon itself to resist all officially sanctioned novelties. With time, the reaction was extended to many issues and came to represent a bitter distaste for the temporal powers standing in support of innovation. Being equally distrusted as a tool of the reformers, the square notation soon became an object of dissent, and the point of view originally advocated in the *Azbuka* of Mezenets was adopted by the traditionalists. The supporters of change meanwhile rallied behind the other influential treatise of the period, the *Azbuka* of Nikolai Diletsky. Written in 1679, this treatise had little to do with the old unison music; it used the square notes and expounded a method of polyphonic writing based exclusively on the Western variety.[20] Subsequent history was to show an increasing divergence between the two practices, with large numbers of Old Believers receding to regions away from the centers swayed by the new style.

Not until two centuries later did research expose the music of the Old Believers as a source of precious information about the early chant (see plate 3). At least a passive awareness of the Old Believer usage is seen as early as the writing of Metropolitan Evgeny who mentions the singing as the sole carrier of the long-lost neumatic tradition.[21] But again, we should turn to the writing of Smolensky to get a clear affirmation of the unique worth of the music, a music that, despite a continuing lack of official tolerance and a stigma of public disdain, was ostensibly the direct descendant of the original Russian chant.

> We have discovered a whole region where the folk arts, both the secular and the sacred song, coexist and are completely alive and thoroughly natural to the people just as they were several centuries ago. . . . We have also discovered that in those places a particularly strict form of the Old Belief survives and preserves for us in a completely live form, aside from the old singing, still much more which is interesting and informative. Of course, we cannot help but welcome these live and simple old practices, and Russian archeology must not neglect to take from them everything possible for our own learning and for the instruction of future artists.[22]

In an earlier publication Smolensky gave special weight to the relationship of the peasant folk song to the chant.

> Underlining here the fact that the Russian folk song, the kindred sister of our old church chant, has not been codified in its melodies, and that the znamenny and demestvenny singing have already been, for a long time, provided with a fine, special notation, I strongly affirm that the knowledge of this living practice of notation has much to reveal in the research on

Plate 3. An Old Believer Choir—early 20th century
(Reprinted from F. Sklemov, *Staroobriadcheskoe
khorovoe penie,* Moscow, 1912)

the structure of the Russian folk melody. We are not at a loss because of the general lack of education of these people: they know their art well. They have not lost the most important details of the theory of znamenny singing and have preserved the fine shades of its performance. Among them are still alive through tradition the many refinements not transmitted in the books, for instance, concerning the pronunciation of the text, the height of the pitch, the speed of the performance, etc. Because of this, musicians and scholars can test their own generalizations and discoveries through these living carriers of antiquity.... [23]

An interest in folk song was by no means a novelty in Russia. But it was Smolensky's awareness of the similar musical principles underlying both the repertory of the Old Believers and the peasant song that gave a new impetus to research. The pursuit of this meant an exploration of both the sacred and secular realms for elements of a national theory of the music. [24]

To this day, the singing of the Old Believers survives as an unexhausted resource. Settlements of Old Believers have spread to many parts of the world including South America, Australia, Canada, and the United States; they are scattered over the entire territory of the Soviet Union, in the faraway regions of Siberia, in Central Russia, and especially in the Baltic countries. Their practice is motivated by an unswerving observance of the ancient Orthodox services in a form closely resembling the common usage in Russia of the seventeenth century. Of course, some changes have been made. But these are small in comparison with the liturgical abbreviation that has occurred in the mainline practice of the Russian Orthodox. From a musical standpoint, perhaps the most interesting of the Old Believer services is the All-Night Vigil, a combination of the morning and evening offices frequently up to six hours long. Especially among the priestless sects—those groups surviving without bishops to perform ordinations—the service is maintained with particular care and offers a unique record of archaic practices in the liturgy. The Old Believer tradition likewise gives investigators a rare glimpse into the theoretical training of singers. Among the many elaborate, hand-copied manuscripts still in use, the grammars of the chant are an important category. Despite some variety in their contents, they reveal a well-established practice whose method has remained largely unchanged.

Long before the azbuka became the bulwark of the Old Believers, lists of musical signs were included in the chant manuscripts. Such antecedents of the azbuka are known as early as the fifteenth century. With time, however, there developed increasingly detailed information about the neumes, and the various manuals came to include not only summary, verbal descriptions, but also the *razvody,* or explanations of the more complex notation through the use of equivalent, simpler signs. By the seventeenth century, the azbuka was at the height of its development, and the core of the treatise was considerably expanded. A variety of additions included appendices of the typical melodic formulas *(popevki),* explications of the unnotated, "secret" melodies *(fity* and *litsa),* discussions of newly developed methods of notation, as well as a number of other occasional insertions. In some cases, the newly acquired portions existed independently. Thus, the popevki could be collected in handbooks known as the *kokizniki,* while the particularly melodious repertoire of melismas was gathered in the so-called *fitniki;* similarly, the azbuka of the *demestvenny* chant could be kept in a separate volume containing music with a special notation. Throughout its development, the azbuka was bound to living practice; it responded to the immediate requirements of the singer and never claimed to teach more than was necessary to perform the chant.[25] The mature seventeenth-century azbuka thus shows a vigorous growth at a time of increasing uncertainty among musicians. On the eve of momentous reforms, its expansion is vivid evidence of a general weakening in an orally based musical tradition.

The seventeenth century also witnessed the appearance of diastematic techniques to enhance the neumatic notation. One of these was the system of *pomety* ascribed to a certain Ivan Shaidurov of the late sixteenth century; according to this method, pitch was indicated by red letters inserted into the manuscripts. A later system, developed by Alexander Mezenets, called for the *priznaki,* or small black tails, to be attached to the existing neumes.[26] Being wholly accurate in respect to pitch, the heightened notation thus gave a new theoretical orientation to the azbuka. Before, in the pre-Shaidurov times, the emphasis had been on the assimilation of the popevki, and the skill of the musician rested on the recognition of standard melodic patterns. With the arrival of the priznaki and pomety, however, the notation lent more importance to the singer's sense of musical scale.[27] Related to this is the usage of the *gorovoskhodny kholm* ("the ascending knoll") which eventually became a common feature of the azbuka, often as a preface to the main body of the treatise (plate 4). Like similar representations in the West, the kholm taught the singer to sing up and down the rungs of "the knoll" using a method of basic solmization.[28] After the schism in the late seventeenth century, the neumes incorporating the diastematic additions survived in the practice of the Old Believers. Their usage is backed by the standard kholm of the modern azbuka.

During the nineteenth and, especially, the early twentieth centuries there was a notable increase in publications on the Old Believer tradition. Evidently, the Old Believers themselves had come to appreciate the growing interest in their music for, on occasion, they cooperated in research and even hailed the work of various authors. Understandably, Smolensky was particularly regarded as the harbinger of a long-awaited thaw.[29] Shortly before the latter's edition of Mezenets, the full repertoire of chant, the *Krug* in the notation of the Old Believers, was published by the Synodal Press.[30] As some thought at the time, this signalled the completion of a task long overdue—one which was supposedly initiated by Bortniansky, who was reputed to have become a private devotee of the old chant in his later years. In fact, it is now known, the story of Bortniansky's "conversion" is apocryphal, and he was not the initiator

Plate 4.   The Kholm
(Reprinted from L. Kalashnikov, *Azbuka tserkovnogo
znamennogo peniia,* Kiev, 1908)

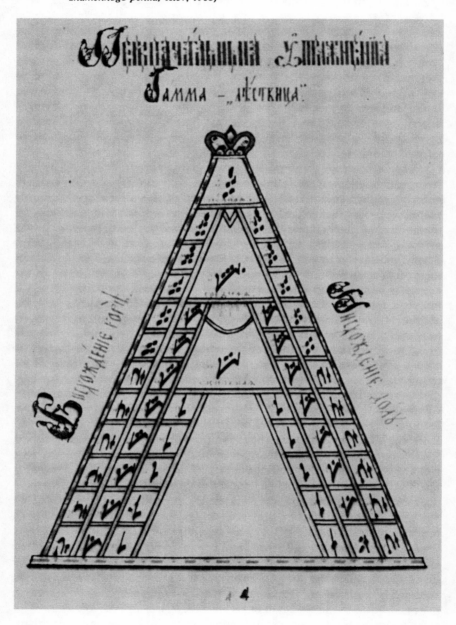

of the project.[31] Apparently, behind the publication were the interests of the Old Believers who saw the mounting concerns of scholars as an opportunity to obtain official recognition for their art. As we read in the preface, despite the collaboration of imperial organs and the editorship of Razumovsky—himself a member of the Russian Orthodox clergy—the funds for the project as well as the original hand-written copy of the music were supplied by the Old Believer community.[32] By the time of the Revolution, several chant books complementing the *Krug* emerged from the independent Old Believer presses in Kiev and Moscow, some of them in the well-known edition entitled *Znamennoe penie* [Znamenny singing].[33] Among the latter were the znamenny and demestvenny grammars of L. Kalashnikov, two good specimens of the Old Believer treatises from the turn of the century.[34] These, however, were not intended for the scientific community, and to teach the neumes they used only the traditional razvody without transcriptions into modern notation. Fortunately, this problem was offset by other publications.

Two of the best introductions to the chant to appear at this time were clearly the *Azbuka* and *Osmoglasie* by Metallov.[35] In accordance with traditional theory, Metallov approached the music through a study of the popevki, litsa, and fity. Perhaps more than any of his predecessors, he had come to see that a knowledge of the notation was essential but insufficient— that the pomety and priznaki make transcriptions of the old melodies possible but give only limited insight into other important realms. A mastery of the chant, he realized, still depended on a basic versatility with the stock of conventional melodic phrases and motifs in each of the eight liturgical modes. Metallov especially stressed this in the supplement to his *Azbuka,* the *Osmoglasie.* Here he provided what is in actuality a combined kokiznik and fitnik, with an extensive list of melodic formulas from the various hymns. Compared with Razumovsky's count of 215, Metallov gathered 283 examples, all of which he conveniently wrote in the square notation.[36] In the edition he explains his method by spurning the use of unrelated theory: "... the eight modes of the znamenny chant," he says, "must be studied not according to a foggy, distant, and for us, extinct system of the ancient modes, but through the live and typical melodic examples of each mode, through the popevki, according to the traditional practice of the singer and the grammars of the neumatic notation."[37] Thus, Metallov's approach was both accurate and realistic. While preserving the fundamentals of the old system, it made allowance for the uninitiated beginner whose greatest handicap was a basic inexperience with the sound of the singing. By side-stepping the difficult issues of notation in the *Osmoglasie,* he moreover showed that, for the novice, the Synodal redaction is a perfectly valid place to start. Against the background of the developing research, the *Azbuka* and *Osmoglasie* by Metallov are important achievements. In these treatises, the fruits of a new historical and theoretical awareness were admirably translated in an accessible, appropriate, and enduring format.[38] Later, Metallov also revealed his extraordinary abilities as paleographer.

In the first decades of the twentieth century, the focus of attention increasingly turned to the earliest history of the chant.[39] Overshadowed by the abundance of material appearing after the fourteenth century, the manuscripts of the pre-Mongol period are comparatively few in number, primitive in appearance, and most importantly, closed to transcription.[40] Although the earlier writers such as Undolsky and Razumovsky had given tentative appraisals of these remote sources, they did little to further an understanding of their history. At the end of the century, as a result, some basic assumptions concerning the Byzantine-Greek origins of the Russian chant remained unexamined. What is more, prevailing ignorance of counterpart Greek manuscripts obstructed the view and even served to lead astray such a figure as Smolensky. In 1901 Smolensky made his notorious conclusions denying the Greek derivation of the Slavic neumes. The evidence, he thought, suggested the contrary—the adoption of Slavic notation by the early Greeks![41]

In 1908, however, Preobrazhensky published his pathfinding essay showing the existence of irrefutable parallels between the Byzantine and Slavic usages.[42] Against the claims advanced by Smolensky he suggested that, although the earliest Slavic notation cannot be transcribed—and it is possible that we will never know its sounds—a comparison of the Greek and Slavic sources shows the occasional use of similar, and in places, identical melodies. Graphic analysis, Preobrazhensky contended, bears this out conclusively and moreover leads to another telling correlation: the use of similar musical signs is apparently related to a closeness in the poetic structure of the Greek and Slavic hymns. This phenomenon in particular seemed to substantiate the Slavic determination to preserve the original Byzantine melodies, a principle which Preobrazhensky believed was deep in the Russian chant tradition and to which he even attributed some of the later curiosities of the music such as the *khomovoe* singing of the Old Believers. In the end, Preobrazhensky asserted that the notation we find is unquestionably of Greek origin and was "completely taken over and assimilated by the Slavic singers."[43] As the author himself noted, it was during an expedition to Mount Athos and Constantinople that he was able to consult the necessary materials.[44] His next and final article on these findings did not appear until almost a decade after the Revolution.[45]

Two books by Metallov represent other milestones in this research. Both published in 1912, the *Simiografiia* and *Bogosluzhebnoie penie* were lasting contributions involving comprehensive studies of the earliest Slavic sources.[46] The breadth of insight exhibited by these publications dwarfed previous pioneering efforts, and if scholars had already surveyed some of the materials, Metallov now showed a masterful command of manuscripts in most of the important archives. In broad terms, he established a useful periodization of the manuscripts and examined the tenth to the twelfth centuries as the formative stage in the znamenny singing. As he put it, the music from the centuries after the Mongolian invasions was "the result of the development . . . of the essential beginnings and elements, the character and organization of the church singing from the pre-Mongol period."[47] Both books by Metallov are still the only ones of their kind, and to the student without simple access to the archives they are of immeasurable importance. If one can learn to account for the new post-revolutionary locations of the documents, the *Simiografiia,* a set of reproductions from the early manuscripts, forms a particularly welcome complement to Smolensky's earlier publication.[48]

By the time of the Revolution, more than a century had elapsed since the first efforts on behalf of the Russian chant, and it seems only fitting that in those years the writers should have turned to surveying the many achievements of the field. We could cite a number of works, all of which gave special acknowledgment to what had already been done.[49] While the publications are useful for a conspectus of the research, they are also important in another way: they stand at the threshold of fundamental changes. The most conspicuous of the coming changes was to be the dissociation of interests from ecclesiastical concerns. If the earlier work had been essentially motivated by reform, in the future, practical aims related to the Church would no longer be expressed. One of the last exceptions was Preobrazhensky, who in 1924 acclaimed the recent stylistic turn—especially in the works of Kastalsky and compositions such as Rachmaninoff's *All-Night Vigil* op. 37—as an important event in the history of Russian sacred music.[50] With the disappearance of the old objectives, a pervasive nationalism occupied the foreground and became the hallmark of postrevolutionary endeavors. New scholarship evaluated the music through the eyes of secular, cultural history, an approach which is already evident in the first large text from the Soviet period by Nikolai Findeizen (1868-1928).[51]

After the Revolution, Metallov not only reviewed the past but suggested aims for the future. Specifically, he wrote about intensifying research on the oldest sources and pleaded for new efforts in the area of facsimile publication.[52] The closing passage from his essay of 1924 is of interest both for the conviction with which it speaks and for the mood which it conveys. Metallov was never to publish again.

To make known the most important manuscript materials of the Greek and Russian church music—at least in the neumes, and, if possible, partly in [modern] notation—is of paramount importance to those interested in this branch of music not only because the time is ripe to size up what these sacred materials and their wealth have to tell us in the context of contemporary musical needs, but also, because these precious materials are subject to the annihilating forces of time, to random destruction, to catastrophic cataclysms and to other dangers; [they] might become inaccessible to Russian music and to the coming generations, which would be an irreparable cultural loss. The present time of increased mobilization of all the working forces of the nation and the people, of both the material and spiritual riches, this is our time, which is especially beneficial for the aforestated goals.[53]

By the mid-twenties, Metallov and Preobrazhensky stood as the last among the eminent prerevolutionary scholars. Eventually, with them vanished a certain generosity of approach. The work of these scholars had relied on unhampered experimentation; it advanced new methods without hesitation and, at the same time, with a certain assurance of results. It remains an open question why, over the years, Soviet research has consistently adopted narrower, more restricted interests, and why comparatively little has been done to continue along the path of renowned predecessors. Thus, for example, Metallov's ideas concerning publication have yet to materialize, and if it were not for a few volumes in the series of Danish *Monumenta Musicae Byzantinae,* the status of research on the earliest repertoire, it is likely, would have remained unchanged for close to seventy years.[54]

Overwhelming credit for contemporary work on the chant belongs to Maxim Brazhnikov (1902-1973). As a student of Preobrazhensky in the late twenties and a prolific writer, Brazhnikov symbolized a continuity between the old and the new research. However, in spite of his claims to broad involvement in all the historical periods and an apparent support of Preobrazhensky's interests, Brazhnikov has concentrated on the later sources beginning with the fifteenth century.[55] As a whole, his research has had only marginal input into the problem of transcription, and the statistical methods which he advanced, unfortunately, have done little to uncover what has not already been known. Among his works, many of which remain unpublished, are included several discussions of archival methodology, transcriptions from the manuscripts, and significant findings on the problem of early Russian sacred polyphony.[56] A history of the azbuka, by far his largest and most valuable contribution, originated in a doctoral dissertation of 1969; it gives a fine historical summary of the contents of the early theoretical sources.[57] The most comprehensive recent account of the history of Russian chant is that of Nikolai Uspensky (b. 1900). In contrast to the long stream of monographs by Brazhnikov, this publication has placed the author in the forefront of Soviet musicology with a single, ingenious stroke.[58] Uspensky gives a chronological survey from the earliest period through the crisis years in the seventeenth century. In doing so, the author has drawn on the important domestic and foreign research and has accompanied his discussion with abundant analyses of musical examples.[59] Uspensky's work is unique in the Soviet literature and offers one of the best aesthetic assessments of the Russian chant to appear in recent years. In the final chapters of the book, the author gives an excellent introduction to the polyphonic art in Russia prior to the arrival of Western theory.

In the absence of a written legacy like that of the West, theory of the Russian chant involves a fundamentally restricted set of concerns. The main subject of technical discussion is the neumatic notation; the essential sources are the grammars and the practice of the Old Believers. Thus, if only for the unsolved questions of transcription, the study of the music faces substantial challenges. Some of these are self-evident. About half of the recorded history of the chant remains silent in the manuscripts, and only the extent to which scholarship is able to uncover the meaning of the neumes delimits what we can know about the repertoire.

From the outset, however, the problems were also of another sort. In the first place, paradoxically, the original challenge had come from the West, and it is probably of more than passing importance that Metropolitan Evgeny composed one of his essays at the request of Anton Friedrich Thibaut, a known advocate of the Cecilian reform movement.[60] This had far-reaching ramifications. Modeled on the Western scholastic approach, the research willy-nilly set out to explain exactly that which for centuries had lacked discussion. The difficulty was not immediately perceptible; hence, the invocation of classical modal theory in the initial response. Secondly, the ideals which gave rise to research confronted scholars with the task of an aesthetic transformation in the Church. Ultimately, the aim was to bridge the deep gulf between two disparate practices. But what this actually implied, and how this was to come about, remained undecided. An intellectual understanding and appreciation of traditional ways was not enough, and because of this, it seems, some genuine interests remained largely by the wayside; others were utterly thwarted. Despite the recovery of historical awareness, in the churches the singing proved capable of change, but only of a limited kind, and it is perhaps indicative of certain misgivings in this regard that in 1904 Smolensky saw fit to acknowledge an important point: neither the old form of chant nor its notation had fallen into disuse through any sanctions of the Church. In other words, conceivably, the practice should be restored.[61] But it is precisely on this crucial question that Living Tradition itself, of which the Church was the official guardian, stepped in with remarkable confidence. Although time had shown a basic failure to implement the facts of discovery, and an incurable distraction with polyphony barred the return to the austere unison of the chant, composers of sacred music increasingly looked to the old melodies for inspiration. And this, finally, was the lesson to be learned. As far as the actual practice was concerned, an intelligent compromise was the only way to go, and "suitability of expression" had to prevail over "purity" and "authenticity" as the underlying motive of new trends. Fortunately, most persons understood this. And in the Church, radical measures were not taken; nor were they necessary in view of the way things existed. The burst of creativity in religious composition just prior to the Revolution is probably the best indication that a path had already been found.

While the notation and facts surrounding it constitute the essential issues, it seems that to grasp the music we should look beyond the overt traces. Here would be the grounds for a more expanded theory treating the lively topics concerning not only the local species, but the early music of the Christian world at large. Apart from the history, the language, and the sacred texts, it is the liturgy that holds the clues to many facets of this repertory, and the liturgical environment is inseparable. The literature on the Russian chant and the history of its appearance above all show the distance of research from the tradition being examined, and if discussions have been prone to conceptual inadequacies, misunderstandings, and a lack of effective terminology, this is symptomatic of an existing tension between native "theory" and what was sought. The materials of the chant are vestiges of a culture founded on oral processes of transmission. To understand the chant and to look beyond the problems of the notation is, first of all, to penetrate the methods which sustained the music throughout the centuries. The results should then be brought to bear in light of similar discoveries with other chant types.

Notes

1. Anton Preobrazhensky, *Po tserkovnomu peniiu ukazatel' knig, broshiur i zhurnal'nykh statei (1793-1896 g.)* [A bibliography of books, brochures, and journal articles on church singing for 1793-1896] (Ekaterinoslav, 1897; 2nd ed., Moscow, 1900).

2. Anton Preobrazhensky, *Slovar' russkogo tserkovnogo peniia* [A dictionary of Russian church singing] (Moscow, 1897), pp. 53-54.

3. Preobrazhensky, *Po tserkovnomu peniiu,* pp. 8-9.

4. Metropolitan Evgeny (Bolkhovitinov), *Istoricheskoe rassuzhdenie voobshche o drevnem khristianskom bogosluzhebnom penii i osobenno o penii rossiiskoi tserkvi, s nuzhnymi primechaniiami na onoe* [A historical discussion generally on ancient Christian liturgical singing and, in particular, on that of the Russian Church, with necessary commentary on the latter] (St. Petersburg, 1804), p. 16, n. 36. (*N.B.* This and other passages from the Russian are in my translation; parentheses are in the original; brackets are mine.) In the *Bibliography,* Preobrazhensky mentions the publication of this essay in 1817 "together with other historical discussions of the author"—but gives no titles. See, however, Metropolitan Evgeny, "O russkoi narodnoi i tserkovnoi muzyke" [On Russian folk and church music] *Otechestvennye zapiski* [Notes of the Fatherland] (1821) and *Strannik* [The Wanderer] (1871).

5. Vladimir Odoevsky, *K voprosu o drevne-russkom pesnopenii* [On the question of old Russian singing] (Moscow, 1864), p. 13. See V. Undolsky, *Zamechaniia dlia istorii tserkovnogo peniia v Rossii* [Observations for the history of church singing in Russia] (Moscow, 1846). Among the other important works of this period are: Nikolai Gorchakov, *Opyt vokal'noi ili pevcheskoi muzyki v Rossii ot drevnikh vremen do nyneshniago usovershenstvovaniia sego iskusstva* [The experience of vocal or singer's music in Russia from ancient times to the present mastery of this art] (Moscow, 1808); idem, "Ob ustavnom i partesnom tserkovnom penii v Rossii" [On unison and polyphonic church singing in Russia], *Moskvitianin* [The Muscovite] (1841); Ivan Sakharov, "Issledovaniia o russkom tserkovnom pesnopenii" [Research on Russian church singing], *Zhurnal Ministerstva Narodnogo Prosveshcheniia* [Journal of the Ministry of Public Education] (1849); Petr

Bezsonov, "O sud'be notnykh pevcheskikh knig" [On the fate of notated singers' books], *Pravoslavnoe obozrenie* [Orthodox observer] (1864); idem, "Znamenatel'nye gody i znameniteishie predstaviteli poslednikh dvukh vekov v istorii tserkovnogo russkogo pesnopeniia" [The important dates and outstanding representatives of the last two centuries in the history of Russian church singing], ibid. (1872); Alexander Riazhsky, "O proiskhozhdenii russkogo tserkovnogo peniia" [On the origins of Russian church singing], ibid. (1866).

6. Dimitry Razumovsky, *Tserkovnoe penie v Rossii* [Church singing in Russia] (Moscow, 1867-69), 3 vols. The work has three parts: (1) early Christian liturgical singing, (2) Russian chant, (3) Russian church polyphony.

7. The following number of entries is given in each category: history (51); theory (39); aesthetics (26); improvement and development of the art (18); pedagogy (19); textbooks (29); biographies, obituaries, and various accounts (30). See Preobrazhensky's table of contents, *Po tserkovnomu peniiu,* p. 3.

8. Potulov's harmonizations are in a somber, modal style evoking the antiquity of the chant melodies. The composer opposed Lvov on all issues except the use of asymmetrical rhythm. Lvov expounded his ideas in *O svobodnom ili nesimmetrichnom ritme* [On free or asymmetrical rhythm] (St. Petersburg, 1858); also published in German translation, A. Lvov, *Über den freien Rhythmus des altrussischen Kirchengesanges* (St. Petersburg, 1859). Potulov's own treatise was entitled *Rukovodstvo k prakticheskomu izucheniiu drevnego bogosluzhebnogo peniia pravoslavnoi rossiiskoi tserkvi* [A guide to the practical study of the old liturgical singing of the Russian Orthodox Church] (Moscow, 1872).

9. In particular see Yury Arnold, "Die Tonkunst in Russland bis zur Einfuhrung des abendländischen Systems," *Allgemeine Zeitschrift für Theater und Musik* (1867); idem, *Teoriia drevne-russkogo tserkovnogo i narodnogo peniia na osnovanii avtenticheskogo i akusticheskogo analiza* [The theory of old Russian church and folk singing based on authentic and acoustical analysis] (Moscow, 1880); idem, "Drevnie tserkovnye glasy" [The ancient church modes], *Pravoslavnoe obozrenie* (1878); idem, *Garmonizatsiia drevne-russkogo tserkovnogo peniia po ellinskoi i vizantiiskoi teorii i akusticheskomu analizu* [The harmonization of old Russian church singing according to Hellenic and Byzantine theory and acoustical analysis] (Moscow, 1886); Dimitry Allemanov, *Garmonizatsiia drevne-russkogo tserkovnogo peniia po khristianskoi-vizantiiskoi teorii* [The harmonization of old Russian church singing according to Christian-Byzantine theory] (Moscow, 1898); idem, *Tserkovnoe pesnotvorchestvo po vizantiiskoi teorii osmoglasiia dlia smeshannogo khora* [Church composition for the mixed choir according to the Byzantine theory of the eight modes] (Moscow, 1899); idem, *Tserkovnye lady i garmonizatsiia ikh po teorii drevnikh didaskalov vostochnogo osmoglasiia* [The church modes and their harmonization according to the theory of the ancient teachers of the Eastern eight modes] (Moscow, 1900).

10. Plates 1 and 2 compare the same hymn in different notations. The former is from a neumatic Old Believer manuscript (see discussion, p. 90) and represents the traditional writing practiced for centuries. The latter is from an edition with the European-like "square" notes introduced in Russia during the seventeenth century.

11. See the discussion in Razumovsky, *Tserkovnoe penie,* 1:90. Historically, the Synodal edition of the chant emerges as a thoroughly surprising undertaking for its time. Coming as it does from the mid-eighteenth century, the standardized compendium was *not* a product of resurgent interest in the old chant, but a demonstration of newly improved techniques in the printing of music. See Boris Volman, *Russkie pechatnye noty XVIII veka* [Russian printed notation of the 18th century] (Leningrad, 1957), pp. 18-21.

12.   Among the otherwise strange, polemical writing of a certain monk Innokenty we find rare
        information on the nineteenth-century performance practice with the Synodal editions. The
        author contrasts the prevailing choral style with the disappearing practice of what was called
        "simple singing," the improvised harmonization of the chant melodies in trio: "We are used
        to calling the cycle of ancient znamenny church singing the 'simple singing.' This name and
        understanding have, in the literal sense, since long ago, become commonplace among our
        Orthodox clergy, which is used to distraction by singing of choirs; because of this, the simple
        singing has long ago been discarded by all as useless, and presently, in our Orthodox Russian
        churches one can usually locate only the abridged Obikhod [in the square notation] and that
        one, not rarely somewhere among the old church rubbish; while the unabridged Obikhod
        and Oktoechos are already a rarity in our churches; and the Hirmologion, by its nature and
        repute, the most valuable [of these] is found even more rarely." A few pages later we read that
        for purposes of reduction the church books are given "in one essential line with the alto clef;
        but the singers must always perform the singing in accordance with chordal laws, with three
        individual voices *(trio)*." See Innokenty, *Drevnerusskoe znamennoe penie i o razumnom
        ispolnenii ego* [On the old Russian znamenny singing and on the reasonable performance
        thereof] (St. Petersburg, 1890), pp. 17, 23.

13.   The codification of local chants was initiated by the Holy Synod. A series of edicts from the
        1840s, mostly inspired by the outspoken opponent of Alexei Lvov, Metropolitan Filaret of
        Moscow (1782-1867), assigned the task to the various dioceses and monastic centers. See A.
        Govorkov, "Golos moskovskogo sviatitelia Filareta v zashchitu pravoslavnogo tserkovnogo
        peniia" [The voice of Metropolitan Filaret of Moscow in defense of Orthodox church
        singing], *Bogoslovskii vestnik izdavaemyi moskovskoi dukhovnoi akademiei* [Theological
        messenger published at the Moscow theological academy] 1912, no. 2, pp. 351-61; no. 3, pp.
        608-28. The following collections appeared: (1) *Sbornik tserkovnykh pesnopenii raznykh
        napevov upotrebliaemykh vo vladimirskoi eparkhii* [A collection of church hymns with
        various melodies used in the dioceses of Vladimir] ed. F. Sokolov, (Vladimir, 1885-86; square
        notation); (2) *Obikhod odnogolosnyi tserkovnogo bogosluzhebnogo peniia po napevu
        valaamskogo monastyria* [Obikhod of unison liturgical singing according to the chant of the
        Valaam Monastery] (Valaam Monastery, 1902; modern notation); (3) *Sbornik tserkovnykh
        pesnopenii raznykh napevov upotrebliaemykh v astrakhan'skoi eparkhii* [A collection of
        church hymns with various melodies used in the diocese of Astrakhan], ed. V. Sevastianov,
        (Astrakhan, 1904; modern notation); (4) *Krug tserkovnykh pesnopenii obychnogo napeva
        moskovskoi eparkhii* [The complete cycle of church hymns with the common chant of the
        Moscow Diocese] (Moscow, 1911; square notation); (5) *Obikhod notnogo peniia po
        drevnemu rospevu upotrebliaemomu v pervoklasnom stavropigal'nom solovetskom
        monastyre* [Obikhod of notated singing according to the ancient chant in use at the first-class
        stauropigial Solovetsky Monastery] (Solovetsky Monastery, 1912; modern notation); (6)
        *Irmologii soderzhashchii irmosy vsego leta... vo obiteli zhivo-nachal'nyia Troitsy i
        prepodobnogo Sergiia* [Hirmologion with the hirmoi of the entire year... in the monastery
        of the Life-giving Trinity and Saint Sergius] (Moscow, n.d.; modern notation). For the
        searching composers of harmonized singing these and similar publications offered a rich
        assortment of cantus firmi. Uncritical use of the edition was, however, a setback to scholarly
        work and continued for a good while even among some of the best writers of the time.

14.   Ivan Voznesensky, *O tserkovnom penii pravoslavnoi greko-rossiiskoi tserkvi—bol'shoi i
        malyi znamennyi raspev* [On the church singing of the Orthodox Greek-Russian Church—
        the bol'shoi and malyi znamenny chants], vol. 1 (Kiev, 1887); vol. 2 (Riga, 1889); idem,
        Osmoglasnye raspevy trekh poslednikh vekov pravoslavnoi russkoi tserkvi [Chants in the
        eight modes of the last three centuries of the Russian Orthodox Church], vol. 1, "Kievan
        chant" (Kiev, 1888); vol. 2, "Bulgarian chant" (Kiev, 1891); vol. 3, "Greek chant" (Kiev,

1893); vol. 4, select examples (Riga, 1893). See a similar but limited undertaking by A. Pokrovsky, *Znamennyi rospev (bol'shoi)—tekhnicheskoe postroenie raspeva na drevne-grecheskikh ladakh i razbor melodicheskikh strok (lits i fit)* [The znamenny chant (bol'shoi)—technical construction of the chant according to the ancient Greek modes, and an analysis of the melodic phrases (litsa and fity)] (Novgorod, 1901).

15.   Vasily Metallov, *Ocherk istorii pravoslavnogo tserkovnogo peniia v Rossii* [A study of the history of Orthodox church singing in Russia] (original edition in *Saratovskie Eparchial'nye Vedomosti* [Reports of the Saratov Diocese] (1893; reprinted in Moscow, 1896, 1900, and 1915); idem, *Tserkovnoe penie kak predmet prepodovaniia v narodnoi shkole* [Church singing as a subject in public school teaching] (Saratov, 1893).

16.   See note 35 below. At the time, Preobrazhensky was not able to include any of his own very useful research which was published in the following decades. See notes 42, 45, and 49 below.

17.   Stepan Smolensky, *Snimki s pevcheskikh rukopisei k opisaniiu (neizdannomu) solovetskikh rukopisei* [Reproductions from chant manuscripts for the (unpublished) description of the Solovetsky Monastery Collection] (Kazan, 1885). The publication, which appeared in a very limited edition, was recently reprinted; see idem, *Paläographisher Atlas der altrussischen linienlosen Gesangsnotationen*, ed. J. von Gardner, Bayerische Akademie der Wissenschaften, philosophisch-historische Klasse-Abhandlungen (Neue Folge), vol. 80 (Munich, 1976). See also idem, *Obshchii ocherk istoricheskogo i muzykal'nogo znacheniia pevcheskikh rukopisei solovetskoi biblioteki i 'Azbuki pevchei' Aleksandra Mezentsa* [A general survey of the historical and musical significance of the chant manuscripts from the Solovetsky Monastery and of 'the Singer's Azbuka' by Aleksandr Mezenets] (Kazan, 1887). Alexei Ignatev later published supplementary research on the materials examined by Smolensky. See the work listed in note 49 below and A. Ignatev, "Kratkii obzor kriukovykh i notnolineinykh pevcheskikh rukopisei solovetskoi biblioteki" [A short survey of the neumatic and diastematic chant manuscripts of the Solovetsky Library], *Pravoslavnyi sobesednik* [The Orthodox companion] (1910).

18.   Smolensky, *Obshchii ocherk*, p. 6.

19.   Smolensky, *Azbuka znamennogo peniia (izveshchenie o soglasneishykh pometakh) startsa Aleksandra Mezentsa* [The Azbuka of znamenny singing (a treatise on the most consonant pomety) by Aleksandr Mezenets] (Kazan, 1888). During these years the author also published other important archival research: *Kratkoe opisanie drevnego (XII-XIII veka) znamennogo irmologa, prenadlezhashchogo Voskresenskomu "Novyi Ierusalim" imenuemomu monastyriu* [A short description of an ancient (12th-13th century) znamenny Hirmologion belonging to the Resurrection Monastery known as the "New Jerusalem"] (Kazan, 1887); and "O sobranii russkikh drevne-pevcheskikh rukopisei v moskovskom sinodal'nom uchilishche tserkovnogo peniia," [On the collection of old Russian chant manuscripts in the Moscow Synodal School of Church Singing] *Russkaia muzykal'naia gazeta* [The Russian musical gazette] (1899).

20.   The first modern edition of Diletsky's treatise was prepared by Smolensky. S. Smolensky, ed., *Musikiiskaia grammatika Nikolaia Diletskogo* [The musical grammar of Nikolai Diletsky], Obshchestvo liubitelei drevnei pismennosti [The Society of Enthusiasts of Ancient Literature] vol. 128 (posthum., St. Petersburg, 1910). For more recent publications see V. Protopopov, ed., *Nikolai Diletskii, idea grammatiki musikiiskoi* [Nikolai Diletsky, an idea of music's grammar], Pamiatniki russkogo muzykal'nogo iskusstva [Monuments of Russian Music] vol. 7 (Moscow, 1979); and Nikolai Diletsky, *Gramatika Muzikal'na* [Musical grammar] (Kiev, 1970). Concerning polyphony in Russian church singing we should note the following: it is certain that it existed before the seventeenth century; but its history is obscure,

and we cannot be sure of the time or the place of its origin. Based on manuscript evidence, the native polyphonic technique is generally regarded as an outgrowth of folk heterophony cultivated in a few centers with privileged status. There is no written theory preserved on the practice, and the surprising dissonance of the music shows a complete independence from Western counterpoint. The practice nevertheless does not survive among the Old Believers. For good surveys and a bibliography see the publications cited below (notes 56, 58, 59).

21.   Metr. Evgeny, "O russkoi narodnoi," p. 12.

22.   S. Smolensky, *O blizhaishikh prakticheskikh zadachakh i nauchnykh razyskaniiakh v oblasti russkoi tserkovno-pevcheskoi arkheologii* [Concerning the immediate practical problems and scientific research in the field of Russian chant archeology] Obshchestvo liubitelei drevnei pismennosti, vol. 151 (1904), p. 26. Towards the end of the nineteenth century there was increasing evidence of an on-coming accord between the Russian Church and the Old Believers. Nevertheless, on an official level the sectarians continued to be regarded as a potentially dangerous, dissident element, and accusations of "backwardness" remained a firmly entrenched obstacle. A popular understanding of the Old Believer music is found in contemporary publications, e.g. Vasily Sokolov, "Razgovor pravoslavnogo s raskol'nikom o tserkovnom penii" [A discussion between an Orthodox and an Old Believer on church singing], *Rukovodstvo dlia sel'skikh pastyrei, zhurnal izdavaemyi pri kievskoi dukhovnoi seminarii* [Handbook of the rural pastor, journal published at the Kiev theological seminary], 1 (1862): 133-48.

23.   S. Smolensky, *O drevne-russkikh pevcheskikh notatsiiakh* [On the old Russian chant notation], Obshchestvo liubitelei drevnei pismennosti, vol. 145 (1901), p. 41.

24.   On the well-known and fruitful liaison of Russian secular composition with folk song see Alfred J. Swan, *Russian Music and Its Sources in Chant and Folk Song* (London, 1973). New sacred composition, however, was similarly inspired. The most brilliant exponent of sacred composition based on the folk idiom was Aleksandr Kastalsky (1856-1926). See his *Osobennosti narodno-russkoi muzykal'noi sistemy* [The peculiarities of the Russian folk musical system] (Moscow-Petrograd, 1923) and *Osnovy narodnogo mnogogolosiia* [The foundations of folk polyphony] (Moscow-Leningrad, 1948).

25.   Unlike many Western treatises, the azbuka contains only what is needed for a basic training of the singer, that is, in the first place, a discussion of the notation. Concepts of humanistic modal theory are an unknown feature, and the eight modes of the Oktoechos are dealt with only to the extent to which the musician needs to recognize and sing the essential melodies.

26.   Although the priznaki were designed to alleviate the difficulty of printing in two colors, after the schism interest in the publication of the old notation subsided. Mezenets's signs thus became regarded as a superfluous invention, and some even superstitiously referred to them as "the black traces of the devil on the page." Nevertheless, most of the Old Believers continued to enter them along with the pomety.

27.   In effect, the role of the popevka was severely reduced, and it became more or less possible to sing the music according to the pitch specified for each neume. Thus, for purposes of modern research, the pomety and priznaki are of fundamental importance. The notation becomes accessible to transcription. Beginning with the seventeenth century and, by retrospective analysis, perhaps as far back as the fifteenth century, we can acquaint ourselves with the actual sounds recorded in the neumatic manuscripts.

28.   Some of the early kholmy included not only the red letters of the new notation, but sometimes also the Western syllables of solmization. See Maxim Brazhnikov, *Drevnerusskaia teoriia muzyki po rukopisnym materialam XV-XVIII vekov* [The theory of

old Russian music according to the manuscript materials of the 15th-16th centuries] (Leningrad, 1973), p. 273. The kholm depicted on plate 4 is entitled: "Pervonachal'nyia uprazhneniia. Gamma—'lestvitsa'" [Beginning exercises. Gamut—'the ladder']. On the left-hand side we read: "Vozkhozhdenie gore" [ascending the knoll]; on the right: "Nizkhozhdenie dolu" [descending the valley].

29.   See anon., *O russkom bezlineinom i v chastnosti khomovom penii* [On Russian staffless and khomovoe singing] (Kiev, 1876); Iakov Bogatenko, *Vopros o staroobriadcheskom kriukovom penii na sobore episkopov* [The question of Old Believer neumatic singing at the council of bishops] (Kiev, 1909); idem, *Metodika peniia tserkovnogo—k voprosu o staroobriadcheskikh pevcheskikh shkolakh* [Methodology of church singing—on the question of Old Believer singing schools] (Moscow, 1910); idem, *'Zabytoe iskusstvo'— doklad prochitannyi na s"ezde khorovykh deiatelei v Moskve 22 iiunia 1910 g.* ["Forgotten art"—a lecture read at the choral conference in Moscow on 22 June 1910] (Moscow, 1910); idem, *Vechnyi vopros—o pevcheskikh kriukovykh knigakh* [Eternal question—on the neumatic chant books] (Moscow, 1916); F. Sklemov, *Staroobriadcheskoe khorovoe penie* [Old Believer choral singing] (Moscow, 1912).

30.   *Krug tserkovnogo drevnego znamennogo peniia v shesti chastiakh* [The complete cycle of old znamenny singing in six parts], Obshchestvo liubitelei drevnei pismennosti, vol. 83, parts 1-6 (1884-85).

31.   See A. Finagin, "'Proekt Bortnianskogo' (k voprosu ob ego avtore)" ["The Project of Bortniansky" (on the question of its authorship)], *Muzyka i muzykal'nyi byt staroi Rossii* [The music and musical life of old Russia], (Leningrad, 1927), pp. 174-88.

32.   *Krug tserkovnogo drevnego,* part 1, pp. i-iii.

33.   See *Kniga glagolemaia irmoloi* [The book called the Hirmologion] (n.p., n.d.); *Obednitsa znamennogo i demestvennogo rospeva s arkhiereiskim sluzheniem* [The small liturgy in the znamenny and demestvenny chants with the archbishop serving] (Kiev: Znamennoe penie, 1909); *Oktai znamennogo raspeva* [Oktoechos in the znamenny chant] (Kiev, 1911); *Sluzhba vo sviatuiu i velikuiu subbotu* [The service of Holy and Great Saturday] (Moscow: Znamennoe penie, 1914); *Obikhod znamennogo peniia* [Obikhod in the znamenny chant] (Kiev, 1910); *Trezvony tserkovnogo znamennogo peniia* [The lesser feasts in the znamenny chant] (Moscow: Znamennoe penie, 1914).

34.   L. F. Kalashnikov, *Azbuka tserkovnogo znamennogo peniia* [Azbuka of church znamenny singing] (Kiev: Znamennoe penie, 1908); idem, *Azbuka demestvennogo peniia* [Azbuka of demestvenny singing] (Kiev: Znamennoe penie, 1911).

35.   V. Metallov, *Azbuka kriukovogo peniia. Opyt sistematicheskogo rukovodstva k chteniiu bezlineinoi semiografii pesnopenii znamennogo raspeva, perioda kinovarnykh pomet* [Azbuka of neumatic singing. The experience of systematic training in the reading of staffless notation of the hymns in znamenny chant, from the period of the cinnabar pomety] (Moscow, 1899); idem, *Osmoglasie znamennogo raspeva. Opyt rukovodstva k izucheniiu osmoglasiia znamennogo raspeva po glasovym popevkam* [The eight modes of the znamenny chant. The experience of training in the eight modes of the znamenny chant according to the modal popevki] (Moscow, 1899).

36.   Cf. Razumovsky, *Tserkovnoe peniie,* 3:287-321.

37.   *Osmoglasie,* p. 6.

38.   Among the other treatises which appeared at the time we can cite the following: M. Ozornov, *Azbuka tserkovnogo znamennogo peniia s prilozheniem azbuki demestva* [Azbuka of

church znamenny singing including an appendix of the azbuka of demestvenny chant] (n.p., n.d.); F. Bornukov, *Azbuka i uroki kriukovogo peniia s prilozheniem polnogo fitnika, pesnopenii osmoglasnika i liturgiinykh staropechatnogo teksta. (Posobie k samoobucheniiu i obucheniiu v shkolakh)* [Azbuka and lessons of neumatic singing including an appendix of the complete fitnik, and chants of the eight modes and the liturgy according to the old printed text. (A guide to self-teaching and teaching in schools)] (Vitebsk, n.d.); A. Pokrovsky, *Azbuka kriukovogo peniia* [Azbuka of neumatic singing] (Moscow, 1901); L. Bystrov, "Azbuka kriukovogo peniia" [Azbuka of neumatic singing], *Tserkovnoe penie* [Church Singing], 1911, nos. 7, 9, 10, 11; idem, *Uchebnik znamennogo peniia v trekh chastiakh—dlia staroobriadcheskikh shkol* [A textbook of znamenny singing in three parts—for Old Believer schools], parts 1-3 (Kiev: Znamennoe penie, 1911). See the survey of such publications provided by Yakov Bogatenko, *Pevchaia azbuka proshlogo stoletiia (ocherk)* [The singer's azbuka of the last century (a survey)] (Kiev, 1909).

39.   The new work was prompted by the surveys of philologists and archivists such as Archimandrite Amphilokhy, I. Sreznevsky, A. Gorsky, K. Nevostruyev, I. Bychkov, A. Pokrovsky, and others, all of whom gave valuable descriptions of resources to be found in many public, private, and ecclesiastical collections. Russian scholarship of this period provided much of the basis for the research later taken up by Western historians of Byzantine and early Slavic music. See note 54 below.

40.   Among these, the oldest exemplar, the so-called Tipografskii Ustav dates back to the eleventh century. For a list of the manuscripts see Miloš Velimirović, "The Present Status of Research in Slavic Chant," *Acta musicologica,* 44 (1972): 262-64. The list is based on a preliminary master catalogue provided by N. B. Shelamanova in "Predvaritel'nyi spisok slaviano-russkikh rukopisei XI-XIV vv., khraniashchikhsia v SSSR" [A preliminary list of Slavic-Russian manuscripts from the 11th-14th centuries in the USSR], *Arkheograficheskii ezhegodnik za 1965 god* [The Archaeographic Annual for 1965] (Moscow, 1966), pp. 177-272.

41.   Smolensky, *O drevne-russkikh,* pp. 20-22.

42.   Anton Preobrazhensky, "O skhodstve russkogo muzykal'nogo pis'ma s grecheskim v pevcheskikh rukopisiakh XI-XII vv." [On the similarity of Russian musical writing with the Greek in the chant manuscripts of the 11th-12th centuries], *Russkaia muzykal'naia gazeta,* 1909, nos. 8-10.

43.   Ibid., p. 9.

44.   Ibid., p. 2. For a detailed account of the first journey by Russian musicologists to libraries of the East see Stepan Smolensky, "Iz dorozhnykh vpechatlenii" [Impressions of the road], *Russkaia muzykal'naia gazeta,* 1906, nos. 42-46. Concerning earlier travel by Russian scholars see Archimandrite Porfiry Uspensky, *Pervoe puteshestvie v afonskie monastyri i skity... v 1845 godu* [First journey to the monasteries and sketes of Athos... in 1845] (Kiev, 1877-80); idem, *Vtoroe puteshestvie po sviatoi gore afonskoi* [Second journey on the Holy Mount Athos] (Moscow, 1880); and A. Dmitrievsky, *Puteshestvie po vostoku i ego nauchnye rezul'taty* [A journey through the East and its scientific findings] (Kiev, 1890); idem, *Patmosskie ocherki—iz poezdki na ostrov Patmos v 1891 g.* [Patmos sketches—from a trip to the island Patmos in 1891] (Kiev, 1894).

45.   A. Preobrazhensky, "Greko-russkie pevchie paralleli XII-XIII vekov" [Greek-Russian chant parallels of the 12th-13th centuries], *'De Musica', Vremennik otdela teorii i istorii muzyki* ['De Musica,' Chronicle of the Department of Music Theory and History] 2 (1926): 60-76.

46.   V. Metallov, *Russkaia simiografiia iz oblasti tserkovno-pevcheskoi arkheologii i paleografii* [Russian notation from the realm of chant archeology and paleography] (Moscow, 1912)

and *Bogosluzhebnoe penie russkoi tserkvi v period domongol'skii* [Liturgical singing of the Russian Church in the pre-Mongol period] (Moscow, 1912).

47.   *Bogosluzhebnoe penie,* p. iv.

48.   See note 17 above.

49.   Some of these are A. Preobrazhensky, "Kratkii ocherk istorii tserkovnogo peniia v Rossii" [A short study of the history of church singing in Russia], *Russkaia muzykal'naia gazeta* (1907); idem, *Ocherk istorii tserkovnogo peniia v Rossii* [A study of the history of church singing in Russia] (St. Petersburg, 1910); idem, *Kul'tovaia muzyka v Rossii* [Music of the cult in Russia] (Leningrad, 1924); V. Metallov, *Ocherk istorii* (see note 15 above); M. Lisitsin, *O novom napravlenii v russkoi tserkovnoi muzyke* [On the new direction in Russian church music] (Moscow, 1909); A. Ignatev, *Bogosluzhebnoe penie pravoslavnoi russkoi tserkvi s kontsa XVI po nachala XVIII veka po kriukovym i notolineinym pevcheskim rukopisiam solovetskoi biblioteki* [Liturgical singing of the Russian Orthodox Church from the end of the 16th to the beginning of the 18th centuries according to the neumatic and diastematic chant manuscripts of the Solovetsky Library] (Kazan, 1916), pp. 27-80.

50.   Preobrazhensky, *Kul'tovaia muzyka,* p. 115. Much of the writing of the Russian émigré musicologist Ivan Gardner (b. 1898) has continued in this tradition. See his recent book *Bogosluzhebnoe penie russkoi pravoslavnoi tserkvi* [Liturgical singing of the Russian Orthodox Church] (Jordanville, N.Y., 1978-82) 2 vols. Portions of this work have been published as: Johann von Gardner, *System und Wesen des russischen Kirchengesanges,* (Wiesbaden, 1976) and *Russian Church Singing* (Crestwood, N.Y., 1980). He has also edited and published an Old Believer azbuka: J. von Gardner and E. Koshmieder, eds., *Ein handschriftliches Lehrbuch der altrussischen Neumenschrift,* Bayerische Akademie der Wissenschaften, philosophisch-historische Klasse—Abhandlungen (Neue Folge), vols. 57 and 62 (Munich, 1963 and 1966). See also the work cited in note 17 above.

51.   Nikolai Findeizen, *Ocherki po istorii muzyki v Rossii s drevneishikh vremen do kontsa XVIII veka* [Studies in the history of music in Russia from ancient times to the end of the 18th century], 2 vols. (Moscow-Leningrad, 1928-29). This does not discount the role of nationalistic prejudices in earlier thinking. For example see V. Metallov, *O natsionalizme i tserkovnosti v russkoi dukhovnoi muzyke* [On nationalism and church piousness in Russian sacred music] (Moscow, 1912).

52.   V. Metallov, "Ocherednye zadachi v izuchenii drevne-russkoi muzyki" [Current problems in the study of old Russian music], *Istoriia russkoi muzyki v issledovaniiakh i materialakh* [The history of Russian music in studies and materials] ed. A. Kuznetsov (Moscow, 1924), 1:91-99.

53.   Ibid., p. 99.

54.   See R. Jakobson, ed., *Fragmenta Chiliandarica Palaeoslavica,* Monumenta Musicae Byzantinae, main series 5 A and B (Copenhagen, 1957); A. Bugge, ed., *Contacarium Palaeoslavicum Mosquense,* ibid., main series 6 (Copenhagen, 1960). For a survey of the research based on these facsimiles see Christian Hannick, "Fragmenta Chiliandarica Palaeoslavica," *Irenikon* 3 (1972): 371-75; and idem, ed., *Fundamental Problems of Early Slavic Music and Poetry,* Monumenta Musicae Byzantinae, subsidia 6 (Copenhagen, 1978). See also the studies by Miloš Velimirović, *Byzantine Elements in Slavic Chant,* ibid., subsidia 4 (Copenhagen, 1960); idem, "Stand der Forschung über Kirchenslavische Musik," *Zeitschrift für slavische Philologie* 31 (1963): 145-69; idem, "The Present Status," pp. 235-65.

55.   See M. Brazhnikov, *Stat'i o drevnerusskoi muzyke* [Articles on old Russian music] (posthum., Leningrad, 1975), pp. 3-22. The article "Novye zadachi issledovaniia

pamiatnikov drevnei russkoi muzyki"[New problems of research on the monuments of old Russian music] was originally published in *Ocherki po istorii i teorii muzyki. Pervyi sbornik nauchnykh trudov i materialov gosudarstvennogo nauchno-issledovatel'nogo instituta teatra i muzyki* [Studies in history and theory of music. First collection of scientific essays and materials of the State Research Institute of Theater and Music] (Leningrad, 1939).

56.   For a complete survey and bibliography of Brazhnikov's work see A. Belonenko, A. Kruchinina, A. Panchenko, eds., *Problemy istorii i teorii drevnerusskoi muzyki* [Problems in the history and theory of old Russian music] (Leningrad, 1979), pp. 62-98. A partial publication of Brazhnikov's candidate's thesis (1943) appears as "Mnogogolosie znamennykh partitur" [Polyphony in znamenny scores], ibid., pp. 7-61. For the published transcription see M. Brazhnikov, *Novye pamiatniki znamennogo raspeva* [New monuments of znamenny chant] (Leningrad, 1967); idem, Pamiatniki znamennogo raspeva [Monuments of znamenny chant] (posthum., Leningrad, 1974); idem, ed., *Fedor Krestianin; Stikhiry* [Fedor Krestianin; Canticles], *Pamiatniki russkogo muzykal'nogo iskusstva* [Monuments of Russian Music], vol. 3 (posthum., Moscow, 1974).

57.   Brazhnikov, *Drevnerusskaia teoriia* (see note 28 above).

58.   Nikolai Uspensky, *Drevnerusskoe pevcheskoe iskusstvo* [The art of ancient Russian chant] (Moscow, 1965; 2nd ed., Moscow, 1971, revised and expanded with forty-one transcriptions from manuscript sources).

59.   In addition to the transcriptions provided in the newer edition of the history, Professor Uspensky has published a unique anthology of early Russian singing: *Obraztsy drevnerusskogo pevcheskogo iskusstva. Muzykal'nyi material s istoriko-teoreticheskimi kommentariiami i illiustratsiiami* [Examples of the art of old Russian chant. Musical material with historical-theoretical commentary and illustrations] (Leningrad, 1968; 2nd ed., Leningrad, 1971).

60.   See Metr. Evgeny, "O russkoi narodnoi," p. 1.

61.   See S. Smolensky, *O blizhaishikh prakticheskikh*, p. 10.

The Theories of Boleslav Yavorsky

Gordon D. McQuere

Boleslav Leopoldovich Yavorsky (1877-1942) has been credited as the first Russian theorist to create a system applying to all music.[1] His body of thought, generally known as "the theory of modal rhythm" [ladovyi ritm], is marked by unusual originality and scope and by its close correspondence to the musical practice of nineteenth- and early twentieth-century Russian composers such as Skryabin. His approach was devised during the first decade of this century. In attempting to deal with his changing musical world as well as with the music of all other times and places, Yavorsky sought to replace the entire corpus of traditional theory with one based on a single principle, the operation of the tritone. The deductive theoretical system that resulted was predestined to fall short of its goal of universality; nonetheless, it provides valuable insights that merit a closer investigation.

Yavorsky's investigations of musical problems use innovative techniques and concepts. His theory abandons acoustical derivations and, instead, posits the triad as the result of tonal motion and not as a given. His concept of tonic as a stable function that may also be dissonant separates consonance and dissonance from stability and instability. He concludes that pitch operations and temporal operations, both manifestations of his unifying principle, are in turn related to dynamics, form, and the setting of texts. His procedures involve reduction theory, linguistic analysis, and hierarchic levels and stress the role of each tone in a musical complex.

It is true that his theory results in a great deal of prescriptive dogma. Like other deductive systems, his is dependent upon the validity of his premises, some of which are unproven and unprovable. To the extent that we accept his premises, his theory is remarkably consistent and believable. To the extent that we question them, the results seem far-fetched and invalid.

Despite objections that may be raised regarding Yavorsky's gospel, his theory contains more value than that of a passing curiosity. Examination of his work forces us to revaluate our own culturally influenced perceptions of music, and to apprehend the culture that engendered Yavorsky's. The Soviet musicologist Valentina Konen states that Yavorsky "was successor to the very high flowering of Russian music of the 1860-90s" and that his modal theories also reflect the newest musical tendencies of his contemporaries.[2] Of his culture's past, Yavorsky's theory most closely relates to the music of Rimsky-Korsakov and others of the Five. Of the composers of his own day, Yavorsky's name has been most associated with the music of Skryabin; he had remarkable insight into the enigmatic works of this composer. His ideas continue to serve as a basis for further analytical experiments in the Soviet Union. Western scholars can, by examining Yavorsky's work, acquire a more profound understanding of Russian music and the society that created it.

Yavorsky's theories also left their mark in Soviet music theory in a more specific sense. He is responsible for introducing a number of accepted terms and concepts, including the concept of "intonation." While some of the prescriptive details of his theory have fallen into the same obscurity that is the fate of all prescriptive theories, much of the conceptual side of his work has become a part of the working assumptions of modern Soviet music theory.

Boleslav Yavorsky, the creator of this remarkable theory of music, was born in Karkov in the Ukraine 10/22 June 1877.[3] His father, of Polish descent, was a soldier, so the young Yavorsky was raised by his mother, two older sisters, a Swedish nurse, and a Ukrainian housekeeper. Both sisters were proficient at languages, and from childhood Yavorsky knew Russian, Polish, French, and Ukrainian. Because their home was located at the edge of town, he came in constant contact with peasant life. Clearly precocious, Yavorsky early acquired a love of reading and developed an inquiring mind. His earliest musical influences were twofold: the piano playing of his mother and sisters, and the folk songs that surrounded him. His own piano lessons began at age six, with his mother as teacher.

An autobiographical sketch tells us that at approximately age seven he decided that each profession must sing its folk songs in a mode corresponding to its physical work. This notion caused him to begin searching through books on music as he was able.[4]

Yavorsky's family later moved to Kiev, where, in 1894, he entered the Kiev music school to study piano and theory, the latter under E. A. Ryb, a student of Rimsky-Korsakov's. In 1897, after completing the Kiev classical gymnasium, he entered the university to study physics and mathematics, while continuing musical studies at the Kiev music school. The university studies were undertaken at the behest of his father, whose death in 1898, coupled with his own illness brought on by overwork, allowed Yavorsky to leave the university. He completed the music school in 1898.

That year Yavorsky and his mother moved to Moscow so that he could enter the conservatory, where he studied theory and piano. At that time Skryabin was teaching piano at the Moscow Conservatory; Yavorsky did not know him, but became interested in his compositions. Among Yavorsky's teachers were Sergei Taneev and Stepan Smolensky.[5]

The importance of Taneev to Yavorsky's musical education can hardly be overstated; Boris Asafiev has called Yavorsky the "successor to Taneev's thought."[6] However, Yavorsky did not continue Taneev's remarkable investigations into strict counterpoint. Rather, the influence is found in Taneev's concept of tonal hierarchy and his disciplined and rigorous approach to problem solving. Sergei Protopopov, Yavorsky's student, quotes his teacher: "The basic task of Taneev as composer and teacher was to reveal the constructive principles that organize musical thinking. Musicality and thinking were the two basic demands that Taneev made on a musician."[7] It is also interesting that Taneev admired Yavorsky's gifts and later often consulted him on contemporary music.

Yavorsky spent five years at the conservatory, where under Taneev he studied counterpoint, canon and fugue, and form. But the conservatory years were profitable for more than formal training. Beginning with the 1899-1900 academic year, he organized an informal group called "Mondays" [ponedel'niki] for the purpose of performance and discussion. At these meetings some of his important ideas developed. Protopopov cites several examples taken from notebooks of those years, including a concept of "intonation"[8] in speech and its possible application to music, inner auditory tuning, four simple modes [lad] (major, minor, augmented, diminished), the so-called turn [oborot], a concept of phrase as a symmetrical arrangement of moments, and the important principle of "comparison and result" [sopostovlenie s rezul'tatom]. The notebooks also present the idea that musical speech is distinguished from verbal speech only by the absence of vowels and consonants. The "Mondays," which sometimes met more than once per week, also performed and analyzed folk songs and even opera. Besides Yavorsky, the original group of four included Nadezhda Yakovlevna Briusova, also a theorist, and later a pupil of Yavorsky's. Through her Yavorsky came to know her brothers, the poets Valery and Aleksandr Briusov, and other poets such as Andrei Bely and Konstantin Balmont, who may have introduced Yavorsky to linguistic theories. In the course of time the group enlarged to include, among others, the composer Reinhold Gliere.

After completing the conservatory in 1903, Yavorsky taught music theory and piano in a variety of situations, and worked for the musical-ethnographic commission of Moscow University. Protopopov relates that in 1905 Taneev recommended Yavorsky as his replacement in counterpoint and canon and fugue at the Moscow Conservatory. Yavorsky allegedly refused, because at that time those subjects did not interest him.[9]

From 1906 to 1916 he taught in the Moscow People's Conservatory, and after 1916 he held the post of professor of composition and piano in the Kiev Conservatory.[10] From 1921 to 1930 he worked in Moscow for Narkompros, and taught in several other schools in Moscow.[11] In 1932 he became an editor at Muzgiz, the Soviet music publishing house, working in particular on the music of Taneev and Bach.[12]

Finally in 1938 Yavorsky was invited to return to the Moscow Conservatory as professor, where he served until his death in 1942. He died on 28 November in Saratov, where the Moscow Conservatory had been moved during the war. He was at the time preparing a major work entitled "Creative Thought of Russian Composers from Glinka to Skryabin."[13]

Yavorsky's first published work, *The Structure of Musical Speech,* appeared in 1908, only five years after he completed the conservatory.[14] Though brief, this volume presents the theory of modal rhythm in a form closely paralleling that of *The Elements of Musical Speech* (1930-31) by Sergei Protopopov.[15] Protopopov, a student and close friend of Yavorsky's, wrote this large work under his teacher's supervision. It remains the only reasonably complete presentation of the theory of modal rhythm. Comparing the two works shows that the theories were essentially in place by 1908. The basic premises and logical framework present in his first publication remained largely unchanged throughout Yavorsky's career.

One must not infer from this, however, that Yavorsky ceased theoretical activity in 1908. His subsequent work included application, expansion, and speculation. The most famous application of the theory of modal rhythm involves the late music of Skryabin. Yavorsky claimed to have discovered the principles behind Skryabin's music before 1915, but they never discussed the matter.[16] Another kind of application is evidenced by Yavorsky's 1929 article, "The Construction of the Melodic Process," where he shows the relevance of the theory of modal rhythm to a single line of music as well as to a more complex musical fabric.[17] As the only mature work by Yavorsky himself that presents his theories, this article is extremely important. The analyses it includes, of melodies from folk song and musical literature, are among the few published ones by Yavorsky. Attempts at a pedagogical application for the theory of modal rhythm include, besides Protopopov's book, two other brief manuals by Yavorsky, *Exercises in Voice Leading* (1913) and *Exercises in Forming Modal Rhythm,* Part I (1915).[18] An early expansion of his work is found in Yavorsky's article "Text and Music," published serially as an additional part to *The Structure of Musical Speech.*[19] This work investigates the analogy between verbal and musical intonations. Later additions to the theories include duplex modes and microtonal modes, the latter probably developed during the 1920s.

Perhaps the most characteristic facet of Yavorsky's later work is its speculation. He ponders how music is, how we should perceive it, and how it will change. A specific instance of this occurs in an article on the perception of music, jointly authored with Sofia Beliaeva-Ekzempliarskaia.[20] Yavorsky's later work also includes speculation into other arts and into linguistics. He considered art as an expression of life, and the various arts as differing expressions of the same human needs. Many of Yavorsky's letters from his last years are devoted to such questions.

These issues are by-products of the basic universal intent of the theory. If art forms are expression of life, they must be interrelated, as must be all aspects of music. To achieve such universality, Yavorsky first had to find basic laws for music and show that music of all times and places is subject to these natural principles. This pursuit occupied the bulk of Yavorsky's efforts and even found reflection in the various names he applied to his theory. Besides "the theory of modal rhythm," the most frequently encountered name, he used "the structure of musical speech," "the theory of auditory gravitation," and finally the all-inclusive "theory of musical thinking."

If his general goal was a universal theory of art, a more immediate goal was to understand music. "Not satisfied with a statement, a description of facts, the theory of modal rhythm attempted to *explain* the meaning of musical phenomena, and to search for the cause-effect connections between them."[21] His search led him to envision a complete revolution in concepts about music. He sought to rid music theory of what he considered artificial distinctions, such as counterpoint, harmony, and form, and replace them with a single theory that would account for all of these. He searched for natural laws that would provide an explanation equally valid for all kinds of music, including folk song. An understanding of folk song was particularly important because he saw it as the purest musical manifestation of life itself.

He reached the conclusion that the basic musical law, the one unifying principle, was the natural instability of the tritone. Its tendency towards motion he refers to as "auditory gravitation" [slukhovoe tiagotenie], the analogue of gravity in the physical world and the result of an "inner tuning" that is present in all human beings.[22] The task of the theory of modal rhythm is to show how all musical phenomena result from the motion of an unstable tritone to its stable resolution.

Yavorsky's theory of modal rhythm is comprised of closely interrelated conceptual strands that cannot be completely unraveled. To aid comprehension, though, the following exposition will separate categories of pitch, duration, and melody and harmony.[23]

Concepts of Pitch

The basic unit of musical structure, the "symmetrical system"[simmetrichnaia sistema], consists of a tritone and its resolution.[24] The tritone is the consistent element; its resolution may take a variety of forms. In the basic symmetrical system (also known as the "single system"), the tritone resolves by converging motion to a major third or by diverging motion to a minor sixth (fig. 1). It is symmetrical in that both voices move an equal distance in opposite directions.

In figures referring to the theory of modal rhythm, unstable tones are given black note heads, and stable ones are given open note heads. The vertical line between them shows the "boundary"[gran'] between the two parts, and the

Fig. 1   The single symmetrical system, converging and diverging

D   T   D   T

slur connects the two parts. The letters beneath stand for dominant and tonic. The term *dominant* designates the unstable portion of any single system. The term *tonic* designates any stable structure to which it resolves.

The next unit, the combination of two single systems one semitone apart, is called a "double symmetrical system"; it contains two unstable intervals and a resolution to a minor third (or major sixth). The first unstable interval, a perfect fifth, is unstable with respect to the double system, although obviously consonant (fig. 2a).

Figure 2b shows the complex of gravitational motions in the double system. Each initial tritone resolves, but one of its tones of resolution coincides with an unstable tone in the other tritone, and thus resolves still further. The unstable portion of the double system is called "subdominant" (*S*), and its resolution, "subtonic" (*t*).[25] Yavorsky asserts that besides the complete double system, incomplete forms are possible. Two of these, the natural and harmonic forms, are shown in figure 2c and 2d. He asserts that the complete form is actually present in the mind, even though only a portion of it is sounded.

Fig. 2   The double symmetrical system in complete, natural, and
         harmonic forms

a   b   c   d

S   t   S   t   S   t   S   t

Each voice of a single or double system is termed a "conjunction" [sopriazhenie] and represents a melodic cell, the product of a systemic gravitation. A "disjunction" [nesopriazhenie] involves a leap from an unstable tone to the opposite stable one, such that the motion is in the direction of gravity, that is, in the direction that normal resolution would take it. Figure 3 shows examples of conjunctions and disjunctions in single and double systems.

Single and double systems may be combined to create modes. An elementary combination uses one single and one double system that share a stable tone. If the double system is above, the mode is major (fig. 4a). If it is below, the mode is minor (fig. 4b). The various forms of the double system result in corresponding modal varieties: complete, natural, or harmonic. The

Fig. 3   Conjunctions and disjunctions as parts of single and
double systems

Fig. 4   The major and minor modes in complete, natural, and
harmonic forms

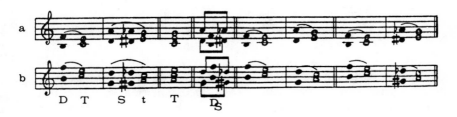

additional tones present in the complete form of the double system provide
some of the more common borrowed or altered tones of traditional harmony.

In Yavorsky's presentation of major and minor each tone has a role to
play and a place in a modal hierarchy. The roles are determined by the tones'
modal gravitations, which correspond, in the main, to the generally accepted
tendencies of the tones of the scales. In addition, a hierarchy exists among the
unstable tones. These are classified as either leading tones [vvodnyi ton] (when
the tone of resolution is part of no other conjunction) or "inversely conjunctive
tones" [obratno-sopriazhennye] (which share a tone of resolution with another
unstable tone).

A second classification shows that dominant instabilities have a clearer
gravitation than subdominants. Thus, the leading tones of the dominant (the
pitch B in the example of C major) has the greatest modal clarity, followed by
the pitches A or A♭ (leading tone of the subdominant), followed by the
inversely conjunctive tones (F and D-D♯, respectively). The combination of all
the unstable tones of a mode, called the "collective moment" [soedinennyi
moment] of the mode, uses both leading tones and two of the possible inversely
conjunctive tones. It is designated by a combination of the letters *D* and *S*,
representing the two unstable functions (see fig. 4). That the major and minor
modes display an inverse symmetry reflects the basic symmetrical nature of the

entire theory and also has ramifications for the theories about sonorities discussed below.

The first nontraditional mode to be investigated by Yavorsky, the augmented mode, combines two or three conjunct single systems. The tonic of the mode is an augmented triad, and the collective moment, designated by two or three *D*s, corresponds to either the sonority of a French sixth chord or a whole-tone scale (fig. 5).

Fig. 5   The augmented mode in complete and incomplete forms

The diminished mode combines two double systems. Its tonic, containing a tritone between outer members, is considered conditionally stable, that is, stable only as a result of its systemic gravitations. Yavorsky asserts that in nature there is no absolute stability, but only relative stability. Because of the two double systems, a great number of incomplete forms are possible. The form given in figure 6 is a common one. The unstable tones of the diminished mode form a tone-semitone series, otherwise known as the octatonic scale.[26]

Fig. 6   The diminished mode

Another mode, the "chain mode" [tsepnoi lad], is formed from two interlocked single systems (fig. 7). Ryzhkin points out that the chain mode resembles the so-called major-minor mode of Catoire; the mode is also called "major-minor" in *The Structure of Musical Speech*.[27]

Fig. 7   The chain mode

Two modes called "variable modes" are formed from three symmetrically arranged systems as shown in figure 8. These probably resulted from Yavorsky's folk-song investigations. Ryzhkin calls them one of the most successful finds of the theory because they more closely account for folk songs than do traditional modes. He also points out that they approach a concept of functional variability in the sense that a tone of the mode may be either stable or unstable depending on its context.[28]

Fig. 8   The first and second variable modes

The last group of simple modes includes three hypothetical modes designated the x-chain, y-chain, and z-chain modes (fig. 9). In *The Structure of Musical Speech* Yavorsky lists several other hypothetical modes that do not seem to have been developed further or were dropped in favor of the duplex modes that he later devised.[29]

Fig. 9   The x-chain (a), y-chain (b), and z-chain (c) modes

The concept of mode as understood by Yavorsky involves two general premises. First, *mode* refers to interrelated gravitations in the patterns given above, which are transposable. Yavorsky uses "modal tonality" [lado-tonal'nost'] to designate a mode at a specific pitch. Thus, major is a mode; C major is a modal tonality. Second, two single systems one semitone apart result in a double system, not a mode. Protopopov provides a chart of the six possible tritones in the tempered system (fig. 10).[30] A mode must involve all six types either completely, i.e., as a tritone, or incompletely, using one tone as part of a stable resolution. Therefore, a single system touches on three types of tritones, and a double system four types. Only by combining systems in a manner that involves all or part of all six tritones does one create a mode. Protopopov includes such a chart for each mode, marking the tones that are used.

Fig. 10   The six possible types of tritones

A major complication occurs at the next step. Yavorsky asserts that since each tritone has two possible resolutions—converging and diverging—it is possible to employ both simultaneously to create a higher order of systems and modes. The resultant structures are prefixed with the word *duplex* [dvazhdy], as in "duplex single system," or "duplex major modal tonality." The number of tones involved becomes much greater, and function becomes increasingly important in resolving ambiguities. The same letter designations are used in duplex systems, but prefixed with a lower-case *d* (fig. 11).

Fig. 11   Duplex single and double systems in converging form

When duplex systems are combined into modes, the results amount to two simple modes separated by a tritone. While this concept causes very complex vertical and linear structures involving all twelve tones (some more than once), each tone has a function that makes it unique. Even the duplex systems taken separately allow complex sonorities. The tonic of the duplex single system coincides with the French sixth chord; that of the duplex double system coincides with the fully diminished seventh.

It is instructive to follow Protopopov's derivation of the duplex augmented mode.[31] First he gives the chart of the six types of tritones, showing with boxes all the tones that are used, most in more than one capacity (fig. 12). Next, the three single systems and their duplex equivalents are given in order of pitch. Finally, he shows the duplex tonic and the unstable tones (fig. 13).

Protopopov points out that since both the stable and unstable tones form whole-tone scales, only two different duplex augmented modes are possible. He might also have used this mode to illustrate the importance of function in determining mode. Since the stable and unstable tones of this mode are both

Fig. 12   The duplex augmented mode as part of the six tritones

Fig. 13   The duplex augmented mode

whole-tone scales, the designation of stability is governed by context, not by structure.

The derivation of the other duplex modes is similar. The duplex chain mode, which also uses only duplex single systems, results in the structures shown in figure 14. Its unstable tones form a fully diminished seventh, and its stable tones form the so-called octatonic scale.

Fig. 14   The duplex chain mode

The duplex major and duplex minor modes are somewhat more complex because they employ duplex double systems. The complete forms of the modes are given in figure 15. Each may have incomplete forms constructed in a manner analogous to the simple major and minor modes. Protopopov points out that in the "classical epoch" simple major was often used with additional tones, e.g., F♯ and A♯ in C major, derived from the duplex portion of the single system.[32] For both the duplex major and duplex minor modes, there are six transpositions. Indeed, six transpositions is necessarily the maximum for any duplex mode, because of the tritone relationship between the parts.

A duplex x-chain mode, a duplex y-chain mode, and a duplex z-chain mode are also hypothetically possible. The first is identical to the duplex augmented mode, the second to the duplex minor mode, and the third to the duplex major mode.

Fig. 15   The duplex major and minor modes

The duplex diminished mode, however, presents a new possibility (fig. 16). The tonic is a fully diminished seventh chord, and the collective moment (the unstable tones) is the octatonic scale. This is just the reverse of the duplex chain mode, where the unstable tones form the diminished seventh chord. In both the duplex diminished mode and the duplex chain mode, three transpositions are possible.

Fig. 16   The duplex diminished mode

Scale patterns seem to have been only indirectly important to Yavorsky. He views them as the fortuitous result of modal gravitations rather than as *a priori* structures. Relationships between his modes and existing scale patterns serve as confirmation of his ideas. Chapter 5 in Part 1 of *The Structure of Musical Speech* is devoted to showing such correspondence in the simple major, minor, augmented, and major-minor (chain) modes. In addition, Yavorsky points out that the whole-tone scale is found in the unstable tones of the augmented mode, and that the "Hungarian" scale equals the incomplete augmented mode.[33]

Vertical relationships in the theory of modal rhythm are governed by only one principle: conjunct tones may not sound simultaneously in order not to counteract the force of gravity. Stable and unstable tones may be mixed in a sonority as long as they are not conjunct. An exception appears in the double system, where the extreme tones of a voice may occur simultaneously if the middle tone is in use. For example, if one voice is A-Ab-G, the A and G might sound together if a complete form of the double system—involving the Ab—is in use. A sonority is stable only if all component tones are stable. But instability is a matter of degree, governed by the least stable member, that is, by the tone with the clearest modal moment. Yavorsky's approach results in a much wider group of available vertical relationships since he is not restricted by preconceptions about chords constructed in thirds.

Any sonority in a mode falls into one of six groups based on its combination of stable and unstable tones (fig. 17). The first group has the least clear modal moment, and so is nearest the tonic. It uses the inversely conjunctive tones and those stable tones that are not conjunct. The result is a group of three- and four-note sonorities that use the labels D, S, D_S, etc. according to their unstable tone or tones, and the subscript Roman numeral I. The combination of symbols identifies both the function and the form of the sonority. Seventh chords in the traditional sense are given the added subscript numeral 7 in Protopopov's text. This seems contradictory in a theory that implies the equality of all sonorities. In general, however, Protopopov's labeling is much clearer than is Yavorsky's in *The Structure of Musical Speech*.

The second group uses one or both leading tones and any disjunct stable tones. The third group uses both unstable tones from one system, that is, the leading tone and the inversely conjunctive tone from the same system, plus one stable tone if possible. Group four uses the leading tone of one system with the inversely conjunctive tone of the other system. Many of the common triads appear in this and the following groups. Group five has both inversely conjunctive tones and one leading tone, but no stable tones. Group six adds the one disjunct stable tone to group five. The entire system for natural major and minor is shown in figure 17.

Protopopov comments on the symmetrical nature of the major and minor modes, illustrating his point with a chart (fig. 18). The modal sonorities of S and D are arranged outward from the tonic in opposite directions, showing the inverse symmetry of major and minor. Consequently, in the minor mode the subdominant and dominant triads of traditional harmony have reversed designations. This is, of course, reminiscent of the theory of harmonic dualism.

Protopopov's investigation of modal sonorities continues with the other forms of major and minor, and with three other simple modes: chain, augmented, and diminished. The results are predictable, but the harmonic variety, particularly in the complete forms of the major and minor modes, is impressive.

Fig. 17   The six groups of modal sonorities in C major and A minor

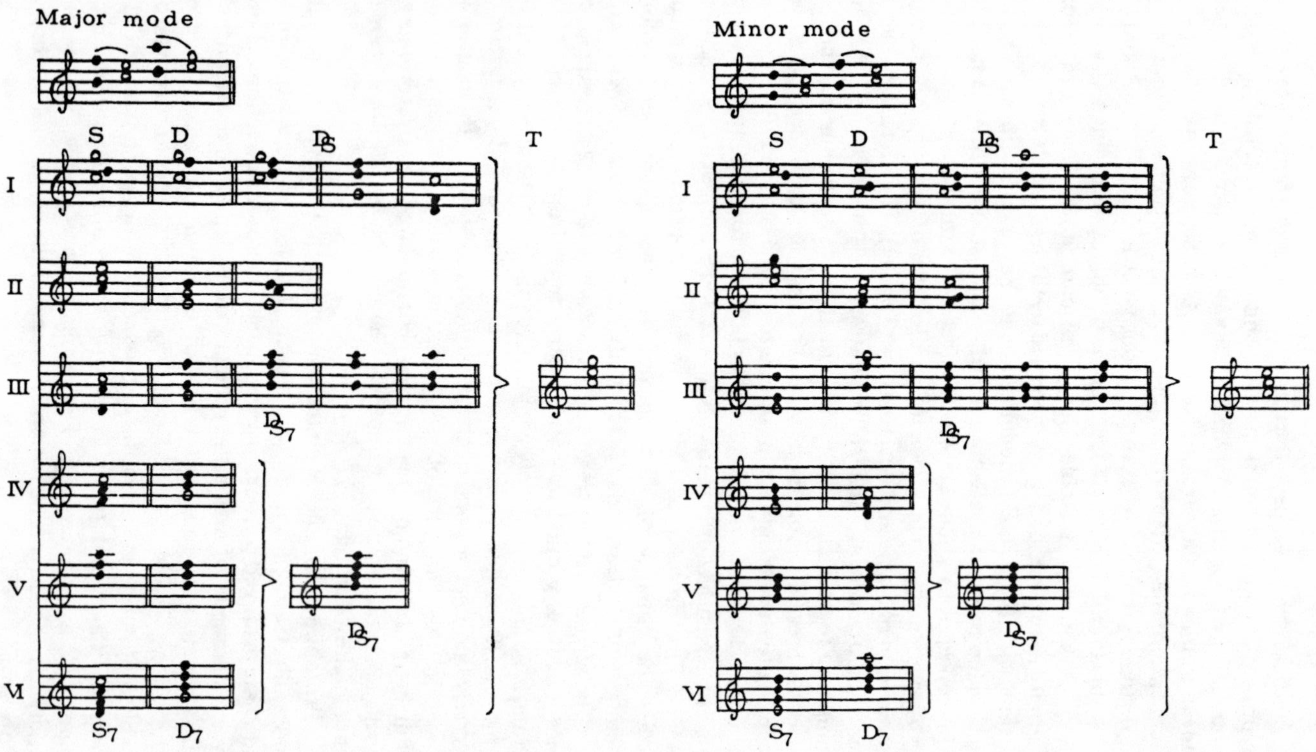

Fig. 18   The symmetry of dominant and subdominant sonorities
in C major and A minor

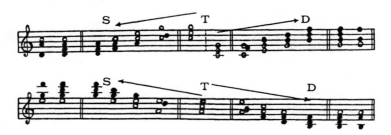

Concepts of Rhythm and Form

In the theory of modal rhythm, the relationship between pitch functions and temporal functions is found in the motion of the tritone towards resolution. It moves in musical space, and it also moves in time. The most commonly encountered definition of modal rhythm underscores this connection: the unfolding of modes in time. There also exists an independent natural origin for temporal events, the motions of the human body: gesture, pace, pulse, and breathing. Yavorsky wrote to Kulakovsky that "rhythm is a living fact, and not a scientific fact...."[34]

In *The Structure of Musical Speech,* Yavorsky asserts the connection between rhythm and life with customary terseness, but Protopopov digresses grandly, quoting extensively from contemporary scientific works on the mechanics of walking and running.[35] He attempts to categorize each position and motion in walking and running, and show how the motion of the two legs can correspond to various kinds of temporal organization, even to that in three pulses.

The point is that all motion is divisible into two parts, a fact he must establish in order to show the natural connection between a variety of metrical patterns and the two parts of the symmetrical system. The connection exists at all hierarchic levels, each level of structure showing a metrical and modal role. In the broadest sense Yavorsky believed rhythm to include all temporal phenomena, small details as well as major sections of a work (e.g., the "rhythm of the main and secondary parts").[36] But the anacrusis and the ictus in a typical symmetrical resolution manifest the most important relationship.

Musical time can be articulated into pulses that have either weak or strong character. In Yavorsky's theory, pulse is the greatest common divisor of the durations in a work. These pulses are combined into two-part groupings, having varying numbers of pulses on each side of the "boundary" [gran'], i.e., the vertical line between the two parts of a symmetrical system. This boundary sometimes corresponds to the bar line. Figure 19 shows the simplest relationship: that having one pulse on each side of the boundary. Either portion is called a moment [moment]. Between groups is a caesura, marked by a comma. The marks above the note heads show weak and strong pulses, respectively, and the slur line shows their connection.

Fig. 19   A two-part relationship of two pulses

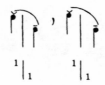

For larger numbers of pulses, more possibilities exist. For example, the three possible arrangements of four pulses are shown in figure 20. A hierarchy among the pulses exists, with the strongest falling on the ictus. To each of these arrangements Protopopov assigns an affective character and includes examples.[37] The first type (fig. 20a) is used for marches with an active character (e.g., Beethoven's Symphony no. 5, first movement, eighth-note pulse), and the second (fig. 20b) for marches with a passive character (e.g., "The Internationale") and for funeral marches (e.g., Beethoven's Sonata op. 26, marcia funebre). The third type (fig. 20c) is inert (e.g., Bach's French Suite no. 6, gavotte). Protopopov treats three-, five-, and six-pulse meters similarly and alludes to even more complex patterns.

Fig. 20   Three possible two-part relationships of four pulses

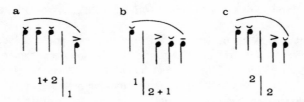

It must be stressed that this process does not happen independently of modal operations. Since the interaction between the rhythmic event and modal meaning occurs at every level, form is seen as a manifestation of the same basic relationships on a much broader scale. Each local two-part pair, with its rhythmic and modal aspects, may be grouped with others on the basis of a number of regularizing principles, the most important of which are symmetry and periodicity. Symmetry is a relationship of parts such that the second half mirrors the first half (ab ba). Periodicity is the repetition of a unit (ab ab). Of these relationships symmetry is clearly the more important, since it reflects the symmetrical nature of pitch structures. Yavorsky does not discuss periodic arrangements in detail, but they are apparently analogous to the symmetrical arrangements.

Four symmetrically arranged moments, two two-part systemic pairs, may create a phrase. The stable or unstable nature of such a phrase depends on the stability of the outside tones. A symmetrical grouping does not form a phrase if an initial unstable tone is resolved in the third moment, shifting the axis and upsetting the symmetry. Figure 21 shows examples.

Fig. 21   The symmetry of four moments in the single system

By analogy, four phrases may be grouped into a symmetry of phrases, composed of 16 moments. In such a structure, successively higher orders of caesurae divide the sections. In order to create a unified whole from the four phrases, two possibilities are available: either the first unstable tone that appears (in the second moment) does not resolve until the last moment, or, before it resolves, another unstable tone appears in its place. This principle is called "crossover" or "coupling"; there are seven possibilities for it. In the examples in figure 22, "+" means stable and "−" means unstable.

Protopopov raises an interesting side issue in the relationship of these symmetrical structures to dynamics. At the level of the phrase and of the symmetry of phrases, he asserts that dynamics should either be equal throughout or should correspond to the functions of the moments, *p* and *f* corresponding to stability and instability.[38]

Periodicity and symmetry may also help to organize larger formal units. Form at all levels manifests modal principles. Those principles that control the functions of tones in a phrase control the functions of sections in a large form, where they become very sophisticated, giving rise to subtle variation.

Kulakovsky reports the following statement by Yavorsky on the relationship of modal rhythm and form:

> Modal rhythm is not form; a form is individual, unique. Schemes, such as symmetrical, periodic, or sonata schemes, may be repeated. Modal rhythm is the principle of impressing a musical process with tones. . . . There cannot be a sonata form; there is a sonata scheme, and there is the form of any sonata of Beethoven, but all the forms of the sonatas of Beethoven are completely different; if there were two sonatas in the same form, there would be creative identity, a tautology, and not one tone would be different from one to the other.[39]

Fig. 22   The symmetry of four phrases with crossover

Yavorsky, seeing schemes as less important, spends little time with them, instead providing guidelines for form as he understands it. These guidelines take various shapes in the several works on modal rhythm, but as a whole shed light on his view. In his first work he gives a definition of a "connected whole," three general laws of form, and some conditions of unity in a connected whole. "A connected whole is a combination of structural elements based on some kind of law that arranges the balance and closed nature of the form that these elements comprise."[40] The three general laws of form referred to are:

1. Every cause has an effect
2. Every action has an equal reaction
3. Balance between cause and effect, action and reaction

The conditions of unity in a connected whole include symmetry of the various modal, metrical, and rhythmic structures, metrical equality of stability and instability, and a stable auditory horizon (i.e., the highest and lowest tones must be stable, relative to the prevailing mode).

Yavorsky next takes up the importance of comparison to perception, stating that every concept is the result of comparing like or unlike things. This idea, reminiscent of Hegel, is fundamental to the theory of modal rhythm. A factor in creating formal structures, it also describes the two tones of the tritone that engender all musical events. Yavorsky briefly illustrates from the physical world, using examples such as light and darkness, hot and cold. Then he lists all the possible musical elements that can be compared and every possible combination of like and unlike structures. Again he stresses that forms are not pre-existent structures, but results, having many possible shapes.

In "The Construction of the Melodic Process," Yavorsky presents six types of organization that specifically apply to melody, but which in a broader sense are applicable to any musical structure.[41] The term *construction* used here refers to the hierarchic level at which modal forces are organized. This will be discussed in the next section. To some of the following he attaches historical significance. They refer to temporal relationships of stable and unstable units, from pulses to large sections.

1. Stability of the whole construction and all its elements.
2. Construction based on a relationship between stability and instability, with stability predominant. The optimum relationship is that of the golden section.
3. Construction based on equality between stable and unstable parts. The seventeenth, eighteenth, and nineteenth centuries embody the change from the second to the third type.
4. Construction with instability predominant over stability, again with the golden section as the optimum relationship
5. Construction based on only unstable forces, typical of some composers of the nineteenth and twentieth centuries
6. Construction based on the motion of unstable phenomena

Viktor Zuckermann, Yavorsky's pupil, reports some other specific formal principles.[42] In these may be seen some correspondence to common schemes, the forms of traditional music theory. First is the principle of comparison in the first half of the form. In two-part form, for example, the first part may begin with a secondary, unstable modal tonality, and the second part has the main, stable modal tonality. The entire form resembles the stable motions *D* to *T* or *S* to *T*. The first modal tonality functions as an anacrusis, and the second, as an ictus. As an example, he cites the beginning of the familiar wedding march by Mendelssohn, which begins in a secondary key but ends in the principal key.

The second principle is digression in the third quarter of the form, an extremely common phenomenon. The third quarter of a form contains a contrasting modal tonality that disturbs the stability. The last quarter restores the stability. He refers to this third quarter as a kind of "dramaturgical knot," pointing out that it contains the golden section. An example is the opening of Chopin's Polonaise op. 40 (*Polonaise Militaire*), where there is a dramatic move from A major to C♯ major in the third phrase of four, followed by a return in the final phrase.

A third principle, the symmetrical comparison of modal tonalities, amounts to a "framing" of unstable modal tonalities by a main, stable modal tonality. While the most obvious instance of this principle is the cadence formula *T-S-D-T*, it may also be seen in larger units. An example is cited from Chopin, Mazurka op. 24 no. 4, mm. 5-12, where in the span of eight measures, the tonalities are, respectively, B♭ minor, D♭ major, F minor, and B♭ minor.

The highest form of tonal relationship is the principle of "comparison and result" [sopostovlenie s rezul'tatom]. In a narrow sense, this is a comparison of two modal tonalities that leads to a third, resultant one. An example of this is a phrase taken from Skryabin's Mazurka op. 40 no. 1, mm. 13-20, in which two measures each of G♭ and A♭ major are followed by four measures of D♭ major. In general, though, comparison and result designate any contrast or conflict with a consequent resolution. This expansion of the idea of comparison as the basis of perception is the foundation of musical development and appears in the operation of the single system as well as in the modal-tonal relationships of the symphonic plan.

The usual tonal forms, schemes, are clearly accounted for in these principles. Only the coda seems to have demanded special explanation, and Yavorsky takes it up in Part 3 of *The Structure of Musical Speech.*[43] He claims the coda results from some incomplete structure earlier in the form. Yavorsky with characteristic thoroughness lists four possible reasons for its appearance.

1. The stable part of a connected whole, if metrically smaller than the unstable part, is completed in the coda.
2. A compared element (a theme, for example) is not unified in the form, and the coda provides unification.
3. Metrical or rhythmic incompleteness of the form is resolved in the coda.
4. An unfulfilled law of the auditory horizon, which requires that the extreme upper and lower tones of a work must be stable, is fulfilled in the coda.

Yavorsky further points out that not only does the coda fulfill various deficiencies in the resultant part of the form, it may also introduce new instabilities or comparisons that will require their own resultant parts. In most cases the beginning of the coda falls on the end of the preceding structure.

Ryzhkin, in his lengthy discussion about the theory of modal rhythm, is more critical of Yavorsky's theories of form than about any other portion of the work. It is instructive to examine some of his points.[44] He observes that, in Yavorsky's theory, sonata form is reduced to a modal relationship, eliminating any melodic or thematic aspects of form. Consequently, Ryzhkin objects, the theory of modal rhythm shows a quantitative relationship between stable and unstable parts of the form, but not a qualitative relationship. He further states that "the theory of modal rhythm ignores the types of structures (schemes) established in the musical practice of harmonic-homophonic writing," and that "to an even greater degree it ignores the question of thematic development."[45] While Ryzhkin's observations are correct, he fails to recognize that Yavorsky was looking past formalized schemes and thematic development to what he considered the controlling factor in music, the modal rhythm.

Yavorsky, in his views on form, attempts to redefine musical concepts as thoroughly as he does in his theories of pitch. Form, as distinct from scheme, is an extension of the smallest rhythmic units in music, which are related, by means of the tritone and its resolution, to the smallest pitch elements in music. Thus, the temporal and tonal aspects of a musical form are interrelated like the temporal and tonal aspects of the single symmetrical system. Yavorsky dismisses the formal categories of traditional theory as completely as he denies traditional harmonic theory.

Concepts of Melody and Harmony

To understand Yavorsky's approach to melody and harmony, it is helpful to examine his concept of the three levels of structure. These hierarchic levels, called construction, composition, and formation, are presented in "The Construction of the Melodic Process."

> *Construction* [konstruktsiia]... is the basic principle of creative work, which consists of the mastery and harmonious agreement of the forces of gravity for realizing a creative act. *Modal rhythm* is the unfolding in time of the construction of a musical work.
> *Composition* [kompozitsiia]... is the articulation of the construction of a work of art with a view to disclosing the creative goal.
> *Formation* [oformlenie]... is the embodiment...of the composition of this construction by means of material standardized for a given art with a view to *expression beyond* the creative goal.[46]

Thus, modal rhythm serves as the background, organizing force that controls the shape of the work but does not deal with compositional detail. Studying the organization of these forces, the construction of a musical work, occupies a large portion of the materials on modal rhythm. Yavorsky explains how vertical and horizontal connections in music are made, and how these are related to the crucial concept of "intonation" [intonatsiia].

In 1908 Yavorsky defined an intonation as "the smallest basic tonal form in time" and "the comparison of two tones (or moments) in a tritone system that have different gravitations, ... the expressiveness of speech, the transfer of its sense and character."[47] In "The Construction of the Melodic Process," he states, "*Intonation* is the disclosing of the expressive possibility of a tonal cell, that is, the unfolding *in time* of the potential energy of a system."[48] Zuckermann provides a more concrete definition by calling intonation the "primary cell of form and expression in music."[49] Protopopov devotes several pages to the relationship of intonation in music to intonation in speech, and observes that speech may be intelligible even without the actual words, if the tone of voice—the intonation—is clear enough.[50] Both verbal speech and musical speech are based on the same intonational principle, the tritone and its resolution. This connection is axiomatic to Yavorsky, and he does not attempt to defend it.

Yavorsky's intonation is the basic linear element in music. Its simplest form can coincide with one voice of a single system (a conjunction), a manifestation of the stable/unstable process. At a more complex level, an intonation may involve a number of tones from several systems. The primary qualification is a clear, bipartite change of function.

The application of intonation, a linguistic concept, to music theory is Yavorsky's own contribution. The concept of intonation in Soviet music is generally associated with the work of the eminent musicologist, Boris Asafiev, who investigated it in detail. Through his broader application, intonation theory has become an important part of Soviet musicology.[51] Even though Yavorsky's intonation theory concentrates on modal derivations, it is clearly the basis of Asafiev's more speculative understanding of intonation.[52]

For Yavorsky, the close connection to modal theory is the most essential aspect of intonation. Here, as in other areas of this involved theory, he indulges in exhaustive lists that categorize every possible combination of tones into intonations.[53] There are two basic divisions of intonations: monopartite and bipartite. Bipartite intonations, the normal form, involve a change of modal function. Monopartite intonations set forth one function; that is, they elaborate a single modal moment. It is not clear how this is reconciled with the need for comparison as the basis of all perception. Zuckermann cites the prelude to *Das Rheingold* as an example of an extended monopartite stable intonation.[54] Yavorsky states that the function may be either stable or unstable, but again does not answer the question of how an unstable modal structure can exist without motion to a resultant stable structure.

Monopartite intonations are further classed as either one-moment or two-moment. The Wagner example cited above would be a monopartite, one-moment intonation, that is, one in which all participating tones have the same modal meaning. In the case of monopartite, two-moment intonations, a change of function of a sort does occur, but the change is between stable and unstable in such a way that there is no natural systemic gravitation. This is to say that an unstable tone moves to a stable tone but in the direction opposite to that which its gravitation would normally take. Although there is a change of modal function, there is no actual manifestation of auditory gravitation, and therefore the intonation is monopartite (see fig. 23).

Fig. 23   Examples of monopartite intonations: two-moment (a),
and one-moment (b)

Bipartite intonations exhibit a clear connection between an unstable tone and its tone of resolution. While the connection may be conjunct or disjunct, the direction of gravitation of the unstable tone is the important factor; it must tend in the direction of the stable tone. Bipartite intonations are also divided into stable and unstable types. Stable intonations proceed from the unstable tone to the stable tone. Unstable intonations begin with the stable tone and move toward the unstable tone. Protopopov cites as analogies instances of one-word questions that elicit the same word as answer.[55] A comparable English example might be the following exchange: "Ready?" "Ready!" The first has unstable intonation; the second, stable. Figure 24 gives examples of bipartite intonations in their simplest form.

Fig. 24   Examples of bipartite intonations: stable (a), and unstable (b)

Not surprisingly, various kinds of bipartite intonations are classified and given names that refer to their functions. Common ones are the following: The combination D/T is called "authentic"; its unstable form, T/D, is, therefore, "half-authentic." Subdominant to subtonic, S/t, is "plagal," and the reverse is "half-plagal." There are numerous others.

A factor in more complex intonations is the distinction between "systemic" and "intersystemic" intonations. Systemic intonations use only tones from one system. Intersystemic involve tones from more than one system, as, for example, from the two or more systems in a mode.

The combination of two or more simple intonations into one larger intonation yields a group of derivative intonations in three classes: complex, composite, and compound. A complex [slozhnaia] intonation combines two simple intonations of the same form (stable or unstable) of the same system (fig. 25).

Fig. 25   Complex intonations

A composite [sostavnaia] intonation combines intonations of the same form (stable or unstable), but from different systems (fig. 26).

Fig. 26   Composite intonations

A compound [smeshannaia] intonation uses both stable and unstable forms from different systems (fig. 27). However, neither half of a compound intonation may form a complete intonation in itself.

Fig. 27   Compound intonations

Both Yavorsky and Protopopov provide many pages of examples of the above types. Even so, their lists and charts only involve the major and minor modes, and the reader is left to work out the intonational systems of the other modes for himself.

The abstract presentations of modal function that constitute the charts on intonations take on more meaning if these functions are given durations. Yavorsky distinguishes carefully between rhythm and meter in intonations. He defines the meter of an intonation in terms of the actual duration of the entire intonation, the modal moments in the intonation, or the individual tones. He asserts that "the greatest and least durations of an intonation correspond to the greatest and least durations of breathing and of continuous consciousness. Intonations of a greater length than the greatest unit of consciousness are not perceived by the ear, and those of a smaller length than the least unit of consciousness are perceived as noise or knocking."[56] He adds analogies to color, smell, and taste.

If meter represents absolute durations, rhythm in intonations is the relationship between various parts, either of one tone to the next, or, what is more important, of one modal function to another, that is, of the anacrusis to the ictus. The possible relationships are exhaustively classified by Yavorsky and elaborated on by Protopopov, who attempts to assign specific affective qualities.

The linear combination of intonations results in melody, which may be organized in any of the usual additive arrangements. One exceptional treatment is the "connective intonation" [soedinitel'naia intonatsiia], an intonation whose resolution delays until after some other intervening intonations have occurred. An example of this may be seen in the principle of crossover discussed above. Connective intonations allow for long-range pitch relationships and also have an important rhythmic role, the relationship of the connective intonation to the work as a whole or to the elapsed time until the instability recurs. The connective intonation also accounts for an important phenomenon of Russian folk songs, their tendency to be repeated many times. Protopopov states that if a connective intonation does not resolve before the end of the song, a repetition is needed to resolve the instability. Such repetition then causes the instability to recur, requiring yet another repetition.[57] It must be inferred from this that a connective intonation can only be stable. Otherwise an instance of resolution coming before instability could be considered a long-range unstable intonation.

If melody results from intonations joined in a linear manner, harmony is their vertical combination. As with intonations, harmonic connections typically exhibit a basic bipartite structure, a motion between two sonorities of different modal functions. The term used to describe this bipartite chord connection is *oborot*, freely translated as "turn." Unlike the word *intonation*, *turn* has no particular musical equivalent in English. An approximation might be *cadence*, but, unlike the cadence, turns form the fabric of an entire harmonic phrase, and not just its close. Zuckermann observes that "as an element of form, the turn is the modal rhythmic equivalent of motive, with which it frequently coincides in practice."[58]

The only rule associated with the formation of turns is that at least one voice should display a clear, bipartite intonation, that is, a change of function. The other voices may retain the same function, or also change. If no bipartite intonation is present, a monopartite structure results. Each sonority taken separately must also subscribe to the principle of chord construction, given above, that no conjunct tones may occur simultaneously. As long as this is heeded, any two sonorities that have at least one true intonation in some voice may be connected. Obviously this allows for a great variety of connections, classified according to the functions of the sonorities that make up the turn. The symbols used to describe a turn show the function (modal moment) and group of each sonority. For example, an authentic cadence, *V-I* in Roman-numeral analysis, will read D_{iv}/T, that is, dominant sonority in group iv followed by tonic. Refer to figure 17 above to see what this means in the natural major mode. An analogous turn exists in every other mode and in the other forms of the major mode.

There are three categories of turn. The first is stable, with all bipartite intonations proceeding from unstable to stable (fig. 28a). The second is unstable, with all bipartite intonations proceeding from stable to unstable (fig. 28b). The third category exchanges one kind of unstable unit for another (fig. 28c). There is no need to review Protopopov's exhaustive lists of all possible combinations. A few more examples showing various types in C major will suffice (fig. 29).

Fig. 28   Three types of turn in C major

Fig. 29   Examples of turns in C major

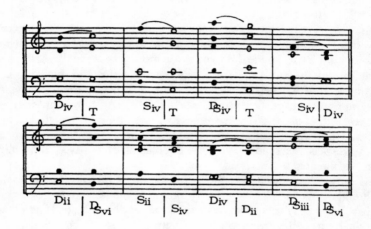

An interesting aspect of Yavorsky's harmonic theory is its ability to account for familiar chord connections while also allowing many unfamiliar ones. Another virtue lies in the relationship between the vertical and linear components of music. The theory is flexible enough to allow a wide variety of textures that are neither strictly linear nor vertical. However, Yavorsky is dealing with only the background organization of music, the construction, and not with compositional details. Thus, a turn may be an abstraction of a substantial quantity of music that exhibits only one harmonic change.

Intonations and turns are grouped into larger structures by systematic relationships such as symmetry and periodicity. This points to one of the shortcomings of Yavorsky's theory of harmony: It has no particular means of describing motion towards a harmonic goal, a cadence. The theory excels in describing the operation of music lacking in such goals, a valid and valuable achievement. But much music of the eighteenth and nineteenth centuries cannot readily be reduced to two-part, additive units without ignoring cadence drive.

Examination of some analyses published by Yavorsky and Protopopov should help clarify how these principles can be applied. It is unfortunate that in

Yavorsky's slim legacy there are so few analytical examples. Those that exist are in the main either very brief, as the second one given below, or are used to demonstrate "errors"[59]

Since the theory is closely related to folk music, it is appropriate to begin with an analysis of a folk song. Protopopov uses elaborate analysis of this song, "Viidi Ivan'ku," as a model of analytical technique (fig. 30).[60]

Fig. 30   Folk song, "Viidi, Ivan'ku"

S t   D T

Protopopov's primary analytical goals are determining the mode and completely breaking down the intonational structure. First, he writes out all the notes used in order of pitch and in the octave where they are found. Next, he locates all tritones (in this case there is just one: F#-C; it is assumed to be part of a single system F#-C, G-B). If two tritones one semitone apart had occurred, it would have signaled a double system. Since the tone E remains alone at the bottom with no conjunction, it is by definition stable; a stable tone can stand alone, but an unstable tone requires resolution. This then mandates that the one remaining pitch, A, be part of an incomplete double system whose tones of resolution are E and G (see fig. 30b). These initial findings he must confirm by the intonational analysis. In many cases, particularly in a more complex texture or in one of the more complex modes, determination of the mode relies to a great extent on the intonational analysis, since the mode would be ambiguous on the basis of pitches alone.

He then divides the entire tune into "structures" [postroenie] determined by "a detailed investigation of the intonations on the basis of modal rhythm."[61] To find the structures one also looks for the repetition of a melodic pattern, articulations of the text, caesurae, and analogy with larger parts. There are seven structures in "Viidi, Ivan'ku." The first six are each one measure long, and the seventh has two measures.

In each structure, he identifies intonations relative to the mode. One must also anticipate connective intonations, that is, ones that do not resolve within the structure. Since the entire song is comprised of only two melodic ideas (called by Protopopov "motive-symbols"), his analysis treats only the first two structures, which are repeated.

Figure 31a shows the first structure, which contains two intonations. The first is a composite intonation formed from two simple ones, B-C and E-C. The pitch A in the second intonation does not participate, but sets up a connective intonation. The symmetry of the structure is shown in figure 31b; the small Arabic numerals given with the function refer to the number of pulses in each part of each intonation. These assume a unit of an eighth note, which is determined in the second structure.

Fig. 31   The intonations of the first structure of "Viidi, Ivan'ku"

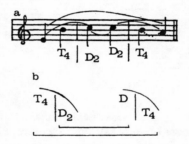

The second structure breaks down into the three intonations in figure 32. These are respectively half-plagal, plagal, and half-authentic. Note also how the tone G is divided in half, half participating in each of the two intonations. This, then, is the greatest common divisor of the temporal units in the work, and so determines the unit of pulse. Figure 32b shows the rhythmic relationships in the second structure. The symmetry is not as clear as in the first structure.

Fig. 32   The intonations of the second structure of "Viidi, Ivan'ku"

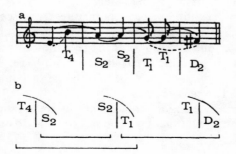

Since both structures end with unstable tones, A and F#, connective intonations occur. Both of these inversely conjunctive tones resolve to the following G when it appears. The last appearance of the F#, in the final structure, can only resolve in the second structure in a repeat of the song. This principle of repetition cited above is illustrated by the circular representation of the whole song (fig. 33). This example is reproduced from *The Elements of the Structure of Musical Speech.*[62]

Fig. 33   Protopopov's analytical representation of "Viidi, Ivan'ku"

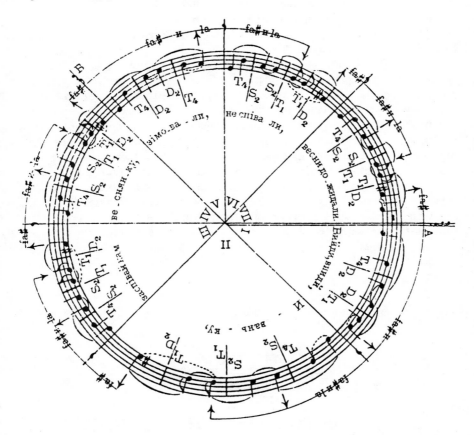

The two major sections of the song are identical except for the extension that occurs in the seventh structure, doubling its length. Protopopov states that this extension stops the periodicity of the structures in order to end the tune. He also calculates the durations of each connective intonation and its recurrence, as well as the durations for each appearance of the tone C and its resolution B, since it is the uppermost pitch. None of these calculations seems to provide particularly significant information.

Protopopov ascribes a symbolic character to the beginning of each structure; he asserts that the rising perfect fifth symbolizes space in nature and that the song is evocative, a spring ceremony calling forth the sun. He points out that this is the tune that Tchaikovsky used in the finale of the B♭ minor piano concerto, and that it is also similar to three fragments from Johann Sebastian Bach, the subject of the Fugue in D♯ minor (*WTC*, vol. 1), the subject of the Fugue in B♭ minor (*WTC*, vol. 1), and the chorale tune "Aus tiefer Noth." The second of these requires a shift of the second tone by one octave, and the third example must begin with its second tone.

The second example (fig. 34), taken from Yavorsky's article, "The Construction of the Melodic Process," analyzes the subject of the Fugue in B major from Bach's *Well-tempered Clavier*, vol. 2.[63] Figure 34b sets forth the systems that comprise the mode, and figure 34c, the most important intonations of the excerpt with the tones shown as either stable or unstable. Yavorsky points out several important properties in this example. First, the construction is basically symmetrical in that subdominant and dominant are both unstable functions (moments). Second, the connective intonations (the unstable tones G♯ and E) both resolve by the end of the subject. Third, the last moment is slightly longer than the other three in order to prevent completeness, so that it can be a part of a larger work. Incompleteness is also achieved by introducing the unstable tone A♯ in the last moment (see *NB* in fig. 34), which is unresolved. This also postpones the D♯ until the fifth pulse, in time for the next entrance of the subject. The other two unstable tones in the last ictus (G♯ and E) resolve immediately to conjunct stable tones, and Yavorsky states that this is part of the "formation," that is, a matter of surface detail.

Fig. 34   Yavorsky's analysis of the subject of J. S. Bach's Fugue in
          B major (*WTC*, vol. 2)

The brevity of this analysis is typical of those published by Yavorsky. Its point is a demonstration of melodic construction; it is not an end in itself.

The final example is reproduced from chapter 18 of Protopopov's *The Elements of the Structure of Musical Speech.*[64] The analyses in this chapter, which is devoted to excerpts in the simple modes, vary as to length of work and depth of analysis, but this twelve-measure excerpt from Liszt's "Die Macht der Musik" is typical (fig. 35).

Below the example are given Protopopov's representations of the pitches used in the excerpt, of the tritone systems, and the scheme of modal rhythm. The mode is E minor, complete form. This determination is made in part on the basis of the pitch G being stable because of its lack of conjunction in the highest register, and on the basis of the tritones marked in the plan. Protopopov identifies three structures, the first two having one turn each, and the third two turns. The first structure has a stable monopartite sonority and a stable plagal turn. The second structure has an unstable monopartite sonority followed by an unstable turn. The third structure has two periodic stable turns.

These analyses underscore a salient feature of Yavorsky's conception of the structure of music, the aggregation of cell-like units into larger groups. Whether there exists any objective connection between the intonations of speech and those of music is not critical to understanding Yavorsky's work. His approach finds a kind of deep structure in music itself and shows how the units that lie there are related to one another. Though his analyses may not account for every important aspect of music, it is difficult to fault a well-ordered system that can account for so many interrelationships while proscribing so few.

Other Concepts and the Evolution of the Theory

In the course of its more than three decades of development, the important aspects of the theory of modal rhythm changed remarkably little. Those changes found in later works are mostly developments of earlier principles. A few ideas seem to have been dropped after their first appearance in 1908, and some others appear in preliminary form in 1931. Both merit at least brief attention as clues to the evolution of the theory. Another group of ideas might be called "working hypotheses." While some of these are implicit in the published writings, they are dealt with in detail only in letters between Yavorsky and his friends. Always evident is a series of assumptions that are basic to all aspects of the theory.

In *The Structure of Musical Speech* (1908), Yavorsky mentions two variant forms of the symmetrical system that apparently do not later recur: the triple symmetrical system and the half-stable system.[65] The triple system is formed by analogy with the double system; that is, a third single system is added to the two already involved in the double system. This may take one of two forms, with a half-step relationship between each single system or with a

Fig. 35 Protopopov's analysis of an excerpt from Liszt, "Die Macht der Musik"

one-fourth-step relationship between each system (fig. 36). Note Yavorsky's symbols for one-fourth-step alterations.

Fig. 36   Two types of triple symmetrical system

The result of the form involving quartertones is identical to the normal double system: it includes perfect fifth, doubly diminished fifth, and minor third, plus an additional pair of unstable tones that form the interval of a diminished fifth. In the other form, the intervals are m6, d5, d4, M2, illustrating the concept that the resolution need not be consonant to be stable.

The "half-stable system," or "half resolution of the tritone," amounts to a single system in which only one tone resolves. The remaining tone is said to be "half stable" during both parts of the system, and Yavorsky uses a note head that is only partially blackened to designate this. It resolves to a perfect fifth. Yavorsky then combines this half-stable system with a normal system to create some unusual modes (fig. 37).

Fig. 37   Half-stable systems (a) and one mode (b)

Like the triple system, the half-stable system seems to have been developed no further. This is unfortunate because the half-stable systems fill two of the most obvious gaps in the modal theories, the raised fourth and lowered second scale steps, which do not occur in any of the usual forms of the major and minor modes. Consequently, these tones must be explained away as "errors," as a change of modal tonality, or as tones from an implicit duplex tonic. The reasons for dropping the half-stable system may be only guessed at, but it is possible that Yavorsky came to consider the role of a tone that was neither stable nor unstable as logically unsound in an otherwise purely binary system.

Another elaboration of the modal theories appears in an annotated response Yavorsky sent to Kulakovsky (1924) regarding an article the latter was writing on modal rhythm. After Kulakovsky had referred to more complex means of organization such as the duplex modes, Yavorsky added "triplex and quadruplex modes, and modes for which a name has not yet been determined."[66] Since he did not elaborate, one can only speculate what form such modes would have taken.

A fascinating later development in the theory of modal rhythm concerns microtones; this appears in the last chapter of Protopopov's *The Elements of the Structure of Musical Speech.*[67] It is speculative in the sense that no mention is made of a practical use. But unlike some of the systematic and modal procedures just mentioned, the microtonal materials are thoroughly formulated, to include detailed charts of interval sizes, symmetrical systems, and even modes for 24-step, 18-step, and 36-step temperament.

Consistent with the entire theory, all systems are derived from the tritone, whether those systems be in 12-step temperament or in any other. Even in the microtonal systems, the tritone is the only unstable interval, and its size and operation never change. What does change is the size of the conjunction, the connection between an unstable tone and its resolution. Thus, in 24-step temperament the conjunction is a quartertone, and the stable resolution is that perfect fourth lying between the tones of the unstable tritone, one-fourth of a step from each. One category of modes takes advantage of this resolution to a perfect fourth by adding an additional quartertone system to the major and minor modes. Its perfect fourth stable resolution is that perfect fourth in the tonic of those modes; in C major the perfect fourth is G-C, and the unstable tones would be a quartertone on either side of that G-C.

Purely quartertone modes are much more complex than the modes of 12-step temperament, because the tones of a mode must still cover all possible tritones. Just as in 12-step temperament there are six distinct tritones, in 24-step temperament there are twelve, in 18-step temperament there are nine, and in 36-step temperament there are eighteen. Since each must be employed in some way, a substantially more complicated modal system results. Protopopov works out eight quartertone modes, each with a corresponding *duplex* quartertone mode. For 18-step temperament, he only gives one sample mode with its duplex counterpart, and for 36-step temperament, he only manages to show the single and double systems. He can hardly be faulted for incompleteness considering the awesome number of possibilities in a temperament involving one-sixth tones.

Protopopov's notation for these materials is fascinating. Figure 38 shows a simple symmetrical system in 24- and 18-step temperaments. The stylized arrows represent alteration in the direction indicated, and the small number 4 indicates a quartertone. For the 18- and 36-step temperaments, the arrow is used as part of a fraction, designating the distance in 36th parts of an octave, where 3/36 is the size of a semitone. One final table in the chapter, comparing the single and double systems in the four temperaments, resorts to 72nd parts of an octave.

Fig. 38   Protopopov's microtonal systems

These theories of microtones, while not practical, are part of Yavorsky's continuing speculation on the development of music. One speculative possibility is overlooked. Since all the microtonal studies involve equal divisions of the octave, and since Protopopov asserts that equal temperament causes even the duplex modes to be approximations, he might well have used microtones to explore various unequal divisions of the octave.[68]

An important benefit of Yavorsky's theory derives from its questioning common assumptions concerning the nature of music. It forces reappraisal of existing presumptions by creating a new set of givens. The first of these is the nature of pitch and of duration. He considers each to be a continuum, but time is expressed as a line and pitch as a spiral. Identical spiral representations of pitch appear in *The Structure of Musical Speech* and in Protopopov's *Elements,* reproduced in figure 39.[69] Octave similarities recur in the same position but on different turns of the spiral. Tritones appear opposite one another on the spiral and resolve by moving symmetrically in opposite directions, either converging or diverging.

Yavorsky also employs a spiral to demonstrate the absence of absolute stability in nature. He places tritone cells on the spiral with their tones of resolution as members of neighboring tritone units.[70] Thus even the tones of resolution are not completely stable. Instability—the tritone—is the governing force in music. While it is the only unstable relationship, there may be many kinds of stable ones. The tritone is natural but not acoustical in the traditional sense. Yavorsky does not invoke the overtone series to demonstrate stability, because many structures not readily found in the overtone series are also stable.

The temporal equivalent of the spiral is a line that represents the infinity of time. Protopopov says that time itself is not articulated, but our perception of time can be articulated by some outside influence.[71] Yavorsky asserts that a necessary condition for perceiving time is a relationship, a comparison of temporal durations, in keeping with his idea of comparison as the source of perception.[72] Therefore, Yavorsky distinguishes between rhythm and meter as follows: meter is the absolute duration of any musical event; rhythm is a relationship among these durations. Modal rhythm sets forth the various modal functions with durations such that the relationship between various units and between the parts and the whole make perceivable rhythmic events.

These pitch and temporal concepts given witness to Yavorsky's essentially binary understanding of music. All pitch events are either stable or unstable,

Fig. 39   The spiral arrangement of musical space

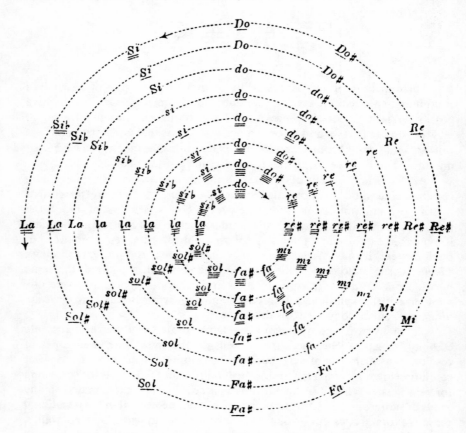

that is, either representative of a tritone or of its resolution and are grouped together by laws of conjunction and disjunction. Temporal events are also essentially binary. Rhythm, a comparison of two durations, relates in turn to the two possible tonal functions, stable or unstable. Therefore, intonations and turns have a bipartite pitch structure, and the rhythmic events attached to them also occur in two parts, even though the number of pulses for each part may not be equal. While monopartite structures are allowed, they only fill out a structure; they are not equal partners in the musical process.

Among the secondary assumptions that result from these premises is Yavorsky's broadened concept of tonic. Tonic is a function, a modal moment that is the product of some other, unstable function. Therefore, tonic takes a variety of forms. It is not just a pitch, the key-note for a mode; nor is it necessarily consonant, a triad. A structure may be dissonant, yet stable in relationship to the tones that evoked it. Therefore the concept of tonic is enlarged to include various structures—triads as well as more complex groupings—that taken as a whole represent the stable part of an interrelated group of functions, a mode.

The emphasis on modal functions stresses the role of each individual tone. For a given modal tonality, a tone has a place in a hierarchy and a natural pairing with some other tone of different function. Sometimes a tone has more than one role, a variable function, as in the case of the two variable modes and the duplex modes. The emphasis on function of tones rather than on form represents an important sophistication in the theory of modal rhythm. A tone's role is determined by more than a theoretical system; it is determined by the tonal context.

Throughout his work, Yavorsky searches for unity in all of music. He attempts to show that all properties of music are subject to the same common laws and that all musics of all times and places are subject to the same set of principles. He successfully shows a kind of unity among musical elements, but the second premise is more difficult to defend. Yavorsky claims that his theories are derived basically from the study of Russian folk songs.[73] He asserts that folk songs are a manifestation of life itself, and so represent music in pure form and are subject to principles innate in man. But if the folk songs of even one culture operate in a manner unlike his theories, the universality of the whole system loses credibility. As shall be seen below, his theories reflect the characteristics of the Russian folk song to a remarkable extent. But, needless to say, Yavorsky did not investigate too widely beyond the boundaries of his homeland.

The importance of the folk song to the theory of modal rhythm is demonstrated by the fact that Protopopov devotes three chapters to the subject. First he attempts to identify the causes of folk song and its specific manifestations in Russian folk art, exhaustively classifying folk songs by purpose, style, and social origin. The next two chapters describe his techniques for analyzing folk song and give sample analyses such as the one discussed earlier, "Viidi, Ivan'ku."

Yavorsky's search for universality included an interest in old music as well. Konen calls him "the first among Russian and Soviet theorists who was really impressed by the musical culture of remote epochs. He was able to trace the successive threads, hidden from the superficial ear, which connect our contemporary era with the art of the past."[74] Yavorsky comments on the music of the past in the last section of *The Structure of Musical Speech,* where he judges it on a modal basis. He finds most of it superficial and filled with errors. He asserts that the folk song was "free as a bird and preserved truth in itself."[75] There follows the most curious part of the entire work, a list of some twenty-nine errors in music, divided into the categories of modal, intonational, and metrical errors and those errors involving text. Each category is reinforced by examples from the standard repertoire, especially at the expense of Beethoven, but also indicting Mozart, Chopin, Liszt, and Grieg.[76]

The future evolution of music is also indirectly addressed by Yavorsky. His hypothetical modes, duplex modes, and especially the microtonal modes represent possibilities, not reality. Even the six principles of construction discussed above in relation to form have an evolutionary sense, since the most complex principles have yet to be exploited.

It was inevitable that Yavorsky would also look to the other arts to find reinforcement for his ideas. The relationship between "musical speech" and "verbal speech" present in his earliest work hints at a connection that goes beyond music and language. Yavorsky says that "human speech... has two forms, tonal and plastic. Musical speech, one of the component parts of tonal speech, derives its material and laws from the same life of which it is a manifestation."[77] Clearly Yavorsky has greatly enlarged the concept of speech [rech'] to mean "expression" or "attempt to communicate." Even more importantly, though, all expressive phenomena originate from the same source, life itself, and adhere to the same laws.

Yavorsky did not formulate a theory of the arts in the sense that Joseph Schillinger did. But references such as the one above are frequent, and it is evident from his correspondence that some hypotheses existed. His first work includes a section on errors involving text in vocal works, and symbols are used that later recur in his correspondence. These symbols attempt to relate the subject and predicate of a sentence to the unstable/stable pairing of pitch processes.[78] In a letter written to Protopopov in 1934, Yavorsky tries to show the structure of a poem by Pushkin using such techniques. He gives the subjects and predicates various durations depending on the number of syllables in each and points out symmetries therein, including the symmetrical use of certain vowels in the poem.[79] Even more remarkable is another letter to Protopopov in 1935 speculating that the dramatic basis of Shakespeare's *Romeo and Juliet* may be compared to a duplex system.[80]

The visual arts are also subjected to this kind of scrutiny. Another letter of 1934 to Protopopov includes a drawing to show the rhythms in "the discus thrower."[81] Other letters include similar musings about paintings he saw in museums during his travel in western Europe. While Yavorsky never systematized his findings, it is clear that they represent a line of reasoning that was important to him.

It is not easy to trace the evolution of the theory of modal rhythm, and finding Yavorsky's theoretical roots, in particular, involves a degree of conjecture. Three general groups of influences are apparent in his work. First is the tradition of Russian music theory instruction, represented chiefly by the teaching of Taneev and Rimsky-Korsakov and secondarily by theoretical approaches to chant and folk song. Second, evidence in Yavorsky's work indicates that he was familiar with the important theoretical ideas of western

Europe. Most obvious are the ideas of François Fétis and Hugo Riemann. The third important influence, which Yavorsky himself acknowledges, is his personal experience with folk song.

The influence of Taneev has already been mentioned. Certainly their relationship occurred at a crucial point in Yavorsky's development—when his theories about modes and auditory gravity developed. Taneev's concept of a unifying tonality may well be the source of Yavorsky's ideas of hierarchy and the application of "comparison and result" to modes. Taneev's own theoretical works are more influenced by western European models than are Yavorsky's; but Taneev's insistence on rigorous logic no doubt had a significant impact on Yavorsky. The willingness to expand on the traditional major and minor categories may show a debt to Rimsky-Korsakov, whose works are filled with examples of symmetrically arranged pitch structures. His later works in particular broaden the concept of tonic in a way that foreshadows Yavorsky's ideas.

Of Western theories, those of Fétis and Riemann left their marks on Yavorsky's theory. Like Fétis, he invoked the tritone as the generating force in harmony. Riemann's powerful influence on the music theory of his time clearly affected Yavorsky, who borrowed Riemann's functional categories of tonic, dominant, and subdominant and his symbols. Furthermore, the symmetrical arrangement of major and minor in the theory of modal rhythm is reminiscent of the theory of harmonic dualism to which Riemann subscribed.

The importance of Yavorsky's study of Russian folk songs can hardly be overstated. In an early letter to Taneev (1906), Yavorsky presents in capsule form the main tenets of his theory, apparently in order to secure his teacher's approval. The opening statement reads, "From my investigation of folk music I have drawn the conclusion that the basic cell of musical speech is the *tritone and its resolution.*"[82] An even earlier specific reference to folk music appears in the notebook of 1899-1900, which, Protopopov reports, contains studies of folk songs and gives examples of street vendors' cries that Yavorsky was investigating.[83]

These three influences stimulated Yavorsky's development of the theory of modal rhythm. However, each is no more than a point of departure. Another potential line of influence, equally difficult to document and equally intriguing, is the relationship of Yavorsky's concept of intonation to contemporaneous linguistic and literary theories. Vadim Baevsky has shown how closely some of Yavorsky's theories correspond to the literary theories of Aleksandr Veselovsky, who died in 1906.[84] Since intonations are mentioned in the notebooks of 1899-1900, it is possible that Yavorsky had come in contact with these ideas through the Symbolist poets who occasionally met with his circle. Both Baevsky and Aranovsky cite similarity with the work of the French linguist Ferdinand de Saussure. Aranovsky believes that Yavorsky knew Saussure's work, but only after he had independently conceived of the relationship of music and speech in his own way.[85] It is not possible to answer all the questions raised by these similarities, but Yavorsky likely acquired his notion of intonation from the linguistic or literary field and freely applied it to music.

Whatever his sources, whether from theorists, peasants, or linguists, the actual fabric of Yavorsky's theory is clearly his own work. Its cells are visible in the notebook of 1899-1900, its outlines are evident in the letter to Taneev in 1906, and in *The Structure of Musical Speech* of 1908, the theory is virtually complete. The ways in which Yavorsky refined and expanded his ideas over the next years may be traced in the published works. His first publication is remarkably concise, containing about 100 pages. Much of this consists of lengthy charts of intonations and other structures and terse assertions about the nature of music and about his theory. Only in the final portion, the polemical section about composers' errors, does the book read anything like normal prose.

Over the next period of years a few other short works appeared, the first of which are two books of exercises.[86] One, *Exercises in Voice Leading,* published in 1913, resembles a primer of strict counterpoint using a very unorthodox method. The astylistic results and rules are only indirectly related to the theory of modal rhythm, but might serve as an introduction to the theory's linear thinking. In 1915 *Exercises in Forming Modal Rhythm,* Part 1 appeared; parts 2-5 were unpublished. This more significant work is cited by both Protopopov and Ryzhkin. The latter calls it an attempt to apply the theory of modal rhythm to the pedagogical field.[87] It begins with vertical relationships in the four simple modes and includes the best explanation of the concept of resultant tonalities. The series of articles called "Text and Music" [Tekst i muzyka], published in 1914, was intended as an additional part to *The Structure of Musical Speech.*[88] They address musical questions only as analogues of speech.

In the first decade following the revolution of 1917, Yavorsky devoted a large portion of his energies to the cause of education. Even so, Averbukh's chronology cites several theoretical studies. One that reached publication is "The Basic Elements of Music," in the journal *Iskusstvo* [Art].[89] It provides some of the rationale for basic concepts that is conspicuously absent in *The Structure of Musical Speech.* In 1926 appeared the first of two works done in collaboration with Sofia Beliaeva-Ekzempliarskaia, entitled "The Perception of Modal Melodic Structures."[90] As its name implies, the article attempts to demonstrate a psychological basis for the theory of modal rhythm; it is highly speculative.

During this period occurs an early reference to the duplex systems and modes. A letter written to Nadezhda Briusova in 1920 distinguishes between "simple modes" and "complex modes," those in which both types of each form of tritone participate.[91]

A climax of interest in the theory of modal rhythm was reached around 1930 following the second edition of *Exercises in Forming Modal Rhythm* in 1928 and the printing of Yavorsky's article, "The Construction of the Melodic Process," in a book co-authored by Beliaeva-Ekzempliarskaia (1929).[92] The latter is the only mature presentation of the theory of modal rhythm written by Yavorsky. Even though it does not treat vertical relationships or the more complex textures, it is valuable for its discussion of folk song and Bach fugue subjects, and for its reflection of Yavorsky's thought processes.

An All-Union Conference on the Theory of Modal Rhythm, presided over by Lunacharsky in 1930, resulted in a resolution in support of Yavorsky's theory.[93] The following year, at another conference, the theory was found to be not sufficiently Marxist.[94] After this, overt interest in the theory of modal rhythm waned. Ironically, the two parts of Protopopov's *The Elements of the Structure of Musical Speech* also appeared in 1930 and 1931. This large, uneven work was intended to be a pedagogical presentation of the theory of modal rhythm. It elaborates on Yavorsky's work published in 1908, from which many passages are taken verbatim. Additions, such as duplex systems and modes and microtonal theories, are evident, but the most significant difference is that Protopopov attempts to support and explain some of the basic assumptions that appear as assertions in Yavorsky's work. The book was edited by Yavorsky and evidently had his full approval. Many of Protopopov's explanations are greatly overdrawn, and, in his attempt to be scientific, he weakens his own case.

The importance of Protopopov's work is that it is the most complete exposition of Yavorsky's theories. Protopopov also presents a number of analyses of folk songs and excerpts from musical literature that, in spite of their shortcomings, shed light on the application of the theory.

Ryzhkin notes the most serious weakness of the book, besides its pretentiousness, when he wonders, if it is a textbook, to whom it is directed. He comments regarding all the above works that "it is possible only for those who already know the theory to use the printed versions of the theory of modal rhythm."[95] Indeed, Yavorsky's work is filled with unsupported assertions, and Protopopov's textbook is cumbersome and opaque. No straightforward presentation of the theory exists.

The final stage in the evolution of Yavorsky's thought is represented by two major manuscripts left incomplete at the time of his death in 1942. The first, *Bach's Suites for Piano,* was compiled by Protopopov from Yavorsky's lecture notes and published posthumously.[96] The theory is presented only in Protopopov's appended notes. The second, "The Creative Thought of Russian Composers from Glinka to Skryabin," examines several composers in turn after an initial discussion on the nature of music. Some interesting material is cloaked in typical Yavorskian jargon. The theory of modal rhythm is present only by implication. An exchange of correspondence with Shostakovich in 1942 indicates that he had read Yavorsky's chapter on Skryabin, found it very interesting and helpful, and hoped to see the remaining portions soon.[97]

It is unfortunate that Yavorsky would leave this major work incomplete. His theoretical legacy includes only a few brief published works, in contrast to the great number of unpublished or fragmentary works that have been preserved. His disinclination to bring his many efforts to publishable form is explained by Zuckermann as "an attraction to the oral circulation of his ideas and a dislike for their final printed form (he saw in this a kind of spiritual hardening)."[98]

Descriptions of Yavorsky's mind and personality also shed light on his work methods. Zuckermann describes him as having "an extremely strong will that subdued those who associated with him, an exceptional force of reason" and "a supernatural knowledge of musical literature, from antiquity to the latest novelties written by his contemporaries."[99] Yavorsky's younger contemporary Boris Asafiev reports that "it was impossible to converse with Yavorsky without in the end feeling oneself in his train of thought."[100] Such encomiums are typical of members of Yavorsky's circle and other admirers. Outsiders and those threatened by his radical ideas can be equally negative. A readily available example of this is found in Leonid Sabaneyeff's *Modern Russian Composers.* Published in 1927 during the apex of interest in the theory of modal rhythm, this volume contains a strong attack on Yavorsky, his pupils, and his theory, branding him with an almost comic succession of epithets.[101]

The aspect of Yavorsky's personality that was most clearly visible in all his endeavors and that gave rise to such hostility is a persistent polemicism. Yavorsky was not content to develop an alternative view of music; an alternative might imply that there were useful aspects to existing theories. Instead he repeatedly calls attention to the errors of other theorists and errors in existing music, even that of the masters. He condemns terms such as polytonality and atonality and cites the inadequacies of Beethoven's modal thinking. In "The Construction of the Melodic Process," he even condemns the misuse of his own ideas, closing with the admonition that only those items should be accepted as correct that appear under his name or editorship.[102] Only as composers develop their sensitivity to modal operations will such errors be eliminated; only as theorists come to recognize the truths implicit and explicit in the theory of modal rhythm will there be successful attempts to explain the music of the past. Such strong convictions could hardly lead to rapprochement with the theoretical community of the day.

In spite of the strongly divided response to his teachings, Yavorsky was a major figure who is now considered an important influence on Soviet music theory. Current interest in intonation theory in the Soviet Union most likely originated with Yavorsky. As noted above, Asafiev received his initial premises from Yavorsky, and through Asafiev the study of intonations has become extremely important. Another significant contribution pertains to modal theory, which Yavorsky was one of the first to apply systematically to modern music. This is now an accepted part of Soviet theory, and Zuckermann says the contemporary concept of mode comes from Yavorsky. The same writer credits Yavorsky with the widespread interest in concepts of stability and instability.[103] All these concepts find reflection in the general interest in scale mechanics, that is, in the function of individual tones in a tone system, that is typical of Soviet theory. In sum, we may echo Zuckermann's position that it is difficult to overestimate Yavorsky's influence on Soviet musicology.[104]

Application and Evaluation

Yavorsky's theory of modal rhythm would be little more than a historical curiosity if it had no application. That it is imperfect and that it falls short of its creator's goal of universality should not obscure its unique contributions. Yavorsky's writings were few and idiosyncratic, and his theory is complex and dogmatic. However, certain aspects of the theory offer particular insight into the music of Yavorsky's own culture. This section will attempt to show such applications and to evaluate the theory's strengths and weaknesses.

One possible application of the theory of modal rhythm is as an approach to composition. Zuckermann says that Yavorsky "refutes the position that 'the theory of music is only the servant of composition.' He aspired to connect theory with creativity by a different path, by disclosing the laws of living musical language and revealing to composers new, as yet unused musical possibilities."[105] In another article, Zuckermann states that an advantage of the theory for composers is that it widens their lexicon.[106] Certainly the broadening effect of such a radically new approach to music could hardly have failed to provide composers with new insights, particularly when seen against the backdrop of the conservative training typical of the day.

The real test, though, must be the results. Yavorsky himself composed, and his letters periodically refer to songs he had written and performed in the capacity of accompanist. None of his works have been published; but his minimal output is consistent with his general lack of interest in publication.

Protopopov, on the other hand, was principally a composer, and one of some reputation. Several of his works were published in both Moscow and Vienna, and excerpts are reproduced in his textbook, where they serve as examples of the duplex modes. His compositions reveal the sort of self-conscious complexity one might expect from a deliberate use of these modes.[107] However, Yavorsky's modes had no other marked effect on the composers of the following generation.

The theory of modal rhythm was also applied with questionable success to elementary music instruction. Several attempts were made to adapt

Yavorsky's ideas to the classroom. The theory instruction at a music school opened in 1912 by Yavorsky's classmate, Nadezhda Briusova, followed Yavorsky's methods.[108] At the All-Union Conference on the Theory of Modal Rhythm of 1930 more than half of the presentations were devoted to using the theory in pedagogical situations.[109] In spite of these attempts, the effect on later elementary instruction was negligible. Among the possible causes are the lack of a suitable textbook (Protopopov's notwithstanding) and the theory's rejection in 1931. But more important, undoubtedly, is that the theories could not be easily adapted to elementary musical training. Elementary theory instruction has traditionally relied on rules, and Yavorsky provides them in ample quantity, but elementary music students may not be capable of dealing with abstractions about time, space, and hearing before matters of musical practice. What may be appropriate for the theorist is not necessarily sound pedagogy. Yavorsky was unwilling to compromise his positions, and only through compromise and simplification could he have fulfilled the practical potential of his ideas. Even so, elementary theory instruction might benefit from some of his ideas. The relationship between melody and harmony and the operation of individual tones in a key or mode are deficient areas in traditional theory that Yavorsky's concepts help to clarify.

Despite his failure to replace all the traditional theoretical subjects, Yavorsky succeeded in creating an effective analytical alternative. His system helps to explain music of all types, both folk song and art music, and the general principles may also be applied with success to some twentieth-century music. Obviously the results vary; the theory does not in every case lend insight beyond that which is available through traditional means. Since his approach reflects the culture in which it was developed, it is most helpful in understanding the music of that culture, particularly folk song.

An example of analysis of folk song was discussed earlier in order to show Protopopov's approach. A few more of his examples can point out some of the ways in which the theory reflects song practice. The first two are drawn from *The Elements of the Structure of Musical Speech.*

Figure 40 is a folk song described as an orphan's song.[110] The three "turn" markings represent a brief vocal ornament that Protopopov claims is too inaccurately transcribed to allow the intonations to be deciphered. Below it is shown the chain mode on A, with the lowest G♯ missing. This mode accounts for the shifting C♯-C, a modal shift rather common in Russian folk songs. Protopopov's analysis of the intonations and structures also shows the last D and the last B to be part of connective intonations that result in a repeat of the song. He again represents the complete modal analysis of the song as a circle.

Another of Protopopov's examples, figure 41, is a folk song taken from the collection of Balakirev and analyzed in the second variable mode.[111] Two of the three systems occur in diverging form, typical of folk tunes with limited compass. While Protopopov only determines the mode, some additional

Fig. 40   Folk song, "Golovka, golovushka"

points may be found. The song is divisible into four parts (structures), each marked by a half-note arrival point. Using a variable mode to describe its operation reflects the two different arrival points. It might also be described as being in modes on Ab and F alternately, but the variable mode allows a unified description. Note further the parallel cadence structures, the third of which is varied in accordance with Yavorsky's principle of "digression in the third quarter." The first cadence is by leap of a perfect fourth (Db-Ab), a cadential figure common in Russian folk songs. This is a disjunction in the middle symmetrical system, and one of Yavorsky's simple melodic units.

Fig. 41   Folk song, "Solntse zakatalos' "

These examples successfully reflect the theory of modal rhythm, and may have been chosen by Protopopov for that reason. Let us now examine two more folk songs chosen independently from Abramsky's *Songs of the Russian North* to see if the theory of modal rhythm contributes to a better understanding of them.[112]

The first, figure 42, is "Vo slobodke vo novoi" [In the new settlement]. An obvious feature is the change of texture between one and two parts, even in the second marked "all." Yavorsky's theory understands texture as the combining of intonations consecutively or simultaneously and so has no difficulty in compensating for these shifts. This is especially true at the final cadence, where the third, D-F, moves to the unison C. Two intonations share the same stable tone of resolution, but one is a conjunction, the other a disjunction. The sections of the tune are loosely related variants of a few common ideas. For Yavorsky these sections would be groups of intonations, illustrating the additive approach to form. Furthermore, there is no need to perceive the vertical relationships (such as in measure 3) in terms of triadic harmony. The theory of modal rhythm can account for two-note sonorities just as successfully as chords. The mode would probably be C major, since the tone C must be stable; the opening pair of tones (C-F) forms an unstable disjunct intonation, which is followed by another unstable intonation (G-A). These are reversed in the last structure (A to G and F to C), showing a general symmetry.

Fig. 42   Folk song, "Vo slobodke, vo novoi"

The second example, figure 43, might be perceived in traditional theory as in F major, but this does not account for the beginning or the end. Such an analysis, or that of the "Locrian mode," is an attempt to force a characteristically Russian pitch process into a Western tradition where it does not fit. On the other hand, Yavorsky's diminished mode on E can account for its operation. The F and A are unstable, and the E, G, and B♭ are tonic. The mode is incomplete. Once again, the structure may be represented as aggregates of small units.

Fig. 43   Folk song, "Prialitsa"

These brief examples are intended to show the relationship between the theory of modal rhythm and the Russian folk song; the theory accounts for individual phenomena and also reveals a deeper organization. Zuckermann's assertion of the applicability of the theory to the folk music of other cultures could be verified only with a separate, detailed study.[113]

The value of the theory of modal rhythm to the analysis of art music varies depending on the kind of music being studied.[114] Nineteenth-century Russian composers, in particular the Five, claimed for their music a relationship to the people similar to that which Yavorsky claims for his system. This is manifested in the use of folk materials in larger works and in the use of folk-like patterns. The structure of their works reveals an openness to modal variation and harmonic variety also seen in Yavorsky's theory.

The theory of modal rhythm finds its clearest musical reflection in the compositions of Rimsky-Korsakov; the next three examples are taken from his work. The first, one of Protopopov's analyses (fig. 44), is cited as an example of the augmented mode.[115] This fragment shows the kind of symmetrical harmony typical of Rimsky-Korsakov. The chord roots (in the traditional sense) are A, D♭/C♯, and F. Major or minor triads, with an occasional augmented sixth or minor seventh, are built on them. The sonorities are related by major thirds, and Yavorsky's augmented mode provides a relationship for them. Protopopov's analysis results in the augmented mode on A♭, the tonic of which is found in the uppermost voice. The chords are all equally unstable relative to the tonic of the mode and of identical function and duration.

Fig. 44   Protopopov's analysis of an excerpt from Rimsky-
Korsakov, *Tale of Tsar Saltan*

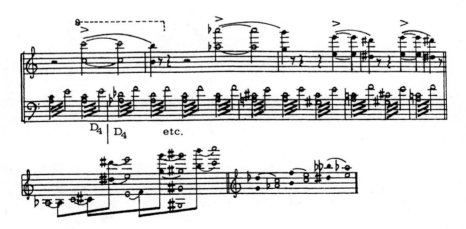

The next two examples (fig. 45) are from scene 1 of Rimsky-Korsakov's opera, *Kashchei the Immortal,* written in 1901 and 1902.[116] These were chosen because the opera exhibits some of the composer's most advanced harmonic language, reflecting the fantastic nature of the plot. The first (fig. 45a) has interlocked tritones in the bass and a contrasting tritone orientation in the upper parts. The bass tritone sequence continues for six measures, uses all twelve tones, and is then repeated exactly. The upper parts sequence every three measures, and each new member of the sequence is a minor third lower. Thus, in twelve measures, the upper parts cover a diminished seventh chord, and the lower parts go twice through the entire tritone sequence, making relatively static harmonic motion. Such obvious use of tritones is common in the duplex modes. The B♭ duplex chain mode, the tonic of which is the so-called octatonic scale, would account for the B♭ diminished seventh in the upper part as well as the lowest pitch, D, which by definition must be stable since no tone is conjunct with it. The periodic structure is natural in the theory of modal rhythm, as are the seemingly arbitrary vertical combinations caused by the overlapping (12 mm. versus 6 mm.) harmonic phrases. In the figure, the unstable tones (relative to the B♭ duplex chain mode) are marked with a square; each falls at the end of a three-measure unit, providing a forward thrust.

Fig. 45   Excerpts from *Kashchei the Immortal* by Rimsky-
           Korsakov

In figure 45b the static nature results from two sonorities that alternate in eighth notes for four repetitions but do not cadence. An augmented triad appears on the first beat and two other augmented triads on the second beat, each one semitone from the first. These chords may be analyzed in the complete augmented mode on G♭. The first sonority is the stable tonic, and the second is the collective moment, the combination of all the unstable tones of the mode, in this instance a whole-tone scale. Yavorsky's system identifies this as a dominant to tonic turn, even though the passage is perceived as static.

Static passages are very common in the music of the Five. The bell chords in the Prologue of Musorgsky's *Boris Godunov* may be conceived of as opposite dominants of the duplex major mode. Pedal tones, such as those in "Il vecchio castello" from Musorgsky's *Pictures at an Exhibition* and in the "Sérénade" from Borodin's Pétite Suite show another kind of harmonic stasis. These persistent pedal tones need not be considered non-harmonic tones. They sound harmonic, and Yavorsky's system clearly can account for their roles. The Borodin example begins and ends with dominant pedals, causing what is perceived as an unresolved tonic six-four chord, a natural possibility in Yavorsky's system since a second inversion does not necessarily create an unstable sonority.[117]

The application of the theory of modal rhythm to Western music yields mixed results. Protopopov's most interesting analytical examples are of music by Chopin and Liszt, although his analyses tend to be superficial. He concentrates on examples in nontraditional modes, and finding the mode is as far as he goes. Yavorsky, on the other hand, was very interested in the music of Beethoven and Bach, sometimes identifying "errors" in Beethoven's music. An exception is the article "Beethoven's Variations in C minor," excerpts of which have been published posthumously in the volume *From the History of Soviet Beethoven Study*.[118] Besides presenting his philosophy of musical evolution and Beethoven's place in it, Yavorsky identifies some important long-range pitch connections in the piece. As a whole, it typifies his personal views of analysis and is much more insightful than Protopopov's analyses. Yavorsky's admiration for the works of Bach is often mentioned, and at the time of his death he was leading a seminar in Bach for the Moscow Conservatory.[119] Unfortunately none of his analyses of Bach works are available.

Using Yavorsky's theories to analyze tonal harmony, one finds an explanation for the common non-harmonic tones flat 6 and flat 3 in major, but not for flat 2, flat 7, or sharp 4. His explanation of flat 2 and sharp 4 as a composer's error or as tones from the duplex tonic avoids the issue. Furthermore, his theory cannot easily show harmonic progression toward a cadential goal. His additive approach to chord connection, so valuable for static music, omits this vital element. The theory explains the local connections and even long-range goals of individual pitches with marked success, but it does not reveal much about harmonic function that is not already clear from traditional theory.

The last analytical possibility for the theory of modal rhythm concerns music of the twentieth century. If we assume that Yavorsky's theories were essentially developed by 1908, any insight they can give into music written after that time is remarkable. The most important instance of this concerns the late music of Skryabin, which shows traits similar to those of the duplex modes. Another line of development of Yavorsky's thought may be seen in the work of the Soviet theorist Yury Kholopov. His most important work to date, *Essays on Contemporary Harmony,* shows some interesting influences of Yavorsky's theories.[120] Among these are complex tonic structures, generalized harmonic functions, and the significance of mode. Another of Kholopov's works, investigating similarities between the modes of Yavorsky and those of Messiaen, successfully analyzes an early work of Messiaen's using Yavorsky's system.[121] A separate study is warranted to determine to what extent the theory of modal rhythm would be helpful in understanding the music of other twentieth-century Russian composers, in particular that of Prokofiev and Stravinsky.

Any attempt to evaluate Yavorsky's analytical approach raises the question of what he considered to be true analysis. Yavorsky comments that there are only two types of musical analysis that yield worthwhile results: the analytical interpretation of intonations and motives as meaningful symbols, and the creation of a historical-psychological typology of musical creativity and performance.[122] It is likely that he would consider the pitch and rhythm manipulation that most often passes for analysis as only the first step, the step that allows true analysis to begin. In this respect, Yavorsky was ahead of his time. He used his system as a means to an end, not as an end in itself.

Evaluation of the theory of modal rhythm reveals substantial weaknesses, some of which are inherent in any highly systematized approach to art, and some that are peculiar to Yavorsky's work. In a deductive theory of music, if the premises are flawed, the entire theory is weakened; if the results of the deductive process are found to disagree with musical practice, either the theory or the music must be in error. Yavorsky's response to discrepancies between his theory and Beethoven's music was predictable, since he thought the theory provided answers to all musical questions. Zuckermann correctly calls this a "naive denial of the importance of facts."[123]

Yavorsky's prescriptive dogma is based on a series of assumptions that must be taken as matters of faith. Among these are that art music follows the same principles as folk music, and that all folk music is organized similarly to Russian folk music. If the second of these is not true, then art music of any but Russian culture may work on some principle other than Yavorsky's. He also assumes that the tritone and its resolution are the most important principle in all music. Yavorsky does not offer, indeed cannot offer, proof of this. The tritone premise seems weakest when he claims that simple, tritone-free diatonic collections must have an implicit, unsounding tritone basis in the human mind. His double tritone system assumes that two tritones separated by one semitone can cause a resultant structure of substantially different form. The diagrams look convincing, but the auditory proof that Yavorsky sought is elusive. As an extension of the tritone premise he assumes that the simple form of a mode or system stands for a complex form; for example, he claims the natural (diatonic) major mode is an "incomplete" form of the complete major mode, which is actually present in the mind of the hearer. Of this Zuckermann says,

"In explaining one or more modes as incomplete forms of more complex modes built on 'single' and 'double' systems, the theory of Yavorsky clearly sins against history."[124]

Some practical weaknesses are also evident in the theory of modal rhythm. The absence of the flat 2, sharp 4, and flat 7 scale steps in major has already been noted. This deficiency could be rectified by a theory of non-harmonic tones, a theory that Yavorsky would certainly have opposed. Zuckermann wisely asks if it is appropriate to ignore non-modal-rhythmic elements.[125] The theory would be more flexible if it had a means to deal with tones outside the mode. Another theorist points out the problem inherent in a second scale step that has only an ascending gravitation.[126] This requirement that the second scale step proceed only to the third step is not supported by musical evidence. Furthermore, one of the theory's greatest virtues, its acceptance of a wide variety of sonorities and chord connections, also has a pitfall. The theory provides a hierarchy of sonorities relative to a modal tonic but cannot distinguish between common and rarely encountered types.

If this discussion were to conclude by listing the flaws in the theory of modal rhythm, its important values might be overlooked. The theory of modal rhythm rightly causes us to reevaluate basic assumptions about music. Yavorsky makes us consider how and what we hear. If he fails in his quest for universality, he succeeds in pointing out common traits in musics of various kinds. If he seems preoccupied with modal operations, he succeeds in renewing an emphasis on the operation of individual tones in a tone system, and in offering an alternative to triadic theory. There is a historical and cultural value to Yavorsky's work as well. His is an early attempt to break free of the restrictions of nineteenth-century scalar and triadic theory. He tried to find connections among the various elements of music, and to deal with the changing musical language of his own time. Even more important, his work clearly reflects the music of his own culture; by examining his theories, we can better understand that culture and its musical legacy.

Notes

1. Viktor Abramovich Zuckermann, "Iavorskii—teoretik" [Yavorsky the theorist], *BYa64*, p. 174. The symbols *BYa64* and *BYa72* refer to the two substantially different editions of vol. 1 of the Yavorsky materials: *Vospominaniia, stat'i i pis'ma* [Recollections, articles and letters], ed. D. Shostakovich (Moscow: Muzyka, 1964), and *Stat'i, vospominaniia, perepiska* [Articles, recollections, correspondence], ed. I. S. Rabinovich (Moscow: Sovetskii kompozitor, 1972).

2. Valentina Dzhozefovna Konen, "Iavorskii i nasha sovremennost'" [Yavorsky and our contemporary], *BYa72*, pp. 69, 71.

3.   The only substantial sources for biographical material on Yavorsky are Boleslav Leopoldovich Yavorsky, "Kratkaia avtobiografiia" [Brief autobiography], BYa72, pp. 31-35; Sergei Vladimirovich Protopopov, "Boleslav Leopol'dovich Iavorskii (biograficheskii ocherk)" [Biographical essay], *BYa64*, pp. 19-40; L. A. Averbukh, comp., "Daty zhizni i deiatel'nosti" [Dates of life and activity], *BYa72*, pp. 611-72. Biographical material is derived from these sources except as noted.

4.   The autobiographical sketch (*BYa72*, p. 32) lists works by Famintsyn and Sokalsky but does not specify which works. On Famintsyn see the entry in Gustav Reese, *Fourscore Classics of Music Literature* (New York: The Liberal Arts Press, 1957), p. 80.

5.   Taneev was at that time the dominant music theorist in Moscow and perhaps in all of Russia. Smolensky is remembered for his work in church music.

6.   B. V. Asafiev, "Glubokii myslitel', tonkii muzykant" [Profound thinker, discriminating musician], *BYa72*, p. 59.

7.   Quoted from an unpublished work, "Vospominaniia o S. I. Taneeve"[Recollections about S. I. Taneev], written in 1938. See Protopopov, "Biograficheskii ocherk," p. 28.

8.   In 1899, called "intonatsionost'." See Protopopov, "Biograficheskii ocherk," p. 30.

9.   Ibid., pp. 37-38.

10.   "Moskovskaia Narodnaia Konservatoriia." See I. A. Sats, "Iavorskii v moskovskoi narodnoi konservatorii (1906-1916)" [Yavorsky in the Moscow People's Conservatory], *BYa72*, pp. 77-98.

11.   *Narkompros* is an acronym for the People's Commissariat of Education.

12.   A list of Yavorsky's editorial activities for Muzgiz appears in Averbukh, "Daty," p. 667.

13.   "Tvorcheskoe myshlenie russkikh kompozitorov ot Glinki do Skriabina." Ibid., p. 661.

14.   *Stroenie muzykal'noi rechi. Materialy i zametki*, parts 1-3 (Moscow, 1908).

15.   Sergei Vladimirovich Protopopov, *Elementy stroeniia muzykal'noi rechi*, 2 parts (Moscow: Gos. izd. Muz. sektor, 1930 and 1931) (abbr.: *Elementy*); Gordon D. McQuere, trans., "*The Elements of the Structure of Musical Speech* by S. V. Protopopov: A Translation and Commentary" (Ph.D. diss., The University of Iowa, 1978) (abbr.: *Elements*).

16.   Faubion Bowers, *The New Scriabin: Enigma and Answers* (New York: St. Martin's, 1973), p. 140. See also Roy Guenther, "Varvara Dernova's System of Analysis of the Music of Skryabin" in this volume.

17.   "Konstruktsiia melodicheskogo protsessa," in *Struktura melodii* (Moscow: Gos. akad. khud. nauk, 1929), pp. 7-36.

18.   *Uprazhneniia v golosovedenii* (Moscow, 1913) and *Uprazhneniia v obrazovanii ladovogo ritma* (Moscow, 1915).

19.   "Tekst i muzyka" [Text and music], *Muzyka*, 1914, nos. 163, 166, 169.

20.   Sofiia Nikolaevna Beliaeva-Ekzempliarskaia and Boleslav Leopoldovich Yavorsky, "Vospriiatie ladovykh melodicheskikh postroenii" [The perception of modal melodic structures], in *Trudy gos. akad. khud. nauk, psikho-fizich. laboratoriia*, vol. 1 (Leningrad, 1926); also in expanded form as "Die Wirkung des Tonkomplexes bei melodischer Gestaltung," *Archiv fuer die gesamte Psychologie* 57, nos. 3-4 (1926), pp. 489-522.

21.   Zuckermann, "Iavorskii—teoretik," p. 175.

22. Yavorsky, "Konstruktsiia," p. 7.

23. The basic material for discussing the theory of modal rhythm is drawn from three primary sources: Yavorsky's *Stroenie* and "Konstruktsiia" and Protopopov's *Elementy*. Additional sources appear in footnotes.

24. Yavorsky refers to intervals by semitone content. Thus, the tritone is a "six-semitone relationship" [shestipolutonovoe otnoshenie].

25. The term *subtonic* first occurs in Protopopov's *Elementy*.

26. Also known as the "Rimsky-Korsakov Scale" in Russia.

27. *Stroenie*, 1:18; Iosif Ryzhkin, "Teoriia ladovogo ritma (B. Iavorskii)" [The theory of modal rhythm], in Lev Mazel and Ryzhkin, *Ocherki po istorii teoreticheskogo muzykoznaniia* [Essays in the history of theoretical musicology], vol. 2 (Moscow: Gos. muz. izd., 1939), 2:125.

28. Ryzhkin, "Teoriia ladovogo ritma," p. 126.

29. *Stroenie*, 1:18.

30. *Elementy*, 1:91; *Elements*, p. 130.

31. Ibid., 2:91-93; pp. 339-41.

32. Ibid., p. 97; p. 347.

33. *Stroenie*, 1:24-25.

34. L. V. Kulakovsky, "Iavorskii chitaet rukopis'" [Yavorsky reads a manuscript], *BYa64*, p. 217.

35. *Stroenie*, 1:8; *Elementy*, 1:43-45; *Elements*, pp. 60-63.

36. Zuckermann, "Iavorskii—teoretik," p. 194.

37. *Elementy*, 1:52-56; *Elements*, pp. 73-79.

38. Ibid., pp. 72, 76; pp. 101, 106.

39. Kulakovsky, "Iavorskii chitaet rukopis'," p. 219.

40. *Stroenie*, Part 3, sec. 1, p. 4.

41. Yavorsky, "Konstruktsiia," pp. 12-13.

42. Zuckermann, "Iavorskii—teoretik," pp. 195-202.

43. Yavorsky, *Stroenie*, part 3, sec. 1, p. 7.

44. Ryzhkin, "Teoriia ladovogo ritma," pp. 185-88.

45. Ibid., p. 186.

46. Yavorsky, "Konstruktsiia," p. 11.

47. *Stroenie*, 2:4.

48. Yavorsky, "Konstruktsiia," p. 35.

49. Zuckermann, "Iavorskii—teoretik," p. 192.

50. *Elementy*, 1:117-19; *Elements*, pp. 167-70.

51. For example, see Malcolm H. Brown, "The Soviet Russian Concepts of 'Intonazia' and 'Musical Imagery,'" *The Musical Quarterly* 60 (1974): 557-67.

52. Kulakovsky, "Iavorskii chitaet rukopis'," p. 218; M. Aranovsky, "Intonatsiia, znak i 'novye metody'" [Intonation, sign, and "new methods"], *Sovetskaia muzyka* [Soviet music], 1980, no. 10, p. 101.

53. The clearest presentation is that of Protopopov, *Elementy*, 1:119-24; *Elements*, pp. 170-78.

54. Zuckermann, "Iavorskii—teoretik," p. 192.

55. *Elementy*, 1:117; *Elements*, p. 167.

56. *Stroenie*, 2:7.

57. *Elementy*, 2:6; *Elements*, p. 231.

58. Zuckermann, "Iavorskii—teoretik," p. 193.

59. *Elementy*, 2:8-17; *Elements*, pp. 234-45.

60. Aleksandr Ivanovich Rubets, *Dvesti shestnadtsat' narodnykh ukrainskikh napevov* [Two hundred sixteen Ukrainian folk songs] (Moscow, 1872), no. 11. A free translation of the text is, "Come out, come out little Ivan, sing a spring song for us; During the winter we did not sing; we await the spring."

61. *Elementy*, 2:4; *Elements*, p. 228.

62. Ibid., p. 12; p. 239.

63. Yavorsky, "Konstruktsiia," pp. 28-29.

64. *Elementy*, 2:109-11; *Elements*, pp. 361-62.

65. *Stroenie*, 1:10-11.

66. "Iavorskii chitaet rukopis'," p. 216.

67. *Elementy*, 2:155-75; *Elements*, pp. 413-38.

68. Ibid., p. 128; p. 382.

69. *Stroenie*, 1:7; *Elementy*, 1:19; *Elements*, p. 28.

70. *Stroenie*, 1:6; *Elementy*, 1:18; *Elements*, p. 27.

71. *Elementy*, 1:6; *Elements*, p. 8.

72. *Stroenie*, 1:8.

73. Letter to S. I. Taneev written in 1906, *BYa72*, p. 256.

74. Konen, "Iavorskii i nasha sovremennost'," p. 72.

75. *Stroenie*, part 3, sec. 2, p. 4.

76. Ibid., pp. 4-12.

77. Ibid., 1:2.

78. Ibid., part 3, sec. 2, p. 12.

79. *BYa72*, 406-7.

80. *BYa72*, pp. 497-500.

81. *BYa72*, p. 389.

82. *BYa72*, p. 256.

83. "Biograficheskii ocherk," pp. 30-31.

84. Vadim Solomonovich Baevsky, "Iavorskii i nekotorye tendentsii kul'tury ego vremeni" [Yavorsky and some cultural tendencies of his time], *Sovetskaia muzyka* [Soviet music], 1978, no. 5, p. 84.

85. Aranovsky, "Intonatsiia, znak i 'novye metody,'" pp. 106-7.

86. See note 18.

87. *Elementy*, 1:3; *Elements*, p. 5; Ryzhkin, "Teoriia ladovogo ritma," p. 105.

88. See note 19.

89. Boleslav Leopoldovich Yavorsky, "Osnovnye elementy muzyki," *Iskusstvo*, 1923, no. 1, pp. 185-212.

90. See note 20.

91. *BYa72*, p. 312. The first published reference to duplex modes is in "Basic Elements of Music," where they are not explained; see note 89.

92. The first retitled as *Uprazhneniia v obrazovanii skhem ladovogo ritma* [Exercises in the formation of schemes of modal rhythm], 2nd ed. (Moscow: Muz. sektor, 1928). See note 18.

93. *BYa72*, p. 650. For a list of the papers see p. 665.

94. *BYa72*, pp. 652, 666.

95. "Teoriia ladovogo ritma," pp. 106-7.

96. *Siuiti Bakha dlia klavira*, ed. S. V. Protopopov (Moscow, 1947).

97. See note 13. *BYa72*, pp. 609-10.

98. "Iavorskii—teoretik," p. 173.

99. Ibid.

100. "Glubokii myslitel'," p. 61.

101. Trans. Judah A. Joffe (New York: International, 1927), pp. 208-13.

102. Yavorsky, "Konstruktsiia," pp. 22-23.

103. "Iavorskii—teoretik," pp. 176, 180.

104. Ibid., p. 173.

105. Ibid., p. 176.

106. Viktor Abramovich Zuckermann, "Teoriia ladovogo ritma i ee primenenie" [The theory of modal rhythm and its application], *Proletarskii muzykant* [Proletarian musician], 1929, nos. 7-8, p. 51.

107. See also Detlef Gojowy, "Zwoelftontechnik in Russland," *Melos; neue Zeitschrift fuer Musik* 39, no. 1 (1972), pp. 130-41. Gojowy cites Protopopov's second Sonata (1924) as an example: Sergei Protopopoff, *II. Sonata op. 5* (Vienna: Universal, n.d.).

108. Averbukh, "Daty," p. 625.

109. Ibid., p. 665. Of 19 papers, 10 appear to be pedagogical.

110. *Elementy*, 2:30; *Elements*, p. 262. Verse one of the text is "Poor little child (wretch), grew up without father, without mother."

111. Ibid., p. 51; p. 288. The text of "Solntse zakatalos'" is "The sun has set behind the dark forest; A dark cloud arose and covered the sky."

112. A. S. Abramsky, *Pesni russkogo severa* (Moscow: Sovetskii kompozitor, 1959), pp. 42, 61.

113. "Teoriia ladovogo ritma," p. 51.

114. See also Gordon D. McQuere, "Concepts of Analysis in the Theories of B. L. Yavorsky," *The Music Review* 41, no. 4 (1980): 278-88.

115. *Skazka o tsare Saltane* [Tale of Tsar Saltan], no. 112. *Elementy*, 2:127; *Elements*, p. 381.

116. Nikolai Andreevich Rimsky-Korsakov, *Kashchei bessmertnyi*, in *Polnoe sobranie sochinenii* [Complete collected works], vol. 40 (Moscow: Gos. muz. izd., 1955), scene 1, mm. 148-51, p. 704.

117. For an interesting investigation of some other phenomena of Russian music see Jurij N. Cholopov, "Symmetrische Leitern in der russischen Musik," trans. Detlef Gojowy, *Die Musikforschung* 28, no. 4 (1975): 379-407.

118. Yavorsky, "Betkhoven. Variatsii do minor," in *Iz istorii sovetskoi Betkhoveniany*, ed. N. L. Fishman (Moscow: Sovetskii kompozitor, 1972), pp. 91-95.

119. Averbukh, "Daty," p. 661.

120. *Ocherki sovremennoi garmonii* (Moscow: Muzyka, 1974).

121. "Simmetrichnye lady v teoreticheskikh sistemakh Iavorskogo i Messiana" [Symmetrical modes in the theoretical systems of Yavorsky and Messiaen], *Muzyka i sovremennost'* [Music and the contemporary], vol. 7 (Moscow: Muzyka, 1971), pp. 247-93.

122. IU. Kon, "Neskol'ko teoreticheskikh parallelei" [Several theoretical parallels], *Sovetskaia muzyka* [Soviet music], 1978, no. 5, p. 91.

123. "Iavorskii—teoretik," p. 178.

124. Ibid., p. 183.

125. Ibid., p. 203.

126. Igor Sposobin, *Lektsii po kursu garmonii* [Lectures for a course in harmony], comp. and ed. Yury Kholopov (Moscow: Muzyka, 1969), p. 20.

Varvara Dernova's System of Analysis of the Music of Skryabin

Roy J. Guenther

Among those composers whose music has been more closely examined recently by theorists interested in that cultural, expressive, and music-structural morass rather loosely referred to as post-romanticism, Alexander Skryabin has proved one of the most fascinating. His lifestyle and quasi-philosophical approach to musical expression attracted much attention already while he was alive. But these surface features, though of a certain interest to students of the period and despite their undoubted relation to the genesis of Skryabin's compositions, have not maintained the degree of fascination for theorists that has always accrued to his handling of the various elements of musical structure, harmony in particular. A probing reexamination of the music and a cogent discussion of Skryabin's organizational procedures, such as have been attempted more than once in recent years, are long overdue. It is to the elucidation and broadened dissemination of one especially significant example of such study that the present article is devoted.

Alexander Nikolaevich Skryabin, who was born 25 December 1871/ 6 January 1872 in Moscow and died there 14/ 27 April 1915, achieved early fame as a piano virtuoso already while a student at the Moscow Conservatory. Only gradually did the focus of public attention broaden to include his piano compositions as well. Though he had performed his own works regularly from his youth on, it was only in the compositions of the turn of the century that Skryabin seemed finally to have evolved a language for expressing in notes that flamboyant, egocentric and, to some, mystical attitude which had even earlier become apparent in his playing. At first, this language was more apt than innovative, containing a mixture of rhythmic imagination, typical late-nineteenth-century chromatic harmonies, and pianistic textures not far removed from Liszt or Chopin. This is not to say that these works, roughly op. 30-44 of 1903-1905, did not bear a unique identity, but rather that in them their composer had not yet moved terribly far from his stylistic predecessors. It was the particular combination of traits and their varied but identifiable repetition, rather than the uniqueness of any one of them, that made the works of this period memorable.

As Skryabin's language continued to evolve through the later op. 40s, various characteristics began to dominate. One particular type of chord—a major-minor seventh chord with various added and altered tones—appeared with increasing frequency. Numerous root progressions involving tritone movement are found. A general fascination with delayed harmonic and melodic resolution is also apparent. For Skryabin, these characteristics answered an expressive need. Ambiguity or lack of completion in the musical character symbolized the striving for perfection and ever greater emotional satisfaction that was central to Skryabin's personal artistic philosophy.

As Skryabin's philosophy evolved in more mystical and less fathomable detail, so did his musical language become more restricted and refined as he sought to find the perfect means for expressing his thoughts and emotions. His music, his life, and his thinking became inextricably entwined. The resulting compositions, from op. 51 on, have piqued analytical curiosity from Skryabin's day to the present. Save for two symphonic poems, all of these are solo piano pieces—miniatures and single-movement sonatas.

It is the harmonic element in these works that has always commanded the greatest attention, partially due to the highly restrictive vocabulary and unconventional syntax involved. Melodic and rhythmic invention are naturally quite prominent in a style so overtly expressive; thematic development, at times quite sophisticated in nature, is handled with technical competence, particularly in the highly compressed last six sonatas. Formal structures are simple and straightforward in the miniatures and are dominated by thematic continuity in the sonatas, but lengthy sections with a texture in which harmony is of secondary importance are relatively rare. (Skryabin himself is supposed to have said that melody and harmony were, for him, but two views of the same musical idea; his term was "melodic harmony" according to Sabaneev.[1]) It is not remarkable, therefore, that most analysts of Skryabin's mature works must at some point, regardless of the specific focus of their examinations, deal with the element of harmonic structure and pitch organization.[2]

Early studies, both in Russia and abroad, sought various explanations for harmonic structure but essentially did not deal with questions of overall organization. For those works of the last seven years of Skryabin's life, works in which the conventional tonic conclusion was apparently abandoned by the composer, analysts found that each work seemed dominated by a specific type of complex chord structure, for expressive reasons, they presumed, and that reiteration of that structure was deemed sufficient enough for unity of organization that a conventional concluding resolution was unnecessary. It was also noted that the prevailing chord structure in each work was transposed freely throughout the course of that work, with a preference for tritone and major third root movement, but that it often appeared above the same root at or near the beginning and end of the piece. As to root analysis, these early theorists noted that the majority of Skryabin's chords had, in addition to various other members, a major third and a minor seventh above the lowest sounding note. Taking this as a holdover from the traditional "dominant"-type, sonority, they looked on the lowest note simply as the root, regardless of overall structural complexity, and even called Skryabin's late-period chords "dominants," despite their lack of traditional resolution.

Ex. 1   a) op. 73 no. 2; b) op. 69 no. 1; c) op. 74 no. 5

Of course, this idea of lack of completion, of a dominant which never finds its tonic, fit perfectly with Skryabin's "striving," "recreative" philosophy, as mentioned earlier. This connection apparently satisfied the needs of scholars of the first quarter of this century, who were much closer in time not only to Skryabin and the memory of his personality, but also to the period in which the mysticism, theosophy, and symbolist poetry which had affected Skryabin so directly had been rampant in both Eastern and Western Europe.

The theorists who studied Skryabin's chords in detail offered various explanations of chord structure. The idea of a dominant derivation, as just mentioned, was one: dominant ninth and dominant thirteenth labels were frequently used. Because Skryabin often voiced his chords such that successive notes in them were separated by fourths of various qualities, the idea that he had invented a system of quartal harmony also became popular. Perhaps the most interesting theory involved speculation that Skryabin was attempting to expand chord structure through use of higher members of the overtone series. Russian theorists in particular were embroiled in controversy over the viability of this solution.

At some point, the conclusion was reached that there was one chord that was basic to Skryabin's vocabulary and that all the others were derived from it. This chord, the "Promethean" or "mystic" chord illustrated below, is mentioned in even the most recent reference books.[3] The very concept of a compositional idiom somehow generated by this single chord has been perhaps the most widespread and durable of all the early theories advanced as explanations for Skryabin's unique language.

Ex. 2

Somewhat later, thanks to the work of the Polish musicologist Sofia Lissa, the relation of Skryabin's harmonic organization to the serial concept was explored.[4] More recently Lissa's theories along that line have been continued and expanded by George Perle[5] and others. Another recent concept has been that of the derivation by Skryabin of his chords (and melodies) from various exotic or synthetic scales. Finally, there is also a "negative" explanation, which is, in fact, no explanation at all but is merely a label frequently used to pigeonhole Skryabin's harmonic idiom: "atonal." Prominent use of this description is a fairly recent phenomenon and is again found in some widely used reference sources.[6] It seems to be a catch-all term which takes over when more traditional analytical terminology is thwarted by Skryabin's failure to provide a concluding tonic, frequently between op. 51 and op. 60, and consistently from op. 61 to op. 74. Despite the somewhat widespread use of the term, little in the way of supporting evidence has been supplied to justify its validity or to explain how "atonal" music can have both a pitch and a chord structure as a focal point.

Let us examine these attempts to deal with Skryabin's unique harmonic language one by one, not with the intention of proving or disproving each (which would be far beyond the scope of this article), but only to point out what aspects of Skryabin's language each theory deals with and what strengths and weaknesses are readily apparent in them. This will provide the background and perspective from which one will be able better to appreciate the scope and applicability of the main analytical approach to be discussed later in this article.

Dominant Derivation

This theory depends primarily on two factors: the traditional tonal character of Skryabin's pre-op. 51 works, and the intervallic structure contained in the chord-types which dominate the later works. The approach of those scholars who use the "dominant" label for Skryabin's unique chords has been to observe that Skryabin, from the early works on, gradually altered and added more notes in his traditionally employed chords. Chords of typically dominant structure—root, major third, minor seventh as basic members—began to appear on scale degrees other than the dominant:

Ex. 3   The concluding measures of *Reverie* op. 49 no. 3, showing
dominant-like structures on scale degrees 7, 4, 5, ♭3, ♭6, ♭2,
and 5 in the key of C major

Finally Skryabin removed the tonic itself from the music; "dominants" only remained, chords which had appeared as truly functional dominants in earlier contexts and which now retained their former structural but not functional character. That is, the word "dominant" was used to signify both a structural peculiarity and a connection with the past; it no longer had a reference to function.[7] This approach was, as far as it went, a sound one, having been based directly on the evidence of the music. It also had the advantage of a theoretical connection to Skryabin's highly personal expressive style. But it began and ended with the isolated chord and was unable to explain anything about chord connection or pitch organization. Not even the use of the word *dominant* was closely examined other than for its aptness to chord structure. Furthermore, if such a chord seems to be a point of focus, both as to structure and as to root location (i.e., the same transposition of a chord stucture appearing at both the beginning and the end of a work), the term *tonic* would seem more appropriate than *dominant*. Of course, both terms carry a number of traditional associations which would have to be severely qualified, if not forsaken, in accepting them for use in this kind of situation. That would be a rather significant step to take for the sake of one specific compositional style, particularly when other related questions would still remain unanswered. However, the fact that these traditionalists noted a gradual evolution of Skryabin's language from the past is important, even if Schloezer, Dickenmann, von Gleich, and others of this group indicated helplessness in dealing with the works after op. 60.[8]

Quartal Harmony

The prominence of fourths of varying qualities has been noted by virtually all students of Skryabin's music.[9] Relatively few have felt compelled to postulate that Skryabin was actually inventing a new system of chord structure—quartal instead of tertian—as the basis of his language. Lack of consistency in the use of quartal structure is one problem with this approach. The use of various qualities of fourths is another: with so many nonperfect fourths in the structure of the various chords, the aural effect of the harmony is often hard to distinguish from other late-romantic, highly chromatic, tertian-based styles.

   From a technical standpoint, complex chord structures can retain their harmonic value, regardless of the distribution of the upper voices, so long as the chord root remains in the bass. If one accepts momentarily the argument that Skryabin's chords are based in tradition, a view supported by the presence in so many chords of the root-seventh-third combination, then it would seem that a logical explanation would be that Skryabin was merely experimenting with quartal *distribution* of chords whose structures were tertian. Thus the description of Skryabin's chords as quartal in *structure* would seem to be a rather hasty assumption based primarily on the observation of surface features. (Various theorists, including Dernova, have asserted this view.) It is not supported by a quartal-based melodic practice,[10] nor is there a hint of a radical change in harmonic structure if one observes the gradual development of Skryabin's late harmonic idiom. In other words, the quartal theory is purely descriptive of chord voicing and thus has little to say about the origins of chords, their connection, or their overall relation to formal structure.

The Acoustic Approach

As was mentioned earlier, this theory of explaining the derivation of Skryabin's chords was particularly prominent among early Russian theorists. Leonid Sabaneev, among the earliest of Skryabin's biographers and apparently the originator of the acoustic theory as applied to Skryabin harmony, described one of his chords (the Promethean or so-called mystic chord) as being arrived at by Skryabin by employing overtones 7, 8, 9, 10, 11, and 13 from the harmonic series.[11]

Ex. 4

Boris de Schloezer, Skryabin's brother-in-law, adopted the same approach. Joining Schloezer and Sabaneev in this acoustic discussion of the World War I years were Boris Asafiev (under his pseudonym Igor Glebov), Arseny Avraamov, and others. The pages of *Muzykal'nyi sovremennik* of 1913-1916 were filled with the debate among these writers.[12]

The primary problems encountered in the theory relate, first of all, to the problem of notation: the ninth to fifteenth members of the harmonic series are, in some cases, quite far from the nearest equal-tempered equivalent. Notation of the harmonic series itself can thus be somewhat arbitrary; how can this fact allow it to relate clearly to specific chord structures? Even more curious is the fact that the vast majority of Skryabin's output is for the equal-tempered piano; of the late-period works under discussion, only two are nonpiano: *Poem of Ecstasy* and *Prometheus*. Such a high degree of compromise on the part of Skryabin seems inconsistent with what is known of his personality.

According to Sabaneev and other of Skryabin's contemporaries, there was some interest on the part of the composer in a new or nontraditional tuning system, perhaps even to the point of altering or redesigning a piano for that purpose. No evidence of actual attempts to carry this out in practice exists. Quite possibly Skryabin was intellectually attracted by the notational similarity between some of his chords and the harmonic series—his sketchbooks (now kept in the Skryabin Museum in Moscow) show one or two labelings of chords which support this—as a seemingly natural justification of his language. His unique and self-centered philosophy would logically have sought to go beyond existing means of expression and, perhaps, systems of tuning. The point is, he was incapable of escaping the equal-tempered piano or of forsaking it for more malleable orchestral instruments because it was *his* instrument, his own personal voice. The acoustic approach to isolated chord analysis may provide interesting observations in light of the philosophical side of Skryabin's art, but it is logically incapable of supporting an entire system of harmonic structure and organization. Nonetheless, references to this theory as an explanation of harmonic derivation persist.[13]

The Mystic Chord

This chord (see ex. 2) has been referred to by almost every study of Skryabin's music, usually with the status of a central chord synthesized by Skryabin as the basis for his harmonic language. Though its specific usage is found in the Fifth Sonata and *Prometheus* (where, in the opening, it has been inverted), Sabaneev, Hull, Swan, and others have found what they call early examples of the chord or its unique characteristics in works as early as the Waltz, op. 1.[14] The label "mystic" apparently was derived from the fact that Skryabin was much involved with mystical spiritualism, satanism, theosophy, and other ideologies as he was trying to focus his own inner feelings and the philosophical ramblings to which his music was giving expression. (It will be remembered that his magnum opus, which remained unwritten at his death, was to have been a gigantic multi-media work called *Mystery*.) The term *mystic* was already in use in England in 1916, its invention credited to Skryabin's "disciples."[15] Focus on this chord's apparently fundamental role probably stemmed from the early writings of Sabaneev, although he only referred to the "chord of *Prometheus*," not to a so-called mystic chord, as the central chord in Skryabin's language.

The fact that the cited chord does contain various features common to Skryabin's harmonic structures is significant: there is the fundamental root, major third, and minor seventh noted by those using the "dominant" label; the expanded forms of the dominant—the ninth and the thirteenth—are also represented; finally the replacement of a perfect fifth by a lowered one is also representative of Skryabin's language (he also used a raised fifth at times). However, focus is still on an isolated structure; no insight to chord relations, pitch organization, or overall harmonic plan is provided. Again, important observations are made but they remain just that—observations. The emphasis on the unique and synthetic nature of the chord obscured its traditional background, despite attempts to find the chord's embryonic existence in early works.

The Proto-serial Nature of Skryabin's Late Works

The idea of the significance of a central chord structure, freely transposable, in each of Skryabin's late works gave rise in the 1930s to the possibility of considering Skryabin's music as yet another style evolving toward a quasi-mathematical organizational method to replace traditional tonality. Sofia Lissa, the pioneer of this approach (see note 4), dismissed the "mystic" chord theory, focusing rather on the technique of building a work around a specific chord structure. This technique she refers to as the *Klangzentrum* technique, with the basic chord for a work being its *Klangzentrum*. Lissa saw this chord as a *Grundgestalt* (a not entirely accurate analogy), a vertical ordering of the pitch collection which provides harmonic unity for the work. The *Grundgestalt* could appear at any pitch level without a functional hierarchy in transposition choice (she says), and could be different for each work. Thus she established independence of the twelve tones and freedom from the major/minor system for Skryabin's works.

The impact of this approach on one's view of Skryabin's historical position is indeed significant. Avoidance of the "mystic" chord theory is also a positive feature, but one problem remains. Transposition of the *Klangzentrum* is said to be arbitrary, and yet even casual observation of Skryabin's late works shows that beginning and ending chords are frequently the same and that, of all possibilities, transposition by tritone and major third are by far preferred, followed by minor third transposition. Rather than the lack of control for chord progression that Lissa cites, there would seem to be very definite constraints that need to be explained.

A step in this direction was taken in the late 1950s by George Perle, who found in the Seventh Sonata a number of passages in which chord transposition seemed to be controlled by common tone. Noting that for thematic purposes Skryabin had made frequent use in this work of a four-note segment of the basic chord, Perle found that this segment could be transposed up a minor third without introducing any notes not already contained in the entire original basic chord.[16]

Ex. 5

Obviously this could provide a controlled system of chord progression based on the chord itself and not on whim. Since a tritone divides equally into two minor thirds, two of the three most common intervals of root movement with Skryabin are involved here; Perle certainly made an important advance over previous explanations, which avoided dealing with harmonic organization almost entirely. Unfortunately, this is the only work examined by Perle and his analysis is quite brief, so one must discover for himself the extent, if any, to which these discoveries would apply to other of Skryabin's late compositions. Two dissertations[17] have gone somewhat beyond Perle in breadth of analysis but, except for important observations on the relation between chord transposition choice and form, little new was added, and much of the problem-laden "mystic" chord theory was retained.

Synthetic Scales in Skryabin's Music

It has been common practice for theorists to discuss various scale formations in relation to the music of a given style period. Thus, one speaks of the medieval modal system, the traditional major/minor system, or the 12-tone system, all having to do with certain pitch and/or interval selections as characteristic of a given body of music. The importance of scalar analysis in explaining the structure of a piece of music varies with the style being considered. Characteristic interval order was the primary concern of the medieval modes; emphasis on a tonal center and pitch hierarchy became more important in the period of the major/minor system; in the 12-tone idiom, neither interval order nor pitch selection nor a tonal center is important to the fundamentals of the system and the use of the chromatic scale as a pitch source is simply a given. Thus, though a horizontalization of primary pitch content can be valid for any piece of music, an analyst must decide whether his pitch abstraction displays an organic connection to the music itself or is merely a convenient means for displaying the composer's pitch choice. Virtually any attempt to show an organic connection between a scale and a piece of Skryabin's music would, it seems, have to deal consistently with foreign tones, melodic presentation of characteristic scalar material, and "modulation," transposition, or change of pitch set. In fact, the theorists who have used a scalar analysis have been unable to do this, choosing simply to present Skryabin's chords in a linear rather than a vertical fashion but otherwise not advancing beyond the "mystic" chord method of simple description. Despite the fact that these analysts—chiefly Manfred Kelkel and Adrian Rațiu, whose scalar analyses are by far the most detailed[18]—point frequently to the whole-tone scale's similar pitch content to the "mystic" chord and also to Skryabin's occasional consistent use of the semitone-tone scale, their fundamental contribution is to show by another means the compactness of Skryabin's vocabulary.

The question here is not one of validity of method, but rather of whether the method is the most appropriate to the style. Given the straightforward vertical organization of Skryabin's language, a vertical, that is, a harmonically oriented analytical system would seem a better choice.

For the most part, these analyses are honest and well-focused attempts to explain a unique and economical compositional language. Each deals in some manner with the most obvious ear- and eye-catching element in Skryabin's music—harmony. All add some point of importance to a total understanding of Skryabin's harmonic language, its nature, origins, and method of organization. Despite surface differences, if added together, these approaches create a picture of Skryabin's late style that would appear somewhat like the following: Skryabin, in seeking a unique language to express his unique ideas, evolved an idiom harmonically oriented around a six-note chord structure, built in fourths of various qualities, retaining some of the structural character of a dominant ninth or thirteenth of traditional practice, and derived perhaps from experimentation with the harmonic series, nontraditional tuning systems, or synthetic scales. This fundamental chord, referred to as the "mystic" chord or the "Promethean" chord, provides the harmonic and melodic material for the last two dozen or so of Skryabin's works, in all of which it apparently appears, though in a number of variant forms.

The fundamental economy and uniqueness of a system thus described cannot be denied, and its level of believability as an explanation for the expressive unity unmistakable in the final works of Skryabin is quite high. And yet questions remain:

1. What organizational means preceded the use of a central "mystic" chord? Are there transition works, or is there a complete break in technique?
2. Is it only the chord *structure* which is central to a given work? Is there any significance to specific pitch content and transposition?
3. Is chord movement and progression arbitrary? Is it controlled only by a preference for certain intervals (tritone, major third, minor third)? Or is there a more all-encompassing, systematic explanation?

It is with the foregoing analytical retrospective and unanswered questions in mind that we approach the contributions of the contemporary Soviet musicologist, Varvara Dernova.

Varvara Pavlovna Dernova[19] was born on 9/22 October 1906 in Elabuga, an industrial town east of Kazan in Vyatka province (now part of the Tatar ASSR, just east of Moscow). After entering the Leningrad Conservatory as a piano student, she transferred to the newly founded Education Department where she completed her basic studies in 1930. During the following years she taught in various music schools. In 1940 she began graduate studies at the Leningrad Conservatory where her principal mentor was Professor Yury Tiulin (1885-1978). Following the war Dernova resumed her studies; her candidate's thesis, "A. V. Zataevich and Kazakh Folk Music," was successfully defended in 1961. Her candidacy for the doctorate led to the awarding of that degree in 1974, her dissertation being "The Harmony of Skryabin."[20]

In 1948, Dernova was appointed lecturer at the new Kurmangazy Conservatory in Alma-Ata, Kazakhstan. She rose to the rank of assistant professor *(dotsent)* in 1961 and is now professor of artistic research. Her main duties center on classes in music analysis. She is also called upon regularly to be a part of the State Examination Commission of the Leningrad Conservatory in connection with the awarding of diplomas. In 1978 she was invited to present a paper at the International Skryabin Symposium in Graz, Austria; ill health unfortunately precluded her attendance but not the presentation of her paper, "The Influence of Skryabin on the Theoretical Thought of Our Century."[21] Earlier in that same year, she had been asked to speak at a conference in Moscow celebrating the 100th anniversary of the birth of the Soviet music theorist Boleslav Yavorsky.

Dernova's research efforts have focused on two chief areas: contemporary harmony, with her study of Yavorsky's theories and Skryabin's music as the starting point; and the folk music of Kazakhstan. In the latter area, she has published several articles and edited collections of music. In particular she has spent a great deal of time with the music of Kazakhstan's most important native composer, Sagyrbaev Kurmangazy (after whom the Alma-Ata Conservatory is named). Her most recent editing work is connected with the *kiui,* a folk instrumental genre of Kazakhstan.

Dernova's concern with the music of Skryabin began before the War. Her initial analytical findings were essentially complete by the late 1940s, but the evolving nature of her system and, perhaps, an unstable political climate delayed their publication until 1968. Although the book *Garmoniia Skriabina* [The harmony of Skryabin] represents the most complete exposition of her ideas, it is by no means the only source.[22] Through the evidence of her publishing as well as through indication in her private correspondence, her application of Yavorsky's theories and her study of Skryabin's music continue to develop and become more refined. Several conservatory students have become involved in the application of Yavorsky's theories to the music of Bartók, Khatchaturian, and others, under Dernova's guidance.

Although it is difficult to gauge Dernova's actual impact on Soviet theory, her enthusiasm for passing on her ideas to her students, her publishing activity, and her proven interest in continung her analytical investigations make it likely that her work will continue to be available for evaluation and continuation. Her work on the State Examining Commission, her being awarded study grants by the Union of Soviet Composers (most recently to Ruza in 1976), and her being approved for travel outside the USSR seem to bear witness to a relatively high level of political acceptance by the Soviet music-theoretical community. It must be noted, however, that awareness of Dernova's work has only recently surfaced in the West, initially in books by Faubion Bowers and Jim Samson, subsequently in the works of Gottfried Eberle and Hanns Steger, and recently in the dissertation-translation of *Garmoniia Skriabina* by the author of this article.[23]

Rather than simply summarizing the findings in Dernova's *Garmoniia Skriabina,* it seems that a more convincing approach would be to examine Skryabin's music from a chronological viewpoint, as Dernova herself did, and then to present her method in a way that shows its parallels to the needs of the musical analysis. For, to anticipate, it is just this close relation with all aspects of Skryabin's output that will be seen as the most revealing and impressive characteristic of Dernova's analytical system.

Dernova's observations and explanations of Skryabin's pre-op. 51 works are not fundamentally opposed to those of other thorough analysts, though her careful observation of certain recurrent techniques led subsequently to important aspects of her method. Thus, only a brief summation of her view of the middle-period works is needed here.

Dernova observes Skryabin's predilection for the altered fifth in dominant and secondary dominant harmony, seen most prominently in the works after op. 23, the Third Sonata. Frequently, as in the following example from that work, the altered chord tone will serve as a melodic link in a succession of chords of dominant-like structure.[24]

Ex. 6   Sonata no. 3 op. 23, 1st movement, mm. 120-23

The first and third measures of this passage are identical except for the tritone transposition. The prominence of a root-minor seventh-major third chord structure with the added sixth (or thirteenth) resolving down to the perfect fifth is obvious. The noteworthy aspect of this example is the first beat of measure two, where the perfect fifth, G♯, is lowered to G♮, the root of the second chord of the passage. For two-thirds of a beat this lowered fifth actually sounds as part of the preceding chord. The succeeding bass movement from C♯ to D in a sense reverses the movement of the upper voice, the C♯ being, in retrospect only, of course, the lowered fifth moving to the perfect fifth of the second chord. The chromatic voice-leading thus makes the tritone movement of the two chords quite smooth. (The first chord is, by the way, a functional dominant; the measures preceding the example are clearly in the key of F♯, as is the movement as a whole.) Other examples similar in nature can be found in the opening measures of the Poem op. 32 no. 1 and in the main theme of the first movement of the Symphony no. 3 op. 43.

Another trait observed by Dernova is Skryabin's frequent use of the flat second scale degree as a chord root, particularly near cadences.

Ex. 7   Prelude op. 35 no. 3, conclusion

Here the triad on flat-II is emphasized by its own dominant. Rather than smoothing out the tritone relation to the main dominant, Skryabin, here and in other such examples, prefers the direct juxtaposition of the two. In op. 35 no. 3, this basic progression, V/♭II–♭II–V–I, appears so frequently that it is really a thematic progression. Tritone root movement itself begins to become a peculiar trait of Skryabin's music from this point on.

Gradually Skryabin's chord vocabulary becomes more restrictive, harmonic rhythm slows, and his preference for chords of dominant-like structure becomes abundantly obvious. The appearance of these chords on scale degrees other than the fifth is more and more common. Observe in the following example that the root progression, ♭II–V–I, is the same as at the close of the previous example, but that the flat-II chord is no longer a triad but a major/minor seventh chord. This connection of two dominant-like chords a tritone apart becomes a virtual style trait of the works after op. 51.

Ex. 8   Op. 51, no.4, final cadence

Though occasionally Skryabin shows his awareness of the resolution tendency inherent in all such chords by including individual resolutions for them (e.g., as would be shown by resolving the chord Db to a triad on Gb in the above example), such instances are infrequent. According to Dernova, Skryabin was at this stage still intent on clearly affirming a single tonic, despite the theoretical dualism implied by duplicating the dominant chord structure a tritone away.

A third observation about Skryabin's evolving language involves his apparent expressive need to delay or weaken tonic resolution. The following examples illustrate that point. In example 9, chromatic voice-leading creates nonharmonic tones in the tonic chord of C major. At the first appearance of the passage, these tones are not resolved; at its second appearance, as the final cadence, they are.

Ex. 9   Op. 45 no. 2, mm. 2-4 and 13-16

In example 10, the same two nonharmonic tones appear at the final cadence. Their disposition and duration almost obscure the fact that the cadence here is bII-V-I in C. Dernova, in fact, calls this cadence "plagal," apparently referring only to the last four measures.[25]

There are numerous examples of the use of extended multiple nonharmonic tones and plagal or quasi-plagal cadences in the period of Skryabin's output under discussion. Dernova sees this tendency as a theoretical complement to the use of two dominant-like structures a tritone apart leading to a tonic. In the latter case, resolution tendencies are in conflict, from a traditional standpoint, though this conflict is exactly what the composer needed, expressively speaking. The former case was an alternative method for achieving a similar expressive result, where Skryabin experimented with altered tonic harmony, specifically with the raised and lowered fifth of the tonic chord. Depending on the context, this may also appear as subdominant

Ex. 10   Op. 56 no. 2, conclusion

harmony (ex. 10), creating at least the feeling of a plagal cadence. In both cases, the very concept of resolution, either linear or functional, is the central theoretical issue.

There is yet one more characteristic feature of these works which Dernova discusses: the nature of the concluding tonic itself. Having evolved expressive means for diffusing the resolution tendency of the approach to the tonic, Skryabin questioned, as it were, the necessity of a pure tonic resolution. This is seen in several works of the op. 50s. For example, *Nuances* op. 56 no. 3 closes with the tonic in the form of a major seventh chord:

Ex. 11   *Nuances* op. 56, no. 3, last measure

In the very next work, the Etude op. 56 no. 4, the first of several appearances of what Dernova refers to as a "bifunctional" closing chord is seen. The dominant of the key of Gb remains as the concluding chord, but with the tonic root added a fifth below; thus, the tonic and dominant functions are combined.[26]

The next and ultimate step for Skryabin was to omit even this weakened reference to the tonic, leaving only the dominant chord as the concluding sonority. This occurs first in the Two Pieces op. 59, but is already anticipated in *Enigma* op. 52 no. 2 and in the Fifth Sonata op. 53. The last work in which an

Ex. 12   Op. 56 no. 4

unobscured tonic triad is used at the conclusion is *Prometheus* op. 60. In the immediately preceding and in the following works, interior or concluding functional progressions which could clarify tonality in the traditional manner are absent. Structurally Skryabin's chord language had been refined to one type, a chord of dominant-like structure, with root, major third, minor seventh, and various other added or altered members. Each of his works from op. 59 onward consisted only of such chords, or segments of them, appearing in both harmonic and melodic form.

By observing carefully the evolution in Skryabin's language, Dernova both justifies a qualified use of "dominant" to describe Skryabin's famous chord structures and even more clearly points out the relation between Skryabin's expressive style and the language he had evolved to match it, giving the latter a sound theoretical and analytical basis. That all Skryabin's late-style harmonies should be thought of as "dominant" in origin is logical and consistent, not only with the transitional style trait of prolonging the resolution tendency, but also with Skryabin's philosophy that creativity was for him an unceasing striving for an elusive goal. The tendency of a dominant chord structure to resolve to its tonic is perhaps the strongest tension-releasing characteristic of tonal music. For Skryabin, the best way to express his feelings and ideas was, ultimately, to compose music that was constantly "dominant" in sound. The idiom might be criticized for lacking potential for subsequent development, but, in retrospect, it seems to have been precisely what Skryabin needed. Thus, the fact that the "dominant" quality exists in these chords is fundamentally significant, while the specifics of the various chord structures Skryabin created are far less important.

One is quite amazed at the unusually clear evolution of Skryabin's language, particularly since there is no evidence that Skryabin was greatly concerned with the theoretical side of his art (he did speak of "strict laws" which governed his late works but, when pressed, failed to explain them). However, the lack of a composer's explicit technical explanations for his particular style and methods can in no way be construed as evidence of unorganized or amorphous procedures. Sensing this, Dernova did not stop at this point in her study, as so many others had. Two aspects of the music discussed above intrigued her: the preference for tritone connection of two dominant-like structures, and the preponderance of common tones shared by these structures. The connection between these points and the more theoretical aspect of diffusing the traditional necessity for chord resolution was found by Dernova in the theoretical work of Boleslav Yavorsky.

Yavorsky was a unique and independent theoretician whose revolutionary ideas of musical structure and syntax are being brought, in detailed form, to the attention of Western scholars for the first time in this collection of essays. The article by Gordon McQuere makes further elaboration here unnecessary. Dernova isolated only a few basic concepts from Yavorsky's work and used them to create a structural model, an analytical system parallel to Skryabin's music. Though this model is not precisely presented in any single composition, it is closely related to all the late works, supplying a basis for understanding chord structure, melody (as derived from harmony), and chord progression, and containing important implications for rhythm and form.

Despite his fascination with and apparently quite detailed study of Skryabin's music, Yavorsky wanted to design a theory of musical structure that was universally valid, that would not be tied to a specific body of music. The result took years to evolve and was finally called the "theory of modal rhythm." It was a complex general concept which assumed the relative instability and stability of certain tones in a musical context. The unstable tones (called "dominant") and the stable tones to which they resolved (called "tonic") were combined into various modal system—modes [lady]. A particularly prominent role in Yavorsky's theory is played by the tritone, traditionally the least stable interval. A tritone can resolve its instability in two directions, outward or inward:

Ex. 13

If a tritone and *both* of these resolutions are considered as part of a single system, the resulting six notes would be part of what Yavorsky terms a "duplex mode" [dvazhdyi lad].

Dernova was particularly attracted to the duplex mode as a means of coping with the analytical problems in Skryabin's music. Of course, this is logical, given the prominence of the tritone in the late works: it seemed to be the basic interval of chord connection, and all of Skryabin's complex chords contained at least one tritone. But Dernova also saw a theoretical connection between Skryabin's detailed evolution of his language from traditional tonality and Yavorsky's duplex mode.

Consider a traditional dominant seventh chord with lowered fifth (an alteration common with Skryabin, which creates a second tritone in the chord, between the root and the lowered fifth) and its normal resolution:

Ex. 14

If the same chord is written in second inversion and respelled enharmonically, the result is another chord of the same structure as the first. However, the resolution of this dominant is a tritone removed from the resolution of the first dominant, despite the fact that the two dominant chords are enharmonically equivalent.

Ex. 15

In other words, despite the "distance" between two tritone-related keys, there can be found a unique link between them through the enharmonic equivalence of their dominant chords with the fifth lowered. This link of the two dominants is termed by Dernova the "tritone nucleus" [tritonovoe zveno]. According to Dernova, the unity of these two chords takes the place of the need for tonic resolution of either of them in Skryabin's music. In her analyses of Skryabin's late works, a basic tritone nucleus is assigned to each work. This forms the reference for chord structure and transposition schemes for that work. The two chords of this basic nucleus are called the "initial dominant" [iskhodnoi dominant—DA] and the "derived dominant" [proizvodnoi dominant—DB]. In analysis, the chords of a nucleus are connected by a square bracket between their roots. (Note that *two* chords form the reference for a work, not one. For Dernova, the directionality and single focus of traditional tonality had been replaced by harmonic stasis and the dual focus of two enharmonically equal dominants a tritone apart. Because they are equal to each other, DA and DB may appear in either order and may even change identity during the course of a composition. However, the basic tritone nucleus does not actually become the "tonic" of the music. As Dernova says, "It both was and remained 'dominant,' since the nonresolution of the dominant and all its enharmonic transformations is understood to be at the basis of Skryabin's duplex mode.... Every such dominant implies a tonic... sounding only in the imagination."[27])

Ex. 16   The Tritone Nucleus

Though Dernova's use of Yavorsky's duplex mode does not involve the stable notes in the mode, i.e., the resolutions (Skryabin's chords do not resolve), the fact that in his mode the two traditional resolutions can be considered as part of the same system leads to the concept of unifying the dominants from two different tonalities, thus dissipating, at least theoretically, the need for tonic resolution. This relates directly to the evidence of Skryabin's music, where we at first see a preference for chords of dominant-like structure and for the tritone relation of such chords, then an occasional experimentation with the tonal resolution of both chords in this tritone relationship, and, finally, a gradual movement away from any tonic resolution. After this point, the music begins to consist only of dominant-like chord structures, most frequently progressing by tritone root movement.

But what of the other principal intervals of root movement—the major third and minor third? Dernova's analytical construct for Skryabin's music explains these as well, but we must first return to the two chords of the tritone nucleus, as seen in example 16. In her system, Dernova expands the four-note basic chords we have been discussing by adding two other members also often seen in Skryabin's music: the *raised* fifth and the major ninth. Upon examination one can see that this structure involves all six notes of a whole-tone scale.

Ex. 17

Naturally, when transposed three whole steps, this chord will acquire no new pitches, because of its whole-tone content. The fact that the entire whole-tone set is used also determines uniformity of structure, regardless of inversion position. In other words, everything which has been pointed out about enharmonic equivalence and unification of the two tritone-related dominants from example 16 applies to this more complex chord as well. It is this dominant ninth chord, a whole-tone chord of six notes, which is the basic chord of Dernova's entire analytical system.

To deal with chord progression, Dernova begins with the basic chord and its tritone-related equivalent, i.e., with the tritone nucleus, and transposes this nucleus twice by whole steps. This sequence of three pairs of tritone-related chords Dernova terms the "major enharmonic sequence" [bol'shaia engarmonicheskaia sekventsiia]:

Ex. 18   Major Enharmonic Sequence

Because of the whole-tone content of the basic chord, the sequence cannot be extended further; that is, the next chord, on the root C♯, would repeat the second chord of the first pair and, with its companion chord, would repeat the tritone nucleus in reverse. This closed system of six enharmonically equivalent chords contains not only the tritone relation, between the chords of each pair, but also the major third relation, between successive pairs (indicated in analysis by a broken square bracket). These two relations, as was mentioned earlier, are the most frequently encountered root relations in Skryabin's late music.

The minor third root relation, third in order of frequency in Skryabin's late works, is derived by interlocking the tritone nucleus of one major enharmonic sequence with the second pair of chords from a sequence using the complementary whole-tone scale (e.g., compared to ex. 18, the one beginning on the root G♭, yielding the roots G♭-C, E-A♯, and D-G♯). This interlocking is done symmetrically, yielding a sequence of minor-third-related chords of identical structure but of totally contrasting pitch content. This is termed the "minor sequence" [malaia sekventsiia] (for clarity, roots only are shown, which generally is Dernova's practice as well):

Ex. 19   Minor Sequence

As will be clarified by subsequent analyses, the minor sequence has strong formal implications, since it provides a means of moving between the two discrete whole-tone pitch sets. The analogy to "modulation" is well worth noting. Except for a series of adjuncts for details of chord structure and voice-leading in specific situations, the structural model described above is the basis for analyzing Skryabin's late works by Dernova's method. It fills a role for that body of music that is analogous to the relation between the tonal system and the works of Bach, Haydn, Schubert, Brahms, etc.: A basic principle of organization exists which provides a chord language and a temporal framework for the style, and there is an organizational focus for pitch, complete with a hierarchy allowing for rhythmic and formal differentiation. Melodic, thematic, developmental, and expressive details remained in the hands of the composer, as with the tonal idiom. Chord structures vary from work to work, but the underlying harmonic organization remains the same.

The all-important demonstration of the viability of Dernova's system will follow subsequently, but first let us examine some of the adjuncts to the system alluded to above. All of these are, in one way or another, attempts to bridge whatever gap may be thought to exist between Dernova's structural model and individual works.

Despite their general similarities to the traditional dominant chord, Skryabin's unique chords are quite distinct from each other if examined closely enough. For the most part, Dernova approaches all specific chord structures as variants, showing that her model chord is just that: a model which allows the demonstration of the basic organization of the system without dictating a practical dependency on only one specific chord (hence, her choosing of the whole-tone chord rather than the "mystic" chord, which would *not* allow for such a demonstration). To repeat, it is the general dominant-like quality of the chords which is significant, not the specific variables of structure.

The chord fifth receives special attention because, in its lowered form, it is so characteristic of Skryabin's harmonic formations and is a prerequisite of the formation of Dernova's system. Dernova speaks of the doubled or split fifth; in her model chord, for example, it appears in both diminished and augmented form.[28] It can also appear in perfect form or in doubly augmented form, combined, of course, with the ever-present lowered form.

The doubly augmented fifth is always referred to as the added sixth (never as the thirteenth, which would seem more consistent with the tertian view of Skryabin's harmonic structure but which would detract from Dernova's emphasis on the role of the split fifth). This tone also is treated in a special manner because its presence in a chord of the tritone nucleus, coupled with the importance of enharmonic relations in Dernova's system, allows for the appearance of the minor third in a chord, an element which detracts from the basic "dominant" nature of the chord. Because of the unique nature of this particular chord member, Dernova gives it a special analytical symbol. As the added sixth in DA it is called "v"; as the minor third in DB it is called "w."[29]

Ex. 20

Dernova notes, based on her observations of Skryabin's music, that this note, the added sixth, usually requires resolution melodically when it appears as the minor third, "w," in DB, because of its conflict there with the major third. The resolution, which may also be dissipated by a return to the initial dominant, DA, can be effected by a chromatic movement up to the major third or down to the major ninth.

Ex. 21

Dernova occasionally uses this chord tone to verify the proper analysis of the reference nucleus. Her logic is that the major third is typical and more likely as a member of a structurally important chord. The minor third will appear, according to Dernova's system, as "w" in DB of a nucleus, and then only if "v" is a member of DA in that nucleus. Thus, if a chord near the conclusion of a work, for example, has a major and a minor third in it, the chord a tritone away will undoubtedly be discovered to contain only a major third and also an added sixth. The former chord will be DB, the latter, DA. In a few of Skryabin's final works, the final chord (and others) is seen to contain both forms of the third, perhaps, as Dernova suggests, for expressive reasons. In such cases, the primary nucleus and the correct labels for DA and DB must be determined by other means.

Besides variation in the use of specific chord tones, there are other ways in which unique chord structures can be derived. One of the more obvious is by inversion. This is the manner in which the opening chord of *Prometheus* is explained by Dernova. In the example below, the first chord is a thirteenth chord with lowered fifth (or a ninth with lowered fifth and added sixth, as Dernova would call it); the following chord is its quartal redistribution; then the root and seventh are exchanged, the seventh becoming the lowest voice; finally, the opening chord of *Prometheus* is shown (in piano reduction):

Ex. 22

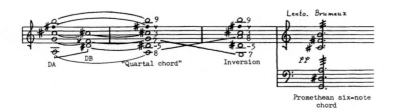

In other cases, what looks to be an unusual chord formation is merely a result of compositional freedom. For example, in the Seventh Sonata, a particular intervallic combination is an important harmonic and melodic unit:

Ex. 23   Sonata no. 7, mm. 10, 17-18

The opening measures contain three of the four notes in this structure:

Ex. 24   Sonata no. 7, beginning

Only in measure four does a chord appear which clarifies these relationships by giving the reference structure for the work:

Ex. 25

This structure is equivalent to the opening structure if one "adds up" all the elements of example 24.

Another method of approaching chord structure follows logically from the preceding example: the combining of two simpler chords into one complex, (usually) thematic chord. This possibility exploits the enharmonic aspect of Dernova's system. Since the two chords of a tritone nucleus are enharmonically equivalent (in Dernova's model, that is), incomplete forms of both chords could be combined to create a more complex chord typical of Skryabin's style. Dernova chooses the following measures from the Sixth Sonata as a typical example of the formation of such a "summary dominant." (The numeral 8 in Dernova's analysis refers to the chord root.)

Ex. 26   Sonata no. 6, mm. 11-12

The ultimate summary dominant contains a tritone, the roots of the preceding two chords, at the bottom of its structure. Dernova, borrowing a term from Arseny Avraamov, calls this double-root phenomenon the "compound bass." There are two reasons why Dernova chooses to refer to this structure as a summary dominant rather than simply as a seventh or ninth chord with lowered fifth. The first is based on the evidence of the music. In the example, the final chord literally results from the combination of the preceding two tritone-related chords. The second reason stems from the predominance of a specific type of structure in the lower part of the texture in Skryabin's late works: the order of chord tones, ascending from the bass, is most often root, seventh, and third. The insertion of the lowered fifth between the root and the seventh is a striking change that makes the chord aurally much more ambiguous, an ambiguity that Dernova attributes to the composer's conscious expressive intention. It is also true, however, that from this ambiguity comes unity, for the two dominants of a tritone nucleus are, theoretically, one. Their separation for the purpose of explaining harmonic progression leads to the simpler and more frequent distribution just mentioned, but this is only one aspect of the application of Dernova's system to harmony. Here we see another, the resynthesis of the chord type from which Dernova's system was developed. The term "compound bass," signifying that *both* roots from a tritone nucleus are at the bottom of a chord voicing, further defines that unity.

The previous examples from the Seventh Sonata illustrate an important aspect of Dernova's approach to melodic analysis, namely, that the notes of recurring motives and themes also have harmonic meaning. Referring again to the melodic form of the chord segment from the Seventh Sonata, we can see that its four notes can be labeled, by referring to measure four (ex. 25), as the seventh, minor ninth, lowered fifth, and "v" of the reference chord, F# thus being the root implied:

Ex. 27

Once labeled accordingly, subsequent appearances of such melodic segments can reveal their harmonic meaning; i.e., the theoretically implied chord root can even be found in a complex polyphonic textural surrounding. This can be an important analytical tool, as will be shown in the subsequent analyses.

Another aspect of Dernova's melodic analysis has to do with the previously mentioned occasional appearance in Skryabin's music of a straightforward statement of a chromatic scale or of one of the so-called synthetic scales, specifically the whole-tone or semitone-tone scale. Dernova explains these also from a harmonic standpoint, through the use of one of her progression sequences. For example, in the work *Strangeness* op. 63 no. 2, a passage appears which contains a clear emphasis on a segment of the semitone-tone scale:

Ex. 28   *Strangeness* op. 63 no. 2, mm. 14-16

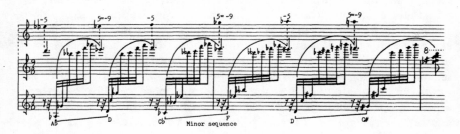

Dernova's explanation uses the minor sequence to explain the harmonic progression. The notes in the scale segment relate quite regularly to the underlying harmony: lowered fifth, fifth= minor ninth, lowered fifth, etc. Dernova is not attempting to deny the validity of labeling this as a scale presentation. Rather, she is only attempting to clarify it as a product of harmonic thinking rather than an element of structural significance, as some analysts have tried to prove. Just as the harmonies in Skryabin's progressions move in symmetrical patterns, voice-leading and melodic patterns are also symmetrical, naturally leading to symmetrical or synthetic scales: chromatic, whole-tone, or semitone-tone.

Although Dernova seems aware of the importance which Yavorsky places on the interrelation of pitch and rhythm, she does not devote a great deal of attention to rhythmic analysis in her work. One very interesting example, however, involves the minor sequence. She observes that "faster harmonic rhythm is more common in interlocked [i.e., minor] progressions than in tritone [i.e., major enharmonic] progressions."[30] A brief example of this is found in *Prometheus* (ex. 29).

Ex. 29   *Prometheus* op. 60, mm. 65-70

Ex. 29 cont.

The chord of the first measure of the example has been sustained for several preceding measures. The pattern of the last two measures of the example—a change of chord on successive downbeats—continues for several more measures. The speed-up of harmonic rhythm is matched by the change in tempo indication also.

Most of the questions of harmonic progression are handled through reference to the major enharmonic sequence or the minor sequence, as is the element of formal structure, as will be shown subsequently. There is, however, one other model sequence which Dernova constructs to explain certain quasi-functional progressions seen in Skryabin's late works. This is called the "functional sequence" [funktsional'naia sekventsiia], the basic form of which is shown below:

Ex. 30   Functional Sequence

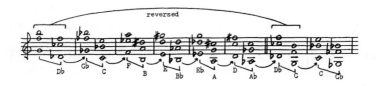

The term "functional" is used, obviously, because there are fifth relations between both the inner and the outer dominants of two successive chord pairs. (Only root movement is being observed; chord structure and function are kept strictly separate.) A wide variety of situations can be explained by use of this sequence or variants of it. One example, of special interest because of its relatively late position in Skryabin's output, is the opening of the Tenth Sonata of 1913. Though the entire segment is too long to quote here, a chart of the root relations of the introduction and the beginning of the main section of the movement will illustrate clearly the application of the functional sequence and the unexpectedly traditional tonal preparation of this introduction:

Ex. 31

The fifth relation between A♭ and D♭, a traditional dominant preparation, is clear from the sketch. The role of the chord on F could be seen as a filling-in of the A♭-D♭ space in a tertian sense. But it also has special meaning in Dernova's system. The roots F and D♭ are related in the major enharmonic sequence; A♭ lies outside that system. Instead of using all the chords whose roots would have provided a clear minor sequence,

Ex. 32

Skryabin, in Dernova's view, allows the F root to take the place of the other elements to which it clearly relates, thus abbreviating and simplifying the connection between the introduction and the following material. Incomplete tritone-related chord pairs, where only one of the two chords actually appears in the music, are encountered frequently in Dernova's analyses, often, as here, with a connection to aspects of formal structure.

This type of analysis acts as a fleeting reminder of the traditional basis of Skryabin's late style. The fact that Dernova's system allows for and, in fact, depends on the retention of certain aspects of the traditional tonal system lends strong support to the validity of her unique and imaginative analytical method.

The following analyses[31] have been included as an attempt to draw together all aspects of Dernova's analytical method. These analyses are strictly the result of the author's understanding of Dernova's system and do not pretend to produce results with which Dernova herself would necessarily be in complete agreement. As with almost any method of analysis, the application of this system to specific details involves certain contextual choices and interpretations. By analyzing entire works rather than excerpts, it is hoped that the individual interpretations can be seen as part of an overall analytical concept of that work, a concept that can display Dernova's fundamental principles faithfully and with maximum clarity.

Several factors were involved in choosing works to analyze. Chronology was certainly important, given the obvious evolutionary nature of Skryabin's style. Therefore it was necessary to choose works that showed both early and later stages of his late style. From the body of Skryabin's works in the so-called miniature forms, two have been chosen which show the variety of applications of Dernova's principles in the most succinct manner possible. This allows the reader to witness the working of the analytical method and also to see the broad-scale structural unity this method can reveal. Finally, the author sought to include works that had not already received abundant attention in the literature on Skryabin, thus emphasizing the all-encompassing applicability of Dernova's analytical system. The complete score for each work analyzed follows the individual analysis; all references are to that copy of the score.

It is not the intent of these analyses to make every possible analytical statement about the works discussed. Rather, they are presented only to demonstrate the use to which Dernova's system may be put and to prove the validity and value her principles have for explaining the complexities of a specific style, that used by Skryabin in the last few years of his life.

Prelude op. 59 no. 2

The *Deux Pièces* op. 59 were written by Skryabin in 1910. Examination of the immediately preceding and following opuses clearly shows the transitional stage of Skryabin's handling of tonal clarification. For example, op. 57 no 1 and op. 58 both employ the bifunctional concluding chords, while op. 57 no. 2 and *Prometheus* op. 60 use traditional tonic conclusions. Neither of the two works in op. 59, on the other hand, shows a direct tonic reference in its concluding cadence, both closing on chords of dominant-like structure. Thus, the first work to be discussed here, the Prelude op. 59 no. 2, would seem to be well-suited chronologically to illustrate Skryabin's nearly fully developed duplex-modal thinking.

Addressing the question of formal structure first, one is struck by the simplicity and economy of material. The overall structure may be labeled "abab," the second half of the work being a virtually intact tritone transposition of the first half, with the addition of a six-measure codetta. The only significant change between the halves is in the "b" material, which shows a different chord voicing in its second appearance (this will be discussed more fully later on). The formal divisions are as follows:

a	mm. 1-10
b	mm. 11-27
a	mm. 28-38
b′	mm. 39-55
codetta	mm. 56-61

Though this structure is quite clear and is in need of no further discussion, the inherent motivic unity, which will be seen to be supported further by the underlying harmonic structure, is worth noting. Pairs of octaves in the left hand, descending a tritone or a perfect fourth, are common to both sections. The "b" section's principal melody, mm. 12-14, is merely a rhythmic transformation of the upper voice in mm. 2-3 of the "a" section. The "a" section is distinguished chiefly by a chromatic line in the inner voice, seen first in the last half of m. 1 and first half of m. 2. The "b" section is set off first by a rest and repeated chords, m. 11, and subsequently by a measure-long arpeggio, beginning in m. 14. This section also closes with repeated chords, which are identical to the opening gesture of the ensuing return of "a," and which thus act as a retransition (mm. 26-27). This same material appears at the end of the second "b" section as a link to the codetta, which begins by repeating the preceding one-and-a-half measure "retransition" and concludes with a single statement of the melodic phrase from "b." Since this phrase had itself been a transformation of material from "a," the codetta effectively rounds off the entire piece.

Proceeding next to the harmonic language, one clearly sees the typical Skryabin trait of emphasizing a restricted vocabulary of chord structure within one work. The "a" section is constructed harmonically from two five-note chords, shown below (Dernova's practice of designating the root as 8 rather than 1 is retained in these analyses):

Ex. 33

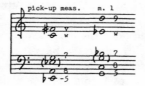

Beginning in m. 8, the second of these chords appears with the fifth lowered; this structure, the fifth alternating between its lowered and perfect form, dominates the first fourteen measures of the "b" section, which of course explains the initial alteration of the fifth at the end of the "a" section.

Before examining the conclusion of the "b" section, some observations on the two basic chords are in order. Root analysis here is complicated by the continuous leaps of a tritone or perfect fourth in the bass. The solution partially depends on an awareness of Skryabin's voicing habits with his characteristic dominant-type chords: the vertical order is generally root, seventh, and third. That is the structure that results if one chooses as the root the initial (i.e., the rhythmically-emphasized) note of each bass pair in the opening measures. This also leads to a root progression which is structurally significant in the overall tonal plan, as will become apparent. It is characteristic of the harmonic unity of Skryabin's style that chords whose roots are ambiguous because of the prominence of the tritone can be clarified either through examination of chord structure or through the broader context in which a chord is found. Such is the case, for example, in mm. 8 and 11, where the order of root and lowered fifth is reversed in comparison to the opening. (In *Garmoniia Skriabina,* p. 98, Dernova analyzes the opening chord of this work as the result of the combination of tones from both chords of the tritone nucleus E♭-A, with E♭ as the principal chord root. The question is not particularly crucial since the central tritone nucleus, C-F♯, is not involved.) A second observation is that the minor third, "w," replaces the usual major third in both chords. The previously mentioned chromatic inner voice in m. 1 results in a vacillation between the minor and major third, the impetus of the chromaticism carrying over into m. 2 where the minor seventh, B♭, is delayed by an accented passing tone:

Ex. 34

m. 1   m. 2

By referring back to example 33, one can also see that there are three common tones beteen the first two chords: "w" in the first chord becomes the root in the second; likewise the seventh becomes the perfect fifth and the lowered fifth becomes "w." These common-tone relations appear again in the progression in mm. 5-6 but are not a prominent feature of the "b" section.

A final aspect of the harmonic texture worth noting is the way in which the upper members of chords are frequently isolated from the root so as to give them emphasis as an independent harmonic entity of a quality generally simpler than that of the basic chord. In the "a" section this isolated structure is a major seventh chord with the third omitted (m. 1, second eighth note). The repeated chords which herald the beginning of the "b" section add a minor third (enharmonically) to this structure (m. 11), perhaps as a theoretical reinforcement of the "w" in the two basic chords. Here, though, the isolated element appears first, with the lower members of the harmony entering only at the end of the measure, in reverse order in comparison to the opening: first the lowered fifth appears, then the root (the slower rhythmic movement—eighths rather than sixteenths—adds support to such an analysis). A final step in the evolution of this isolated element appears in m. 14 where, because of the nature of the melodic phrase, the major seventh no longer appears and the structure is simply a minor triad, enharmonically. The three isolated structures discussed above are shown in the next example:

Ex. 35

At this point the slight variation in texture in the second "b" section can be explained. There are two aspects of change. First, the melody is doubled in octaves in the right hand; this is seen first in m. 40 and continues through m. 49. Second, though all of the music of the repeat of "a" and "b" is in a higher register, because of the tritone transposition, the left hand part of the isolated element just discussed has been inverted. The reason is clearly because of the doubled melody in the right hand, which adds moving notes in the middle of the texture. The left hand inversion accommodates this need for space but, of course, in no way alters the harmonic structure of the section. The following example clarifies this change:

Ex. 36

In the concluding measure of the "b" section, mm. 24ff., the first noticeable change is the prominent introduction of the major third in place of "w," not as part of melodic activity as in m. 1 and elsewhere, but as an integral part of the chord. This occurs at the beginning of m. 24 and again one and two measures later.

Ex. 37

Of course, this use of the major third appears again, transposed, at the end of the second "b" section, mm. 52ff, and is retained throughout the codetta. The fact that the major third replaces "w" at the end of the "b" section, and even more prominently at the end of the work, lends a certain feeling of repose or resolution, perhaps compensating, if only theoretically, for the lack of a tonic cadence. It should be noted, however, that, coinciding with this introduction of the major third, the minor ninth also appears. The significance of this lies in the other appearances of the ninth, all of which were major (see ex. 33, second chord). In other words, balancing the change from the minor third to the major, Skryabin changes the major ninth to the minor.

An examination of the overall tonal structure of this work supports various aspects of the foregoing analysis and yields interesting results itself. The polarity of this work, that is, its reference tritone nucleus, is C-F#. Of course, this can be most easily verified by examining the ending, where the last chord is on the root C, which must then, according to Dernova, be DA. However, the harmonic organization of the whole prelude also leads to this analysis, and this is, after all, the important factor in determining the polarity.

Example 38 is a sketch showing all the root progressions of the work, arranged by formal sections.

Ex. 38

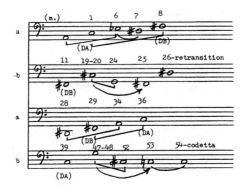

There are several important points to be made from examining this chart. The initial formal analysis was made on a motivic basis; here, it can be seen that differentiation in harmonic movement supports that analysis. The "a" sections show directed movement, first toward DB, then toward DA. The "b" sections show stability, the first one emphasizing DB, the second emphasizing DA. Within the "a" sections, the harmonic plan derives from a minor sequence. The "b" sections, on the other hand, display one type of functional sequence, the dominant on C# "resolving" (i.e., moving by fifth) through its theoretical equivalent in the tritone nucleus (on G) to the dominant on F#; in the second "b" section, the dominant on G "resolves" through its equivalent on C# to the dominant on C. This movement toward and emphasis on F# and C as the two focal points of the work conclusively support the linkage of C-F# as the central tritone nucleus.

The foregoing analysis demonstrates clearly that Dernova's system is capable of explaining much about the harmonic language and tonal order in Skryabin's music and that it also can support analytical observations made on the basis of principles not related to the duplex mode.

PRELUDE op. 59 no. 2

PRELUDE cont.

PRELUDE cont.

Poem op. 71 no. 2

The *Deux Poèmes* op. 71, dating from 1914, belong to those smaller piano works Skryabin wrote during the final months of his life. The formal structure of the second of these is exactly that of the prelude just examined. That is, it is in two halves, the second being a transposition (here, at the interval of a minor third) of the first half. In this case, the transposition is exact; nothing is changed. Likewise, each half may be further divided into two sections which are differentiated in various ways, but chiefly melodically. The first section is built from an ascending motive which is heard three times, each slightly different from the others. The second section is built from a contrasting motive which begins with a sustained trill leading to a descending line. This too is repeated and then fragmented as the trill is omitted. Thus we again have an overall structure which can be labeled "abab":

a	mm. 1-11
b	mm. 12-18
a	mm. 19-29
b	mm. 30-36

The final two measures of the piece are simply cadential: m. 37 repeats the top voice of m. 36 in a changed rhythmic guise; m. 38 brings back the opening chord of the entire piece, with the addition of the minor third, "w." Thus the initial impression of this work is one of even greater simplicity than in the earlier work, op. 59 no. 2. This simplicity extends, at least initially, to the area of harmonic language too, for the opening chord displays the typical root-seventh-third disposition that is such a characteristic stamp of Skryabin harmony. But it is just this simplicity of voicing which leads to the more complex chords encountered in the "b" section, about which more will presently be said.

It would seem advisable to deal first with harmonic material and tonal organization since melody is relatively more prominent here than in the work previously discussed. Because of the straightforward nature of the foundation of the chords of the "a" section—root, seventh, third, as previously mentioned—one encounters no problem in assigning chord roots there. The root progression of the "a" section is as follows:

Ex. 39

The brackets, as usual, show the tritone nuclei. The two ties indicate the repetition of the initial chord of a nucleus. The basis for this passage is a minor sequence, but it is handled in a unique manner. Here is the underlying minor sequence:

Ex. 40

The plan of the section is a movement from the basic DA-DB nucleus to first one and then the other chord of the second pair (see ex. 39). The reason for the minor third transposition for the second half of the work is now clear: it results in a reversal of the two chord pairs in example 40, DA now being the last chord of the sequence. Example 41A shows this reversal; example 41B shows its realization in the second "a" section.

Ex. 41

The middle and upper voices in the texture of the "a" section fill in the remaining chord tones in various ways. The stability of the three-part harmonic foundation allows a great deal of freedom in the upper voices; each note could simply be assigned a harmonic label according to Dernova's system (as she herself occasionally does), but to do so here would put too little emphasis on the melodic character of these voices. In the following discussion, only significant harmonic relationships will be emphasized. Thus, in m. 1, following the left-hand statement of the harmonic foundation, the half-note B♭ adds the raised fifth (A♯). In m. 2, the three-note figure beginning on the second beat descends to this same raised fifth in relation to the chord on G♯. This brief motive recurs in mm. 7 and 9-11, and is absorbed into the end of the descending melody of the "b" section (m. 13, last three notes in the right hand, and mm. 15-18 in comparable positions). The harmonic significance of a part of this motive—its consistent conclusion on the raised fifth of the supporting harmony—is particularly important in explaining some of the more complex chords of the "b" section, as will be seen.

The principal melody of the "a" section begins, in m. 1, on the minor ninth, E_b, of the first chord and ascends to the lowered fifth, D, of the second. This relationship remains consistent at the melody's repetitions in mm. 6-7 and 8-9. In mm. 3-4 the melody descends chromatically, ending in a trill on, again, the lowered fifth, B (C_b), of the supporting chord, on F, the first chord of the second pair of the minor sequence (see ex. 39). This chromatic descent is accompanied by an inner voice which begins in m. 2 on the lowered fifth, D (doubling the melody), and ascends to the ninth, G, in m. 4. A third chromatic line begins at the end of m. 3, connecting the third of the chord on D with the seventh of the chord on F at the beginning of the next measure. Still another chromatic line appears briefly at the end of the arpeggio in mm. 4 and 5, perhaps preparing the slow chromatic ascent in the melody which ends the "a" section, mm. 9-11. This abundance of chromatic movement gives variety to the otherwise static harmonic language and also lends motivic coherence to this section.

The "b" section begins with simultaneous contrast and similarity. The three-note harmonic foundation, ascending to the raised fifth as a half note, is retained from the opening of "a." The trill in the melody is reminiscent of the sustained trill in mm. 4-5, but harmonically it represents "w," the minor third of the chord, appearing simultaneously with the major third in a lower voice:

Ex. 42

m. 12

The minor third, "w," only appears once in the "a" section, and then only as a passing tone (F, m. 3). Thus, the prominent appearance of it here gives a striking means of articulating the second section of the work. At the end of m. 12 "w" descends to the ninth, G (F##), which is carried over to the next measure as an anticipation of the raised fifth of the following chord, on B. This line continues, ending with the three-note motive from m. 2 of the "a" section, as mentioned earlier.

In m. 13, the harmonic foundation is changed for the first time; in place of the seventh, the lowered fifth, E#, appears between the root and the third of the chord. This lends particular ambiguity for two reasons: this lowered fifth is equal to the root of the preceding chord, and the interval between the lowered fifth and the third is a minor seventh. Since the third and seventh of chords a tritone apart exchange identity in a tritone progression, and since the seventh, A, does appear in m. 13, there is the very pertinent question of whether the harmony of this measure is the root position of a chord on B, or the second inversion of a chord on E♯. Both possibilities are shown by the labels in example 43.

Ex. 43

The solution is found in the upper voices. First there is the appearance of the half-note C, coming at that point where, in m. 2, the harmonic foundation had led to the appearance of the important three-note motive. In that measure, the motive began on the minor ninth and descended to the raised fifth. In m. 13, C is a minor ninth above B and, though that voice does not continue the three-note motive, it prepares the motive's appearance in the upper voice, C-A-G. Thus, it appears that B should be considered the chord root at this point.

Ex. 44

As the "b" section continues, it becomes apparent that the introduction of this ambiguity was not whimsical or fortuitous. For, in m. 16, following the repetition of mm. 12-13, a chord appears which makes the question of proper root analysis even more difficult. It appears as an articulating element for the two-measure thematic unit of this section and coincides with what Dernova terms "structural dissociation"; i.e., the melody is fragmented: mm. 16-18 present three statements of the last half of the thematic unit. As an articulating chord repeating the harmony of mm. 13 and 15, the root of this chord could still be considered as B, as it was analyzed above. However, to the seventh, A, has been added the sixth, G♯; the lowered fifth, E♯, now appears below the root:

Ex. 45

Though the above analysis of this chord as an inversion of a chord on B poses no problems, the context suggests another possibility, one that Dernova applies in similar situations: the concept of a summary dominant. Though this view of the chord is a highly theoretical one, it includes interesting relationships with the "b" section as a whole. Example 46 shows this analysis.

Ex. 46

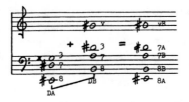

(The designation of DA and DB here are only for the purpose of chord designation and have no relation to the basic nucleus for the entire piece, which is D-G#, as will be discussed below.) From this analysis we can see the interconnection of the two principal chords of the "b" section as well as a possible explanation for the use of "w" in mm. 12 and 14. Viewed this way, the initial ambiguity is actually a basic characteristic of this segment, both expressively and theoretically; the summary dominant of m. 16 demonstrates the fundamental harmonic unity of the section.

There is one more item of interest related to the preceding. In m. 18, the third statement of the fragmented "b" theme, the relationship between the previously discussed melodic elements and the underlying harmony (see ex. 44) has changed. Instead of the root appearing first, followed by the lowered fifth, the reverse is seen. That this is the correct way of viewing the harmony is demonstrated first of all by the melody:

Ex. 47

In other words, this analysis allows the harmony and melody to retain the same relationship seen in every previous statement. Further support for this analysis is found in m. 19, where the return of "a" begins with a chord in F. The last chord of the "b" section thus becomes a logical preparation for the return of "a." (Note also the change in notation: compare m. 16 with m. 18.)

All of the preceding commentary applies similarly to the second half of the piece, since the transposition is exact. Before overall tonal order is examined, however, the concluding cadence deserves discussion. By analogy with m. 18, the root of the harmony in m. 36 is G♯. Since m. 37 repeats the same melodic notes found in m. 36 with changed rhythm, the harmony should be viewed only as an inversion of the harmonic foundation of m. 36, the root, G♯, now appearing as the lowest-sounding note. The final chord forms an effective cadence (in the best sense of the word) for several reasons. It is less ambiguous than the preceding chord since its lowest notes are the root and major third. It forms a tritone nucleus with the preceding chord, thus reversing the opening two chords of the work, a progression from D to G♯. Finally, the last chord contains as its highest note a reminiscence of the minor third, "w," which opened the "b" section; here F conflicts with the major third F♯. In addition to the reappearance of "w," the final chord brings back the entire opening chord of the piece, distinguished particularly by the minor ninth and the raised fifth, as was previously pointed out. Thus, the concluding cadence brings not only a feeling of relative repose but also fulfills an extremely concise coda-like function for the rest of the work.

Since harmony, melody, and form have all been discussed, the overall tonal plan of this poem can now be shown in example 48.

Ex. 48

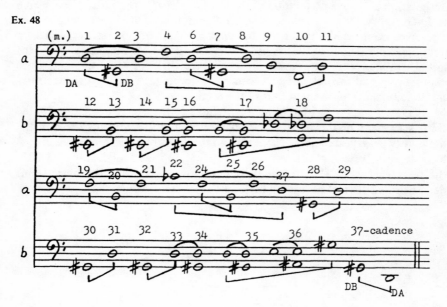

Ex. 48 cont.

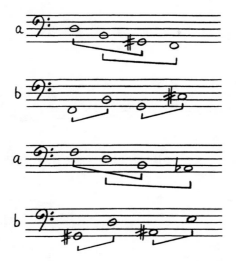

The organization within each section has already been treated, with the exception of noting the whole-step relation near the end of each "b" section: mm. 16-17 and 34-35. This relationship comes, of course, from the major enharmonic sequence. In addition to the second "a" section being a reversal of the minor sequence of the first "a," each "b" section is now seen clearly to be but an extension of the nucleus closing the preceding "a." Again, as with the other work analyzed, one cannot help but note the close connection between the tonal plan and formal structure, a traditional concept applied here in a unique manner, as revealed by Dernova's analytical method.

POEM

En rêvant, avec une grande douceur

Op. 71 Nr. 2

POEM cont.

Having thus explained and demonstrated the fundamental principles of the tritone nucleus system which Dernova derived from Yavorsky's duplex mode, it remains only to attempt to put her work into perspective as regards both Soviet and non-Soviet theoretical work of this century. Of course, her system was derived specifically in relation to indications in the music of Skryabin. Although she and a few students have attempted to apply the system to music by other composers, there is as of yet no convincing evidence that such applications are leading to results as significant as with analysis of Skryabin's music. This, perhaps, is to be expected, given the unique language and thought of Skryabin; it in no way diminishes the importance of Dernova's discoveries. However, a comparison of Dernova to other theorists is generally of value only if their work touches on Skryabin's music, since Dernova, unlike Yavorsky, was not attempting to devise a universal analytical theory.

It is important from the standpoint of logic that Dernova's theory does not totally refute all of the analytical work done by other Skryabinists. In many cases it amplifies and clarifies their work. It is equally important that her theory, despite its relationship to the concepts of Yavorsky, basically grew directly out of the music itself, much as the difficult late style of music is seen to have grown directly out of the post-romantic tradition. To elaborate, Dernova gives a sound theoretical basis to the term *dominant* as applied to Skryabin's harmony, showing the degree of qualification involved and establishing a clear connection between the term and Skryabin's evolving technical and expressive language. In addition, she has finally established a system for discovering organization in chord progression. The question of resolution, always a problem in former uses of the term *dominant,* can thus be dealt with for the first time. Finally, the term *atonal* can be justifiably dropped from the analytical vocabulary for Skryabin; the long-observed uniformity in beginning and ending harmonies in many of his late works has now been incorporated by Dernova into a system based on the supremacy of a specific enharmonic relationship as the harmonic focus of a given work.

Dernova's system is, of course, based on a single chord, a common thread with those analysts who espouse the "mystic" chord theory. The important difference is, as was stated earlier, that Dernova's chord leads to the creation of a structural model that can then be used to answer satisfactorily important questions in addition to those simply dealing with chord structure (e.g., chord progression and connection). The "mystic" chord has no such capability, providing only a standard against which to measure as variants other of Skryabin's unique chord structures.[32] Furthermore, Dernova uses her chord *only* as a source of the structural model; nowhere does she claim that Skryabin used it as a fundamental structure himself. Rather, it is the dominant-like nature of that chord and all its variants which was important to his music, a point particularly well taken in light of the clear evolution of Skryabin's harmonic thought.

As to the theory of quartal harmony, Dernova convincingly demonstrates the fundamental tertian nature of Skryabin's harmonic vocabulary, properly relegating its quartal aspect to the area of chord distribution rather than chord structure. The totally correct and, from an expressive standpoint, important observation that Skryabin preferred chords voiced in fourths is not weakened at all by this. Likewise, the view that Skryabin was unconsciously working in a proto-serial manner is not totally incompatible with Dernova's system, at least not with its structural model. The fact that the model is based on a closed set of six pitches, that there is a means for progressing logically to the other closed set, that both harmonic and melodic material can be derived from the set—all of these are characteristics which point even more clearly than before to yet another anticipation of the serial technique.[33] Of all the methods of analysis mentioned at the beginning of this article, perhaps the only one to receive no particular support from Dernova's research is the so-called ultrachromatic or acoustic theory. However, its speculative nature and logical fallacies were already realized shortly after Skryabin's death; its persistence in contemporary Skryabin literature is a lamentable but altogether predictable facet of the renaissance of interest in the composer.

There are various other important studies of Skryabin's music, several of which are essentially nonharmonic in nature. Study of the music's scalar nature has a minor echo in Dernova's work which causes little if any disagreement except as to the level of its overall importance. The study by Ellon Carpenter on thematic unity arrives at many conclusions totally in agreement with Dernova's harmonic theory; studies by Hanns Steger on the motivic basis of Skryabin's sonata forms proceed on a level essentially removed from detailed considerations of harmonic organization (see note 2). A recent dissertation by James Baker on the evolution of Skryabin's tonal thinking remains unavailable for study but an article by the same author involving a Schenkerian approach to analysis indicates again an individuality of aim but not wholly incompatible results.[34] In other words, despite the extremely important role of Dernova's work in the field of Skryabin analysis, it does not preclude the use of other techniques to examine or emphasize other compositional traits. Rather, its thorough handling of questions of harmony and harmonic organization can allow other approaches to proceed on a more uniform and firm basis.

As far as Dernova's fellow theorists in the USSR are concerned, the matter of their relationship to her work is only partially clear. It can be seen, after studying this article and the McQuere article on Yavorsky, that Dernova, despite her avowed esteem for the theorist, used his concepts only in a very general way. This may partially explain her lack of enthusiasm for the work of Protopopov who, while claiming to be speaking for Yavorsky in his analyses of Skryabin's music, is said by her to be guilty both of a misunderstanding of Yavorsky and of faulty analytical procedure.[35] No contemporary Soviet analytical work on Skryabin's music has dealt seriously with Dernova's revelations as a basis for related studies. Sergei Pavchinsky's 1969 study of Skryabin's late period[36] makes only passing, though favorable, mention of Dernova's article analyzing *Enigma* op. 52 no. 2. Viktor Delson's 1971 biography of the composer[37] contains no thorough analyses, despite a great deal of attention to the music from a descriptive standpoint. The work of Dernova's mentors, Tiulin in fact and Yavorsky in spirit, is mentioned in Delson's biography; Dernova herself is not. Dernova's own article in the Skryabin centenary collection mentioned earlier is one of several analytical views presented there, along with those of Pavchinsky, Dobrynin, and Zhitomirsky. The last-named author also wrote the article on Skryabin for the new *Muzykal'naia entsiklopediia;*[38] it too is essentially nonanalytical. The only mention there of Dernova's contributions is the listing of *Garmoniia Skriabina* in the bibliography. In another article, presented as a lecture for the Moscow Symposium observing the Skryabin centennial in 1972,[39] Zhitomirsky credits Dernova with finding the connection between traditional tonality and tritone enharmonic relations, but the focus remains on the apparently widespread Soviet view that the Promethean chord was merely the "tonic" of a new brand of tonality. Thus, despite the professional status Dernova seems to have achieved in the Soviet Union, as a Skryabin analyst she seems to be regarded only as one of many who have been fascinated enough by the unique idiom to write about it.

And what of these other modern analysts and their approaches? Surprisingly, in light of Dernova's innovative and very fruitful study, little new has surfaced in other studies. The one-chord theory (with its *Klangzentrum* counterpart in German research) is most prominent, describing all other late-period harmony as variants of the Promethean chord. Traditional terminology is stretched quite far at times to attempt to retain its applicability to Skryabin's late works. Pavchinsky and Zhitomirsky go so far as to assign traditional keys to some of these late pieces, retaining major/minor mode references as part of an apparently expanded view of what can constitute an extension of traditional tonality. Generally speaking, there is a diversity of viewpoints and an emphasis on detailed description rather than on overall structural organization. Dernova's study seems unique both in its comprehensive approach and in its freedom from ideological or philosophical constraints.

In sum, Dernova seems to have accomplished what any astute analyst should always hope to accomplish. She examined the music thoroughly, ascertaining that a basic analytical problem—harmonic organization—was of fundamental importance but was not sufficiently or accurately understood by the theorists who preceded her, and then devised a method of analysis to solve the immediate problem in a way that was not only compatible with the musical evidence, but also applicable to other parameters of the music. In the process she uncovered a relation between Skryabin's music and the theories of Boleslav Yavorsky which had long been known and which Yavorsky himself had discussed and demonstrated for his students, but which had never before been so thoroughly and convincingly revealed. Finally, and of the greatest general significance, Dernova's study proves that Skryabin was not simply a maverick forging totally new paths or given wholly to atonal meanderings dictated by whim or impossible-to-fathom philosophies. Rather, he was a true heir of nineteenth-century tradition who found, perhaps quite unconsciously, a means of squeezing yet one more expressive language out of what seemed to some in his day to be a totally depleted tonal system. He refined this language with a highly restrictive technique into a cohesive unity of style that contained, among other qualities, a clear and logical bridge over the chasm between traditional tonality and certain aspects of serialism. Dernova has revealed a unique Janus-like image of Skryabin, one that has been sensed by many listeners and students of his music, but one which now has been supplied with a solid theoretical foundation.

Notes

1. Leonid Sabaneev, *Vospominaniia o Skriabine* [Reminiscences of Skryabin] (Moscow: Music Division of the State Publishing House, 1925), p. 47. Cited in Varvara Dernova, *Garmoniia Skriabina* [The Harmony of Skryabin] (Leningrad: Muzyka, 1968), p. 69.

2. There are various theoretical studies with a principally nonharmonic focus: Ellon Carpenter, "Thematic Development and Continuity in Skryabin's Ten Piano Sonatas" (M.A. thesis, Kent State University, 1971) and Hanns Steger, *Der Weg der Klaviersonate bei Alexander Skrjabin* (Munich: Wollenweber, 1979), to name but two. The final statement here is not to be construed as a refutation of the validity of these and other types of examinations, but rather is made to emphasize the extreme importance for Skryabin's music of relating the results of such examinations to the harmonic context.

3. For example, in Willi Apel, *Harvard Dictionary of Music,* 2nd ed. (Cambridge: Belknap Press of Harvard University Press, 1969), p. 562, there is a brief article, "Mystic Chord," discussing its significance in Skryabin's output; and Hugh MacDonald, in his article on Skryabin in *The New Grove Dictionary of Music and Musicians,* ed. Stanley Sadie (London: Macmillan Publishers Ltd., 1980), 17:373, says that "Skryabin's last works, from 1910 to 1915, are constructed from... variants of the so-called 'mystic' chord...."

4. Sofia Lissa, "Geschichtliche Vorform der Zwölftontechnik," *Acta Musicologica* 7 (January, 1935): 15-21.

5. George Perle, *Serial Composition and Atonality,* 4th ed. (Berkeley, University of California Press, 1977), pp. 41-43.

6. Donald Grout, *History of Western Music,* 3rd ed. (New York: W.W. Norton, 1979), p. 659: "The last five [piano sonatas]... attain a harmonic vagueness amounting at times to atonality." Stanley Krebs' article on Skryabin in *Dictionary of Contemporary Music,* ed. John Vinton (New York: E.P. Dutton, 1974), p. 667, includes this statement: "His fourth chords, invented modes and scales, and harmonic motionlessness were synthesized into an impressionistic atonality."

7. G.H. Clutsam, in "More Harmonies of Skryabin," *The Musical Times* 54 (August, 1913): 512, says that the Promethean chord, statements of which "Skryabin persists in with unvarying deliberation, becomes an essential in his harmonic methods . . . based functionally as they are on . . . the dominant thirteenth."

8. Paul Dickenmann, *Die Entwicklung der Harmonik bei A. Scrjabin* (Bern and Leipzig: Paul Haupt, 1935); Boris Schloezer, *Alexander Scriabine,* trans. Maya Minoustchnie, intro. Marina Scriabine (Berlin: Grani, 1923; Paris:Librairie des Cinq Continents, 1975); Clemens-Christoph von Gleich, "Skrjabin, Alexander Nikolajewitsch," in *Die Musik in Geschichte und Gegenwart* (Kassel: Bärenreiter, 1951-67), vol. 12, cols. 751-58.

9. See Stanley Krebs' article. Gerald Abraham, in *The Modern Age,* vol. 10 of *The New Oxford History of Music,* ed. Martin Cooper (London: Oxford University Press, 1974), says: "The only composer to construct a system of fourth-chords was Skryabin" (p. 133).

10. Ellon Carpenter, in the work already cited, shows clearly that thirds and sixths are by far the dominant motivic intervals in Skryabin's themes.

11. Leonid Sabaneev, *A.N. Skriabin,* 2nd ed. (Moscow, 1923), pp. 115-17.

12. Arseny Avraamov, "Ul'trakhromatism ili omnitonal'nost'" [Ultrachromaticism or omnitonality], *Muzykal'nyi sovremennik* [The musical contemporary] (April-May, 1916); Leonid Sabaneev, "Ul'trakhromaticheskaia polemika" [Ultrachromatic polemics] *Muzykal'nyi sovremennik* (February, 1916), pp. 99-108.

13. See Abraham and Krebs.

14. Sabaneev, *A.N. Skriabin;* Arthur E. Hull, *A Great Russian Tone-Poet—Scriabin* (London: Kegan Paul, Trench, Trubner and Co., Ltd., 1916); Alfred J. Swan, *Scriabin* (1923; reprint ed., New York: Da Capo Press, 1969).

15. Arthur E. Hull, "The Pianoforte Sonatas of Scriabin," *The Musical Times* 57 (November and December, 1916): 492-95; 539-42.

16. Perle, *Serial Composition,* p. 41.

17. John E. Cheetham, "Quasi-serial Techniques in the Late Piano Works of Alexander Scriabin" (Part I of D.M.A. dissertation, University of Washington, 1969); Felix Loren Powell, "Grouping of Vertical Structures in Selected Later Piano Works of Alexander Scriabin" (Part I of D.M.A. dissertation, University of Washington, 1970).

18. Manfred Kelkel, *Alexandre Scriabine; sa vie, l'ésotérisme et le langage musical dans son oeuvre* (Paris: Editions Honoré Champion, 1978); Adrian Raţiu, "Sistemul armonic al lui Skriabin" [Skryabin's harmonic system], *Muzica* 22 (February and March, 1972): 17-23; 15-20.

19. Information for this biographical sketch was put together primarily from Dernova's letters to the author. A brief biography and list of works may be found in *Kto pisal o muzyke* [Writers on music], vol. 1 (Moscow: Sovetskii kompozitor, 1971), p. 272.

20. Varvara Dernova, "Garmoniia Skriabina" (unpublished dissertation, Leningrad Conservatory, 1973); this is a somewhat abbreviated version of her book of the same title.

21. Included in *Alexander Skrjabin; Studien zur Wertungsforschung,* vol. 13, ed. Otto Kolleritsch (Graz: Universal Edition, 1980).

22. Besides her doctoral dissertation, there is an article in the collection *A.N. Skriabin; sbornik statei* [A.N. Skryabin; collected articles], ed. Sergei Pavchinsky and Viktor Zuckermann (Moscow: Sovetskii kompozitor, 1973); her analysis of *Enigma* op. 52 no. 1, in *Teoreticheskie problemy muzyki XX veka* [Theoretical problems in 20th-century music], ed. Yury Tiulin

(Moscow: Muzyka, 1967); an analysis of op. 59 no. 1 to be published in Leningrad as part of the collection *Russkaia muzyka* [Russian music]; and finally her paper for the Graz symposium.

23. Faubion Bowers, *The New Scriabin: Enigma and Answers* (New York: St. Martin's Press, 1973); Gottfried Eberle, *Zwischen Tonalität und Atonalität. Studien zur Harmonik Alexander Skrjabins (Berliner Musikwissenschaftliche Arbeiten,* vol. 14 (Munich and Salzburg: Katzbichler, 1978); Roy J. Guenther, "Varvara Dernova's *Garmoniia Skriabina;* A Translation and Critical Commentary" (Ph.D. dissertation, The Catholic University of America, 1979); Jim Samson, *Music in Transition: a study of tonal expansion and atonality, 1900-1920* (London: J.M. Dent & Sons, Ltd., 1977); Hanns Steger, *Der Weg der Klaviersonate.*

24. For the sake of faithfulness to Dernova's study, her use of "dominant" as a convenient label for any chord structure containing a root, major third, and minor seventh will be retained. To maintain clarity, however, the discussion which follows will always indicate whether a true functional dominant is involved or whether it is only that chord structure which is being referred to.

25. Dernova, *Garmoniia Skriabina,* p. 38.

26. Though Skryabin had by this time abandoned key signatures, the V-I progression at the beginning of the cited passage justifies both the assignment of G_b as the key (though admittedly it is weakly felt) and the unusual explanation of the final chord.

27. Dernova, *Garmoniia Skriabina,* p. 48.

28. Dernova actually ascribes an element of "control" to this split fifth, saying that it controls the motion between chord transpositions. For example, she observes that the split fifth separates into a major ninth in the tritone nucleus (*Garmoniia Skriabina,* p. 25, ex. 9; the numeral 8 refers to the chord root):

Ex. A

In a major third relation, that is, between pairs of chords in a major enharmonic sequence, the split fifth separates into a minor seventh (Dernova's ex. 9 continued):

Ex. B

These observations are correct, of course, and they happen regularly in the major enharmonic sequence, but they are a product of the whole-tone nature of the system, not a controlling factor in it. Because of the closed pitch set and repeating chord structure of the model, various observations could be made about a pitch and its position in the chords, but to call such relations "regulatory" only obscures the importance of the whole-tone scale in determining the unique properties of Dernova's theoretical construction.

29.   Note that other forms of the fifth create no such problem. The lowered and raised fifths form the root and major ninth respectively of the other chord in the nucleus. The perfect fifth would form a minor ninth, creating merely another variant chord structure; it alters the whole-tone nature of Dernova's model chord but it does not detract from its dominant-like quality as determined by the root, major third, and minor seventh.

30.   Dernova, *Garmoniia Skriabina*, p. 51.

31.   The author wishes to note here that these analyses, as well as many of the ideas expressed in this article, appeared first in similar form in his doctoral dissertation, listed in note 23. Anyone familiar with that work will notice a few changes in basic vocabulary, made for the sake of uniformity within this collection: tritone nucleus rather than tritone link; duplex mode rather than dual-polarity; modal rhythm rather than polar attraction.

32.   Manfred Kelkel, in the book mentioned earlier (note 18), derives a system of progression based on common tones between transpositions of the "mystic" chord. This is parallel to the work of Dernova, to which Kelkel makes no reference, but is limited because of the non-whole-tone nature of the "mystic" chord.

33.   For the sake of accuracy, it should be noted that Dernova's model is, in a serial sense, more closely related to the tropes of Josef Hauer than to the full-blown technique of Arnold Schönberg, since pitch *order* is not a matter of concern.

34.   James M. Baker, "Alexander Scriabin: The Transition from Tonality to Atonality" (Ph.D. dissertation, Yale University, 1977), and "Scriabin's Implicit Tonality," *Music Theory Spectrum* 2 (1980): 1-18.

35.   Dernova, *Garmoniia Skriabina*, pp. 15-16, and in a letter to the author, dated 21 December, 1975.

36.   Sergei Pavchinsky, *Proizvedeniia Skriabina pozdnego perioda* [The works of Skryabin's late period] (Moscow: Muzyka, 1969).

37.   Viktor Delson, *Skriabin: Ocherki zhizni i tvorchestva* [Skryabin: essays on the life and works] (Moscow: Muzyka, 1971).

38.   Daniel Zhitomirsky, "Skriabin, Alexandr Nikolaevich," in *Muzykal'naia entsiklopediia*, ed. Yu. V. Keldysh (Moscow: Sovetskaia entsiklopediia, 1973-1982), vol. 5, cols. 66-76.

39.   Published in German as "Die Harmonik Skrjabins" in *Convivium Musicorum: Festschrift Wolfgang Boetticher* (Berlin: Verlag Merseburger, 1974).

Boris Asafiev and *Musical Form as a Process*

Gordon D. McQuere

Of the numerous studies in the vast legacy of Boris Vladimirovich Asafiev (1884-1949), one major work, in two parts, falls under the heading of music theory. Its title, *Musical Form as a Process,* indicates that it is anything but a conventional survey of traditional forms. In fact, it is an attempt to express his unique, personal concept of the origins and operations of music, coming closer to music philosophy than to a survey of forms. As a prime example of twentieth-century *musica speculativa,* it offers the reader nearly equal measures of frustration and reward. The difficulties in studying Asafiev's theories are of a different sort from those found in the study of other Russian and Soviet music theorists. Certainly there is no shortage of data. Possessing seemingly boundless energy, Asafiev, who is considered the founder of Soviet musicology, left hundreds of written works about a wide range of musical topics. This legacy has been continually reissued and investigated by Soviet scholars, and several important works have appeared in English translations.[1] The challenge is that of drawing this diverse, sometimes contradictory but always stimulating, body of material into focus, of finding the essence of Asafiev's thought. His opaque, complex style and his penchant for undefined neologisms exacerbate the problem. The rewards of such an effort lie, however, in the opportunity to follow in the path of a vast intellect that unfailingly precipitates a revaluation of the commonplace and to observe as he helps to found Soviet musicology.

Even determining Asafiev's role in musical society is difficult. Not only a musicologist and theorist, he also functioned as a composer of substantial repute, an influential critic, an educator, a pianist, an authority on the theater (and especially the ballet), and above all, a "publicist" who carried art to the masses. But for Asafiev, each of these roles was a different manifestation of the same musical essence. His scholarly works take up the same themes found in his popular pamphlets; only the emphasis shifts. Even his compositions betray his ideas about music as an intonational language. And in all his works he writes with the passion of someone in a hurry to get on with an overwhelming task.

Asafiev's theoretical statement, *Musical Form as a Process,* contains two substantially different parts. The first part, published in 1930, bears the same title as the entire work. The second, entitled *Intonation,* appeared in 1947.[2] Along with these two works, which are usually (but perhaps not correctly) considered as two volumes of one work, there are a number of other publications, about composers and repertoire, that function as practical reflections of these ideas.[3] In all his works, Asafiev attempts to explain the processes at work in music, from the nature of forms and their evolution to the nature of musical communication. He is not diverted by issues of harmony or technique; even in his vast output, one finds almost nothing related to the pedagogical aspects of music theory.

This remarkable musician was born in 1884 in St. Petersburg, the son of a minor official.[4] Even though the family was not particularly musical, Boris showed talent at an early age. Musical studies at home were continued part-time during his years of study at the Kronstadt gymnasium, from which he graduated in 1903. His education continued at the University in St. Petersburg in history and philology, with specialization in the Renaissance and in nineteenth-century Russia; he graduated in 1908. Meanwhile, Asafiev was continuing musical studies. Rimsky-Korsakov had been amply impressed with Asafiev's talent following their meeting in 1904, for he encouraged him to take instruction in the conservatory along with his university study. Lessons there in composition were under Anatoly Lyadov, and instrumentation under Rimsky-Korsakov. Among his student associates were the young composers Myaskovsky and Prokofiev. In the summer of 1904, Asafiev had also met Vladimir Stasov, who, while not a composer, had been a member of the Balakirev circle and remained an important critic. Through him, Asafiev managed to secure a position in the St. Petersburg Public Library, where he worked with Stasov in the history of art and music, and on bibliographic and archival techniques. "[My] acquaintance with Stasov," Asafiev writes,

> had the great significance of enabling me to work with him in the Public Library and to obtain the books I needed besides allowing me to be present (at his Sunday gatherings) in an artistic atmosphere (Repin, Chaliapin, Glazunov, the Blumenfel'd brothers, Lyadov, and others).[5]

On Stasov's influence he continues, "I am indebted to him for persistence and a stubborn belief in the invincible strength of an idea, if only it be organically vital."[6]

The death of Rimsky-Korsakov in 1908 presented Asafiev with a crisis, since he had hoped to study composition with the eminent composer. Having just completed the university, Asafiev decided to cease further formal training at the conservatory in order to work on his own. He did continue lessons with Lyadov, but privately. Through about 1910, Asafiev composed a number of works, including some large ones such as the children's opera *Snezhnaia koroleva* [The Snow Queen] in 1907; it was produced in 1908.[7]

In 1910 he secured his first professional position, starting as rehearsal pianist for the ballet troupe of the Maryinsky theater. This experience undoubtedly contributed both to his later success as a ballet composer and to his considerable insight into and appreciation for musical theater. The summer months he spent abroad, studying in the museums of France, Germany, and Italy; these trips enabled him to continue the broad intellectual and aesthetic development he had begun at the university and under Stasov.

The year 1914 marked a turning point for Asafiev, for at that time his first attempts at music criticism appeared in the journal *Muzyka* [Music]. These appeared under the pseudonym of "Igor Glebov," who became something of a sensation and a mystery in the St. Petersburg musical community. For a brief time in 1916 Asafiev also wrote for the journal *Muzykal'nyi sovremennik* [The musical contemporary], but, after a dispute with the editors, left to help establish a new journal *Muzykal'naia mysl'* [Musical thought] early in the year 1917. While this journal was never published, some of its contents appeared in two separate volumes entitled *Melos.*[8] These already betray Asafiev's strong opinions and highly developed aesthetic sense.[9] Thus, just at the time of the Revolution, Asafiev emerged as a completely formed scholar and musician, one whose later course became closely bound up with that of the new regime.

From 1919 to 1930 Asafiev worked in the Russian Institute for the History of the Arts (RIII), after 1920 serving as head of the section for the history of music. This first decade of the Soviet era, a time of optimism for many scholars, saw an initial flowering of Asafiev's mature scholarly work. His vast production was very influential and helped to establish standards and directions for incipient Soviet musicology. Three works of the period, each relating in some measure to music theory, deserve mention here. The first is *Symphonic Etudes,* 1922, a collection of articles on a wide variety of topics in Russian music, but especially stressing opera.[10] Of particular interest is the organization of the work, in which a number of short essays called "etudes"— in the sense of exercises that might be used later in some other way—are marked off by set pieces, called "intermezzos." The title of the last essay is "In lieu of a Finale" [Vmesto finala]. The idea that a book might be organized in a kind of musical structure foreshadows some of his later works, particularly *Intonation.*

The second major work, *A Book about Stravinsky,* written in 1926 and published in 1929, gives witness to Asafiev's love of Russian music and to his perceptive understanding of what at that time seemed like imponderable complexities in Stravinsky's music.[11] The third work is *Musical Form as a Process,* 1930, the first volume of the work that is the primary subject of this essay.[12] As the culmination of his studies up to this time, Asafiev presents his ideas on the nature of musical forms and their relationship to musical language and to society. Using polemical language and controversial themes, he sharply distinguishes between his ideas and those current in his day.

In his role of educator, Asafiev led seminars at the Russian Institute for the History of the Arts and also taught a wide range of subjects at the Leningrad Conservatory, where he was named professor. This position was continued until 1943, at which time he moved to Moscow to become professor at the Moscow Conservatory and to direct its research section.[13]

During the late 1920s and early 1930s, Asafiev came under ever increasing criticism from the proletarian factions in the musical community for his strong defense of contemporary music and advanced ideas, both domestic and foreign.[14] The Party Resolution of 1932, which established the Union of Soviet Composers (including musicologists), helped to alleviate the situation. However, the resolution, which marked the beginning of Party control over music, led eventually to the ascendancy of a much more conservative approach to music and music scholarship.[15] These general changes presented Asafiev with a great personal crisis. His conciliatory attitude showed a determination to cooperate, but his practical response was to return to composition, where he found a successful means of expression as a composer of ballets.[16] Thus came into being the compositions for which he is most famous, *The Flames of Paris* [Plamia Parizha] (1932), *The Fountain of Bakhchisarai* [Bakhchisaraiskii fontan] (1933), and *A Prisoner of the Caucasus* [Kavkazskii plennik] (1936), plus a great many others. At least one work, *The Fountain of Bakhchisarai,* has entered the standard Soviet ballet repertoire.

Even as a composer, however, Asafiev could not free himself completely from his scholarly bent, and at one time referred to himself as a "composing historian."[17] Thus, for example, while working on a ballet or opera he would attempt to immerse himself in the musical and verbal language of the appropriate era in order to convey more accurately its intonational essence. Such a connection with his theoretical ideas may be observed in the ballet *The Flames of Paris,* which uses intonations derived from songs of the era of the French revolution. For another work, the opera *Altynchech,* he undertook the study of the Tatar language, as well as its folk music.[18]

The pent up scholarly energy from the 1930s resulted in another flowering of theoretical and critical works in the decade preceding his death in 1949. The culmination of his theoretical efforts was reached in the second volume of *Musical Form as a Process,* entitled *Intonation* [Intonatsiia].[19] Taking the ideas of the preceding volume as givens, it explores the historical development of musical language from the aspect of intonation theory. As in the earlier period, Asafiev in the 1940s also wrote works related to specific composers or pieces. The most significant of these are *Eugene Onegin, Lyric Scenes of Tchaikovsky: An Attempt at Intonational Analysis of Its Style and Dramaturgy* (1944), *Glinka* (1947), and *Grieg (1843-1907): Research* (1948), plus many smaller works.[20] A number of these were projected as parts of a larger cycle of investigations to be called *Ideas and Thoughts,* which was to include works of all types in three categories: (1) about himself and his works, (2) monographs, and (3) historical and theoretical experiments.[21] The work on intonations fell in the latter category. Although the cycle was left unfinished, the completed portions represent a cross section of the kinds of ideas that interested Asafiev in this period.

During World War II, Asafiev found himself trapped in the blockaded city of Leningrad for about a year and a half. In typical fashion he used the time to continue his writing even under the most adverse circumstances; it was at this time that *Intonation* was born. In 1943 Asafiev was elected to the Academy of Sciences of the USSR, an honor never before accorded a musician. This honor firmly established him as the focus of Soviet musicology. Just before Asafiev's death in 1949 another difficult era for Soviet musicians occurred, and a question is sometimes raised concerning Asafiev's role in the attacks on composers and scholars of the year 1948, because a speech was delivered in his name. Both Alexander Werth and Andrey Olkhovsky express doubt at any complicity on Asafiev's part, and Olkhovsky sees his former mentor as attempting to maintain intellectual freedom during that very trying era.[22] Whatever the truth, it seems clear that Asafiev was throughout his life able to adjust to changing conditions in very resourceful ways in order to preserve his ability to communicate his ideas on music.

That Asafiev dominated the development of Soviet music scholarship is illustrated by the variety, and also by the staggering number of his works. Elena Orlova lists some 944 literary works and 202 compositions.[23] Besides the many brief works—reviews, introductions, and the like—he wrote a substantial number of major works. Likewise the list of compositions includes eleven operas and twenty-eight ballets, along with five symphonies. The bibliographies also show how his emphasis shifted from scholarly writing to composition in the 1930s. For example, the year 1926 provided 112 written works but only one composition. On the other hand, the year 1938 yielded only three brief written works but ten compositions, among them three symphonies, an opera, and a ballet. After 1942 the number of compositions again decreases, with a commensurate increase in the literary output.

In all of Asafiev's writings, his own inner contrasts and conflicts are evident. On the one hand, he is clearly an exponent of the unique nature of Russian music; on the other, he is a great admirer of the latest trends in Western music. While the works of Glinka and Tchaikovsky are perhaps the most frequently cited, there also appear works about Krenek, Hindemith, and Berg.[24] He even carried on a substantial correspondence with Berg in 1928-1929.[25] Boris Schwarz cites a related contradiction: "a passionate interest in musical newness, and an equally passionate belief in music as a reflection of the people."[26] The author of *A Book About Stravinsky,* he also composed remarkably conservative ballets, written with intonational authenticity and communication as their objective.

Asafiev's intellectual roots stem from widely disparate sources that may be traced to his university studies and his time with Stasov. His knowledge of Hegelian philosophy led to his emphasis on contrast as the most important motivating force in music.[27] This, in turn, accounts for some of the similarities between his ideas and Marxist philosophy, which is also derived from Hegel.[28] In *Musical Form* other Marxist elements seem to be superimposed on a Hegelian theory. In *Intonation,* however, the two parallel streams are more successfully integrated.

The influence of nineteenth-century Russian musical thought came largely through the prism of Vladimir Stasov. Orlova asserts that, as a musicologist, Asafiev is "the continuer of the best pre-revolutionary traditions," citing especially Stasov and Serov. From Serov, she believes he acquired a "deep interest in the theoretical and esthetic problems of the art of music," and a belief in the "leading role of melody."[29] The direct influence of Stasov is acknowledged by Asafiev himself in an essay written in 1947 about his conservatory years:

> [The year 1906 was] memorable for me for the strengthening of my friendship with Stasov. I had met Vladimir Vasilevich before [attending] the conservatory, and my acquaintance with him and his circle were for me my second, parallel university, because, among the many persons besides musicians who frequented his gatherings, Gorky, Repin, and Chaliapin were especially dear and memorable for me. At the Public library, Stasov introduced me to the musical manuscript archives and taught me how to use them. There I first got to know the manuscripts of Musorgsky and copied out his "Zhenit'ba" [The Marriage]. Stasov introduced me into Alexandra Molas' circle, where I absorbed the very "atmosphere of *kuchkism*" and the realistic bases and traditions of Russian singing. In the summer of 1906 I composed, at the insistence of Stasov and to his scenario, the children's opera "Zolushka."[30]

Certainly, the composers Rimsky-Korsakov and, especially, Lyadov were also important to his development. He credits Lyadov with first showing alternatives to the prescriptive view of musical forms[31] The cases of the Austrian theorist Ernst Kurth and of Boleslav Yavorsky are more difficult to trace. Kurth and Asafiev were almost exact contemporaries whose theories overlap in several important respects, but most of all in the sense that both had a dynamic view of form. Asafiev, who very much admired Kurth's work, edited and wrote an introduction for the Russian translation of Kurth's counterpoint text, but this appeared in 1931, after *Musical Form as a Process.*[32] The Russian theorist Yavorsky, whose career began about one decade earlier than Asafiev's, devised a theory of "modal rhythm" that addresses in a practical way some of the same ideas that Asafiev explores. In a letter written in 1915 about Yavorsky, Asafiev wrote, "In his method I have found that for which I have long searched—a firmly scientific basis for music theory...."[33] The extent of Yavorsky's influence, however, is difficult to determine.

Orlova cites another possible influence on Asafiev that could help account for his concept of intonation. This was the famed theater director Stanislavsky, who used the term in a manner related to Asafiev's later usage.[34] This possibility has yet to be investigated in detail.

Asafiev's two major theoretical statements represent the culminations of the two important eras of his literary work. For all their similarities in style and in terminology, their substantial difference in purpose makes it preferable to regard them as separate works, not as consecutive volumes of the same work. Only the first deals with the nature of musical forms; it is an attempt to correct seeming deficiencies in traditional form instruction. The second endeavors to account for the evolution of music. Each presents a different aspect of Asafiev's basic premise that music is an intonational art; each, however, makes a complete theoretical statement in itself. Both volumes are highly speculative, and assertions are sometimes presented as fact. Both also suffer from deficiencies in style and presentation that make a proper understanding and assessment a difficult task. The most obvious of these are redundancy and a complex, discursive, and figurative style. Also trying are the lack of logical flow and a certain amount of inner contradiction. The greatest problem, though, is the result of his insistence on new uses for old terms and his many neologisms, in both cases usually lacking clear definitions. The neologisms are most often successive stages of abstraction of familiar nouns: "tone" leads to "tonation"; symphony to "symphonism." These idiosyncracies may be accounted for by his method of writing. "I think with the tip of my pen," said Asafiev.[35] "I am accustomed to writing as I speak, as though leading a discussion."[36] Even more telling is the following description of his method, written in the late 1920s:

> My language results from this constant temptation to convert music into words, but not to retell "programs." I always search for expressions, but not agonizingly on paper; rather before writing them down, thinking to myself about the music, almost unconsciously; even I cannot explain exactly *how.* Then after long nervous vacillation I feel that something is ready. Then I sit down and write without stopping, *without corrections,* which I cannot endure, and without drafts and copies. I have all the material, strictly worked out, in my head, and I cannot bear copying over rough drafts.[37]

Since his style is most complex in the theoretical and esthetic works, it is tempting to see in them an attempt to camouflage his advanced ideas with verbiage such that they would be intelligible only to the professional community. Whether or not this is true, it is possible to find in his style a literary manifestation of his musical theories. He writes in a symphonic, developmental style, and not in a systematic, logical one. The entire structure of *Intonation,* for example, is based on the themes that are only touched on in the first chapter. These are then repeatedly taken up in various contexts during the remainder of the volume. The organization might be represented by circles surrounding a central core of ideas about intonation rather than by a straight line of logical flow toward a conclusion. Some of the individual chapters also manifest this kind of symphonic organization. That the experiment is not altogether successful may well point out that the close relationship between musical and verbal communication, so important to Asafiev, is not completely tenable.

Of all Asafiev's neologisms, three are so basic to his thought (not just in this work) that separate treatment is in order. *Symphonism* [simfonizm], one of Asafiev's earliest concepts, is the potential of music to be symphonic, to be developmental. The term may apply to any kind of music, even opera. In 1918 he described symphonism as the "continuous nature of a musical thought [soznanie]."[38] In the early 1920s he called it the "creative comprehension and expression of the world of feelings and ideas in a continuous musical current. . . ."[39] In his last years he distinguished between two types of symphonism: intellectual and pictorial (or representative).[40]

Melos [melos], a term borrowed from classical Greek theory, is the horizontal correspondent of harmony; it is the linear dimension of music. *Melos* might also refer to the melodic style of a place or kind of music, such as the *melos* of Russian folk music. He saw it as the musical equivalent of the Greek work *logos,* meaning "word."[41] Melody is a specific instance of *melos.*

Intonation [intonatsiia], Asafiev's most important term, is the relationship of music to the environment, the way the nature of life is expressed in sound. While intonation is also a factor in speech, purely musical intonations are his specific concern. The term underwent substantial evolution; in about 1920 he wrote:

> I understand the process of intoning to be . . . the embodiment and reproduction of music in all its varied branches; the composer, while writing, is already internally intoning the music that is being born.[42]

In the mid 1920s, in *A Book about Stravinsky,* he writes:

> I often use the term "intonation," and I therefore state that I mean thereby the totality of sounds from whatever source, not only the *audible* music but the whole phenomena of sound, actually or potentially audible as music. To intone means to define a system of sound-relationships.[43]

Much later he described his concept of intonation at the time of writing *Musical Form as a Process* thus:

> At the end of the book *Form as Process* I had already approached the concept of intonation as the emotional ideational *pronouncing* of sound, as a quality determining the direction of meaning in musical speech . . . [44]

Still later, at the time of *Intonation,* he distinguished two meanings for the term, one wide and one narrow. In the first sense music is equal to intonation: the phenomenon of intonation is all and explains all of music. In the second sense, intonation is "the designation of separate representative phenomena of meaning in musical art.... "[45]

The next section of this essay attempts to present the most important material of *Musical Form as a Process* and *Intonation* in the form of a chapter-by-chapter abstract of its contents, which makes it possible to avoid much of Asafiev's most confusing terminology while attempting to convey his essential meaning. The terms and wording are based on James R. Tull's translation, with quoted material adapted from his text. Numbers in square brackets refer to page numbers in his translation. After the abstract, the most important themes will be discussed and evaluated.

Musical Form as a Process

Introduction

Musical form [forma] is a "socially determined phenomenon" [184]. Intonation [intonatsiia] is the basis for the interaction between music and society, and that basis is socially determined and continually evolving. Musical intonations are particular to a given era and culture, and may be anything from the simplest musical materials to the largest complex forms.

"Form is not merely a constructive framework. Form, verified by listening, sometimes by several generations (i.e., socially discovered . . .) is the organization (the purposeful distribution in time) of musical material, or, in other words, the organization of musical motion, for, generally speaking, there is no stationary musical material" [185-186]. While classical forms result from relatively stable intonations, the process of musical forming remains dialectical, always changing. Form is at the same time both a process and a crystallized scheme, manifesting:

> a contradictory quality...: a tendency toward crystallization—toward the exposure of similar intonations, similar and parallel constructive landmarks, such as cadences—and a tendency toward a progressively more intense feeling of destabilized equilibrium, i.e., toward the destruction of identical and repeated features by the introduction of unfamiliar, unexpected capricious intonations, and by means of the breaking down or expansion of structural norms. [194]

Because new intonations periodically displace familiar ones, it is possible to trace the development of music and forms in Europe from the time of the earliest polyphony.

Part I: How Musical Formation Occurs

Chapter 1. Facts and factors of musical motion and organization. Musical organization relies on the phenomena of motion and memorization, that is, the ability of the listener to recollect and redefine music as it moves in time. The limitations of notation qualify the study of this process, however. Other factors, such as breathing, the environment during composition and performance, the choice of timbre, and the manner of execution also relate to musical organization. "People instinctively compare the 'features' of music as it transpires and remember similar, frequently repeated complexes" [207], rejecting or only gradually accepting unfamiliar combinations. Professional listeners, who already know many sound complexes, may exhibit a greater disinclination to accept the new.

> The inertia or the vitality in the creative work of composers depends on just such a choice between combinations long since assimilated, which remain passively in the memory..., and "material not yet mastered."...[209] The successive stages in the art of composition are concerned with overcoming the inertia in one's own consciousness, and with an increased striving toward the mastery of purely musical relations—this may be called the origin of a "professional musical consciousness." [214]

Chapter 2. Principles of identity or repetition; imitation; canon and fugue; concept of theme; musical kinetics and statics. Repetition, the simplest way to continue motion, is also the easiest for the memory to assimilate. Whether exact or varied, repetition in more than one voice is called imitation. "Literal repetition will be perceived as motion only as long as there is some interest in comparison, discernment, and memorization" [219]. Even slight intonational variety such as octave transposition generates a comparison and hence the perception of movement.

Strong contrasts, those engendering a greater stimulus to comparisons, require more repetition, either immediately or after entire sections, themselves repeated, as in the exposition of the classical sonata form. A shift in tonal level allows for a fairly simple type of varied repetition, whereas a shift in mode evokes a stronger contrast. Thus, a variation in a minor key in variation form promotes a stronger sense of motion. Theoretically, variation forms are open-ended, always permitting yet more variations. The most successful variations are those that do not "entirely lose the feeling of connection between the links in a single chain" [224]. Examples are Beethoven's C-minor Variations and his "Diabelli" Variations. The earliest stage in the evolution of variation forms is typified by the ground bass and related procedures where the basis for variation remains present throughout. The second stage uses a decorated repetition of the whole, such as is found in French doubles. The third stage gradually unfolds the possibilities for variation that are inherent in a theme.

The simplest type of repetition also involves reverse symmetry, including the important device of a leap followed by conjunct motion in the opposite direction. This last is a basic principle in the music of Bach.

In the case of imitation, the impetus toward movement must come from within the theme or subject. The first instance is canon, which "as a crystallized form...is a static formation and a mechanical phenomenon" [232]. On the other hand, "Fugue...represents not only a rationally constructed mechanism, but also a kinetic formation" [233]. The theme of a fugue must be "of a maximally distinct character, flexible, and potentially active" [234] in order to generate motion.

Chapter 3. Study of the motive forces of musical organization and the concept of energy: the kinetics of impetus. The perception of motion in music is the product of sound relationships which are culturally determined. Some relationships are static, some kinetic. For example, in the romantic era composers tried to replace the tonic-dominant relationship with third relations, but the latter were inert and only served as coloristic devices.

> If one examines a musical composition in its concrete reality...one must inevitably pass from the stage of the study of form-schemes...to the observation of the stages of motion in music or the processes of its organization, and...to the study of the *forces* which serve as causes or stimuli of motion. This is the area of musical kinetics. [241]

The striving for motion results in the attempt to put off a state of equilibrium for as long as possible. A good example of a moving force that organizes music is the leading tone. The suspension and the deceptive cadence are examples of phenomena that postpone equilibrium. Such motions result in an expenditure of musical energy and constitute part of a complex chain of energy transfers that connect the composer and listener. "The kind of energy that results in musical motion is intonational energy, unfolded in the motion of sound" [249].

> The totality of these phenomena and forces...permits one to examine the process of the formation of music as a dialectical process with the continuous coexistence of opposites. [254]

For a given epoch and composer, either vertical or horizontal forces predominate, but both work as motive forces.

> The epochs of academicism in music are the epochs of the predominance of combinations which are pleasing to the majority of people and are...habitual. The epochs of crisis and struggle are the result of the search by musicians for more intensive and unfamiliar combinations....[257]
>
> Musical motion...must be considered as a *condition of destabilized equilibrium* enclosed between the first impetus...and the final formula...which terminates the motion. [258]

One must be aware of the limitations of studying forms as schemes independent of their intonational content, because music is form in motion.

Part II: The Stimuli and Factors of Musical Forming

Chapter 4. Impetus and termination of motion (cadence).

> Each musical composition unfolds between a primary impetus (point of departure, moment of pushing off) and a braking or termination of motion (cadence). [263]

While the first moment or pitch in a work helps establish its character, it is not necessarily an impetus. The initial impetus derives from that pitch or series of pitches that first stimulates motion. In large forms this role may be played by the slow introduction of a sonata-allegro form or by an opera overture. In smaller forms it may be the opening melody, ritornello, or rondo theme. The braking or termination of motion may occur in a cadence or a coda. Indeed, an entire musical formation is a series of impetuses and brakings, all gravitating toward the final cadence.

> The first function of an impetus is to engage the ear in the basic *tone* (tonal sphere) of the music which is about to be unfolded. [269]

Examples include the introductions of Beethoven's Seventh and Ninth Symphonies, a single chord or tone as in his overtures *Egmont* and *Coriolanus,* and triadic passages, either within a tonality, as in Glinka's *Ruslan* overture, or in third relations as in the introduction to Rimsky-Korsakov's *Christmas Eve.*
   Other functions of impetus include reaffirming the tonality after a digression. This is sometimes accomplished by means of a pedal point, which accumulates energy that can be discharged in a single gesture, as happens before a reprise or coda. Highly dissonant or unstable intonations are strong local impetuses. The end of the introduction of a large form discharges its accumulated energy into the following section, which, in relation to that which follows it, becomes a new stimulus.
   Within a given section of music, the kinetics that cause impetus stem from several sources. One of these is intervals; the resultant comparison of pitches is perceived as either consonant or dissonant. Another source involves the augmentation or diminution (either vertically or horizontally) of intonational material. Other types include the exchange of conjunct and disjunct lines and shifts of tonality.
   The point of maximum tension in a work is most often located just before the final fundamental tone complex, whether it be a medieval cadence or a Beethoven coda. Internal cadences may act as strong stimuli, changing the direction of motion.

Chapter 5. Development of motion; uniform and uninterrupted motion, and other types. A medieval psalm tone provides a simple example of motion. After an initial impetus or ascent, a tenor or reciting tone appears on a pitch different from the stable beginning, and later still a braking device occurs. One might even create linear representations of a melodic shape such as this one. Other melodies have more complex shapes. (Here, Asafiev analyzes the main theme from Beethoven's *Prometheus* overture and a long melody from Wagner's *Siegfried* for their melodic operations.)

> A musical formation always occurs as follows: an impetus, or starting point of sound, and a displacement; the motion or state of destabilized equilibrium; a return to the source, to the condition of equilibrium (to the basis), or the closing of motion, i.e., the correlation *i* (*initium*—beginning): *m* (*movere*—to move): *t* (*terminus*—close, ending). [310]

This formula, i:m:t, is found in music at all levels.

In the middle portion of the formula, the sense of disequilibrium is caused by contrast, which can either be resolved or intensified. It may also dissipate if the sense of motion becomes inert. Sequence provides less impetus, since there is no growth or transformation.

In larger sections of music, at least a phrase, a kind of "muscular" expansion and contraction is also evident, which is perceived as vitality. The kinetic, linear quality of *melos* results from a variety of inner contrasts that cause motion towards some point of repose.

> A musical formation cannot be assimilated unless it contains ... repeated irritants that evoke repeated reactions and a consequent, natural memorization of identical formations. [322]

Thus, musical perception depends on comparisons of similarity and difference.

> Whether we listen to Russian peasant polyphony ..., or delve deeply into the flexible and resilient lines of ancient singing of Gregorian Chant, or comprehend the *Five Orchestral Pieces* of Schoenberg ..., musical formation is always revealed in an uninterrupted series of alterations. [324]

Chapter 6. Dissonance and consonance, sequences, modulations, parallel constructions. Contraction and expansion of the musical fabric, as factors that stimulate motion, are achieved by many devices, including phrase elision, two-beat combinations in a three-beat rhythm, irregular measures in a regular pattern, contraction of the melodic line, and combination of duple and nonduple measures. Even more important to the stimulus of motion is the relationship of consonance and dissonance, because dissonance evokes intonational impetus and displacement. Like other phenomena, what is perceived as dissonance is historically changing and even varies among composers of the same era.

By the romantic era, the sequence has developed into a powerful structural factor, a favorite means for any transfer of motion and for an "arbitrary" change in its direction; it has also become a means, easily available at any moment, for contracting or expanding the fabric. This is not only the case in music for the theater, ... but is also the case in symphonic music. [345]

The sequence enabled composers to write ever larger works and to heighten emotion. A related device is parallel construction, the sequential repetition of a large, closed episode in another tonality. In symphonic works, parallel constructions allowed for " ... increasing the intensity of motion at the expense of novelty of invention" [347]. Parallel constructions by third, which are effective in Schubert, quickly become static and unsatisfactory as stimuli for later composers, although Rimsky-Korsakov used them effectively for pictorial purposes.

Part III: Principles of Identity and Contrast: Their Exposure in Crystallized Forms

Chapter 7. Forms based on the principle of identity (variation, canon, fugue, rondo, etc.). The two principles basic to the process of musical forming and to the crystallized schemes are the principles of identity and contrast. Each represents a category of forms in which it predominates. Forms relying on the principle of identity evoke motion by the repetition of similar elements, ranging in size from two beats to entire, complex sections.

The principle of identity is not necessarily more primitive than that of contrast, but it does prevail in the early, developmental stages of a formal process. For example, at the same time that Gregorian chant was already showing contrast in a highly developed horizontal style, the newer polyphonic forms exhibited a greater degree of identity through repetition.

Variation forms operate on the basis of progressively more complicated transformations of a stimulus, the theme. Canon and fugue are made possible by the development of the theme in imitation: "the material engenders motion by means of an uninterrupted coupling of *identical* elements in different voices, i.e., it forms a firmly cohesive fabric" [364]. If canon had a limited development, fugue offered new possibilities because it was "a more flexible formal process full of intricate comparisons on the basis of a controlling core" [366].

Even though the sonata-allegro form eventually gained dominance over identity forms, the latter continued to develop, and not just as further examples of variations and fugues. If one assumes a kind of cantus firmus principle in the subject and answer of a fugue, then it is possible to see yet further development of the principle in the Wagnerian leitmotif. Thus the structure of Wagner's operas lies in between the principles of identity and contrast. *Die Meistersinger,* which is particularly fugue-like, uses the densest polyphony at points of greatest tension; *Tristan* is more harmonic.

Chapter 8. Forms based on the principle of contrast (1). The sonata-allegro form is the highest expression of the principle of contrast.

> The scheme of the allegro is simple: exposition, working-out, reprise. Within it is concealed the following process: impetus, the removal of equilibrium, restoration of equilibrium. The formula of the perfect cadence represents a microcosm into which this process has been compressed. [384]

The most important kind of contrast evident is that of the material associated with the "tonic" and "dominant" groups. Their contrast necessitates further motion. The sonata form has always evolved towards more contrast; such contrast is intensified if a slow introduction is present.

The repeated exposition resulted from the need to reinforce thematic interrelations for the purposes of memory. The strong dominant cadence at the end of the exposition sharpens the contrast of tonalities. The instability so created is emphasized in the central development ("working-out"), where the material encounters new types of contrasts.

> Through understanding the functions of contrast inherent in the basic sound complexes... of the European intonational system from Bach to Schoenberg and Stravinsky and through analyzing the formal process on the indispensable basis of *hearing* (the constant sensing of intonational energy, its fluctuations, its shifts both sudden and gradual, its accumulation, and its discharge), each organically created musical form is perceived as kinetic and, in terms of this perception, represents a complete contrast both to the predominantly sensual enjoyment of the separate elements of music, and to the abstract comprehension of form as a scheme for the visual analysis of soundless horizontals and verticals. [390]

Chapter 9. Dialectic of musical forming; consecutiveness and simultaneity; form in the process of forming and form in the process of crystallization. Motion or development may be consecutive and rational, using stable formulae, or nonconsecutive (irrational), using shock, elision, or mutation.

> The combination of periodic changes of filled-in and unfilled ascent and descent, and also of consecutive and nonconsecutive motion... creates a complex of mutually contradictory and, at the same time, mutually counterbalancing sound conjugations, which evoke the perpetuation of the condition of unstable equilibrium. [402]

Music, then, amounts to a chain of contrasts, each evoking motion toward synthesis and new contrasts. The formula i:m:t (impetus, motion, termination) illustrates this. In the course of a work the functions are variable. The chord in an elided cadence, for example, changes from termination to impetus.

Likewise, the last material of the exposition of a sonata-allegro form sometimes is repeated with a new function at the beginning of the development.

> In connection with the continuous transfer of functions and their transition into their opposites, all this taken together raises a complex network of *mutual gravitations* operating on one another at various distances and with varying force, or a system of crossing, *intonational arches* [intonatsionnaia arka] [412-413]. Music, to repeat, is a system of organized motion; it is not an *anarchistic* succession of sound complexes, but rather, their strictly and mutually conditioned *exposure* in the process of intoning. [413]

Part *m* of the formula is represented in the sonata-allegro form by the development. Various parts of *m* function as *i* or *t* or both causing a "dialectically contrasting formation" [415].

(There follows a lengthy analysis of the intonational complexes of the first 13 measures of Movement I of Beethoven's Sonata op. 2 no. 3.)

Chapter 10. Forms based on the principle of contrast (2). In all types of sonata formations, not just Beethoven's, successive stages of departure, development, and return are in evidence. The reprise is a synthesis of the preceding, in more ways than just tonally; it must synthesize the *ideas* of the exposition and development. The synthesis can be delayed or extended into the coda, which for Beethoven takes on the character of another basic section, similar to the development, but whose forces work toward synthesis, not contrast. In a sense, this causes a two-part division of the sonata-allegro form: exposition and development plus reprise and coda. In another sense, the exposition and development are thesis and antithesis to the synthesis of the reprise and coda.

The first movement of Beethoven's Ninth Symphony is an outstanding example since its four sections manifest four variant stages of the same ideas. It represents a landmark after which several types of symphonism are possible. The first is that represented by Beethoven himself who,

> a contemporary of Hegel (1770-1831), highlighted the dialectic of the sonata and intensified the functional interconditionality of the formative elements of the sonata and symphony to the highest degree of expressiveness. [438]

Three other streams of nineteenth-century symphonism may be identified: The first is the songlike sonata, as in Schubert and Bruckner, whose development is a "blossoming of melody, of *pro* and *contra* ideas..." [439]. The second, the virtuoso salon sonata, such as Weber's, was "weak dramatically, but saturated with refined lyricism" [440]. The third is exemplified by the program music of Berlioz and Liszt, in which the contrast is in part dictated by the external program.

Chapter 11. Formation of cycles on the basis of contrast. A sonata-allegro form typically occurs as a part of a cyclic form such as of a sonata or symphony. The origin of cyclic forms is found in the sixteenth century, perhaps in such paired dances as the pavanne and galliard. These, when grouped with other types of paired dances, developed into the suite, which manifests principles of both similarity and contrast. Instrumental canzoni, such as those of Frescobaldi, had the advantage over the suite of not being confined to dance rhythms.

Those factors contributing to unity in these works are (1) modal unity, (2) motivic relationships, (3) periodicity (or symmetry) of meters and rhythmic formulae, (4) regularity of motion, and (5) imitative textures. Those factors evoking contrast are (1) chromaticism, (2) juxtaposition of contrasting rhythmic formulae, (3) juxtaposition of regular motion with improvisational motion, (4) contrast between a spaced-out and a filled-in fabric, and (5) contrast of linear and chordal motion.

Other seventeenth-century examples of cyclic forms include types of variation forms, church sonatas, and chamber sonatas, all leading to the works of Domenico Scarlatti and J. S. Bach. The latter "in his concerti, stood on the border of dialectical sonata thinking, and was almost ready to exceed the limits of monothematicism or psychologically undifferentiated polythematicism ... " [466].

Chapter 12. Suite and symphony. The eighteenth-century suite had a four-movement core with various additions. Its highest manifestation is found in the works of Bach. While there is no tonal contrast in his French Suites, there is a kind of gradation of tempi, the final gigue being the fastest. The sarabande provides a break in the center. In the English Suites, weak tonal contrasts are encountered and an introductory prelude "enlivens the suite" [478]. The orchestral suites have massive overtures counterbalanced by several contrasting dances.

The advantage of the sonata in comparison with the four basic movements of the suite lies in its "kinetic clarity and lucidity of gradation" [481]. The symphonic finale plays an important psychological role, ranging from joy (Beethoven's Ninth Symphony) to pain (Tchaikovsky's Sixth).

> It seems to me that it would be most correct ... to characterize the meaning and development of the finale's formation as a wave-like intensification of unified feeling, or as an ascent, in opposition to the dramatic formation of the first movement of the symphony which is characterized by conflict, by the overcoming of contradictions. [483]

The recognition of the importance of thematic contrast is the key to the idea of development.

I emphasize once more that the growth of the symphonic, sonata form coincided with the growth of social contradictions and conflicts of ideas which gave rise to a mighty upheaval, and that the symphony attained the apex of its development in the creative work of Beethoven, a contemporary of Hegel. [492]

Since intonational material comes from a composer's environment, Beethoven is indebted to many generations of musicians.

Supplement 1. Generalizations and Conclusions That Systematize My Observations of the Processes of Musical Forming and the Crystallization of Forms in the Human Consciousness

Theoretical positions.

    a. "Form as a process . . . is comprehended by our consciousness as the co-existence of opposites" [504].

    b. Form, like a musical instrument, is a tool for treating the material of music.

    c. Musical rhythm is a factor in intonation, and thus is socially determined, related to work or games. "Meter and bar are gauges of measurement, but rhythm is that which is measured . . . [512].

    d. Rhythmic formations are kinetic, not static. "In fact, in music there is no equality without inequality, there is no symmetry without asymmetry. . . . Rhythm exists only in the mutual conditionality of contradictions" [514].

    e. "*Melos,* harmony, and timbre . . . all define form . . . as a growth process" [517].

    f. Tempo is a factor in form, as in the sonata-allegro form.

    g. Form is affected by environment, such as the size and location of the place of performance.

    h. Crystallized forms are either cyclical or self-contained.

There are five kinetic factors in the formation of music and crystallized forms.

    1. The principles of identity and contrast.

    2. The various degrees of contrast.

    3. Identity as repetition or variation.

    4. Single-line or multi-line texture.

    5. The interaction of horizontals and verticals.

Supplement 2. Bases of Musical Intonation.

This supplement is part of an unpublished work called "The Bases of Russian Musical Intonation," written in 1925-26.

To understand the dialectical nature of music, one must study the nature and process of intoning. Music must be perceived as "changeable in conformity to place, time, epoch, and properties of the media of reproduction" [537].

> The musician must hear and evaluate the intonations of twelfth-century organum, archaic heterophony, and the instrumental fabric of the music of the seventeenth-century lutenists; he must perceive folk creation, not with a view toward the esthetic selection of beautiful themes, but as music of a concrete social environment, constantly changing in its formations. [537-538]

Music is neither visual systems nor theorists' rules. One must avoid convenient but static terminology. Terms must themselves evolve. *Melos* is a concept that "embodies the *quality* and the *function* of melodic forming"[541], its melodiousness. It is governed by the complex interrelationships of linear forces in music. These forces, perceived as repeated or contrasting parts, result in tension and gravitation.

Musical intonation, a related concept, is "the interpretation of sounds already placed in a system of ... tones and tonalities. ... Without intoning and apart from intoning there is no music" [543].

The act of creation engenders a new, original intonation which results in a new type of motion. Later, this intonation may be assimilated by other composers and by listeners, and still later it ossifies.

> The concept of "intonation" as the interpretation of sound correlations, in the very process of sounding assumes societal conditionality or social justification as the highest criterion of any musical phenomenon [560-561].

Both *melos* and intonations help to reveal the figurative content of music, its extra-musical associations.

Intonation

In Lieu of an Introduction

"This work is not so much a continuation as a development of my book, *Musical Form as a Process,* which was published in 1930" [600]. There, the issue was *how* sound is organized. Here, the issue is *why* music is formed in the manner that it is, what the principles of intoning are, how they are manifestations of thought, and how they are related to verbal speech.

> Thought, intonation, the forms of music—all are in continuous connection; a thought, in order to be expressed aloud becomes an intonation—is intoned. The process of intoning, in order to become not speech but music, either merges with speech intonation and is transformed into a unity, into a rhythmic intonation of word and tone ... or else, having

escaped the word (in instrumentalism),...the process of intoning becomes "musical speech," "musical intonation." [600-601]

The connection between musical intonations and their understanding by the intellect is achieved by means of intervals, which were probably identified gradually in religious rites or declamation.

This book, which aims to explain and elaborate the concept of intonation, will begin with the presentation of several themes as "nuclei." It is, unfortunately, necessary to use neologisms to convey nuances of meaning different from those of conventional terminology.

Chapter 1

"Many people listen to music, but few hear it, especially instrumental music" [609]. Music that is sung, on the other hand, is easier to perceive; for example, a fine instrumentalist is said to have a "singing quality." This quality results from the attempt to intone accurately, with meaningful materials, and, thus, to communicate.

The people, the culture, and the historical epoch define the stages of intonation, and through intonation are determined both the means of musical expression, and the selection and interconnection of musical elements. [613]

In seventeenth- and eighteenth-century Russia, cultural changes caused an "intonational crisis"—the need for a new method of hearing and understanding music. During such an era, the intonational expectations of society are rapidly changing.

The following are "prerequisite positions and definitions, which are absolutely essential to understanding the development of my thoughts"[615]. As the distinctive difference between speech and music, the interval becomes the expressive basis of music and is necessary to intonational understanding.

Thus, intervals, as a form of expression in any given system of tones, any scale, comprise intonational indicators which are in constant operation (with respect to stability, pitch range, the degree of tension of a tone, all of which are qualitatively different for different instruments). [616]

From this arises style, the prevalence, for example, of one interval in some period or genre (such as the sixth in some types of nineteenth-century opera), which is the result of intonational selection.

Motives and their groupings result from "living intonational formation and stylistic selection as expressions of figurative thinking" [619].

There are four principles of intoning.

1. Intoning by leap evokes the eventual filling in of the empty space;
2. the stable pitches in a mode may be constantly shifting;
3. a pitch or interval may have its intonation colored by a neighboring one;
4. tonality may be defined by harmony or by melodic intonation.

A song is a "concise intonation," and a symphony is the interaction of "two or three short, 'fundamental' intonational theses" [625]. "European harmony...is the cooling lava of Gothic polyphony" [626]. A theme is an identifiable intonation that is conducive to development. The proper use of commonplace intonations by a composer is basic to the acceptance of his new intonations. Such proper use stems from his ability to sense the role of intervals in a "vocal" way. Instrumental music, in particular, requires a "vocal intonational essence" [634] to enhance intelligibility. It must also contain a dramatic quality. In the modern era, timbre has become the new bearer of intelligibility, as in the *Rite of Spring*.

The leading tone is the "verb" of a mode:

> One may say that there is only *one* mode in European music, for it has a single and most characteristic indicator—the quality of the leading tone. Major and minor are, in fact, only inclinations, or rather, "tendencies." [641]

The leading tone, as the representation of the dominant, is contrasted with the subdominant. The dominant and the subdominant are the "aggravation and softening" [643] of a mode.

Musical development is the culmination of a search for purely musical formations. To the listener it is "living intonational speech" [655]. The technique of development had a long, complex evolution. From roots in Renaissance polyphony, it developed into "the essence of European symphonism" [656].

The rise of the tritone (and consequently the enhanced role of the leading tone) greatly altered existing intonational norms and organized an important system of interrelationships among the pitches of a mode. The Russian theorist Yavorsky recognized the significance of the tritone, but the functional system of Riemann has "enslaved the ear and consciousness of composers with its conservative, mechanical 'predetermination'" [672]. The functional system is alien to the polyphonic *melos* of Russian folk music. Glinka, in particular, knew to use the dominant only sparingly, and that the subdominant must provide equilibrium. This criticism of functionalism, on the other hand, must not be construed as denying the rise of nineteenth-century harmony from the earlier practice of figured bass, to which functionalism is also indebted.

Chapter 2

The mechanism of intonational change can be observed in the changes in music that occurred between the seventeenth and nineteenth centuries, and especially in the decline of polyphony in the nineteenth century. The difficulty of hearing the intonations of Renaissance polyphony lies in the fact that we now hear them through contemporary theoretical systems, and not as they were heard then. While early instrumental polyphony did not survive in the nineteenth century, it resurfaced in the twentieth. The works of Hindemith, for example, manifest not so much harmony or polyphony as intonation, "the statement of thoughts *in voice-leading,* governed by rhythm, not formally, but so that the rhythm helps to interpret the developmental course of ideas" [688].

In early cities, the "dividing line between performance and creation... was almost obliterated" [691-692]. New instrumental possibilities and solutions generated new intonations. The reflection of reality and the mastery of early instrumentalism evoked joy and emulation, and thus, the individuality of the concertante style. The intellectualized techniques of the *concerti grossi* and suites that followed led to solo virtuosity, which limited the polyphonic potential of the ensemble. The ensemble (in the form of the orchestra) tended towards homophonic harmony with polyphonic techniques.

The decline of polyphony in the nineteenth century also relates to the intonational needs of the changing era.

> Music entered ever more intensely into the sphere of contemporaneous ideas, and its development inclined toward the mastery of symphonic sonata form, the dialectic of the sonata quality, because only through the evolution of this form was it possible to express the stormy nature of the epoch, the collision of ideas and sensations, and to raise music to a still higher level of ideational content, to provide a more profound analysis of the human heart. [701-702]

The new intonations, the reforms, of Gluck reflect the era of "storm and stress." Likewise in the music of the French revolution, "there is brilliant proof that rhythm and intonation are the chief bearers of musical expressiveness and persuasiveness" [710]. Beethoven, much influenced by these intonations, contributed the idea of development as basic to symphonism. Beethoven "understood the significance of form as a scheme..., but, overcoming the inertia of these norms, he subordinated theme to development..." [714].

> The independence of music as an art is inconceivable without the organization of the elements of music in a form, as a process of forming intonations, i.e., a process that follows a constructive principle; the temporal nature of music—its unfolding in time—demands this. [714]

Eras of intonational crisis result in the selection, evaluation, and reinterpretation of musical materials.

Chapter 3

A musical composition has a life that depends on its performance, subsequent recollection, reinterpretation, and discussion. If the work succeeds and is understood, fragments enter the musical consciousness of the general public as "memorable moments of music" [724] that have an "independent artistic life" [725]. Thus, living intonations are created; a dictionary of them might be made up for a given era. *Intonations*...are a *complex* of *musical thoughts,* persistently occurring in the consciousness of a given social environment" [725]. The "oral vocabulary of intonations" [727], while always evolving, has stable elements.

> Therefore, the more subjective a composer's intonational language and its constituent elements, the more difficult it is for them to enter into the "sphere of sound ideas" of the epoch.... The best of the symphonies of Beethoven...advanced slowly, but, as we can see, their basic intonational content was deeply rooted in the social milieu. [727]

On the other hand, if properly used, popular intonations are not vulgar but "native to mind and heart" [729].

Realism in music stems from intonational communication, and must be the basis for critical evaluation. Haydn and Mozart provide good examples of the "realistic" use of intonations. Both used common intonations of their era, but with individual deviations characteristic of their backgrounds and inclinations.

> Haydn is a monolith, a model of "sensible meaning." But the creation of Mozart is always an art of experiencing, the experiencing of a limitless world of sensations, and, through it, of objective reality.... [735]

"In its essence [Beethoven's music] is reality and his reflections on it, which have become intonations (i.e., his thought about reality transformed into sound)" [740].

> Beethoven is the most convincing example, to me, of the revelation of European music as a reflection of reality through intonation, and in this lies the force and persuasiveness of his art as an art well-grounded in reality. [745]

Chapter 4

An intonational crisis occurs when the existing body of intonations seems decayed or artificial to a new group of listeners; it is especially significant at times of political or social change and often involves a quest for simplicity.

> For Beethoven, the revolution is first of all one of rhythm. Of course, only rhythm, as an organic, organizing, and disciplining *principle,* fused with the intonational content of all

music, emerges as the "motive force" of music and the "builder of form in time.". . . Beethoven employs the simplest of meters, but within these "mile markers,". . . the rhythm rages, continually breaking the metric regularity. . . . In a word, *rhythm* is heard as the directing thought, as the motivating will. [748]

Particularly interesting are his triple meters, which exist in a great many types, interacting with duple meters.

The creative imagination of Beethoven carves figuratively striking rhythmic intonations— sections of a profoundly intelligent development of musical ideas—out of the "opposition of rhythmic rudiments." [760]

Intonations may have an affective character, particularly in vocal music. For Beethoven, this is realized in the relationship of tonic and dominant, and especially in the various harmonies involving the leading tone. He affirms the tonic by means of a dominant-tonic balance, imbuing the tonic with a *"tense stability."* [763]

Here is the principle difference between Beethoven's symphonism and the symphonism of the Romantics, and even psychorealistic symphonism. There is no "irritation," no "unevenness," no "sensuality" in Beethoven's dominant as a stimulus of intonational tension, but there is "passion," ardent pathos, anger; there is no tonic as the formal resolution of dissonances, no tonic as a state of rest, but there is the tonic as the governing intonational sphere of affirmation, of firm conviction—the tonic as "tense stability." [765-766]

Chapter 5

The *kant* [kant] (an unrecognized form and style in Beethoven) is "a choral, *eulogistic song,* sometimes achieving the structure and scope of the ode"[769]. It must not be confused with the motet, which is "more contemplative and static. In the rhythmic intonation of the *kant* there is always motion; it is a procession of jubilation"[769]. Although known in Russia even in pre-Petrine times, the *kant* flourished in the works of Bortniansky. As an element in a larger work, it is seen in the finale to Glinka's *Ivan Susanin.* Among its traits are the following: choral style even when written for instruments alone, a clear, but not march-like rhythm, a natural, simple harmonic structure, and a memorable, singable melody. These are seen in various parts of Beethoven's symphonies, such as at the beginning of the funeral march of the Third and the finale of the Fifth symphony.

The rule of tonic intonations in the *kant* and its "processional rhythm" exerted tremendous influence on all of Beethoven's symphonism, with its "open-air character" and aspirations toward "human expansiveness," with its positive, emotional inclination—its ethos. . . . Finally in the finale of the Ninth Symphony, Beethoven creates the most perfect *kant,* the well-known theme-melody "To Joy," intoning it first instrumentally, then vocally, and varying it powerfully. A monumental *kant* rises whole, as a symphonized form with a huge performing apparatus.... [775]

Chapter 6

Nature influences music, but the result need not be imitation.

In the creative work of Beethoven (as in his life) the influence of nature is unquestionable. To establish the presence of the intonations from nature (except as in the Sixth Symphony where they are concrete) is very difficult; they are converted into symphonic thinking so thoroughly that they enter the fabric of music organically and indistinguishably. [778]

Beethoven's close relationship with nature created a "tremendous code of intonations" [781] for listeners, which became part of their consciousness.

Such is the true life of the "sounding art" of each composer; it lasts while its intonations live and operate, while its creative experience continues to function, being transformed and converted. Such is the real history of music.... [782-783]

When intonations are exhausted, they become part of "musical antiquity" [782] and cease to play a part in "living perception."

Changes in the perception and acceptance of intonations create an intonational crisis. Once intonations become fixed in the public consciousness, they are long-lived because of the conservatism of the public memory. This creates a problem in the acceptance of new works. Sometimes, however, the public is more accepting and accurate than the professionals, as in the case of *Boris Godunov.*

The conclusion is clear; the conservatism of listeners...is, to a considerable extent, conditioned by the sluggishness of performers, or by their enthusiasm for the superficially virtuoso "work of the fingers and vocal chords." The limited performance repertoire and senseless brilliance evoke in the listeners a deadening of attention and little interest in new creative facts. [791-792]

In the past, improvisation allowed a closer contact between composer and listener, but the decline of that ability caused the rise of an independent virtuosity, unrelated to creation, that separated composer and listener.

Chapter 7

The process of intoning is basic to all parts of musical creation, including performance and listening. The performer either co-creates the composer's intonations or merely reproduces the notation. A performance is at its best, its most sensitive, if the performer (especially a conductor) can intone the music silently beforehand as a part of study. The art of performance is not interpretation but rather intonation. "Musical content cannot exist without breathing, governed by natural rhythm, but these are qualities which are organically inherent in intonation" [800-801].

The evolution of music is periodically interrupted by crises of intonation that may foreshadow political and social change. The French revolution, for example, is foreshadowed by the intonational crisis of mid-eighteenth-century France, which led in turn to the new possibilities of nineteenth-century music.

Chapter 8

The Mediterranean origins of the intonations of European music are still little understood. The Greek doctrine of ethos is a descriptive phenomenon related to intonations. Some evidence exists of crises of intonation in Ancient Greece; Aristoxenus seems to be sensitive to these problems.

The fact that Gregorian chant shows evidence of a continuing reinterpretation of existing intonations marks it as a crisis of intonations. One factor in this process has been *rhythmic intonation* [ritmo-intonatsiia], "the combination of word and sound, from which various vocal genres of that period were derived" [817].

> Gregorian Chant contains "deposits" of the most diverse stages of the intonational struggle; in it, one may discern and distinguish the strata of different "intonational cultures.". . . Its impact "on the centuries ahead" was exceptional, in terms of the depth and force of its intonational and emotional influence, imparting an ever new artistic quality to the individual art of the great musicians of the nineteenth century. [818-819]

Medieval folklore and domestic music-making probably served as a source of nonreligious intonations. Unfortunately it is impossible to reconstruct this accurately.

The gradual shift from freely expressive intonations toward those specifically controlled by interval relationships

> made European polyphony possible, not as a heterophonic complex, but with voice-leading distinctly differentiated according to the auditory combinations of horizontal and vertical... which apparently struck the imagination and the intellect as an absolutely new quality. [822]

The *Ars antiqua* and *Ars nova* helped to separate music from words, but still involved rhythmic intonation. During the fourteenth century, a series of intonational crises occurred based on the developing sense of *melos,* the determinant quality in musical intonation. The complex, polyphonic style of the fifteenth and sixteenth centuries did not fulfill the popular need for familiar intonations.

The Reformation chorale contributed a new quality of "rhythmic, verbal, and musical unity" [837]. The intonational crisis that engendered these was the most important one before that of the French revolution. In seventeenth- and eighteenth-century Germany,

> the chorale tunes and their elements were not only the formal cores and "girders" of polyphonic construction, they were thoughts and figurative ideas which had become intonations. Out of this intonational essence of the chorale style there developed, almost everywhere in Europe, the melodics of concentrated reflection, of serious and profound meditation and thought.... [839]

During the same era, the Italian madrigal contributed to the developing sense of melody and of *bel canto,* natural singing at the end of the Renaissance.

> The birth of the *new musical practice* of Italy, which soon conquered the entire world, and the soul of which was *melody,* was not a consequence of strivings within music itself, within its technique and style, but a consequence of a *revolution of intonation.* One may say that music before this was rhythmic intonation, utterance, and pronunciation. Now it began to *sing;* breathing became its fundamental principle. Here, at just this time, opera arose. [844]

Chapter 9

Three phenomena resulted from the crisis of intonations in Italy during the sixteenth and seventeenth centuries:

1. There arose a new concept of melody, with smooth, logical motion.
2. "*Bel canto* singing strove to become '*bel canto* playing.' The instrumental culture of that epoch took possession of melody, resulting in the emergence of the concerto style..." [851].
3. Opera, the addition of musical intonation to theater, emerged as a "barometer of all the 'changes in the intonational atmosphere' of society" [855].

Chapter 10

The nineteenth century presents no great post-Beethovenian crises of intonation comparable to those already enumerated. Its music is based on the "rhythmic forms and *voice-leading* worked out by the Classicists and breathed into long life by the genius of Beethoven" [859]. Even the music of Debussy, Stravinsky, and Hindemith follows this path, manifesting logical voice-leading, the norms of which were made possible by the popular acceptance of equal temperament. The seeming contradiction between the tremendous variety of nineteenth-century music and the relatively little new intonational material is accounted for by the fact that the possibilities of the intonations of

Beethoven's world have still not been exhausted; we still identify with his intonational language.

A new development in the course of the nineteenth century led to the fact that we now can hear timbre as intonation, perhaps even well enough to eliminate instruments, to use pure timbres. The origins of this are found in the music of Berlioz and Chopin, who thought in terms of the orchestra and piano and used timbre as intonation. Chopin "proved that the piano is, in essence, a 'speech of timbres,' sensitive, passionate, contrasting in its pathos" [870]. In fact, the use of timbre unites the music of the nineteenth and twentieth centuries.

Chapter 11

Composers of the nineteenth and twentieth centuries employed timbre to avoid the stagnation of formal norms.

> The concept of "artistic form" as unity of content and its figurative realization has begun to be confused with the genres and kinds of music-making, with constructions, theoretical schemes, and forms as manifestations of construction. [876]

The development of timbre, as with the other aspects of the language of intonations, was a gradual process. The early shift of the interval from consecutive intonations to simultaneities, the establishment of modes, the increase in the force of the leading tone, and the various nineteenth-century modal alterations also had complicated, gradual histories. Chopin's music shows a complex relationship between "an intensified leading tone quality and...folk-modal diatonicism" [882]. Chopin's forms have a "persuasive naturalness, thanks to an ineradicably persuasive intonational logic" [883].

As the summation of this development, the nineteenth century proved to be an "arena for the exposure"[884] of the intonational wealth accumulated up to that time.

> Music, in Beethoven's hands, matured to the level of the highest intellectual manifestations of the human brain. Therefore, it could participate in all the purposefulness of the intellect, and in emotional life, the life of feeling[885]. Music, sensitive to the ebb and flow of the sea of life, again verified, in living creative experience, its own expressive possibilities, to which were adapted the norms of musical grammar. Intonation tested the vital capacity of these norms, and not the contrary. The intensity of this testing also created a perfect musical technique for the nineteenth century, which seems self-sufficient, since it is lifeless only in the music schools. [886]

Chapter 12

The development of symphonism in the nineteenth century was based on Beethoven, whose music relies on the principle of "gradation of sonority"[888] where tonic prevails. Gradually dominant instability became more important.

The intonational force of the "leading tone" operates in two ways: as a tendency, a purposefulness toward the tonic, and as a delay, a "prolongation" of the tension related to this tendency. [890]

This resulted in a change in emotional impact:

The intonational "nervousness," characteristic of the nineteenth century, is a reflection of all the changes in the psychological makeup of mankind, and it would be difficult for music, as the art of intonation, not to "reflect" phenomena, commonly called "nervousness" or "nervous life," without itself growing numb and being diverted from the mainstream of the contemporaneous emotional order. [891-892]

Vital forms such as Beethoven's replace inert schemes; but even so, his intonational material is that of his own time. All music after Beethoven is influenced by the principle of development. This is as true for the music dramas of Wagner as it is for the chamber music of Brahms and Taneev. Each tried to reduce the importance of the "constructive framework" of the sonata-allegro. Every section of the sonata-allegro became developmental.

Conclusion

Music is wholly an intonational art and is neither a mechanical transference of acoustical phenomena into the area of artistic imagination, nor the naturalistic exposure of the sensual sphere. [904]

Unlike speech intonations, musical intonations depend on the concept of intervals. Various eras prefer certain characteristic intervals, such as the sixth of the romantic era. This phenomenon also applies to tonalities.

Modes are expressive, not structural devices. The idea of leading tone has now resulted in a semitone mode—a chromatic scale with "differentiated components" [909]. The tritone has become a "compressed mode of six semitones" [909]. The importance of the sixth in the nineteenth century has resulted in a "revival and firm consolidation of the hexachord, now as a mode" [910]. The medieval modes have been reactivated by contact with folk diatonicism. In a mode, stable tones act as focal points, which attract neighboring tones. European harmony amounts to "a unique system of resonators for the tones of a mode" [918]. The component intervals of a mode possess great expressive value, but may later degenerate into vulgarization.

Musical forms, from the standpoint of intonational evolution, manifest a natural tendency toward continuity, which conflicts with the tendency to mark off rhythm that results from the natural processes of breathing and moving. These two contrasting tendencies find their reflections in the continuity of the symphony and the measured nature of the suite.

The concept of intonation also accounts for other musical phenomena such as tonalities and their change (modulations), harmony, texture, and cadences.

Intonational sensitivity with respect to melodic and harmonic content and the construction of cadences constitutes a characteristic sign of intellectual activity in the area of style, intelligent mastery, and the revealing of the "personal handwriting" of a composer.... [928]

Epilogue

1. The arts may be divided either into the intonational arts of expression and poetry or the "mute" arts, i.e., the visual.
2. "*Tone* [ton], the tension or effort required to express an affect... evolved in close association with the evolution of the human, 'public' ear" [929].
3. Tonation [tonnost'], the manifestation of tone, possesses continuity and timbre, which permit identification and character.
4. "Intonational complexes" [930], in both music and speech, provide intellectual meaning.
5. The phenomenon or "condition of tonal tension" that conditions both "verbal speech" and "musical speech," I call *intonation*. The separation... of the "tonal art" of the word (poetry) from the "tonal art" of musically organized sound was determined by the rise of... the *interval*, the precise *determinant* of the emotionally meaningful quality of *intonation*.... [931]
6. The dissociation of music and poetry was gradual, caused by rhyming, cadences, and other phenomena.
7. The process of intoning brings music to life; it is the medium between the material and public consciousness.
8. Intonations, which unite all aspects of music with culture, enter the public consciousness as part of an "oral, musical, intonational vocabulary" [935], which helps to explain the demand for melody. A "reserve of living, concrete sound formations, even including characteristic intervals" is formed [936].
9. Crises of intonation change this vocabulary in relationship to parallel social change.
10. Such crises establish those new intonational phenomena that were prepared by the preceding era. Great composers often chose simple, vital intonations. The public spontaneously supports that which is intonationally fresh and vital.
11. Instrumental music possesses some independent intonational characteristics, which stem in part from its percussive origins and a consequent striving for fluidity.
12. The organ has a particularly fluid, melodic nature.
13. "I still emphasize that the changing nature of scales is a consequence of social selection, carried out 'by the ear' of social man" [950].
14. The problem of the interrelationship of form and style, which is intonationally based, needs further study.

Generally speaking, the confusion over the nature of Asafiev's ideas on music stems from the complexity of his expression (as discussed earlier) and the fact that his ideas were continually evolving, perhaps in a manner analogous to his model for the evolution of music. By pursuing that analogy it is possible to see the two volumes of this work as crystallized points in a life-long development. The first volume, *Musical Form as a Process,* aspires to a systematic treatment of musical forms and allows Asafiev to insist that the traditional static view of form misses a crucial aspect of music as an art that operates in time. In *Intonation* he endeavors to trace the evolution of musical language; the concept of form as intonation is now axiomatic. *Musical Form* shows how, by conceiving of music as an intonational art, form and content are closely related, not separate phenomena. By the same means, *Intonation* points out that the changes in musical language evolve through a coherent process, one that relates music to its environment.

It is possible to identify a number of recurrent themes that are basic to his thought. Most of the ideas that dominate *Intonation* are present in some embryonic state in *Musical Form.* As might be expected, these themes naturally cluster into two categories: form and intonation.

The essential issue of musical form for Asafiev is the nature of form as process. While all forms operate in time, a given form may be perceived as relatively kinetic or static. Sonata-allegro form, the highest point of evolution of the symphonic, developmental idea, stresses the kinetic element, the process. Even in its least kinetic manifestations, however, form must not be confused with a kind of musical architecture that is static, frozen in time, able to be perceived as a whole. Music requires the action of the memory, constantly reinterpreting that which has already been heard. Forms may be classified in another way, as based on either the principle of identity or that of contrast. Since contrast (dialectic) is the source of motion in music, those forms are the most kinetic that make the most use of *symphonism,* the linear, developmental aspect of music, in which contrast is essential. Not only sonata-allegro forms but even opera may fit into this category. But even those forms based on identity, such as variation forms, fugue, and rondo, have a dialectic source of motion, one that exists within the unit that provides identity. The contrast that provides motion may then be as small as the tones in a fugue subject or as vast as the thematic relationships of a symphonic movement. The relationship of the process to form is demonstrated by the formula i:m:t (impetus:motion:termination). The three functions occur at various hierarchic levels and may change roles. For example, a cadence chord, obviously a unit of termination, may also be the impetus for the next musical event. Thus, form results from the dialectic process and not from some formula that is chosen a priori. In *A Book about Stravinsky* Asafiev writes:

> Form in music is no abstract scheme into which materials are poured like wine into a crater. Form is the end result of the complicated process by which associations of sound elements crystallize themselves into our consciousness.[46]

The relationship of form as process to form as crystallized scheme results from the fact that musical forms are always evolving. A given formal description may be valid only for one era, one composer, or even for one work. Both *Musical Form* and *Intonation* emphasize that the evolution of musical language, and musical form as a part of it, is a socially determined process. The forms reflect the communal will of society as it chooses those intonations that adequately communicate between composer and listener. In some cases, however, a form becomes relatively stable for a period of time, probably, in Asafiev's view, because of relatively stable social forces. This results in a crystallized formal procedure, a classical norm.

Those themes that deal with the subject of intonation represent a more difficult, but at the same time more rewarding side of Asafiev's work. The connection between intonations and the culture that produced them is brought out in both volumes and is crucial to his hypothesis of the origin and development of musical language. From obscure origins intoning developed into a marriage of music and words—the rhythmic intonation of chant—and only later into purely musical intonation, potentially or actually free of verbal intonation. The freeing of music from words depended on the establishment of the interval as a distinctive feature, a measurable quantity in music. The evolution of music can be traced through the many rises and falls in specific intonations. The term here is used in the narrow sense of an identifiable fragment of music that is culturally determined, can be musically developed, and reflects life. The so-called life of an intonation ends when it ceases to be meaningful to a group of listeners or composers. A successful composer senses the balance between using familiar intonations that readily communicate and new intonations, the products of his creativity, that are more difficult to assimilate. In those eras when, because of social or cultural unrest, intonational requirements are changing rapidly, a "crisis of intonations" results. Asafiev's best example of this is the era of the French revolution that he says resulted in the new intonations of Beethoven's music. Asafiev asserts that it would be possible to compile a "dictionary of intonations" for a given era, made up of those intonations that most accurately reflect the time.

Thus music for Asafiev is intonation: all aspects of the musical art, including language, technique, form, style, and evolution are subject to and accounted for by the concept of intonation, music's basic communicative element. His obsession with this dominating theme is the work's strongest contribution and also its greatest weakness. By means of intonation as *melos,* he calls attention to the essential linearity of music. By means of intonation as communication, he shows how composer, performer, and listener are linked. Through the idea of form as process he finds the importance of contrast in music. But to assume that all music depends on dialectic, and that all change is rooted in the needs of society carries the theme further than it will easily go. It becomes too easy to identify contrast and then find a way to make it the source of motion, or to find a societal relationship and assume that it is the dominating force. But the value of Asafiev's ideas does not lie in consistency of thought, rigorous method, or accuracy of historical speculation, all of which may be found to be flawed. Rather, his controversial, polemical insights become a catalyst for thought and the basis for a new appreciation of the nature of music and of musical change.

That Asafiev's ideas are similar to those of Yavorsky has already been mentioned. Even a superficial examination of Asafiev's *Musical Form as a Process* and Yavorsky's *Structure of Musical Speech* shows some remarkable similarities in the face of radically different purposes and styles.[47] Both theorists are obsessed by the need to find a universal explanation for music. Both find it in dialectic and in the process of intonation. Yavorsky is interested in the mechanics of musical motion; Asafiev in its broad kinetics. Yavorsky studies intonations as cells in modal structures; Asafiev sees them as reflections of society. For Yavorsky, dialectic contrast makes a tritone resolve; Asafiev assumes that dialectics operate even in large forms. Yavorsky's universal theory is based on tritone systems; Asafiev's universal is the intonational communicative basis of music. In sum, Yavorsky and Asafiev developed theories that seem like the practical and philosophical sides of the same questions. Each seemingly developed those hypotheses that most favorably suited his intellectual makeup. Taken as a pair, the two theories make a remarkable complement that reflects the Russian theoretical thought of the era.

In terms of influence on subsequent thought, however, Asafiev's is both broader and deeper than Yavorsky's. As early as 1927, Asafiev was called "the founder of Russian musical science," and "the creator of an independent school of musicology."[48] Decades later Boris Schwarz reported the following:

> Asafiev shaped Soviet musicology in his own, wide-range image, and he established a tradition that balanced the study of the past with an awareness of the present. This—until today—is the profile of Soviet musicology, moulded through trial and error by one dynamic personality—Asafiev.[49]

The influence of Asafiev is felt as more than just a teacher and role model. His doctrine of intonation has become a cornerstone of modern Soviet thought on music. Its many potentials and contradictions are still being grappled with, and will be for many years to come.[50]

In the West, however, where his works are barely known, a proper assessment of his thought and its application awaits a substantial amount of basic study, including translations of important works such as *Symphonic Etudes* and *Glinka,* and a comprehensive survey of his writings. More important questions such as the history of the concept of intonation, the place of Asafiev in the development of Soviet musicology, and the relationship of intonation theory to analysis can then follow.

Notes

1. *Russian Music from the Beginning of the Nineteenth Century,* trans. Alfred J. Swan (Ann Arbor: J. W. Edwards, 1953); *A Book about Stravinsky,* trans. Richard F. French (Ann Arbor: UMI Research Press, 1982); and James R. Tull, "B. V. Asaf'ev's *Musical Form as a Process:* Translation and Commentary" (Ph.D. diss., The Ohio State University, 1977). In addition the following article has been translated: "The Great Russian Composer," in *Russian Symphony: Thoughts about Tchaikovsky* (New York: Philosophical Library, 1947).

2. *Muzykal'naia forma kak protsess* (Moscow: Muzsektor Gosizdata, 1930); *Muzykal'naia forma kak protsess kn. 2-aia* [book 2]. *Intonatsiia* (Moscow-Leningrad: Muzgiz, 1947). *Intonation* was reissued separately in *Izbrannye trudy* [Selected works], vol. 5 (Moscow: Izd. Akademii Nauk SSSR, 1957), pp. 163-276. Both parts were republished in an edition by E. M. Orlova (Leningrad: Gos. Muz. Izd., 1963). There is also a German translation, Boris Assafjew, *Die musikalische Form als Prozess,* ed. Dieter Lehmann and Eberhard Lippold, trans. Ernst Kuhn (Berlin: Verlag Neue Musik, 1976), and the English translation noted above.

3. Among these are *A Book about Stravinsky* [Kniga o Stravinskom] (Leningrad: Triton, 1929; Leningrad: Muzyka, 1977; and the English translation noted above); *Simfonicheskie etiudy* [Symphonic etudes] (Petrograd: State Philharmonic, 1922; Leningrad: Muzyka, 1970); *Glinka* (Moscow, 1947, 1950); *Evgenii Onegin, liricheskie stseny P. I. Chaikovskogo: opyt intonatsionnogo analiza stilia i muzykal'noi dramaturgii* [Eugene Onegin, lyric scenes by P.I. Tchaikovsky: an attempt at an intonational analysis of the style and musical dramaturgy] (Moscow and Leningrad, 1944); *Grieg (1843-1907): Issledovanie* [Grieg: Research], (Moscow, 1948), and numerous others.

4. The best sources for biographical data and the basis of this biographical sketch are the following: E. M. Orlova, *B. V. Asaf'ev, put' issledovatelia i publitsista* [The path of a researcher and publicist] (Leningrad: Muzyka, 1964); A. N. Kriukov, comp., *Materialy k biografii B. Asaf'eva* [Materials for a biography] (Leningrad: Muzyka, 1982); and his autobiography, "B. Asaf'ev o sebe" [About himself], in *Vospominaniia o B. V. Asaf'eve* [Recollections about B. V. Asafiev], comp. A. N. Kriukov (Leningrad: Muzyka, 1974), pp. 315-508. As yet there is no complete biography. See also M. Montagu-Nathan, "The Strange Case of Professor Assafiev," *Music and Letters* 38 (1957): 335-40; "B. V. Asafev et la musicologie russe avant et après 1917," in *Bericht uber den siebenten Internationalen musikwissenschaftlichen Kongress Köln 1958* (Kassel, 1959).

5. *Materialy,* p. 6. (All translations from Russian publications are mine except as noted.) See also Yury Olkhovsky, *Vladimir Stasov and Russian National Culture* (Ann Arbor: UMI Research Press, 1983).

6. *Materialy,* p. 7; also see the descriptions of Stasov and Rimsky-Korsakov in "B. Asaf'ev o sebe," pp. 379-433.

7. *Materialy,* p. 5.

8. *Melos. Kniga o muzyke pod redaktsiei Igoria Glebova i P. P. Suvchinskogo* [Melos. A book about music edited by Igor Glebov and P.P. Suvchinsky], Book 1 (St. Petersburg, 1917) and Book 2 (1918).

9. *Materialy,* pp. 10-11.

10. See note 3. For a summary of contents see Orlova, *Asafev*, pp. 95-99.

11. See note 3.

12. See note 2.

13. A more detailed summary of his positions appears in *Materialy*, pp. 166-69.

14. Orlova, pp. 241-43.

15. See Boris Schwarz, *Music and Musical Life in Soviet Russia, 1917-1970* (New York: W. W. Norton, 1972), pp. 109-19.

16. "Volnuiushchie voprosy" [Exciting questions], *Sovetskaia muzyka* 1936, no. 5. Reprinted in *Izbrannie trudy*, vol. 5, pp. 116-19.

17. Orlova, p. 9.

18. Orlova, p. 253. For an evaluation of his music see Stanley Dale Krebs, *Soviet Composers and the Development of Soviet Music* (New York: W. W. Norton, 1970), pp. 86-95.

19. See note 2.

20. See note 3.

21. *Mysli i dumy;* see the plan of the work in Orlova, pp. 330-31.

22. Alexander Werth, *Musical Uproar in Moscow* (London: Turnstile Press, 1949; reprint ed., Westport: Greenwood, 1973), pp. 96-98; Andrey Olkhovsky, *Music under the Soviets: The Agony of an Art* (New York: Praeger, 1955), pp. 81-85.

23. For complete bibliography see *Izbrannye trudy*, vol. 5, pp. 293-347; for a list of compositions, pp. 350-80.

24. Orlova, pp. 154-55.

25. Five letters are reproduced in *Materialy*, nos. 99, 106, 109, 115, 117.

26. Schwarz, p. 125.

27. Orlova, p. 172.

28. See Tull, pp. 107-41, for a discussion of this relationship.

29. Orlova, p. 7.

30. *Materialy*, p. 33. See also his essay, "O V. V. Stasove" [About V. V. Stasov], in the same work, pp. 40-43. Alexandra Molas, a singer, was a sister-in-law of Rimsky-Korsakov. *Kuchkism* refers to the Balakirev circle.

31. *Materialy, p. 36.*

32. Ernst Kurth, *Grundlagen des linearen Kontrapunkts* (Berlin, 1917); Russian translation by Z. Evald, edited and with introduction by B. V. Asafiev, *Osnovy linearnogo kontrapunkta* (Moscow, 1931). Kurth (1886-1946) was professor of musicology in Berne, Switzerland. In an article in *Sovetskaia muzyka* (1957, no. 3, pp. 73-82) entitled "O muzykal'no-teoreticheskoi kontseptsii B. Asaf'eva" [The musical theoretical conception of B. Asafiev], Lev Mazel carefully distinguishes between the two theories in such a manner that it underscores their similarities.

33. Letter to V. V. Derzhanovsky, May 3, 1915. B. Yavorsky. *Stat'i, vospominaniia, perepiska* [Articles, recollections, correspondence], ed. I. S. Rabinovich, 2d ed. (Moscow: Sovetskii

kompozitor, 1972), pp. 296-97. See also Jaroslav Jiranek, "K otázce tzv. dynamických muzikologických koncepcí poriemannovských (Javorskij, Kurth a Asafjev)" [Concerning the so-called dynamic post-Riemann musicological concepts (Javorsky, Kurth, Asafiev)], *Hudební věda* (1967): 71-105, English summary, pp. 176-78.

34. Orlova, pp. 412-13.

35. Schwarz, p. 391.

36. Orlova, p. 14.

37. *Materialy,* p. 31.

38. *Materialy,* p. 231.

39. Orlova, p. 119.

40. Orlova, p. 306; *Glinka,* p. 94.

41. Orlova, p. 49.

42. Orlova, p. 86.

43. p. 7; trans. Richard French.

44. *Izbrannye trudy,* vol. 5, p. 145.

45. Orlova, pp. 401-402. For a further discussion of this last sense, see Malcolm H. Brown, "The Soviet Russian Concepts of 'Intonazia' and 'Musical Imagery'," *The Musical Quarterly* 60 (1974): 557-67. A chart showing the development of several of these concepts appears in Orlova, pp. 444-51 and in German translation in *Die musikalische Form als prozess,* pp. 402-10.

46. p. 11; trans. Richard French.

47. See my article,"The Theories of Boleslav Yavorsky," also in this volume.

48. *Materialy,* p. 15.

49. Schwarz, p. 90.

50. See Malcolm Brown, op. cit.; also B. M. Yarustovsky, ed., *Intonatsiia i muzykal'nyi obraz* [Intonation and musical imagery] (Moscow: Muzyka, 1965); Jaroslav Jiránek, *Asafjevova teorie intonace, její geneze a význam* [Asafiev's theory of intonation, its significance and outline] (Prague: Academia, 1967); Jaroslav Jiránek, "Assafjews Intonationslehre und ihre Perspektiven," *De musica pragensis,* 1 (1972): 13-45.

The Contributions of Taneev, Catoire, Conus, Garbuzov, Mazel, and Tiulin

Ellon D. Carpenter

When, in the twentieth century, the theory of music in Russia became established as a discipline with serious research objectives (as part of the science of music, and later theoretical musicology) rather than a field with purely practical, pedagogical intentions (the theory of composition), it was due in large part to the efforts of the theorists Sergei Ivanovich Taneev, Georgy Lvovich Catoire, Georgy Eduardovich Conus, Nikolai Alexandrovich Garbuzov, Lev Abramovich Mazel, and Yury Nikolaevich Tiulin. Taneev especially, in the early years of this century, contributed his scholarly and organizational energies towards creating a Russian science of music. But each of the theorists in his own way made valuable contributions to the overall development of theoretical thought in Russia.

The purpose of this article is to investigate in detail the theoretical ideas of each of these scholars and to point out their significance for the future development of music theory in the Soviet Union. These theorists have not been grouped here because of any common theoretical approach or concept, but because, along with Yavorsky and Asafiev, they were the most influential and important theorists of their time. Therefore, because of their differing theoretical approaches and periods of activity, each theorist will be discussed individually and chronologically.

Sergei Ivanovich Taneev (1856-1915)

Of the six Russian theorists discussed in this article, Sergei Ivanovich Taneev is probably the best known to Western theorists. His reputation as a composer and as a teacher, and the availability in English of his major work, *Moveable Counterpoint in the Strict Style,* have resulted in an acquaintance among Westerners with his achievements not possible with lesser-known theorists.[1] Nevertheless, aside from some articles in English by former pupils regarding his counterpoint method, little has been written in the West about Taneev's theoretical views.[2] Yet his theories of counterpoint and of form profoundly influenced the growth of music theory in Russia, the development of theory pedagogy, and the compositional and theoretical abilities of his numerous pupils.

Taneev was born in the year of Mozart's centennial, which must have pleased him, considering his high regard for Mozart's music. He valued most highly the works of the masters—Palestrina, Bach, Mozart, and Beethoven— and used them as models for his own compositions and as sources for his theoretical studies. Indeed, as one of his later projects he traveled to Salzburg to examine Mozart's counterpoint notebooks.[3] Among Russian composers, he admired and performed works by Tchaikovsky, his teacher and friend.[4] Taneev also admired and encouraged the compositions of his own numerous pupils, but he stopped short of accepting Skryabin's later works, for example, considering them to be beyond the acceptable limits of tonality.

Taneev, perhaps the leading teacher of his day, was revered by students and colleagues alike, not only for his brilliance, but also for his devotion to music and to his students. During his twenty-seven-year tenure at the Moscow Conservatory (1878-1905), he taught a variety of subjects: harmony, instrumentation, piano, elementary theory, composition, counterpoint, and form. In later years he concentrated on counterpoint (both strict and free, beginning in 1886) and form, a course he initiated in 1897; these two subjects became his specialties.

Unfortunately, during his lifetime Taneev published only one book, his treatise on moveable counterpoint. However, he also had completed a sequel, *The Doctrine of the Canon,* which was published posthumously.[5] His plans for six other counterpoint works were never completed.[6] He had also hoped to write a book on form, and to that end made analyses of Bach fugues and Beethoven sonatas; but this project, too, remained incomplete. Many of these analyses and his letters have been published in recent years; from them it is possible to obtain some insight into Taneev's views on the subject of form.[7]

In his approach to theory pedagogy, Taneev was influenced to a great extent by the writings of Hermann Larosh, to whom Taneev dedicated his counterpoint treatise. Taneev fully concurred with Larosh's idea of the historical approach to the study of theory, and eventually provided the practical fulfillment of Larosh's views.[8] Thus his courses in strict counterpoint, fugue and free counterpoint, and form, in the words of one student, "compelled students to experience for themselves the entire historical process of the evolution of music, taught them to separate in art the essential from the secondary, [and] to evaluate also in the past the strong, the fantastic, the eternal."[9]

Taneev himself had not undergone such a regimen of instruction at the Moscow Conservatory; only after his graduation in 1875 did he begin to study counterpoint in earnest.[10] During the 1880s he began to work out more systematic methods for such studies, which he applied in his classes and eventually published in his treatise. Therefore he did not derive his pedagogical methods from his professors; rather, he developed them according to his own needs and aspirations as a composer. He passed them on to his students, hoping to prevent in them deficiencies such as he had experienced.

Taneev's more systematic, scientific approaches countered the empirical method, the "trying-on method," as one student put it, that prevailed in the conservatories during Taneev's student years and later.[11] Taneev's approach was also flexible and historically accurate:

> The rules and norms of music were not "absolute" or self sufficient... but were only conditional rules, characteristic of a particular style, which was studied at a given time. What was not acceptable in one style was completely acceptable in another. And the observance of these rules is not *the observance of the rules of music in general,* but only the practical study of music of some particular style.[12]

In his theoretical studies and teachings, Taneev aspired to one basic goal: the enrichment and improvement of compositional technique. This, he believed, could be achieved not so much through the development of new harmonic means, which composers were rapidly exhausting in their search for original ideas, but through counterpoint, which was capable of providing endless opportunities for the derivation of new and interesting material.[13] As substitutes for the hyperbolic, chromatic excesses and the gradual dissolution of tonality in music of his day, Taneev advocated two techniques—the infusion into a composition of more counterpoint, resulting in a more varied thematic design, and more attention to the overall structure of a composition, expressed through the use of a modulatory plan coordinated with the thematic design. Regarding the application of counterpoint in new music, he wrote:

> In multi-voice music, melodic and harmonic elements are subject to the influences of the time and to the nationality and individuality of composers. But the forms of imitation, canon, and complex counterpoint—either as actualities or as possibilities—are universally valid; they are independent of such conditions, capable of entering into the plan of any harmonic system and adaptable to any melodic idiom.... As for the music of today, the harmony that has gradually lost its virility would be greatly benefited by the strength that the contrapuntal forms can infuse. Beethoven, who in his later works reverted to the technical methods of the old contrapuntalists, sets the best example for composers of the future. The music of today is essentially contrapuntal. Not only in large orchestral works, where the abundance of independent parts often results in obscurity, or in opera, where leitmotifs are worked out contrapuntally, but even in pieces of insignificant dimensions, can counterpoint be employed to the greatest advantage. The study of free counterpoint is therefore indispensable for the technical training of composers, but because of its melodic and harmonic intricacy it cannot be studied first. The foundation must be laid by counterpoint of the strict style, more accessible because of its simplicity.[14]

Thus he devoted his first work to one aspect of the strict style, that of moveable or shifting counterpoint, which he considered "the most important and extensive phase of complex counterpoint."[15] He analyzed exhaustively the concept of voice-shifting, both vertical and horizontal, following

> the principle that in complex counterpoint both the original and the derivative combinations must satisfy the requirements of simple counterpoint. The analysis of the concept of shifting governs the general plan of the book and it includes in its scope shifting counterpoint in all of its many phases, where each form has a definite place, irrespective of whether or not it is used. The consistent application of these principles gives the system of rules for shifting counterpoint.[16]

Moveable Counterpoint in the Strict Style actually fulfills two functions: On the one hand, it is a scholarly treatise presenting a detailed study of the technical achievements of the masters of the strict style in the sphere of moveable counterpoint; and on the other hand, it is a textbook for the systematic exploration and mastery of moveable counterpoint with the goal of developing the compositional technique of composers of any era. Thus it may be read and studied with a view towards enriching one's knowledge, one's technique, or both.

However, Taneev's objective, as he stated it, was

> not to analyze and classify examples from musical literature but to develop the deductive faculty.... The deductive method can be applied without difficulty in a given case, owing to the fact that... [the] capacity [of the voices] to shift and the resulting relationship are completely subject to mathematical treatment. Basing the study of shifting counterpoint on elementary algebra renders possible exhaustive statement together with a conciseness otherwise unobtainable. A cursory view of the program of shifting counterpoint leads to the conclusion that musical literature uses only a few of the resources available.... Many of the examples quoted ... refer to forms of shifting counterpoint never before actualized in music.
>
> It is believed that the study of this book will lead to the conviction that only on the basis of mathematics can be built a clear and rational theory of shifting counterpoint; that it is no longer possible to revert to the redundant, vague, inaccurate, and confused explanations of former times, and that only the method of mathematics can rend the veil of semi-mystical secrecy that for such a long time has obscured the study of convertible counterpoint.[17]

Taneev based his application of mathematics to counterpoint on an elementary but very important procedure: He designated the intervals (diatonic), not by ordinal numbers as they are usually named, but by cardinal numbers, from 0 for unison to 7 for octave. He applied these designations to the measurement of time as well as to intervallic distance. This "audio-visual approach to the subject" enabled Taneev to formulate simple algebraic equations representing original and derivative contrapuntal combinations.[18] Numbers representing intervallic distances of either time or pitch can be easily added to or subtracted from these equations to represent new possible combinations.

Another important device that Taneev developed involves the graphic representation of dissonances, which in strict counterpoint must be carefully controlled, with various symbols: the line, "−," the line with parentheses, "(−)," or the line with an x, "−x." Used in conjunction with the intervallic numbers, these symbols designate which intervals are dissonances, the type of dissonance, and the appropriate treatment of the dissonance. Placed above the number, the symbol refers to the upper voice; below, to the lower voice. For example, the number three with a line over it, $\overline{3}$, represents a suspension of a fourth in the upper voice and its resolution one step downward.[19] These symbols, together with Taneev's attendant simplification of the rules regarding dissonances, greatly facilitated this aspect of strict counterpoint.

The two-voice contrapuntal combination forms the foundation for multi-voice counterpoint, for Taneev regarded "multi-voice counterpoint as the union of various combinations of two-voice counterpoint," which he considered "as a basic principle of the strict style":

> From this principle may be deduced both the conditions of simple multi-voice counterpoint, beginning with the first species, and the conditions of complex counterpoint in all of its many phases.... To know the rules [of two-voice counterpoint] is to possess the key to the whole domain of strict counterpoint.... Due to the simplicity on which it is based, counterpoint of the strict style is an art unique with symmetry, naturalness, and logic as its foundations. All its infinite variety is but an evolution from the basis, easily comprehensible, of two-voice counterpoint.[20]

In two-part counterpoint, the upper, first voice is designated by I, the lower, second voice, by II. Adding them together, I + II, gives the formula for the original two-voice combination. The formula for a derivative combination, the result of the shift of one or both of the voices, results from the addition to the original formula of superscripts denoting the intervallic distance shifted, designated by the interval numbers, and the direction of the shift, designated as positive or negative. Voice I moving up and voice II moving down are both positive shifts. Movements in the opposite directions are negative, as shown: $\overline{\text{I}}$ $\underline{\text{II}}$. In the superscript, the letter v indicates a *vertical* shift. Thus, the formula $\text{I}_{v=-2} + \text{II}_{v=-7}$ designates a combination in which the upper voice has moved down a third (−2) and the lower voice has shifted up an octave (−7). The formula for the derivative combination will differ depending on the size and direction of the shifts.

The algebraic sum of the vertical shifts of the two voices $(\text{I}_{v=-2} + \text{II}_{v=-7})$ equals the index of the vertical-shifting contrapuntal combination, indicated Jv.[21] For the example stated, $Jv = -9$. As Taneev stated,

> Adding the value of the index to an interval of the original combination gives the corresponding interval of the derivative.... The important idea implied by the use of the symbol Jv simplifies the study of vertical-shifting counterpoint; it yields numerous possibilities of voice-shifting with a comparatively small number of indices.[22]

Example 1 illustrates an original combination and three derivatives obtained from it. The formula for the original (a) is I + II. The formula for derivative (b) is $(\text{I} + \text{II}_{v=3})$ $Jv = 3$; for derivative (c), $(\text{I} + \text{II}_{v=-2})$ $Jv = -2$; for derivative (d), $(I + II_{v=-9})$ $Jv = -9$. Adding the Jv to the intervals in the original results in the intervals in the derivative; for example, in (d):

original:	4	7	6	5	4	2	3	4
Jv:	−9	−9	−9	−9	−9	−9	−9	−9
(d):	−5	−2	−3	−4	−5	−7	−6	−5

Ex. 1   Vertical-shifting counterpoint: a) original combination: I +
II; b) derivative: $(I + II_{v=3})$ $Jv = 3$; c) derivative: $(I + II_{v=-2})$ $Jv = -2$; d) derivative: $(I + II_{v=-9})$ $Jv = -9$

In this case, the shift is inverse, meaning that both voices change their relative position; therefore, the intervals in the derivative are represented by negative numbers.[23]

Horizontal-shifting counterpoint involves "combinations giving derivatives by means of the temporal shifting of voices, i.e., by changing the relationship between the time-intervals of their entries."[24] The formula for a horizontal-shifting contrapuntal combination is represented similarly to that for a vertical-shifting combination. In the superscript, *h* represents a *horizontal* shift, the cardinal number indicates a measure (or fraction, if a portion of a measure) as the unit of distance, and the shift direction is, for I, positive to the left, negative to the right, and for II, the reverse: + I − II +. The positive and negative directions of voices I and II for both vertical- and horizontal-shifting counterpoint may be summarized in this way: + $\overset{.}{I}$ − $\overset{.}{II}$ +. The algebraic sum of the two voices is *Jh,* the index of horizontal-shifting counterpoint. Example 2 illustrates two versions of horizontal-shifting counterpoint based on the original in example 1a. In example 2a, the formula is $(I_{h=-\frac{1}{2}} + II)$ $Jh = -\frac{1}{2}$; in example 2b, $(I_{h=-1} + II)$ $Jh = -1$.

Ex. 2   Horizontal-shifting counterpoint: a) derivative: $(I_{h=-\frac{1}{2}} + II)$
Jh $= -\frac{1}{2}$; b) derivative: $(I_{h=-1} + II)$ Jh $= -1$

Double-shifting counterpoint combines both vertical- and horizontal-shifting counterpoint. Example 3 illustrates several derivatives, again based on the original in example 1. The formula for example 3a is:

$$(I^{h=-\frac{1}{2}}_{v=-9} + II) \; Jh = -\frac{1}{2}, \; Jv = -9;$$

for example 3b:

$$(I^{h=-1}_{v=5} + II) \; Jh = -1, \; Jv = 5;$$

for example 3c:

$$(I^{h=-1\frac{1}{2}}_{v=0} + II^{h=0}_{v=5}) \; Jh = -1\frac{1}{2}, \; Jv = 5.$$

Ex. 3   Double-shifting counterpoint: a) derivative: $(I^{h=-\frac{1}{2}}_{v=-9} + II)$
Jh $= -\frac{1}{2}$, Jv $= -9$; b) derivative: $(I^{h=-1}_{v=5} + II)$ Jh $= -1$,
Jv $= 5$; c) derivative: $(I^{h=-1\frac{1}{2}}_{v=0} + II^{h=0}_{v=5})$ Jh $= -1\frac{1}{2}$,
Jv $= 5$

Taneev represented three-part counterpoint as three separate two-part combinations. The third, lowest voice is indicated by III, resulting in three different formulae: I + II (index Jv′ or Jh′), II + III (Index Jv″ or Jh″) and I + III (index JvS or JhS).[25]

Horizontal-shifting counterpoint involves an element not encountered in vertical-shifting counterpoint—the addition of a voice in canonic imitation with one of the original voices. Taneev labeled this derivative, imitating voice as *R*, for *risposta* (Italian for answer or reply). He called the original voice *P*, for *proposta* (proposal), and the nonimitated voice, *CP*, for counterpoint. This combination of three voices "that serves as the basis for horizontal-shifting counterpoint, and of which the indispensable attribute is canonic imitation, is termed the basic version."[26] The basic version contains both the original two-voice combination, *P* + *CP*, and the derivative combination, *R* + *CP*. Example 4 illustrates horizontal-shifting counterpoint as created by Palestrina. In the basic version, example 4a, *P* is imitated by *R* and accompanied by *CP*. In example 4b, *P* + *CP* make up the original combination, and *CP* + *R*, the derivative combination.

Ex. 4   Horizontal-shifting counterpoint: a) basic version by
         Palestrina; b) original combination (top) and derived
         combination (bottom): $(I_{h=0} + II_{h=-2})$ Jh$= -2$

The principles and rules formulated by Taneev in *Moveable Counterpoint in the Strict Style* remain essentially the same for his sequel, *The Doctrine of the Canon.* Since they are not repeated in the later work, study of this volume should be preceded by study of *Moveable Counterpoint in the Strict Style.* In *The Doctrine of the Canon,* in which he investigated the application of shifting counterpoint to canonic imitation, Taneev concentrated first on the two-voice canon, which forms the basis for the multi-voice canon, and then the three- and four-voice canon. He distinguished two types—the "finite" canon, which concludes with a cadence, and the "infinite" canon, in which the voices may be repeated from their beginnings. Each type of canon contains two categories, depending on the distance between the voice entries and, consequently, the method of shifting counterpoint applied. Canons in the first category contain the same distances between the entries of the voices; they are written by the rules of vertical-shifting counterpoint. Canons in the second category contain different distances between the entries of the voices; they are written by the rules of horizontal-shifting counterpoint.

In both categories, Taneev differentiated between the infinite canon in which P *(proposta)* repeats on the same degree or the infinite canon in which P transfers to different degrees. He called the latter occurrence a canonic sequence. Of the two types of two-voice canon, only the infinite requires the application of shifting counterpoint. And within this type, the infinite two-voice canonic sequence of the first category has the most significance for composition. In general, the multi-voice canon has greater possibilities for practical application than the two-voice canon. Finite canons and infinite canonic sequences of the first category are the types of multi-voice canons most frequently met in the literature. As Taneev pointed out, the remaining types of infinite multi-voice canons belong in the realm of theoretical works. To illustrate Taneev's methods, only the infinite two-voice canon of the first category will be examined here.

As in *Moveable Counterpoint in the Strict Style,* Taneev applied an audio-visual approach to the study of canon, devising schematic diagrams and the like to illustrate visually the various characteristics of the canonic schemes: distance, direction, and the number and combinations of the various entries. Example 5 illustrates an infinite two-voice canon of the first category in which P repeats on the same degree. He represented the "distance of entry" between P and R, and R and $_n P$ (the repeated imitation of P) with vertical slashes on a horizontal line (ex. 5c). He designated the "interval of entry," the interval at which R enters in relation to P, by a cardinal number, and the "direction of entry" by an arrow accompanying the interval number. In example 5a, the downward-pointing arrow and the number 7 indicate that the appearance of R is an octave below P.

This canon requires the application of vertical-shifting counterpoint. To accomplish this, the original and derived combinations must be determined. For this purpose Taneev divided the canonic voices into motivic segments

Ex. 5   a) Infinite two-voice canon of first category; b) distance,
direction, and interval of entry of the voices; c) equal length
of the distance of entries

which, when combined initially, represent the original combination, and when shifted, the derived combination. For instance, in example 5a, *P* is divided into the segments *A* and *B*, *R* into *A'* and *B'*. The original combination, which in the two-voice canon occurs beginning with the entry of *R*, is B + A'; the derived combination, which occurs beginning with the entry of ₙ*P*, is A + B'. Figure 1 illustrates the resulting combinations in a two-voice infinite canon of the first category with *P* repeating on the same degree.

Fig. 1   Two-voice infinite canon of the first category with *P* on
the same degrees

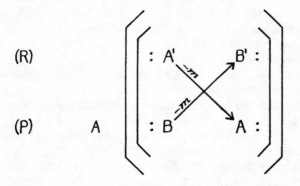

Since this type of canon contains equal distances between the entries, the number of segments equals the number of voices. The algebraic sum of the intervals of entry (designated *m*) of the two segments equals the vertical index *(Jv)*. In figure 1, both *m*s are negative because the voices are moving in directions opposite to their usual placement. Consequently, $Jv = -2m$ represents the general formula for a two-voice infinite canon in the first category with *P* repeating on the same degree. Example 5, a canon at the octave ($m = 7$), illustrates one of the most frequently used Jvs, double counterpoint at the octave, also equivalent to $Jv = -14$. The Jv may be reduced by 7, an octave; if Jv is not an even number, in order to find m, one must add 7 and then divide by 2. Other frequently used Jvs include −9, double counterpoint at the tenth (canon at the ninth: $m = 8$, $Jv = -16$), and −11, double counterpoint at the twelfth (canon at the tenth: $m = 9$; $Jv = -18$).

The second type of the infinite two-voice canon in the first category, in which P transfers to different degrees, either in ascending or descending order, is known as a canonic sequence of the first category. The most frequent instance of this occurs when A (the original segment of P) is transferred in the direction opposite to the direction of its first imitative entry, shown in figure 2.

Fig. 2   Two-voice infinite canon of the first category with P on
different degrees

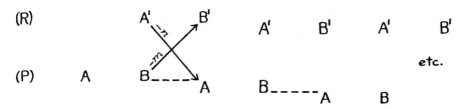

Taneev designated the letter m for the original interval of entry, as in the previous case, and the letter n for the derived interval of entry, which in this type of canon differs from the original interval of entry. The formula $Jv = -m-n$ therefore becomes the general formula for all infinite two-voice canons in the first category in which the intervals of entry have different direction. The formula $Jv = -2m$ designates a partial case of the formula $Jv = -m-n$; since P is repeated on the same degrees, the derived interval of entry (n) equals the original interval of entry (m). If the direction of both of the intervals of entry (the original and the derived) were the same—a case rarely met because the upper voice would get too high—the formula would be $Jv = -m+n$. Thus, the general formula for all canonic sequences must be $Jv = -m(\pm n)$. In example 6, which illustrates a canonic sequence such as that diagrammed in figure 2, the formula is $Jv-3-4$ or $Jv = -7$; in other words, the original combination should be written in double counterpoint at the octave.

Ex. 6   Canonic sequence: $Jv = -7$

Ex. 6 cont.

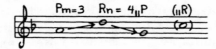

As an example of a canonic sequence in free style, Taneev quoted an excerpt from Mozart's *Ave Verum,* shown in example 7. He stressed that the infinite canonic sequence has wide application in composition, and is found both in works in the strict style, particularly of the Netherlands composers, and in works in the free style.

Ex. 7   Mozart, *Ave Verum*

Thus, these elements constitute the basic application of vertical-shifting counterpoint to the two-voice infinite canon of the first category. In expanded versions, they apply also to multi-voice canons of the first category. The application of horizontal-shifting counterpoint to the two-voice infinite canon, for example, again requires the addition of a third voice ($R\ldots$), which carries the same intervallic relationship to P as $_{,,}P$ does to R. The original combination thus becomes $P + R\ldots$ and the derived, $R+_{,,}P$. Only through this device is it possible to determine, as one is composing P, the correctness of further combinations, in this case $R+_{,,}P$. Taneev followed this basic procedure as well for the application of horizontal-shifting counterpoint to multi-voice canons.

As in two-voice canons, three-voice canons require separate applications of either vertical- or horizontal-shifting counterpoint, depending on the category. The four-voice canon, though, may require the simultaneous application of both types of shifting counterpoint in mixed cases in which both equal and different distances of entry appear, designated as *aba, aab,* or *abb.* The letter *a* refers to the original distance of entry between P and R and all subsequent equivalent distances; the letter *b* refers to subsequent different distances. Other four-voice combinations are *aaa* and *abc.*

These unique features of Taneev's methods of writing and teaching counterpoint enabled students to master easily what had previously been a very difficult subject. As one student explained, "Now there are no 'difficult' and 'more difficult' double counterpoints—since they are all equally easy."[27] Taneev's systematic, logical, and thorough approach to contrapuntal composition, aided by the application of mathematics, gave composers an invaluable compositional tool, one which, if applied properly, would reap wide benefits for musical composition. Equally important, his creative and scholarly methods set an example for numerous young Russian theorists at a time when he was most in a position to be influential, the time when Russian music theory was beginning to expand beyond its pedagogical, practical origins into scientific and speculative realms. Taneev's work in counterpoint, containing as it does both pedagogical and scientific significance, helped Russian music theory to make this transition.

Had Taneev written his proposed book on form, he might be known today not only as a master of polyphony but also as a master of form. Certainly his students saw him in that light, owing to his conservatory course in form, upon which he placed great importance. The content of this course ranged from small forms such as the sentence (phrase) and the period to large forms such as the song, rondo, and sonata. Taneev emphasized particularly the sonata form, which, in his view, embodied all the elements contributing to the artistic unity of a successful musical composition—thematic transformation and development, a reliance on tonality and a tonal scheme, and a logical structure. The sonata form provided an important compositional model, Taneev felt, primarily because of the delicate interrelation between thematic content and tonality inherent to the form.[28]

By the time students arrived in his class on form, they had already taken two years of counterpoint, also from Taneev. Thus they were able to work out problems of thematic development and variation with little difficulty. Taneev therefore concentrated on the modal-harmonic and rhythmic-structural aspects of form. For Taneev, the foundation of diatonic tonality served as the principle means of formal organization in instrumental music. He outlined the contribution of tonality to the development of form:

> The free style enables entire groups of harmonies to be consolidated into one organic whole and then by means of modulation to dissect this whole into factors that are tonally interdependent. This characteristic, absent in the former harmony, provided the conditions for the development of the free forms of instrumental music that appeared at the end of the eighteenth and during the first half of the nineteenth century. This new tonal system made possible the writing of works of large dimensions that possessed all the qualities of effective structural style and that did not have to be reinforced by texts or by imitative forms *per se,* but contained within themselves the necessity for the latter. By degrees this system widened and deepened and its spreading circle embraced newer and newer resources and laws governing the relations between remote harmonies. Such were the broad horizons opened up for harmony; the creative activity of Beethoven then appears, and he, by a further expansion of the modulatory plans as they stood at the end of the eighteenth century, showed how much variety of key-relationship a composition could exhibit, both in its larger and smaller aspects.[29]

He thus considered Beethoven's music the apogee of the application of diatonic tonality to formal unification. Taneev did not approve of the chromatic harmony that followed, though:

> This tonal system was in turn affected by a new one that tended to endanger key sense by the substitution of a chromatic for a diatonic basis; this led to a transformation of musical form. Applying the principle that by the use of chromatic progression any chord may follow any other, and pushing it too far, is likely to compromise key-relationship and to exclude those factors by which the smaller units of form are grouped and amalgamated into one organic whole.[30]

This new "omnitonal" harmony—so named by Fétis, as Taneev pointed out— "is inimical to the logic of tonality and forms"; while it may add "to the resources of composition," it nevertheless "lacks the virility of the diatonic method."[31]

> To remain for a time in one key, as opposed to more or less rapid modulation, the contrast afforded by passing gradually to a new key, with a return to the principal key—all this, by contributing to the clearness of long movements and enabling the listener to comprehend their forms, has little by little disappeared from contemporary music. The result has been the production of small works and a general decline in the art of composition. Unity of construction appears with less and less frequency. Works are written not as consistent organisms but as formless masses of mechanically associated parts, any of which might be replaced by others.[32]

Therefore, the disintegration of the diatonic tonal framework has led to the disintegration of formal logic and unity as well. In his counterpoint treatise, Taneev advocated the infusion of contrapuntal technique to revive music, following the example of Beethoven, "who in his later works reverted to the technical methods of the old contrapuntalists."[33] He considered the music of his day to be "essentially contrapuntal":

> Not only in large orchestral works, where the abundance of independent parts often results in obscurity, or in opera, where leitmotifs are worked out contrapuntally, but even in pieces of insignificant dimensions, can counterpoint be employed to the greatest advantage.[34]

At the same time, though, Taneev urged young composers not to ignore the benefits—the necessity, even—of formal logic expressed through tonality, i.e., modulation:

> I believe that in the area of modulation we have made a great step backwards compared with the musicians of former times and, having complicated its means, have become entangled in this complexity and have lost the sensitivity to modulation that nearly correctly guided previous masters, creating logical and expedient modulatory plans.[35]

For Taneev the modulatory plan needed to exhibit some unifying principle as well, and to that end he conceived of the idea of a *unifying tonality* to provide it:

> As a tonality brings a connection and a unity to the series of chords belonging to it, so a series of tonalities may by joined into a tonality of a higher order. We call such a tonality *unifying*. If, for example, in the cadence of C major [ex. 8a], deviations into the tonality corresponding to its separate chords are made [ex. 8b], then these tonalities preserve among themselves the same connection that the chords of the cadence had, and so their unifying tonality will be C major [ex. 8c].[36]

Ex. 8   Formation of a unifying tonality

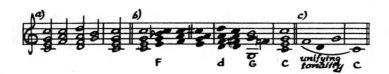

Taneev derived this principle of a unifying tonality, as he derived all his theoretical ideas, from his observations of actual practice. He observed it particularly in the music of Beethoven. In one study he analyzed twenty-one different modulating passages taken from transitional, developmental, and episodic segments of various movements in Beethoven piano sonatas.[37] The various tonalities touched upon in these modulations (which also include deviations and passing modulations) "belong to" (in the sense that individual chords "belong to" or are "in" a certain tonality) or are related to, a unifying tonality. "The relation of tonalities of the middle part [of a work] to the main [tonality] and between themselves (the juxtaposition of tonalities) is the same as for separate chords.... If one takes a row of tonic chords, they should form a satisfactory progression."[38] For example, in the Trio from the Piano Sonata op. 2 no. 3, measures 9-16 (the contrasting "B" section) exhibit in clear succession the tonalities C major, D minor, and E major, all of which are subordinated to the unifying tonality of the tonic A minor (ex. 9).

Ex. 9   Beethoven, Sonata for piano op. 2 no. 3, Trio, mm. 9-16

As in this example, the unifying tonality is often the main tonality; this occurs in nine of the twenty-one passages. The unifying tonalities of the other passages are related to the main tonality, either as parallel minor (seven passages), relative minor (two), the dominant (two), or the minor dominant (one). The subordinate tonalities vary in their relationship with the unifying tonality. Most of their tonic triads may be found among the chords of the unifying tonality; others may be found among the chords belonging to the parallel major or minor mode of the unifying tonality. Such altered harmonies as the lowered II and the lowered VI, which occur often, are borrowed from the parallel minor mode. Frequently, Taneev explained, these altered harmonies, occurring in the context of a major mode, recall the minor mode so strongly that the parallel minor mode unexpectedly becomes the unifying tonality, as in example 11 below. Also, the lowered submediant frequently substitutes for its minor tonic. The passage shown in example 10, from the Rondo (third movement) of the Sonata op. 14 no. 1 "presents an example of the juxtaposition of the major and minor subdominants in the capacity of unifying tonalities."[39] Here, Taneev regarded F major as a substitute for A minor, the minor subdominant of E major.

Ex. 10   Beethoven, Sonata for piano op. 14 no. 1, Rondo (third movement), mm. 90-108 (repeat of first episode)

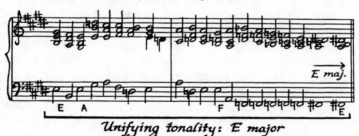

In the passage shown in example 11, from the Rondo of the Sonata op. 2 no. 2, "the deviation into the major tonality a major third below may be explained as an aspiration of the harmony to a unifying tonality equal to the parallel minor."[40] In this case also, F major, VI in A minor, substitutes for its tonic.

Ex. 11   Beethoven, Sonata for piano op. 2 no. 2, Rondo, mm. 139-148 (third return of theme)

In two of his analyses, Taneev carried the hierarchy of tonalities one step further, to what he called "a unifying tonality of a higher order." From the Scherzo of the Sonata op. 2 no. 3, the passage shown in example 12

represents *a unifying tonality of a higher order.* We will use this name for the case when a tonality, subordinate to the unifying [tonality], itself becomes unifying. So, for example, the deviation from A♭ major and the deviation into G major following it point to the unifying tonality, C minor. At the same time the tonality A♭ major is a unifying tonality in relation to the progression of tonalities: C minor, B♭ minor, A♭ major.[41]

Ex. 12   Beethoven, Sonata for piano op. 2 no. 3, Scherzo, mm.
            17-28 (contrasting "B" section)

As may be observed in the examples presented here, Taneev notated the rate of harmonic change only in a general way, with whole notes and fermatas for lengthier occurrences. The other harmonies, although notated identically, actually vary in length from one beat to five measures. He certainly was not unaware of this aspect, though, according to his students.[42] But he apparently preferred to concentrate on correlating harmonic change and important moments in the other elements of the music. In a letter to the young Russian composer Nikolai Nikolaevich Amani, for instance, Taneev pointed to the correspondence between the elements of melody and rhythm and significant occurrences in the modulatory plan in his explanation of a passage from the Scherzo from the Sonata op. 2 no. 2, shown in example 13:

[In this passage] the dominant is the unifying tonality [ex. 13a]. After the appearance of E major, all the while having been prepared by the previous tonalities, a deviation into D major follows directly. This juxtaposition of E [major] and D [major] points to a new expected tonality of A major, and the appearance of the 4/3 inversion [of the dominant] of A major is the result of the entire previous movement of the harmony [ex. 13b]. We turn attention to the fact that the important moments of the modulatory plan are marked thematically. When the development begins, the first two tonalities [E major and F♯ minor, in measures 9-13] still do not point to the unifying tonality (E major); they both could belong also to A major. But the appearance of G♯ minor [measures 15-25] points without a doubt to E major as the unifying tonality, and this moment is marked by a change in motion (eighth-notes in the accompaniment) and by a new theme [ex. 13c].[43]

Ex. 13   Beethoven, Sonata for piano op. 2 no. 2, Scherzo, mm. 9-
           32 (B section)

This illustration becomes clear when compared to Taneev's earlier analysis of
the modulatory plan of the same passage, shown in example 14. He defined E
major as a lower-level unifying tonality and A major as a unifying tonality of a
higher order.

Ex. 14   Beethoven, Sonata for piano op. 2 no. 2, Scherzo, mm. 9-
           32 (B section)

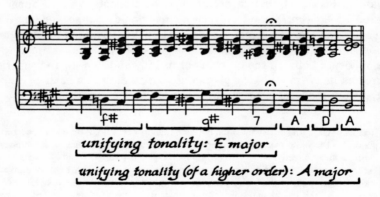

In another, more complicated example, Taneev shows that the
modulatory plan of the development section of the first movement from the
Sonata op. 14 no. 2 (ex. 15) is influenced by the rhythm, dynamics, and theme:

The first five modulations belong to the unifying tonality of E♭ major. The moment where this tonality is defined as a unifying tonality is marked: the sudden shift from *pp* to *f,* the introduction of the motion [of sixteenth-note triplets] and the appearance of the main theme [m. 81]. Another important moment of the approach [of E♭] after the prolonged preparation is marked by a long stop on its dominant, with a fermata; a change in motion (a cessation of the triplets) and the appearance of the main part coincide with the appearance of the tonic triad E♭ major [m. 98]. The tonalities [C minor and G minor] following E♭ major are apportioned little space (two bars) [mm. 104-106], but then great significance is given to the pause on the D major triad (dominant of G minor, preparing for the appearance of G major in the recapitulation). The movement of thirty-second [notes], hitherto absent in the development, is introduced on this chord [m. 107]. The triad itself is repeated faster. A new section with triplets in the left hand appears [m. 115]. Thus, the attention of the listener is concentrated on the juxtaposition of E♭ [major] and D [major], which attracts the main tonality [ex. 15b].[44]

Ex. 15   Beethoven, Sonata for piano op. 14 no. 2, first movement,
          mm. 64-124 (development section)

This example resembles example 4 in that the unifying tonality is the parallel minor of the main tonality of the movement, reinforced by the appearance of lowered VI.

Taneev called this modulatory plan "a model of logic and expediency."[45] However, any modulatory plan with a unifying tonality exhibits these characteristics to some degree. A unifying tonality is manifested only when the tonalities making up the modulatory plan are chosen and grouped in such a way that they point inexorably, logically, to a definite tonality, the unifying tonality, frequently also the goal of the modulatory plan. But which factors or which harmonies contribute to the creation of a unifying tonality? What governs the choice of a unifying tonality? Taneev revealed the important role of the interval of the tritone in this regard. He repeated the thought, "expressed by Fétis . . . that the augmented fourth, the tritone, which was so feared in the epoch of the strict style, was made a foundation of our harmonic system."[46] The two notes of the tritone, the fourth and seventh degrees of the diatonic scale, "mutually pushing away and attracting us to tonic, bring to harmony an element of movement or aspiration"[47] (ex. 16a). The chords that form this interval, which in Taneev's illustrations are either II and V or IV and V, aspire to tonic. From their juxtaposition, a given tonality may be sensed before the appearance of its tonic triad (ex. 16b and c). According to Taneev, the same effect occurs between unified tonalities:

When a similar tritone relationship does not occur in a succession of tonalities, the harmony develops smoothly, quietly and does not aspire to a definite point.... In such a case the unifying tonality is not expressed clearly, and frequently a succession [of tonalities] might belong to two or more unifying tonalities. But when a tonality carrying the above-mentioned tritone relationship occurs, the harmony aspires to a definite point that is expected by the listener. It is customary ... to modulate into the dominant of the dominant of the secondary part [of a sonata form, for example], so that a progression is formed in which the beginning tonality is in a tritone relationship to the concluding tonality. [This custom] is rooted in the essence of the harmony itself [ex. 16c].[48]

Ex. 16   Tritone relation: a) resolution to major sixth; b) tritone
between chords; c) tritone between tonic and dominant of
the dominant

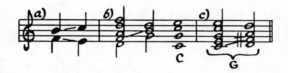

Thus the juxtaposition of the original tonic, in this case C major, with the new dominant, D major, creates the tritone C-F♯, which aspires to the now tonic, G major, the unifying tonality. This progression may also be identified as IV-V-I. Within a tonality, this tritone juxtaposition occurs between the subdominant (II or IV) and the dominant, as in the progression *T-S-D-T*. Taneev pointed out that the augmented second between the lowered sixth degree and the leading tone may substitute for the tritone to a certain extent. Such is the case in example 15, in the juxtaposition of the E♭ major and D major triads preparing for G. The augmented second E♭-F♯ resolves to D-G. The tritone in this progression, E♭-A, would lead to the tonality of B♭ if it were regarded as the subdominant and the leading tone.[49]

Taneev graphically illustrated this juxtaposition of the subdominant and the dominant in his tonal schemes of the development of sonata movements from the Beethoven piano sonatas. Figure 3 illustrates the development section of the first movement of Sonata op. 13.[50] The straight line represents the main tonality of the movement, C minor; all tonalities above it are on the dominant side, below it, the subdominant. Approximately in the middle of the development, the tonalities of the subdominant and the dominant are directly juxtaposed, indicating the tonic as the eventual goal. Here again, the lengths of the tonalities are not represented accurately. The subdominant actually takes up about one-fourth of the development, and the major dominant, one-half. Nevertheless, Taneev clearly depicted the interaction between the dominant and subdominant "spheres" in the development section, which culminated in their juxtaposition and the aspiration towards tonic.

Fig. 3   Beethoven, Sonata for piano op. 13, first movement,
development section

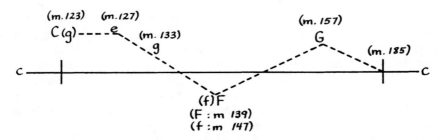

Outside of the modulatory plan and its attendant unifying tonality, attention to structural logic, particularly as manifested in the thematic and harmonic development within a movement, also concerned Taneev. For the development section of the sonata, for instance, Taneev differentiated seven types of formal sentence structure. Each type he isolated (such as the modulating sentence repeated sequentially in the first movement of the Sonata op. 14 no. 2) illustrates the coordination between the sentence structure and the variations of the thematic and harmonic material.[51] He also compared the recapitulation of the sonata form with the exposition to determine the types of structural changes in the recapitulation.[52] His findings reinforced his propensity for variety in structure as well as in melody, harmony, and rhythm within the limits of a recognizable form such as the sonata.

Taneev carried out his theoretical studies of both counterpoint and form with a practical goal in view—the education and development of composers and theorists.[53] Through his meticulous work, he removed some of the old empirical fetters from music theory and also some of the mystical aura surrounding musical creation. He provided students with precise methods and models that coincidentally gave the development of Russian music theory a much needed impetus. Although his studies on form did not lend themselves to the kind of mathematical verification applied to his counterpoint studies, they nonetheless benefited from his unerring observations and deductive reasoning.

Georgy Lvovich Catoire (1861-1926)

Georgy Lvovich Catoire never received a formal music education; he originally studied mathematics, graduating from Moscow University in 1884. But in 1886, on the advice of Tchaikovsky, Catoire went for a year to Berlin to continue piano lessons (begun in 1875) and to study composition with Tirsh and Rufer. Later he took private lessons in counterpoint from Lyadov in St. Petersburg and in Moscow consulted with the esteemed Taneev, who, like

Tchaikovsky, came to value Catoire's compositions and his friendship. After Taneev's death, Catoire assumed his unofficial role as leader of the theory and composition "schools" in Moscow. He composed most of his works—including two symphonies, a cantata, a piano concerto, and chamber and vocal works—during the years 1888 to 1916. For the last nine years of his life, from 1917 to 1926, he taught theory and composition at the Moscow Conservatory and devoted his attention more towards theoretical matters than towards composition. His interest in theory resulted in two works: *The Theoretical Course of Harmony* and *Musical Form.*[54] With these two works Catoire made such fundamental contributions to Soviet music theory that a student of his later commented, "Practically no new book on questions of music theory manages without mention of and reference to works of Catoire."[55]

Catoire's primary achievement as a theorist rests in his adaptation, enrichment, and, in certain aspects, correction of the tenets of the functional school of music theory. Incipient functionalism in harmony had already entered Russian music theory through Rimsky-Korsakov's textbook. Riemann's functional approach developed along the same line of thought, and thus Russian theorists were congenial to its acceptance. Catoire, though, was the first Russian theorist to adapt Riemann's approach for a practical, pedagogical use, and to publish textbooks based on it.[56]

As a starting point for *The Theoretical Course of Harmony,* Catoire borrowed from the treatise of the Belgian theorist François Auguste Gevaert, *Traité d'harmonie théorique et pratique,* which incorporates Riemann's theory of harmonic function into a tonal scheme that encompasses chromaticism as a natural extension of diatonicism.[57] Catoire adopted Gevaert's four-tiered hierarchy of harmonic systems—protodiatonic, diatonic (major and minor), diatonic major-minor, and chromatic—and also Gevaert's system of chord nomenclature based on function and formation, which differed from Riemann's. To this latter system, though, Catoire made extensive changes and additions, based on harmonies found in Romantic and modern Russian music, such as that of Skryabin. He incorporated numerous examples of these in the text.[58]

The fundamental principle of functional harmony provides that the three principal triads, tonic, dominant, and subdominant, give rise through their transformation to all other chords, which are therefore closely connected to the principal triads and may share their functions. This principle is basic to each of Catoire's systems beginning with the diatonic. Even more basic to Catoire's approach, though, is the degree of relationship of tonalities and harmonies through the circle of fifths: "The fifth is the first degree of relationship of tones.... The major third is the second degree of harmonic relationship of tones."[59] Catoire used the circle of fifths to determine intervallic content within the various systems. The number of fifths separating any two tones determines the nature and frequency of occurrence of the interval. The greater the number of fifths between them, the more chromatic the interval and the less it occurs.[60] Diatonic intervals from the unison to the tritone contain from zero to six fifths between their tones. Chromatic intervals contain from seven to twelve fifths; they include all augmented and diminished intervals except the tritone. Ultrachromatic intervals—so named by Catoire—contain from thirteen to fifteen fifths and beyond; they include all doubly augmented and diminished intervals. Knowledge of the frequency of occurrence of intervals allowed Catoire to determine the frequency of occurrence of chords containing the intervals. Since he constructed chords using only thirds, based on Rameau's principle of the superposition of thirds, this task proved to be not as cumbersome as it might appear. Catoire called any group of tones not constructed from thirds an "accidental combination."

The four systems contain the scale degrees shown; Roman numerals refer to scale degree and not to chord.

Protodiatonic						I	V	II	VI	III				
Diatonic: major					IV	I	V	II	VI	III	VII			
minor		bVI	bIII	bVII	IV	I	V	II						
Diatonic major-minor		bVI	bIII	bVII	IV	I	V	II	VI	III	VII			
Chromatic	bV	bII	bVI	bIII	bVII	IV	I	V	II	VI	III	VII	#IV #I #V #II #VI

The protodiatonic system equals the pentatonic scale. The diatonic system, equal to the major or minor mode of the diatonic scale, consists of the tones of a major triad and of the two major triads most closely related to it: tonic *(t)*, dominant *(d)*, and subdominant *(s)*.

> The chord *t* appears as the center of the system, as the moment of full equilibrium, from which we make deviations in the direction of chords adjacent to it [in the circle of fifths]; each time the equilibrium is broken, a conflict and an attraction back to the center, to full equilibrium, is created. Such deviations from our basic chord to the chords adjacent to it and the return form an embryo of our art, the essence of our music.[61]

To illustrate this relationship between tonic and the adjacent dominant and subdominant, as well as between these triads and secondary triads, Catoire developed a theory of chordal formation based on the "displacement of voices," which gives rise to harmonic deviations. The displacement of the root or the fifth of *t, d,* or *s,* by the tone below or above it, respectively, leads to the formation of the secondary triads, III, VI, II, and VII, which carry "an indecisive, indefinite character."[62] These triads may serve as substitutes for the main triads and as such fulfill their functions:

tonic:	I	IIIt	VIt
dominant:	V	IIId	VII
subdominant:	IV	II	VIs

The triads III and VI are each equally related to two of the main triads; therefore they have dual harmonic functions and must carry a designation as to which function they are performing, *t* or *d* in the case of III, and *t* or *s* in the case of VI. The triad III, though, is primarily tonic; the triad VI is shared equally by tonic and subdominant. In minor, the triads function the same as in major:

minor tonic:	Imin	♭IIIt	♭VIt
minor dominant:	Vmin	♭IIId	♭VII
minor subdominant:	IVmin	IIdim	♭VIs

Regarding substitution in the other systems, Catoire mentioned only that chromatically altered chords may substitute for their diatonic counterparts, such as ♭VI for VI, ♭III for III, minor *s* for *s*, and minor *d* for *d*.

The displacement of two tones of the tonic triad illustrates the relationship between *t* and *d*, and between *t* and *s*. The total displacement of all the tones of all the triads illustrates the relationship between *t* and *d*, *t* and *s*, and *s* and *d*. It leads in turn to the formation of chordal groups—the tonic group from the subdominant, the subdominant group from the dominant, and the dominant group from the tonic. These functional groups contain within them the different higher tertian structures of the main triads *t*, *s*, and *d*, as well as the secondary triads related to *t*, *s*, and *d*. An exception occurs in the dominant group; the missing triad III is primarily tonic and therefore may be found in that group. Thus the dominant group is the only group that uses the fundamental tone of the group to represent its basic function.[63]

Dominant Group

$$\begin{bmatrix} VI \\ IV \\ II \\ VII \\ V \end{bmatrix} \quad [D^1]$$

$$D^1 \quad D$$

Tonic Group

$$9[T^1] \quad \begin{bmatrix} \begin{bmatrix} \begin{bmatrix} II \\ VII \\ V \\ III \\ I \\ VI \end{bmatrix} \end{bmatrix}_{[t^1]} \end{bmatrix}_{[[t^1]]}$$

$$T^1 \quad T$$
$$11T^1$$

Subdominant Group

$$9[S^1] \left[\underbrace{\left[\underbrace{\left[\underbrace{\begin{matrix} V \\ III \\ \left[\begin{matrix} I \\ VI \end{matrix} \right] \\ IV \\ II \end{matrix}}_{11S^1} \right]}_{S^1} \right]}_{S} \right]}_{[S^1]} \right] [[S^1]]$$

These groups occur in the diatonic major system. In the diatonic minor system the groups are derived differently and therefore differ somewhat in makeup. Like Riemann and Gevaert, Catoire derived the minor triad and mode from the undertone series. But calling this method of derivation only a hypothesis, Catoire concluded, "We hear the harmonic foundation [of the minor triad] not in the upper but in the lower voice of the chord."[64] However, although Catoire preferred to designate the triads of the minor mode by their bottom pitch, he persisted in constructing them inversely symmetrically to the major triads. Thus he formed the chordal groups of the diatonic minor system in the manner shown in example 17.

Ex. 17   Inverse relationships between functional groups in major and minor

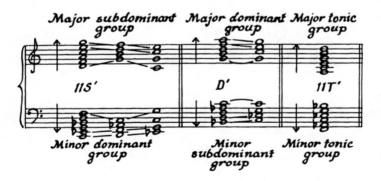

Since he constructed the seventh chords of the major mode by adding an additional third to the top of the triad, in the minor mode he constructed the seventh chords by adding an additional third to the bottom of the triad.

In the major-minor diatonic system, the chord groups retain their fundamental construction as in the major diatonic system. The additional altered tones—♭III, ♭VI and ♭VII—create new chords within each group, although ♭VII is not included in the dominant group.[65]

Dominant Group

VI	♭VI
IV	IV
II	II
VII	VII
V	V
D^1	D^2

Tonic Group

II	II	II	II
VII	♭VII	VII	♭VII
V	V	V	V
III	III	♭III	♭III
I	I	I	I
VI	♭VI	VI	♭VI
$11T^1$	$11T_♭^1$	$11Q^1$	$11Q_♭^1$
maj.	mel.	mel.	min.
	maj.	min.	

Subdominant Group

V	V	V	V
III	♭III	III	♭III
I	I	I	I
VI	VI	♭VI	♭VI
IV	IV	IV	IV
II	II	II	II
$11S^1$	$11S^2$	$11Z^1$	$11Z^2$
maj.	mel.	har.	min.
	min.	maj.	

This system contains six major and six minor triads:

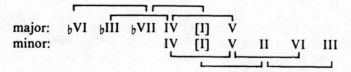

major: ♭VI ♭III ♭VII IV [I] V
minor: IV [I] V   II   VI   III

The brackets indicate the four different diatonic systems contained within each mode of the diatonic major-minor system. Each consists of the tones of three chords, with the center chord acting as tonic, within each mode. The primary major diatonic system contains I as tonic; all other systems therefore become "subordinate tonalities." A deviation into such a subordinate tonality, an "inter-tonal deviation," may occur, but only into the four major diatonic systems and the minor system equivalent to the parallel harmonic minor. The remaining three minor systems are natural minor and, according to Catoire, deviations into them are not possible, since no major dominant triad for them exists in the diatonic major-minor system.[66]

The seventeen-tone chromatic system, which contains five enharmonic duplications, encompasses six different twelve-tone chromatic scales.[67] Catoire divided these scales into chromatic major scales, which include all six scales, and chromatic minor scales, which include only three of the six scales. All six scales contain a nucleus of the seven diatonic degrees. The most common major chromatic scale substitutes #V for ♭VI and #II for ♭III of the diatonic major-minor system, and adds #IV and #I. The most common minor chromatic scale adds ♭II and #IV, two frequently used chromatic degrees, to the ten degrees of the diatonic major-minor system.

The existence in the chromatic system of thirteen major thirds gives rise to thirteen major triads and ten minor triads, plus three minor triads of secondary significance, #I, #V, and #II. The major triads may be grouped into eleven diatonic systems, one main and ten subordinate; the minor triads—eight diatonic systems, one main and seven subordinate.[68]

In the chromatic system, the functional equilibrium of the diatonic systems becomes disturbed: "In the chromatic [system], the tonic and the subdominant functions of our diatonic system retire into the background; they are substituted for by dominant [functions]"[69] (ex. 18).

Ex. 18   The substitution of dominant function for tonic and
subdominant in the chromatic system

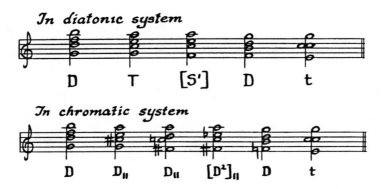

One need only look at the chord structures introduced by the chromatic system for evidence of the validity of this statement. Catoire distinguished twenty-three different chords, which may be reduced to five basic types, each identifiable by the chromatic or ultrachromatic interval in its construction. Only one type occurs solely in the subdominant group; the others occur in the dominant group. A chord with a subdominant function may occur in three of the four other types only when it is constructed on II as a dominant of the dominant. All remaining functions are dominant. This overriding dominant function may be seen in the music of Skryabin, from which Catoire took the majority of his examples for this portion of his text.

To form these chords, Catoire turned to "the intervals of higher order": the chromatic interval of the diminished third, and the ultrachromatic intervals of the doubly diminished fifth and the doubly augmented unison. Catoire did not choose these intervals arbitrarily, but on the basis of his stated premise of chord construction by the superimposition of thirds and on his observations of contemporary harmonic practice.[70] The interval of a diminished third occurs in three types of chords distinguished from one another by the position of that interval. As bases for these chords, Catoire used chords from the diatonic major-minor system, primarily D^1 and D^2 from the dominant group. In $\sharp S$ and $\sharp Z$ the diminished third occurs between the raised basic tone and the third of the seventh chords from S and Z of the dominant group. In the U chord, the diminished third occurs between the third and lowered fifth of D^1 and D^2. In the J chord, the diminished third occurs between the raised fifth and the seventh of D^1.

Subdominant Group

I	I
VI	♭VI
IV	IV
♯II	♯II
♯S	♯Z

Dominant Group

VI	♭VI		VI	♭VI
IV	IV	IV	IV	IV
♭II	♭II	♭II	♭II	♭II
VII	VII	VII	VII	VII
V	V	V		
U^1	U^2	U	$[U^1]$	$[U^2]$

VI	♭VI		VI	♭VI
IV	IV	IV	IV	IV
♯II	♯II	♯II	♯II	♯II
VII	VII	VII	VII	VII
V	V	V		
J^1	J^2	J	$[J^1]$	$[J^2]$

VI	♭VI			♭VI
IV	IV	IV		IV
♭II ♯II	♭II ♯II	♭II ♯II		♭II ♯II
VII	VII	VII		VII
V	V	V		
UJ^1	UJ^2	UJ		$[UJ^2]$

Subdominant Function

	III	♭III
	I	I
I		
♭VI	♭VI	♭VI
♯IV	♯IV	♯IV
II		
U_{II}	$[U^1]_{II}$	$[U^2]_{II}$

	III	♭III
	I	I
I		
♯VI	♯VI	♯VI
♯IV	♯IV	♯IV
II		
J_{II}	$[J^1]_{II}$	$[J^2]_{II}$

The interval of a doubly diminished fifth occurs in ♯Z between the raised basic tone and the fifth, and in J^2 between the raised fifth and the ninth of the chord (from D^2). The interval of a doubly augmented prime occurs in the UJ chord between the raised and lowered fifths of D, D^1, D^2. These three chords ♯Z, J^2, and UJ, constitute "ultrachromatic" chords, so named because of their doubly augmented and diminished intervals. Even though he created this category, Catoire provided no illustrations of ultrachromatic chords from musical literature.[71] However, from Skryabin's *Poème Satanique* op. 36, he furnished examples of U^2, U_{II}, and $[J^1]$ chords (ex. 19). He analyzed the opening chord of Wagner's *Tristan und Isolde* as a U_{II} chord in second inversion (G♯ is nonharmonic) resolving to the dominant; in this sense it carries a subdominant function.[72]

Ex. 19   Alexander Skryabin, *Poème satanique* op. 36: a) mm. 13-14; b) mm. 17-19; c) mm. 29-31

Catoire examined or mentioned the occurrence in harmony of all but two of the chromatic and ultrachromatic intervals found within the span of sixteen fifths: the augmented prime or diminished octave and the doubly diminished fourth or doubly augmented fifth. He left these out intentionally, concluding, "The possibilities of further enrichment of our music with new chromatically altered *correct* chords is almost exhausted."[73] He therefore turned to "another source of enrichment of our harmony... the sphere of 'accidental combinations,' that is, harmonies, formed by suspensions, such that in their resolution the function of the chord is not changed."[74] Yet, since Catoire viewed accidental combinations as simply "enharmonically correct chords," differing only in their treatment and resolution, these accidental combinations resulted in no new harmonies, only in new contexts for correct chords.

Aside from his discussion of nonharmonic tones used in the creation of accidental combinations, Catoire, in the application of the diatonic and chromatic systems and the functional chord groups, concentrated on the topics of sequence and modulation. Concerning the latter, he departed from Gevaert's example by substituting a less rigid system, one more consistent with Russian harmonic theory. He combined chord function and the hierarchy of systems with the means of modulation advanced by Rimsky-Korsakov—modulation through a common chord based on the relatedness of keys, and through enharmonism.

Both methods require the presence of a connecting or intermediary chord, which changes function and which signals the switch from one tonality to another. This chord belongs to both tonalities of a common chord modulation, and therefore occurs only between related tonalities. In Catoire's approach, related tonalities differ in their key signatures by one to six accidentals. Depending on their system—diatonic, diatonic major-minor, or chromatic—these tonalities have in common certain chords that fulfill more than one function. Therefore, only bifunctional or multi-functional chords, which Catoire identified as triads and dissonant chords such as augmented and diminished triads and certain seventh chords, may serve as common chords. In general these chords originate either from the diatonic system or from the harmonic mode of the diatonic major-minor system. The original tonality should preferably be in one of these systems; the second tonality may be in any of the three systems. However, the reverse situation may also occur, as long as one of the tonalities is predominantly diatonic. Catoire recognized only two dissonant chords from the chromatic system that fulfill a dual function.[75] The other chromatic and ultrachromatic chords usually do not have more than one function. Since they are unifunctional, so to speak, they may not successfully be used as common chords. For modulation by means of enharmonism, no such restrictions apply. Diatonic, chromatic, and ultrachromatic chords and accidental chords may all be used.

The "intertonal deviation," which involves a brief sojourn into a tonality subordinate to the main tonality within the limits of the diatonic or major-minor system, usually is effected by means of a common chord. It occurs most frequently within a period or in a two-part or simple three-part form, such as the Chopin or Skryabin preludes, which adhere to one main key. The second type of modulation identified by Catoire establishes a new, temporary main tonality, which in its relation to the main tonality may be subordinate, closely related, or remotely related. Either common-chord or enharmonic means may be used. As a short modulation into a more remote key within the limits of a period, this type becomes a substitute for an intertonal deviation. Such a substitution takes place in the third and fourth appearances of the opening theme in the Prelude to Act I of Wagner's *Parsifal:* a $[J^2]$ chord with no fifth in $A\flat$, a tonality that falls within the major-minor system of C minor, is replaced with an E minor triad (ex. 20).

Ex. 20   Richard Wagner, Prelude to *Parsifal:* a) mm. 28-33; b) analysis of chord, m. 30

Catoire's *Theoretical Course of Harmony* lies within the tradition of Russian harmony textbooks established by those of Tchaikovsky and Rimsky-Korsakov. In that it presents a detailed description of chord construction based on intervals and of chord classification, it resembles, especially in its complexity, Ippolitov-Ivanov's textbook, *The Study of Chords, Their Construction and Resolution.*[76] But Catoire's focus on chord function within an organized framework, the diatonic-chromatic hierarchy, provides an organization lacking in Ippolitov-Ivanov's book and other similar textbooks of the early twentieth century that attempted to provide a comprehensive examination of chromatic harmony.[77] The introduction to the theory of functional harmony in Catoire's textbook was unique among Russian textbooks of this time. Although Catoire invented neither the idea nor the method of its presentation, his adaptation of the principles of Riemann's theories as interpreted by Gevaert became a permanent part of the Soviet theory of harmony. Various aspects of Catoire's approach may be found in almost any contemporary Soviet harmony textook as well as in a number of recent Soviet studies devoted to questions of harmonic language or analysis.[78]

Another factor undoutedly contributed to the wide influence of Catoire's theories. His teaching career at the Moscow Conservatory coincided with the first nine years of the new Soviet regime, which turned out to be formative years for Soviet music theory.[79] During those years Catoire taught a number of students, who, after having become teachers themselves, continued and developed Catoire's tradition of theory pedagogy. Several of his students collectively wrote a harmony textbook containing a simpler but more extensive application of his theories for pedagogical use. Several other of his students completed and published his *Musical Form,* also for pedagogical use. In this way Catoire's views were widely disseminated in conservatories and other music schools during the 1930s and later.

Before his death Catoire had prepared for publication only the first volume of his *Musical Form,* which discussed the elements of musical form. So his students Lev Mazel, Dmitri Kabalevsky, and Leonid Polovinkin, working from separate analyses and notes made by Catoire and from their own extensive notes of his lectures, put together volume 2, on particular musical forms. They completed only those chapters which Catoire himself had outlined—those on two- and three-part forms, the rondo, and the sonata.[80] Catoire had already outlined the general approach and scope of the work in his introduction to the first volume. The two basic problems in any study of musical form involved, as Catoire saw it, "the study of the laws of metrical structure of the sound fabric forming musical speech," i.e., "the study of metrics"; and "the study of the laws by which musical structural units are combined together and create one artistic whole," in short, "to establish the regulating laws of the structure of an artistic work."[81]

Again, as a starting point, Catoire used books on form by others, namely Bussler, Riemann, and Prout.[82] But, as in the harmony book, while he adopted many of their ideas, he also supplemented or changed many others, those he found too "one-sided" or that distorted "the musical thought of the composer."[83] Thus he rejected, for example, Riemann's more dogmatic approaches to metrical construction and form, such as those concerning the omnipresent upbeat and the iamb, and the eight-measure period. He accepted the motive as the musical embryo from which form grows, but resisted the arbitrary breaking up of phrases into motives.

Catoire defined the study of metrics as "the study of the interrelation of tones by the great or small weight with which they are perceived, [and] of the division of musical speech into bars and the grouping of [these bars] among themselves."[84] Metrics is based on "symmetry in time," the "juxtaposition of two moments directly following each other, while in the second, answering the first, normally lies the weight."[85] Catoire differentiated between symmetry in time and symmetry in space:

> Whereas symmetry in space represents the correspondence at *any distance of identically constructed* parts of a building, symmetry in time... represents the juxtaposition of *two absolutely adjacent, but not always identically constructed* parts, answering each other as thesis to arsis; moreover on the second (that is, on the answering—the thesis) lies the weight. Obviously, the idea is a completely different cateogory. Here we will apply together with Riemann the term "symmetry" in this new, metrical significance.[86]

This symmetry is expressed at each level of Catoire's hierarchical metrical organization—the motive, phrase, small structural unit, and large structural unit. Its most basic manifestation takes the form of the iamb; other manifestations include the anapest and amphibrach. Catoire frequently disagreed with Riemann's "artificial interpretations," as he called them, of joining an unaccented beat following an initial accented beat to the following accented beat or motive; so he accepted as well the metrical grouping of the trochee. He mentioned the dactyl also as a possible grouping, but never illustrated it. Figure 4 illustrates the hierarchical relationships of Catoire's architectonic levels up to the period, expressed in end-accented groupings.

Fig. 4   Hierarchy of formal units

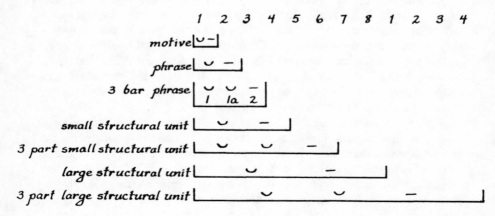

The motive, "the smallest musical symmetry" is equivalent to "a musical embryo," since it provides the foundation for all succeeding levels and, ultimately, the form of the music itself.[87] Catoire interpreted the next level, the phrase, not as a "structure" but as "an element of musical structure."[88] He named as the smallest *structure* in music the "small structural unit," a symmetry of the two phrases. A symmetry of two small structural units forms "a large structural unit." "All our musical structures may be reduced to a row of small and large structural units, which also may be accepted therefore as bases of our analyses."[89]

Catoire distinguished three basic forms of large structural units—one iambic and two trochaic (fig. 5). The iambic structural unit is a normal structural unit made up of iambic phrases. The trochaic structural unit, type 1, consisting of trochaic phrases, ends with a cadence in the penultimate measure. The trochaic structural unit, type 2, contains an abbreviated first phrase; the remaining phrases are iambic, or, in certain cases, amphibrachic. Catoire considered this last form to be trochaic because, as in type 1, all odd bars are accented. The last uncompleted phrase concludes in the following structural unit, forming what he called "an intruding cadence," since it intrudes into the next structural unit.[90] Throughout, Catoire provided metrical groupings only for the phrase level, as illustrated in figure 5. Concerning the higher-level structures, he stated that at each level the metrical weight lies in the last segment of the structure, whether it is two-part or three-part. Thus large and small structural units may normally be regarded as end-accented groupings, such as the iamb or anapest. Catoire labeled them "iambic" or "trochaic" depending on the metric grouping at the phrase level, not on the metric relationship between the small structural units within the large structural units.

Fig. 5   Types of structural units

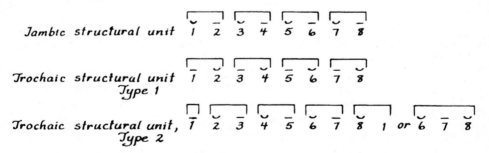

The elements and structural units shown in figure 5 may be mixed, abbreviated, or expanded. In general, each level may be expanded by the addition of one element or unit from the previous level. This results in expanded three-part structures instead of the normal two-part structures. A three-part large structural unit, for instance, generally contains three small structural units. On the lower levels—motive and phrase—such additions frequently take the form of repetitions, either exact or varied, and are represented through the repetition of numbers. A phrase expanded through the repetition of an unaccented motive thus becomes $\bar{1}$ 1a $\bar{2}$. The repetition of an accented motive would result in a change of metric grouping. A repeated phrase would be represented as $_{\lrcorner}$1 2$_{\lrcorner}$ $_{\lrcorner}$1a 2a$_{\lrcorner}$. For the large three-part structural unit, the additional small structural unit is represented by the numbers 1 2 3 4 added to the original eight (fig. 5). In other words, Catoire never ventured beyond the number 8 in his numbering of metrical units or motives. Twice he added the number 9 to account for a final unaccented bar after an accented cadence in the eighth bar, but those were exceptions. These procedures are mostly consistent with those of Prout, who was less insistent than Catoire about exceeding the number 8. But Catoire's numberings are not so much measurements of quantity as they are designations of definite metrical function. Thus Catoire's adherence to the number 8 for large structural units results from the practical, functional significance of using number repetitions to denote expansions and number deletions to denote abbreviations, not from a preconceived notion of the hegemony of the eight-bar structural unit. The accented number 8, for example, generally represents the concluding cadence. In the Haydn excerpt shown in example 21, for instance, Catoire illustrated the expansion of a phrase through the addition of a motive (3ă) and the expansion of one phrase into two through the repetition of two adjacent motives from two adjacent phrases (6ā/7ă). The Haydn excerpt thus consists of a five-bar small structural unit and a seven-bar three-part small structural unit. The excerpt from the third movement of Mozart's Symphony no. 40, K. 550, shown in example 22, contains two large structural units six and eight measures long, respectively. Both contain abbreviated phrases and the second contains an expanded small structural unit. An abbreviated phrase occurs when the unaccented portion of the phrase has been omitted; in such a case the number of the omitted motive is left out as well. Both excerpts are iambic.[91]

   Unlike Riemann, who concentrated in his metrical analyses on the melodic line, Catoire considered not only the metrical division and motivic content of the melody, but also other factors such as harmony, cadences, the type of accompaniment, and the movement of the other voices. He also stressed the cohesion and indivisibility of structural units in those cases where the seamless texture of the melodic line disallowed any low-level divisions. The large structural unit at the beginning of Skryabin's Mazurka op. 25 no. 9, for example, allows only a "theoretical" division into two small structural units. "The half cadence serves as a direction to us that this eight-measure musical thought still is not expressed; one or more such structural units should follow it"[92] (ex. 23).

Ex. 21   Joseph Haydn, String Quartet op. 76 no. 3, Minuet, mm. 1-12

Ex. 22   W.A. Mozart, Symphony no. 40, K. 550, Minuet, mm. 1-14

Ex. 23   Alexander Skryabin, Mazurka op. 25 no. 8, E♭ minor,
          mm. 1-8

Catoire also rejected Riemann's interpretation of the period:

> Theorists usually call any eight measures a period, by virtue of which a musical work is
> broken up somehow *mechanically* into a row of periods; such a simplistic view helps us little
> in explaining the principles of musical form.[93]

In contrast, Catoire defined a period as

> a symmetry of two musical structural units, completed with a full (in exceptional cases half)
> cadence, and having the significance of a more or less self-sufficient whole.... The musical
> thought (theme) from which the work is created always is stated as a period.[94]

Thus for Catoire the musical content of the period had an importance equal to
that of purely formal considerations. The smallest period consists of two small
structural units; if one large structural unit satisfies the requirements of a
period—a cadence and self-sufficiency—it may be considered a period. Two
sentences, the stressed part of the symmetry on the answering sentence, make
up the component parts of a period. In a simple period they equal the small
structural units; in larger periods, the large structural unit. In more complex
periods, the sentences may be compound, consisting of several large structural
units. The resulting period, in Catoire's view, may therefore be nearly any

length, depending on its internal structure, ranging from 8 measures to 140 measures, as in the Scherzo of Beethoven's Fifth Symphony, which Catoire analyzed as one period.[95] Many of the preludes of Chopin and Skryabin are written in such expanded periods. Within the compound sentences, Catoire analyzed the structural units as serving various functions—modulation, supplement, cadence, introduction, and transfer.

As in his textbook on harmony, Catoire devised a system of symbols to designate graphically the form and function of these various components of form. When combined, these symbols make up representative formulas depicting the content of a period. Some of the most commonly used symbols include:[96]

f	phrase
m	small structural unit
b	large structural unit
m3p	small three-part structural unit
b3p	large three-part structural unit
abb	abbreviation
abb (1)	abbreviation by one measure
exp	expansion
exp (1)	expansion by one measure
expf	expansion by a phrase
d	supplement

The Haydn excerpt in example 21 would be represented in this manner:

m exp + m3p expf
  (1)   (1)

The Mozart excerpt in example 22 is more complicated:

b [m abb + m abb] + b [m expf abb + m abb]
   (1)   (1)   (1)   (1)

This attempt by Catoire to devise a graphic representation for metric analysis proved to be the least successful aspect of his approach to form. Like his chord symbols, these structural symbols are too complex to be pedagogically useful, and were not widely used.

Catoire did not apply metric groupings beyond the phrase level within the large structural unit. But he did apply the concept of metrical symmetry to such higher-level forms as the simple two-part form, both as an independent form and as part of a larger form, for example the exposition of the sonata form.

Since he viewed the simple two-part form as having generated other forms such as the three-part form and the sonata form, then perhaps he intended his application of metric symmetry to be broadened to include these more complex forms as well.

He focused his study of the larger forms on their evolution. He discerned two directions in this development: On one path, new structures were joined to the simple two- or three-part forms, leading to the complex three-part form and to the simple rondo. On the other path, the two- and three-part forms were expanded from within, leading to the formation of the sonata form. The inner expansion of the simple two-part form, through a new middle section at the beginning of the second section, gave rise to the simple three-part form. In tracing this evolutionary development, Catoire observed the subtle stages between forms, such as between the simple two- and three-part forms. He classified these connecting links as "intermediary forms" that arose during this evolution. For example, between the simple three-part form and the sonata form exists an intermediary form that contains an abbreviated exposition, a tonally unstable middle section, and a recapitulating section. The difference between this form and the sonata form lies in the first and third sections, which, although they contain the tonal pattern of a sonata form, lack the thematic differentiation expressed in the transitional and secondary parts of the exposition and the recapitulation. Catoire cited the final movement of Beethoven's Piano Sonata op. 10 no. 2 as an example of this form.[97] He considered the sonata without a development section not an intermediary form but an abbreviated sonata, which developed directly from simple two-part form. Other notable features of Catoire's theory of form include his derivation of the rondo form from the complex three-part form, his analysis of the sonata-rondo form, and his observations on the use of form, particularly the unusual manifestations of the rondo principle in the works of romantic and modern Russian composers.[98]

As with his theories of functional harmony, Catoire pioneered in Russia the development of a theory of metrical structure and analysis that had practical application as well as theoretical significance. Although he did not entirely overcome Riemann's dogmatic metrical interpretations—for instance, his insistence on the number 8 and accompanying number manipulations—nevertheless he broadened the concept of metrical grouping beyond Riemann's limited scope and developed for it a more realistic and flexible application.

Catoire's views on music and music theory closely resemble those of his friend and colleague Taneev. Both remained opposed to the loss of tonal structure and the breakdown of form in the music of their day, and reflected these views in their research. Although functional distinctions become blurred in Catoire's chromatic system, it is nevertheless firmly rooted in the lower-level diatonic systems. And Catoire's examinations of form presuppose the participation of tonality in those forms. Both also applied some aspects of mathematics in their research. Taneev was more successful in this regard; mathematics actually verified his findings and simplified the results, whereas mathematics merely illustrated and at the same time complicated Catoire's findings.

Catoire developed his innovations in music theory from the foundations created by Riemann, Prout, and Gevaert. In all, though, his most valuable contribution remains the introduction into Soviet music theory of several concepts. The most prominent of these include the idea of chord function, the hierarchy of systems, and the general approach to formal analysis, all of which remain important elements in contemporary Soviet music. Catoire's own contributions stemming from these ideas include his development of the chromatic system and "ultrachromatic" chords, his harmonic and formal analysis of modern Russian music, his discussions of certain types of form such as the rondo, and his detection of "intermediary" forms. These concepts, too, remain. Missing, though, are the the more cumbersome aspects of his theory, such as the chord designations, the derivation of minor from major, and the formulas representative of metrical processes.

Such problems, however, did not prevent Catoire's works from being widely used and accepted. During the 1920s and 1930s, when these works were written, a real need for such books existed. Just such a need for a textbook on form led Soviet theorists in the 1930s to complete Catoire's manuscript. That they chose to complete and publish his work rather than write a new text testifies to his influence. In addition, aside from his lack of attention to "the musical art as a part of social practice," Catoire's views conformed with those of Soviet theorists attempting to build a Marxist musicology.[99] For example, his treatment of form as a manifestation of "artistic content" as well as of purely formal delineations and functional (dialectical) properties, rendered his approach acceptable to Marxists.[100] His emphasis on the practical and pedagogical applications of his views was also considered significant.

It is probable that Riemann's theories of harmonic function and of metrical analysis would eventually have entered Soviet music theory through other means, but Catoire's logical and accessible presentations of them accelerated their widespread acceptance. He must be viewed then as the founder and chief representative of the functional school in Russia, the main tenets of which, largely through his efforts, were accepted into the legacy of Soviet music theory.

Georgy Eduardovich Conus (1862-1933)

Georgy Eduardovich Conus published the first written statement of his theory of "metrotechtonicism" in 1924, when he was nearly 62 years old[101] and a professor and dean of the composition faculty at the Moscow Conservatory. This was not the first public presentation of his theory, though. After his return in 1919 from a seven-year sojourn teaching at the Saratov Conservatory, he began lecturing on metrotechtonicism, and took part in the research activities then being initiated in Moscow. In 1920 he was appointed director of the department of the analysis of form, the first such department in Russia, at the Moscow Conservatory; in 1922 the State Institute of Musical Science (GIMN) established a laboratory of metrotechtonic analysis, with Conus as the head. Clearly, by the time his article was published, Conus's theory had already received a certain amount of attention. During the next nine years (until his death in 1933), Conus published three articles and two books on metrotechtonicism; in addition, several of his manuscripts were published posthumously.[102]

Conus graduated from the Moscow Conservatory in 1889; he studied composition and theory with Arensky and Taneev, respectively. From 1891 to 1899 he also taught there. During this time he began to develop his theory of metrotechtonicism:

> Having come upon [the theory of metrotechtonicism] accidentally 30 years ago (1894), thanks to a special technical method of writing that put very remotely distant parts of a musical whole into a single field of vision, in a striking regularity of musical structures absolutely unknown to science, I dedicated myself to the laboratory testing of the laws I discovered for a quarter of a century (until 1919). Almost 1000 musical creations of different epochs from the fifteenth century to our day were subjected to precise analysis. I researched in detail whole cycles of works: all 48 fugues of Bach, all the Chopin etudes, all the songs of Mendelssohn, all the sonatas and symphonies of Beethoven, etc. And only in 1919 on the basis of a great amount of accumulated factual material did I allow myself to undertake the first presentation of the theoretical bases of the method and of the details of separate cases.[103]

Conus did not remain totally silent about his theory during those twenty-five years of research. Already by 1902 he had revealed some of its secrets in discussions with Arensky and Taneev.[104] During the 1900s he gave a few lectures on the topic before such groups as the Moscow Scientific Musical Society, of which he was an active member.[105] His interpretation of his theory at this early stage does not greatly differ from that expressed in the 1924 article. But in succeeding publications, he refined, revised, and elaborated on his views.

Metrotechtonicism's basic principle had two aspects: first, the graphic representation of a musical composition allowed all segments of its form, notated according to temporal size, to be seen at once; second the patterns that these schemes exhibited showed that each composition, or at least each movement of a composition, was inherently symmetrical. The term "metrotechtonicism" means "measured construction," from the Greek words *metron* (measure) and *tektonikos* (constructor or builder). Since a musical work exists in time, its temporal limits may be measured exactly. Fundamental to a metrotechtonic analysis is "the discovery of the temporal coordinate, to which the structure of any musical work is unconsciously subordinated."[106]

This temporal coordinate is nothing less than "symmetry in time"; it reveals the temporal relationships within parts, between parts, and between the parts and the whole, all more or less symmetrical. The discovery of the temporal coordinate is accomplished by measuring in time the various segments of a composition and providing hierarchical groupings for them: "First we divide the organism into parts, and then, as a synthetic collection of parts, we mentally restore the whole."[107]

As the basic unit of the measurement of time, Conus designated what he called the "cell," or the "structural pulsating wave," comparable in size, usually, to the musical measure. He defined both the wave and the cell as "the largest common measure of all the component parts of a given musical creation."[108] Conus considered them equal in measurement and in size, but not in concept. The structural pulsating wave is the largest common measurement of a regularly occurring phenomenon, akin to a wave in physics or a pulse in the human body. In metrotechtonicism, it most frequently equals the measure in length, sometimes a half-measure, or sometimes two measures. Conus described it variously as "the length of time, limited by the two nearest pulsating stimuli of uniform frequency," a "form of musical cell."[109] In an earlier description, he defined it as "the primary temporal cell, the most elementary form," the "embryo" of a musical organism, "from which the entire musical piece is constructed and grows."[110] He described an accented wave as "a supporting wave."[111] The cell, by comparison, is "the concrete sound content of the wave," not the thematic content of the wave, but the metrical or temporal content.[112]

Conus stressed that the idea of the structural cell, which in one of his works receives more emphasis than the pulsating wave, was a new theoretical idea. Neither the term "structural cell" nor the idea of it as "the sound content of the structural wave," as "the greatest common measure of all the organic parts of a given musical organism," even existed previously.[113] "Not knowing the origins of musical creation (not knowing the structural cell) deprived theory of the possibility of solving the problem of musical form, and of even raising rational questions concerning this problem."[114]

To designate the next higher unit of measurement, the intermediate level, Conus invented a number of terms which he used at varying times: simple and compound structural units, "metrically pulsating accents," "structural musical meters," "measures of higher order," "organic part of the whole," and "musical creative volitional act." In his earlier writings, Conus used the term, "measures of higher order," which, in the later works, was supplanted by "musically creative volitional acts." Three of these terms—measure of higher order, organic (or architectural) part of the whole, and musical creative volitional act—came to represent three different aspects of the same phenomenon:

> The psychological conception—the creative volitional act—is synonymous with the structural conception—the architectural part—and both of these are synonymous with the

musical technological conception—the measure of higher order. This triad of terms illuminates a single object from three different sides.[115]

He subsequently increased this triad to a tetrad by adding the syntactical term "musical phrase."

Conus formed the musical creative volitional act by grouping the pulsating waves or cells, as shown in example 24, measures 8-22 of the Chopin Ballade op. 52 in F minor. Here the structural cell equals a dotted-quarter note, one-half of a measure (meter: 6/8). Conus grouped the twenty-nine pulses into seven creative volitional acts of three, four, or five pulses each. He then grouped these seven musical creative volitional acts into three larger groups, containing nine, eleven, and nine pulses, respectively. These groupings form a nearly symmetrical equilibrium, broken only by the reverse order of the musical creative volitional acts in the outer nine-pulse groupings:

$$4\text{-}5\text{--}4\text{-}3\text{-}4\text{--}4\text{-}5.$$
$$9\text{----}11\text{----}9$$

However, in order to follow the pattern established in the first three volitional acts, in which the phrasing coincides with the grouping of the pulses, he should have appended the second half of measure 16, containing the cadence of B♭ minor, to the previous volitional act. The shortened cadence on F major in measure 18, which elides in the first half of the measure with the beginning of the next phrase, would then leave the fifth volitional act with only three pulses instead of Conus's four. This action would, of course, destroy his near-symmetry on the lower level:

$$4\text{-}5\text{--}4\text{-}4\text{-}3\text{--}4\text{-}5.$$
$$9\text{----}11\text{----}9$$

Conus chose instead to shorten the previous phrase to create a more symmetrical grouping.

Conus's criteria for forming the musical creative volitional acts, the grouping of the pulsating waves or cells into the volitional acts, vary and are often indefinite. Whatever these criteria are, though, they must exhibit what Conus called "elements of community," "cementing traits of a familial, so to speak, relatedness," "distinguishing signs joining groups of measures into a metric structural unit."[116] A metrical structural unit, or a musically creative volitional act, therefore, exhibits a certain completeness, which allows it to be viewed as an "isolated part of the work.... The musical completeness of a structural unit is confirmed by the formula of some kind of cadence completing it."[117] In Conus's analyses, the elements of community may range from an unbroken series of eighth notes in the bass to an organ point on the dominant. In one of his earliest analyses, he applied a variety of criteria, including cadence type, pauses, repetitions, the introduction of new thematic content (differences in melodic phrasing, accompanying rhythm, etc.), harmony (stable, unstable), and tonality.[118]

Ex. 24   Fredrich Chopin, Ballade op. 52, F minor, mm. 8-22

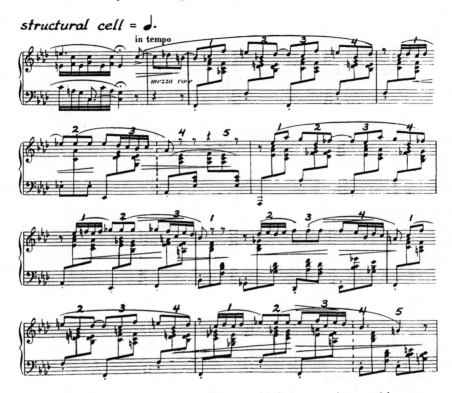

In his later writings, though, Conus paid little attention to this matter, never explaining why a certain grouping was formed. One fact becomes certain, however: each creative volitional act begins with an accented wave or cell. Invariably the pulsating waves form trochees, dactyls, a mixture of the two, or a combination of one with a single cell (accented or unaccented). The three basic possibilities—one cell, two cells (trochee), and three cells (dactyl)—occur universally: "In the end *all music* of all epochs and all genres breaks down into these three basic forms."[119] Conus applied the term "metrical accent" to the beginning (normal) accent of these forms, and "episodic accent" to one "manifested in an inappropriate place."[120] Such an "inappropriate place" may be observed in Varlaam's song from Musorgsky's *Boris Godunov* (ex. 25). Here the accent, which is episodic, falls on the fourth beat instead of the first beat of the phrase. In Conus's view, though, misplaced accents were no obstacle: "Metrotechtonicism worked out the idea of supported points in music *irrespective* of the accent sign."[121] Conus firmly rejected Riemann's view of the iamb as a type or *ur*-meter, substituting for it the beginning accented meter, which he considered "the true nature of musical structural meter."[122]

Ex. 25   Modest Musorgsky, *Boris Godunov,* "Varlaam's Song,"
mm. 1-5

At the next level of the hierarchy, Conus grouped musical creative volitional acts to form larger and larger units. The highest level usually represents the division of the composition (or movement) into two or three parts. Inevitably this level also exhibits some type of symmetry, or what he called, "the law of reflected size," or, later, "the law of the equilibrium of temporal size." This reflection or equilibrium occurs in three types:

Symmetry, or mirror similarity:	(2-3-4)	(4-3-2)
Periodicity, or direct similarity:	(2-3-4)	(2-3-4)
Mixed order, partly symmetrical, partly periodic:	5 (2-3-4)	5 (4-3-2)
	7 (2-3-4) or	7 (2-4-3)

Since this law may be observed in all levels of a musical work, Conus concluded, "The principle of equality lies, thus, at the foundation of musical architecture."[123]

Conus's analysis of the Adagio from Beethoven's Sonata op. 13 (fig. 6) shows a mixed order of symmetry. It is partly symmetrical, and partly periodic, if one disregards the extra measure at the end (m. 73), which lies outside the symmetry. The scheme reproduced here combines two different schemes Conus made at different times. The earlier version included lower-level groupings and individual cells that the later version omitted.[124] The meter of the movement is 2/4, and each cell equals a measure. Concerning this movement Conus concluded:

> The varied structural units, both in their interrelation and also in their relation to the whole, are subordinate to the laws of symmetry and identity. In respect to form, the composer

creates one half freely. For the other half he unconsciously reflects the form already created in the first half.[125]

Fig. 6   Ludwig von Beethoven, Sonata for piano op. 13, Adagio: metrotechtonic analysis

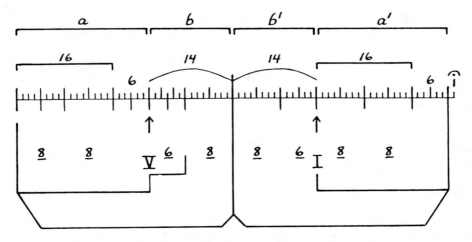

However, while this movement may be divisible into two nearly equal parts, thematically and harmonically this reflected symmetry does not exist. Although Conus's six- and eight-cell volitional acts are grouped correctly, his groupings on the next level—and subsequently on the highest levels as well—do not properly represent the musical content.

Most analysts would see in this movement a rondo or perhaps a complex three-part form with an abbreviated return:

Measure nos.:	1-16	17-23	24-28	29-36	37-50	51-66	67-73
Conus's groupings:	8+8	6	6	8	8+6	8+8	6+1
Rondo:	A	B		A	C	A	coda
Three-part:		A			B	A′	
Conus:		a		b	b′		a′

The measures in dispute are measures 23-28, which, according to Conus, belong to the following eight measures, measures 29-36, the return of A in the rondo form. Harmonically, being on the dominant, they anticipate the return of A and the tonic. But thematically, these measures are not related to the main theme in A and should not be grouped with it. Conus did not adequately demonstrate any thematic connection between measures 23-28 and the main theme, but merely stated, "Both melodically, harmonically, and also by the unbrokenness of the movement, the concluding measures of the fragment examined by us [measures 23-28] *are as if instilled* into the main theme."[126] Instead, he dwelled primarily on the differences between the two six-bar fragments in measures 17-22 and 23-28, in order to justify their separation. Metrically, he divided the first segment (mm. 17-22) into two groups, 3 + 3, each a dactyl, which do not reflect their true metrical or formal natures. His general observations concerning the first segment, though, are accurate:

> We have here not a twelve-measure [phrase], but two independent six-measure phrases, isolated from each other; the first of these, possessing a full close in the tonality V and a completely independent beginning, by no means aspires to join into a single large structural unit either with the previous or with the following [phrase]; the second, on the contrary, by many signs shows an inclination to join with the following eight-bar [phrase].[127]

Separating measures 23-28 from measures 29-36, though, would result in a disproportionate grouping of measures and would spoil the near-symmetry of Conus's analysis. Because of this discrepancy, Conus's symmetry has little validity thematically or tonally, and his letter designation "a b b' a'" reflects only his arbitrary groupings.

Although Conus concentrated less on naming the higher levels of the hierarchy than the lower levels, he did relate all levels to the measure of higher order: "The parts of a musical organism are measures of a higher order of different degrees. The organism as a whole is a huge measure of higher order, the measured portions of which are those measures of lower orders of which it is constituted."[128] The boundaries of these upper-level measures of higher order, as seen in the analysis of the Adagio, must coincide with existing boundaries of measures of lower order:

> The partition of a musical work should be made exclusively at the points of union of its composite parts, that is, at the ideal boundary where the preceding measures of higher order come into contact with the following [measures of higher order].[129]

Not only do the boundaries of the upper-level groupings coincide with certain of those of the lower-level groupings, but they also occur before an accented cell, since Conus used trochees and dactyls exclusively. The concept of hierarchical grouping on different levels of metrical units may be broadly related to Schenker's structural levels. Taneev and Catoire attempted to apply this concept at the lower levels, to harmony and metrics, respectively, but Conus was the first Russian theorist to develop this concept and apply it in a systematic fashion.[130]

The division of a musical composition into its various temporal components—the discovery of its temporal coordinate—results in what Conus called "the techtonic skeleton" of the work, its "autonomous, musical architectural" "structural skeletal" aspect, which formed Conus's primary analytical interest. Antithetical to this "techtonic skeleton" is the "external sound covering," the "integumentary, syntactical" aspect, which has its own "metrical fabric" in which the meter may differ. In fact, these two aspects usually do not agree in metrical construction: while the skeletal meter is always trochaic or dactyllic or a mixture of the two, the covering meter may be iambic, amphibrachic, anapestic, or some other type. In Conus's view, Riemann and other theorists were unable to keep these aspects separate, leading Riemann to insist on the hegemony of the iamb.

Conus provided illustrations of agreement and nonagreement between the integumentary (covering) whole and the skeletal whole. Although agreement between the two aspects is normal and nonagreement abnormal, the latter occurs more frequently. As an example of agreement, Conus selected the first two measures of the second movement of Tchaikovsky's Sixth Symphony (ex. 26), which exhibit a symmetrical equilibrium of two volitional acts, each five quarter-note pulses, agreeing therefore with the 5/4 meter. As an example of nonagreement, Tchaikovsky's *Elegie* op. 55 no. 1, measures 1-3 (ex. 27), displays in its integumentary structure an anapestic anticipation of the six-part skeletal meter:

Syntactical integumentary:

$$\overline{5\ 6\ \underline{\dot{1}\ 2\ 3\ \overline{4}\ 5\ 6}\ 1}$$

Skeletal integrity: 6

Ex. 26   P.I. Tchaikovsky, Symphony no. 6, second movement, mm. 1-2

Conus related the breaking-up process of analysis, the uncovering of the boundaries of the various groupings, to the skeletal aspect of a composition:

> Metrotechtonicism establishes that the breaking up of musical bodies should be done by the principle of a *skeletal,* and not an integumentary division, since the second may give an arbitrary and particularly irrational relation of parts, while the first reveals the structural regularity of the interrelation between parts and of the parts to the whole. Here is why one

Ex. 27   P.I. Tchaikovsky, *Elegie* op. 55 no. 1, mm. 1-3

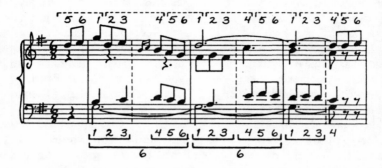

ought to divide musical creations at the boundary points of their skeletal parts. . . . These are chronometric points, not having a dimension—equal to zero—and mathematically agreeing in the musical body with the rudimentary pulsating stimuli of the first supported cells of any musical creative volitional act. In view of the unbroken continuity of a musical body in time, the concluding point of each previous volitional act is at the same time also the beginning point of the following [volitional act]. These points, invariably supported, we call points of the skeletal (or architectural) union of parts. They are the points of origin of the bars of higher order.[131]

These points of the skeletal union of parts are found between succeeding volitional acts; they correspond to the seams of the musical fabric but without any overlapping, since they have no dimension. The skeleton of a musical organism consists of "a regular system of points, intuitively formed in musical time, in which parts [of the organism] are joined with parts."[132]

Dividing up a composition at the skeletal point tends to break up the thematic content unnaturally, for example, severing upbeats (as in ex. 27) or downbeats (as in ex. 24) from the thematic material to which they belong. Conus affirmed, though, that an upbeat, while appearing to be the beginning of an integumentary phrase, is "in reality the architectural end of the previous skeletal part of the musical organism"; the downbeat, the integumentary end, is "in reality the architectural beginning of the following skeletal part."[133] The upbeat and downbeat are severed from their respective beginning and ending integumentary positions by the points of skeletal joining, the points appearing as the boundaries of measures of higher order. When no upbeat exists, the integumentary and skeletal limits of the grouping agree. When án upbeat precedes the first pulse (accented) of Conus's grouping, the integumentary and skeletal limits diverge.

The value of the discovery of the skeletal structure of a musical work had a wide application for Conus:

The revelation of the skeletons in musical organisms clearly shows the crystallike structure of the temporal plan of sound architecture. Having at one's disposal the skeleton of a musical organism, one obtains a firm basis for definitive and exhaustive judgments about its metrics, rhythmics, melodies, harmony, modulatory plan, factors of its presentation, its thematics, instrumentation, etc. All these factors are closely connected with the skeleton of the organism, since they all agree in the points of temporal division.... Dissecting the musical body, defining the mutual disposition and correlation of the organic parts of the whole in time, we may diagnose their functional purposes.[134]

Concerning the usefulness of his theory of metrotechtonicism, Conus wrote:

The discovery of the temporal coordinate... solves the complex... problem of musical form. The solution is expressed in the following highly valuable scientific generalization: the form of an audible creation is defined by the measurement of its *temporal* coordinate just as the form of a visual creation [is defined] by the measurement of its spatial coordinate.

The discovery of temporal coordinates in musical architecture firmly established that intuition in the process of creation secretly is based on sober equality (mechanics), on perfectly measured computation (mathematics), and on pure deductions (logic). The existence of musical coordinates in each audible creation irrefutably points out that even *the most emotional* audible phenomenon is in its inner constitution servilely submissive to the eternal laws of *impassive* numbers.[135]

The advantages of such a system, Conus determined, narrow down to two areas: practices of orthography and methods of study. Conus wanted to enrich orthography with a system of punctuation marks, which he did not divulge, with the invention of "a syntactical codex" that would establish the "architecturally strictly proportionate nature of musical speech,"[136] and with a new form of writing bar lines, as dotted, unbroken, double, etc., that would reflect the syntactical thought of the composition. Changes in study methods, such as decreased time needed for memory work, less difficulty in understanding a composition, increased accessibility of the formal aspect of compositions for research purposes, would result from the republication of the masterpieces of world musical literature using these new notational practices. He also suggested that students be educated in metrotechtonic analysis and in the metrotechtonic methods of notation, resulting in the correct notation of new compositions. Thus for the first time, music would be provided with its own language, its own syntax.

Conus viewed musical form as a strictly temporal embodiment:

The form of a musical creation is a kind of method that limits its creation in time. Metrotechtonic research established that musical forms belong to the category of regularity.... Form is a necessarily copresent component part of a unified whole, which finds its expression in *a temporal projection* and illuminates the organization of its parts *in time*. Form is perceived as unified because the participation of *all* available factors of musical content is concentrated collectively in its formation.... [Form is] the side of living musical content that is imprinted on the passive temporal substrata.[137]

In Conus's interpretation, the realization of the musical syntactical process unfolds in stages beginning with "pure time," which is calm, impassive, and is symbolized by a straight line, and ending with "musical time," essentially, musical form. This development of musical time from pure time involves four steps: (1) the rise of the concept of "measure" (not a musical measure, but a means of regular measurement; the cells or waves in metrotechtonicism), symbolized by points equidistant from each other on a straight line; (2) the rise of "supported points," accented cells occurring periodically from within one to three cells, functioning as natural borders between the musically creative volitional acts and measured by whole numbers representing the cells; (3) the rise of "architecturally measured parts," designated by brackets, by numbers reflecting the numbers of cells, and by letters identifying parts; and (4) the rise of the "regularities of symmetrical, periodic, and mixed orders. Music, formed in time, is invariably subordinate to one of these regularities."[138] Conus called these regularities "the laws of sound architecture," which "are the greatest relation among the parts of a musical organism but by no means should be applied to the sound content of the cell."[139] These laws apply to all the parts except the cell: "One and the same general structural law of proportionality directs the creation both of small parts (in their details) and also large [parts] in music."[140]

In his last work, Conus distinguished between the "technical content of musical creation," consisting of "all the varied material used for its manufacture," and the "artistic content of musical creation," consisting of

its influence on the listener, caused by tonal perceptions of the psychic experience.... The technical content of musical creation is a phenomenon of the first order, perceived by our ear from without; the artistic content of musical creation is a phenomenon of secondary order, perceived by our psyche from within as an echo, a reflex.[141]

The technical content includes four kinds of factors—the factor of time, factors of physical order (acoustics), factors of physiological order (music perception), and factors of psychological order, which include such concrete elements as mode, rhythm, polyphony, and such abstract elements as stasis or kinesis, similarity or contrast, etc. Metrotechtonicism is concerned not so much with the artistic content of a musical work as the technical content, specifically the factors of time and of psychological order.

Conus's most detailed and comprehensive example of the metrotechtonic approach is his analysis of the first movement of Beethoven's Piano Sonata op. 90 shown in figure 7. In it he illustrated graphically the syntactical division of the movement, from the lowest level, the grouping of the structural cells, to the highest, the three parts plus codetta, of the sonata form. To this scheme he appended a portion of the movement printed in his metrotechtonic notation, in which he separated the cells with dotted bar lines, the volitional acts with solid bar lines, and the measures of higher order with double bar lines and a blank space. The portion shown in example 28 illustrates these procedures.

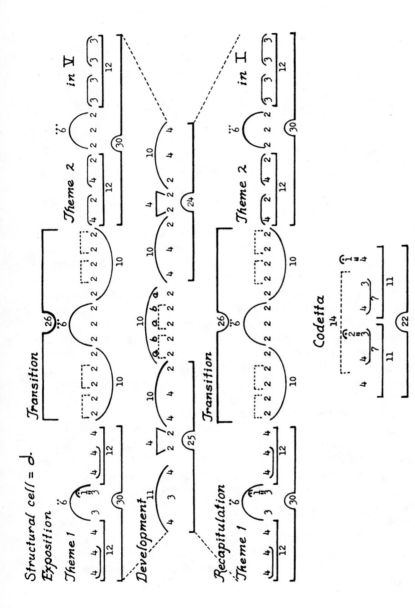

Fig. 7   Ludwig van Beethoven, Sonata for piano op. 90, first
movement, "Metrotechtonic plan of the syntactical
motion"

Ex. 28   Beethoven, Sonata for piano op. 90, first movement, mm.
12-17

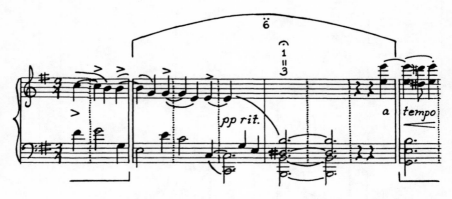

Conus also made a detailed survey of the musical creative volitional acts of this movement, from which it appears that changes in tonality and cadences were the determining factors in the groupings. Certainly the thematic content did not contribute. The nonagreement between the integumentary and the skeletal aspects is evident from the excerpt shown in example 28: frequently, as in the sixteenth and eighteenth cells, for example, an upbeat at the beginning of a phrase or a downbeat at the end of a phrase falls outside the joining points, and is excluded from the volitional act containing the theme to which it belongs. The metrical analysis poses no problem, even though Conus did not indicate it: the two-and four-cell groupings may be interpreted as one or two trochees, or perhaps, in the case of the four-cell grouping, a dactyl with an extra unaccented cell; the three-cell groupings may be interpreted as dactyls. The structural cell equals one measure, a dotted half note.

Although the movement contains 245 measures, the total number of cells is 253. The discrepancy exists because of Conus's practice of interpreting fermatas as extra cells (from one to three), as in measure 16 (ex. 28). While this approach may appear to be a practical one since time, not space, is being measured, in application it becomes a subjective matter. In this analysis Conus added eight cells in all, two to measure 16 and its equivalent, measure 159, in the recapitulation, and in the codetta, one to measure 237 and three to the final measure of the movement, measure 245. However, he omitted from consideration the fermatas in measure 24 and its equivalent in the recapitulation, measure 167, which mark the end of the first theme and the beginning of the transition to the second theme. Consequently, it becomes difficult not to believe that Conus manipulated these lengths so that the various sections of the composition would become more nearly equal in length to support his "laws of sound architecture."

Conus's metrotechtonic plan illustrates the symmetry of the movement, the tripartite division of which coincides with the three main sections of the sonata form—exposition, development, and recapitulation. Symmetry also occurs at each level within these sections. Only the development section contains minor discrepancies between the first and third segments. The exposition and recapitulation also exhibit a tripartite division, which, according to Conus, coincides with the first theme, the transition, and the second theme. In order to determine the validity of Conus's analysis, I have compared it with the analysis of this movement by Donald Francis Tovey:[142]

Exposition:	Theme 1	Transition	Theme 2				
Conus:	1-28	29-54	55-84				
Tovey:	1-24	24/25-54	55-81				

Development:	Part 1	Part 2	Part 3	Part 4	Part 5	Part 6	Part 7
Conus:	85-95	96-99	100-109	110-119	120-129	130-133	134-143
Tovey:	82-91	92-99	100-109	110-117	118———————132		132-143

Recapitulation:	Theme 1	Transition	Theme 2				
Conus:	144-171	172-197	198-227				
Tovey:	143/144-167	168-197	198-221				

Codetta:	Part 1	Part 2	Part 3				
Conus:	228———————237		238-245				
Tovey:	222-231	232-237	238-245				

Conus's interpretation agrees with Tovey's at many of the major structural points, namely, the beginning of theme 2 (m. 55), the beginning of the recapitulation (m. 144), part 3 of the development (mm. 100-109), and the concluding phrase of the codetta (mm. 238-245). Concerning other major structural points, such as the beginning of the transition and the beginning of the development, Conus's analysis differs from Tovey's by four and three measures, respectively. In both instances, the disputed measures are ambivalent thematically and could belong either to the previous grouping, as in Conus's analysis, or to the following grouping, as in Tovey's analysis. Harmonically, these measures should be considered as belonging to the previous grouping; however, structurally, they belong to the following grouping, since they occur after important strong cadences, in the tonic and the dominant, respectively. Thus, although Conus successfully demonstrated a certain degree of symmetry in this movement, the extension of that symmetry to the rigorous proportions he claimed remains in doubt.

Conus strongly criticized other methods of analyzing musical form, particularly those of Riemann and his followers, who made up a large segment of the group of theorists Conus called "traditional" (which included virtually all theorists from Reicha up to Conus's time).[143] Conus attempted to prove the validity of his theory of metrotechtonicism by pointing out the faults of the traditional school and offering metrotechtonicism as the correct alternative.[144] His list of fifteen points, concerned primarily with the metrical division of music, includes the following criticisms: the hegemony of the number two and its multiples in analysis; the dogma of the iamb; the insistence on an accented concluding cadence; Riemann's idea of the "bar triplet"; the impossibility of separating form from content, skeletal meter from integumentary, and episodic accent from metric; the inability of one measure to possess dual function, acting both as the beginning of one phrase and the end of another; and the concepts of expansion and contraction within a metrical analysis. Regarding musical form in general, Conus's criticisms include: the nonexistence in traditional theory of general guiding principles concerning the formal articulation of music; the inattention of traditionalists to the questions of general laws concerning the relation of the parts to the whole and the structure of the whole, and to the laws of proportionality; the inadequacy of the existing classification of forms; the secondary status of vocal and instrumental forms in traditional theory; and the overabundance of unnecessary syntactical terms.

To some extent Conus's criticisms are valid, but his theory does not provide all the solutions to the problems. In certain respects his theory merely replaces one dogmatic approach with another, such as its insistence on trochees over iambs. In addition, in his haste to condemn traditional theory for its faults, Conus neglected to consider the many areas where his theories coincide with—and perhaps were influenced by—the theories of Riemann concerning formal analysis. One can see similarities in several areas: the idea of the measure as *ur*-motive (in metrotechtonicism, cells or waves); the grouping of these measures into larger units (Riemann: symmetries of higher order; Conus: measures of higher order); the application of Greek metrics to these measures (for Riemann the iamb was omnipresent; for Conus, the trochee), and so on. In addition, Conus applied Riemann's statement that "musical metrics is, consequently, the study of symmetries"[145] to the work of music as a whole. For Riemann, though, the law of strict metric proportionality applied only to small structures, such as the period: "The largest forms are constructed not with the aid of purely metrical structure, but on the basis of the grouping of their thematic content."[146] Conus, apparently, had in mind phrases such as this one when he criticized the traditionalists for confusing form with content and integumentary structure with skeletal structure.

Conus also shared with Catoire some similar approaches to questions of musical form: denouncements of Riemann and his one-sided interpretations; attention to the metrical analysis of music; dissatisfaction with certain aspects of traditional theory (different for each, however); and a hierarchical approach to formal analysis. Yet Conus did not approve of Catoire's more traditional approach to formal analysis; nor did Catoire approve of Conus's revolutionary method, as he implied in his book.[147] Overall, the differences between the two theories far outweigh their similarities.

However, despite the attention given to Conus's theory of metrotechtonicism in the 1920s and 1930s, it turned out to be less significant for Soviet music theory than Catoire's approach. Conus's attempts to prove the existence of universal laws of architecture in music led him to disregard much that is useful in distinguishing one form from another, such as thematic content and tonality. And yet in his analysis of Beethoven's Sonata op. 90, Conus reconciled somewhat the traditional approach with the metro-techtonic approach. Although he had nearly 1,000 analyses to his credit, he never grouped them according to general characteristics, except those of symmetry or periodicity on the lower levels and proportionality on the higher levels. He only wished to prove that each piece of music was inherently subordinate to the laws of architecture.

Such a unilateral and frequently illogical approach proved unacceptable to many musicians. As early as 1902 Conus demonstrated his method to Arensky and Taneev, applying it to their own works, and they both reacted unfavorably. Taneev wrote to his former student: "You must recognize that the 'schemes' of the system of calculation represent an imperfect instrument so poorly worked out that by means of it you not only fail to reach the truth but also become entangled in very simple things."[148] Arensky complained to Taneev about Conus's "absurd" theory:

> The qualities ascribed by Conus to the forms of works are the qualities of *numbers*, of *figures*, and not at all of musical structures, since the graphic structures made by him bear a completely arbitrary character.
> It is possible to see this from the following:
>
> 1. Conus arbitrarily takes 2, 3, 4, etc. measures (sometimes 1 and sometimes none) and designates this the middle.
> 2. He is not able to say whether there is *equality* or *symmetry* and ascribes to form arbitrarily one or the other.
> 3. He divides movements not on the basis of their logical meaning, but completely arbitrarily, beginning with whichever measure he pleases.
> 4. Along with this he sometimes still uses neither equality nor symmetry.
> 5. If one considers that the majority of musical structures consist of an even number of measures, it becomes understandable that one can easily determine such a combination of numbers in which it is possible to find either equality or symmetry.
>
> It seems to be that this fascinating work in the analysis of form may also do essential damage to the weak health of Conus, and absolutely will not be useful to art.[149]

In his reply to Arensky, Taneev revealed how Conus reacted to criticism:

> G[eorgy] E[duardovich] relates very strongly to those who do not agree with him. For example, in the concluding part of my symphony, he did not observe the place where the main sentence finished, but placed the boundary earlier than its conclusion; when I

protested, he said that his division does not have anything in common with the division into sentences, periods and such. When you ask him what criteria guide him in placing the boundaries, he evades the answer, saying that theoretically he himself does not understand this.[150]

Taneev also pointed out Conus's false logic:

Frequently in his discussions one meets what in logic is called *petitio principio*, or, "false circle.".... For example, he says, "Look, what symmetry! On one side of the 'center' there are 8 and 6 measures, on the other, 6 and 8," etc. When you ask: "On what basis is the 8 measures divided from the 6?" he frequently answers: "Because otherwise there would not be a symmetry!" Thus, in order to show the essence of symmetry, he operates on a given division of measures into groups, and in order to justify this division, he operates on symmetry.

When you point this out to him, he is dissatisfied and answers that whoever has not drawn as many schemes as he may not criticize him, for he has been studying this for two years.[151]

Leonid Sabaneev first criticized Conus's theory of metrotechtonicism in an article appearing one month after Conus's first article.[152] Sabaneev disputed nearly every point made by Conus, from Conus's "hypertrophy" of time to his disregard for other elements. Sabaneev wrote:

Form is the result of the complex interaction of all the elements of a musical whole.... The method of Conus is completely saturated with scholasticism—it is the living negation of art. Besides, it is completely unscientific—for it is based on *a priori* structures ... and therefore does not give an idea of the true structure of a musical organism. One should be more objective. This is why we consider that the method of Conus is not useful, and is also in many ways harmful.[153]

In a subsequent article defending his theories, Conus appended testimony from prominent musicians who praised his analytical approach. Yavorsky's remark (made February 2, 1922) typifies these laudatory comments: "The Metro-architectonic method of research of musical works appears to be a solution for one of the more important problems related to finding the processes of thought in the sphere of musical poetry."[154]

Other critics of Conus's theories tended to express more moderate views, both positive and negative. The musicologist Valentin Eduardovich Ferman, for example, approached the analysis of musical form from a materialistic point of view and divided it into organic and historical aspects.[155] In his opinion, the organization of the tonal artistic process takes place in several directions: the intonational melodic, modal harmonic, factural instrumental, metrical rhythmic, and structural temporal directions.[156] He agreed with Conus that "the organization of the musical material by temporal means is the primary organization both in biophysical and in historical relations; it makes possible all other types of organization."[157] Therefore, in the narrow sense, musical form may be understood generally as "the metrical structure of a given piece," expressed through the organization of the musical pulse. But Ferman disagreed with Conus concerning the method of measuring these pulses:

> Essential [elements] in the temporal structure of a work are the number of pulsating units being measured, the number of strong beats, and the principal kind of succession of strong and weak parts, not the isochronism of the distances between them, and not the mathematically equal lengths of the structural pulsating waves.[158]

Ferman stressed that irrational tempo changes, including fermatas, do not allow exact calculation, but may be subject to various interpretations. While admitting that in music, as in all art and in nature, there exists a definite tendency towards equilibrium, towards structural proportionality expressed in a work's temporal structure and also in its thematic structure, Ferman emphasized that "in music, as in the other arts, symmetry is manifested not mathematically exactly, but only as an aspiration to equilibrium that arises on a biological basis."[159] Most importantly, he stated:

> A different type of musical, architectural symmetry characterizes each historical epoch.... But it is possible to reveal the individual particularities of separate authors and whole schools only when seen from a historical viewpoint, from the viewpoint of living activity, of gradually changing facts and phenomena.[160]

Sociology, and not biology, becomes the center of gravity for this approach, since "art is a social-historical category, a category subordinated to the laws of the historical process in all its dynamics, in all its varieties."[161] Nonetheless, Ferman praised Conus "for shaking loose many old pseudo-scientific... positions of the old German School of musical theorists," for arousing greater interest in the problem of musical form, and for playing a great revolutionary role in musical science.[162]

Lev Abramovich Mazel, the foremost critic and interpreter of Conus's theory during the 1930s, saw both positive and negative aspects in it. He argued against its lack of attention to the dynamic aspect of music and its neglect of the elements of form other than the metrical element: "One should not construct a *closed, finished,* and 'absolute' theory of form on the basis of the study of *one* element."[163] He also disapproved of metrotechtonicism's equating of spatial symmetry with temporal symmetry, and its inability to reveal anything about the evolution of musical form or style or the structure of a musical work. He pointed to Conus's failure to provide definite criteria—except perhaps that of symmetry—for the division of works into measures of higher order. Given all the "apparatus" of Conus's method, all the variables Conus allowed in his analyses, it would be "completely improbable" to find a work that

> could not be divided... in order to fulfill one of the many possible schemes of "equality." There is nothing "miraculous" in this; only the laws of probability are demonstrated here,

and thus the "law of equilibrium" in its absolute form says nothing about the specifics of musical art.[164]

However, Mazel did reveal a positive side of the theory:

> Very many metrotechtonic analyses turn out to be very satisfactory and uncover essential correlations; without knowledge of these, the understanding of the structure of a given work would be incomplete. This is explained by the fact that all the arts are related, and in particular, many musical works demonstrate architectural properties.... Metrotechtonicism, undoubtedly, enriches our perception and calls attention to these architectural correlations in musical works; in this lies its merit.[165]

He added that it is not necessary "to develop the entire cumbersome theory of metrotechtonicism" in order to show these architectural correlations:

> These correlations should be studied not in opposition to musical syntactical correlations, but in close connection with them.... The perceived structure of a work in an architectural plan should be only one component element in our perception of form and should not be the principal one; this should be the perception of the development of musical thought.[166]

In a later work, Mazel developed more fully his interpretation of the positive aspects of metrotechtonicism. He pointed to Conus's "brilliant and witty criticism of the traditional school and Riemann's conception of form," and to the "possibility of a similar sort of opposition among various 'layers' of the musical fabric" as between Conus's idea of "skeleton" and "integument."[167] In addition, Mazel gave examples of metrotechtonic analyses that help to illuminate the structure of certain forms, such as the sonata form without development.

Soviet musicology in general, though, has criticized Conus for ignoring the historical, philosophical, and sociological aspects of musical analysis, as in this comment from 1935:

> The outstanding trait... of the work of Conus is its attempt to find some common principles of structural order in the variety of musical forms.... However, the musical creative process is examined by [Conus], not as a socially conditioned, complex ideological process... but as an immanent, outer historical act, subordinated to the self-sufficient abstract laws of numbers and relations. Instead of establishing the connections of cause and effect and the interdependence of musical forms in the concrete social historical conditions, Conus considers it possible to speak about "the beginning in musical time of the important regulatory laws of symmetrical, periodic and mixed orders," and about the fact that "compositional geniuses are servilely submissive to all of the same laws of impassive numbers."[168]

Conus replied to such criticisms with a few feeble apologies such as this: "I consider musical creation the object of exclusively *scientific* research, and refrain absolutely, by incompetence, from a judgment of [its] sociological and philosophical bias."[169] He similarly justifies his distinction between the technical and artistic content of musical creation: the interpretation of the artistic content of music takes place in the listener's psyche and is secondary to the technical content.[170] But Conus failed to acknowledge most of the valid criticism directed against his theories; he only grew stronger in his conviction that metrotechtonicism as he developed it was a valid analytical method.

Had Conus overcome the deficiencies in his approach, had he developed the possibilities inherent in his methods, rather than blindly adhering to tenets established before he had conducted sufficient research, his theory of metrotechtonicism might have found wider application in Soviet music theory. Even so, his reputation remains secure. He is remembered as the creator of one of the more original theoretical concepts of the early twentieth century, who

> showed the significance of temporal proportions... to musical form as a whole.... Conus illuminated one aspect of the musical manifestation of general esthetic laws—measurement, symmetry ..., harmonic... order—and substantiated one of the so-called precise musicological methods that helps to disclose structural regularities in music.[171]

In this endeavor Conus joined Taneev and Catoire in directing attention in Russia to questions of formal analysis and to the impracticality of Riemann's approach. Therein lies his main contribution to the development of Soviet music theory.

Nikolai Alexandrovich Garbuzov (1880-1955)

Nikolai Alexandrovich Garbuzov, like Catoire, turned to the serious study of music only after he had completed his education in another field, the physical sciences. After graduating from the Gornyi Institute (The College of Mines) in St. Petersburg in 1906, he taught inorganic chemistry at a Moscow technical school from 1911 to 1921. During this time, he began studying music composition at the Musical Dramatic School of the Moscow Philharmonic Society, and received his degree in 1916. His abilities in both music and science led to his interest in acoustical research. In 1921 he became the director of the State Institute of Musical Science [Gosudarstvennyi institut muzykal'noi nauki], taking an active part in acoustical research there. After it was disbanded in 1931, he continued to conduct research, from 1931 at the State Academy of the Arts [Gosudarstvennaia akademiia iskusstvoznaniia] and from 1932 at the Scientific Research Institute at the Moscow Conservatory [Nauchno-issledovatel'skoi institut pri Moskovskoi konservatorii], which he directed from 1934 to 1937. He also taught at the Moscow Conservatory (1923-1954) and directed its acoustical laboratory (1933-1948). When the Institute for the History of the Arts [Institut istorii iskusstv] was organized in 1944, he directed the musical section.

Garbuzov believed in the mathematical verification of all sciences, including musical science. He found the realization for this belief in the application of acoustics to music theory. Unlike the pseudoscientific efforts of such researchers as Leonid Sabaneev and Arseny Avraamov in acoustics, Garbuzov applied a more rigorous approach and established acoustics as a legitimate branch of Soviet music theory. This constitutes perhaps his most important contribution. During the 1920s and 1930s, he advanced a theory of the acoustical basis of harmony, particularly the harmony of such modern Russian composers of his day as Skryabin, Prokofiev, and Stravinsky. This he published in a two-volume work, *The Theory of Multi-based Modes and Chords.*[172] He also published a number of articles on this and other topics related to acoustics.[173]

Garbuzov's theory of multi-based modes and chords rests on the assumptions that (1) the tones of modes and chords are derived from the overtone series; (2) only certain tones of the overtone series contribute to these constructions; (3) more than one overtone series may enter into the construction of modes and chords; and (4) the various overtone series contributing to such constructions are related. Garbuzov developed this theory while attempting to determine scientifically whether chords originate in the overtone series, and specifically, to explain, through the application of the higher partial tones, harmonic constructions used by such composers as Skryabin. He pointed in particular to the acceptance by some theorists of the partial tones 7, 11, and 13, which previously had been unacceptable.[174] With the aid of a five-octave harmonium, Garbuzov determined that "the uselessness of the overtone series as a whole for the purpose of harmonic construction was completely clear, and the inaccuracy of explaining all chords as parts of an overtone series proved convincing."[175] He also subjected to scrutiny the theory of the contrapuntal origin of chords of Ernst Kurth and found it insufficient as well.

In an attempt to determine the true structure of modes and chords, he began a systematic examination of modes, beginning with simpler ones such as the church modes.[176] He concentrated on the ionian mode as the most historically complete and the simplest in construction. Perceiving that the first tetrachord of this mode gives the impression of F major, while the second tetrachord that of C major, he sensed a modulation from F major to C major. He therefore assumed that the tones of the ionian mode were a combination of certain partial tones from the overtone series on C and on F. To determine which partial tones from these two series made up this mode, Garbuzov followed this line of reasoning: the tones F and A do not belong to the overtone series on C; moreover, the fractions corresponding to the coefficients of these tones are not multiples of 2 (ex. 29a). Therefore, only C, D, E, G, and B belong to C. By reducing the fractions of these tones by the lowest common denominator, which is 8, the resulting numbers are identical to the numbers of the corresponding tones in the overtone series from C (ex. 29b). He obtained this order of tones in the overtone series by eliminating lower octave duplications (the partial tones 1-6), and the approximate partial tones 7, 11, 13, and 14. By taking the same pattern of notes from F in the overtone series on C, dividing their fractions by 4/3 (the relation of F to C) and multiplying the results by 8, he obtained the same pattern from F (ex. 30). Both these pentachords are what Garbuzov called "natural pentachords," that is, they exhibit the same structure, with the partial tones 8, 9, 10, 12, and 15. Garbuzov concluded, "The natural major or ionian mode originates therefore from the connection of two natural pentachords in the relationship of a perfect fourth"[177] (ex. 31).

Ex. 29   a) ionian mode; b) partial tones from C used in
construction of mode

Ex. 30   Partial tones from F

Ex. 31   Construction of ionian mode from partial tones on C and F

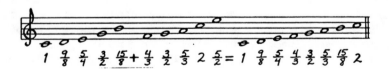

Garbuzov analyzed the other church modes in a similar manner. The aeolian mode (on A), for example, originates from three pentachords on C, F, and B♭, related to each other through the intervals of the perfect fourth (4/3) and perfect fifth (3/2).[178] He added the B♭ pentachord because only from it could he obtain the correct coefficients (from B♭, F is 8/5 and D is 4/3, ex. 32). Garbuzov called this mode "an incomplete mode," since not all of the tones produced by the three pentachords participate in the actual constitution of the aeolian mode. Garbuzov explained the one nonparticipating tone, B♭, by citing its use in the Neapolitan sixth chord, as in the cadence I-♭II^6-V-i. He also called the aeolian mode a "commatic mode," because it contains degrees—two D's— separated by a comma (81/80), which occurs in pure tuning.

Ex. 32   Construction of aeolian mode from partial tones from F, C, and B♭

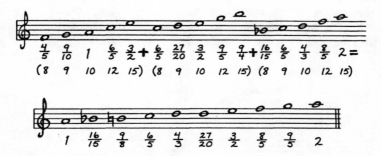

Garbuzov showed the remaining church modes and the harmonic major and minor modes also to have originated from the joining of pentachords— specifically, from two, three, or four pentachords related by the intervals of a perfect fourth, a perfect fifth, a major third, a major second, and a minor seventh. Since all the modes he examined result from the combination of two or more pentachords, he called them "multi-based modes." More specifically, he referred to each mode by the number of pentachords it employed as "duple-based," "triple-based," or "quadruple-based." Ionian (C and F), dorian (C and B♭) phrygian (C and F), and lydian (C and F) are duple-based modes; mixolydian (G, C, and F) and aeolian (F, C, and B♭) are triple-based modes; and the harmonic major (F, C, B♭, and A) and harmonic minor (F, C, B♭, and A) are quadruple-based modes. Garbuzov designated the fundamental tones of each pentachord in the modes as its "acoustical bases." Within each mode the pentachord most clearly related to the other pentachords serves as the main pentachord; its base is usually tonic. Depending on the degree of acoustical relatedness between its constituent pentachords, determined by the number of common tones between them, each mode exhibits a certain level of stability or instability. Modes with pentachords sharing the maximum number of three common tones, indicating relatedness by a perfect fourth or perfect fifth, exhibit the highest degree of stability. Modes with pentachords containing two common tones, a relatedness by major or minor thirds or sixths, exhibit a lesser degree of stability. Garbuzov considered those modes with pentachords containing one common tone, a relatedness by major or minor seconds or sevenths, to be unstable. Of the modes examined, only the dorian mode, with one common tone between its pentachords on C and B♭, fits into this last category.[179] These modes in their complete forms are shown in example 33.

Ex. 33   Church modes and harmonic major-minor mode: complete

Garbuzov classified modes in three groups according to the number of common tones between the constituent pentachords and the agreement between the tonic and the basic tone of the main pentachord. Among the modes with three common tones between constituent pentachords, Garbuzov distinguished two types, "primary modes," whose tonics equal the basic tone of the main pentachord, such as the ionian and lydian modes, and "derived modes of the first order," whose tonics equal the third of the main pentachord, as in the aeolian and phrygian modes. This latter characteristic occurs mainly in modes with minor quality. Among the modes with fewer than three common tones between constituent pentachords, Garbuzov distinguished only one type, "derived modes of the second order," or "modes with unstable tonic," whose tonics agree with the basic tone of the main pentachord, as in the harmonic major and minor modes and the mixolydian mode. Thus, the modes in each of the derived groups share one characteristic with modes in the primary group. Garbuzov should have designated a fourth category for the dorian mode, whose pentachords share only one common tone and whose tonic equals the third tone of the main pentachord, but he chose to overlook its instability and include it with the derived modes of the first order.

He also named modes according to the intervallic relationships between the acoustical bases of the modes. The derived modes of the first order, whose tonics equal the third of the main pentachord were named relative to the mode whose tonic equals the basic tone of the main pentachord:

1. Ionian: quartal mode (complete)
2. Dorian: third derived from major secundal mode (incomplete)

3. Phrygian: third derived from quartal mode (complete)
4. Lydian: quintal mode (complete)
5. Mixolydian: minor quartal-sextal mode (incomplete)
6. Aeolian: third derived from quartal-quintal mode (incomplete)
7. Harmonic major-minor mode: minor secundal-tertial-sextal mode (incomplete)[180]

Garbuzov applied the same methods to the synthesis of modes:

> Using the theory of multi-based modes and chords, I would be able to construct these modes through the analysis of the chords encountered in the works of contemporary composers, but I preferred the path of the synthesis of modes, since it made it possible to show that theory may go *ahead* of practice.[181]

He constructed all the possible stable modes up to sextuple-based modes inclusively, adhering to the following rules: (1) joined pentachords should contain no fewer than three common tones; (2) each higher multi-based mode (from four to six pentachords) should be formed from lower multi-based modes (from two to three pentachords); and (3) the main pentachord of the primary mode should be the natural pentachord sharing the most common tones with each of the other constituent pentachords. Including most of the modes already analyzed, Garbuzov constructed 42 different modes, each consisting of from seven to fourteen notes, some with commatic pairs (counted here as one note). In equal temperament this number would be reduced to 34 different modes.

Number of bases:	2	3	4	5	6
Primary modes:	2	3	10	6	3
Derived modes					
first order:	1	3	6	3	
second order:	0	2	2	1	1

For example, one of the three primary sextuple-based modes, the minor-major-minor secundal-tertial-quartal-quintal-sextal commatic mode, contains fourteen different notated pitches with one commatic pair (A♮). Its acoustical bases are, C, D♭, E, F, G, and A♭ (ex. 34).

Ex. 34   The minor-major-minor secundal-tertial-quartal-quintal-sextal commatic mode

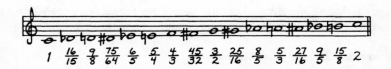

Garbuzov realized chords in a manner similar to his realization of modes. He analyzed or synthesized mono-based, duple-based and triple-based chords. He designated the chords as "full" if all the notes of the pentachord(s) are present and in ascending order, "derived" if the same tones are present but in a different order, and "incomplete" if tones are missing. Example 35a-c illustrates three different manifestations—full, derived, and incomplete—of a mono-based chord on C; example 35d-f illustrates the full, derived, and incomplete manifestations of a triple-based chord with bases on C, E, and B♭. If the base(s) is present in the chord, Garbuzov called it a "real" base; if the base(s) is missing from the chord, he called it an "imaginary" base. The minor triad exemplifies a chord with an imaginary base. The base of the minor triad from E, for example, is C; it is an incomplete mono-based chord (example 36a). The major triad may be analyzed as having a real or an imaginary base. The C major triad such as in example 35c, constructed from the pentachord on C, has a real base (C); but if constructed from the pentachord on F, it has an imaginary base, as shown in example 36b, and is an incomplete mono-based chord.

Ex. 35   Mono-based chord from C: a) full; b) derived; c)
          incomplete; Triple-based chord (C, E, and B♭): d) full; e)
          derived f) incomplete

The chords studied in harmony courses, Garbuzov discovered, usually contain from one to four bases. All are incomplete, and the majority of them are unstable, and therefore dissonant. The mono-based chords, containing five types plus inversions, include triads and some seventh chords; they

Ex. 36   a) Minor triad, imaginary base C; b) major triad,
imaginary base F

contain no tritones, augmented intervals, or diminished intervals. The duple-based chords, eleven different types plus inversions, are more diverse; they include such chords as the diminished triad, the dominant seventh chord, other seventh and ninth chords, and augmented chords. The triple-based chords, twelve different types plus inversions, include reinterpretations of some duple-based chords, and many altered chords. The two quadruple-based chords Garbuzov borrowed from Catoire's harmony textbook.[182] Catoire's J^2 chord, the minor ninth chord with a raised fifth, here constructed on G, has two real bases (G and F) and two imaginary bases (D♭ and E) (ex. 37a). Catoire's UJ^2 chord, the minor ninth chord with both raised and lowered fifth, here constructed on G, has three real bases (G, D♭ and F) and one imaginary base (E) (ex. 37b). The simplest mode in which these chords are found is the primary sextuple-based minor-major-minor secundal-tertial-quartal-quintal-sextal commatic mode with bases C, D♭, E, F, G, and A♭, already illustrated in example 34. In fact, Garbuzov discovered that all the "textbook" chords he analyzed, including some "accidental combinations," may be found in just seven modes: the duple-based quartal mode (the natural major mode), the triple-based quartal-quintal mode (C D E F F♯ G A B C), the quadruple-based minor tertial-quintal-sextal mode (C D E♭ E♮ F F♯ G A♭ A♮ B♭ B♮ C), the quadruple-based major tertial-quintal-septal mode (C C♯ D D♯ E F♯ G G♯ A B C), the quintuple-based minor secundal-quartal-quintal-sextal mode (C D♭ D♮ E♭ E♮ F F♯ G A♭ A B♭ B C), and the mode in example 34, the sextuple-based minor-major-minor secundal-tertial-quartal-quintal-sextal mode.

For additional, nontextbook chords, Garbuzov concentrated on the music of such contemporary composers of his day as Skryabin (the late sonatas), Debussy, Ravel, Prokofiev, Stravinsky *(The Rite of Spring),* and Schoenberg *(Erwartung):*

The progress of the newest music compared with the music of past epochs derives not so much from the complication of *modes* as from the complication of *chords.* Research into the

Ex. 37   a) Catoire's J^2 chord on G; b) Catoire's UJ^2 chord on G

modes of past music and folk music shows that these works frequently were constructed using very complicated modes, but their authors used similar modes for the creation of complex melodic designs (the horizontal development of bases); the newest composers use them for the construction of complex chords (the vertical development of bases).[183]

In Garbuzov's analyses, Skryabin, Debussy, Ravel, and Prokofiev used only a small number of triple-based chords, mainly four types from the dominant group (in the functional sense). In addition Prokofiev employed triple-based chords from the subdominant group (on the lowered second degree), and Stravinsky, triple-based chords from the tonic group that included some perfect fifths. For example, Garbuzov analyzed the bitonal chord from the "Dance of the Adolescents" in *The Rite of Spring* as a triple-based, incomplete major quintal-septal chord, with acoustical bases F♭, C♭, and E♭ (ex. 38). It may be found in a quadruple-based major tertial-quintal-septal mode on F♭ (bases F♭, A♭, C♭, and E♭). Two characteristic chords from Skryabin's Piano Sonatas are the beginning chords of the Seventh and Eighth Sonatas. Garbuzov analyzed the first of these as a triple-based incomplete diminished-minor quintal-septal chord (ex. 39a). It occurs on the fifth degree of the quintuple-based minor secundal-quartal-quintal-sextal mode on F (bases F, G♭, B♭, C, and E♭). He analyzed the beginning chord of the Eighth Sonata as a triple-based incomplete major-minor tertial-septal chord (ex. 39b). It occurs on the fifth degree of a quintuple-based major tertial-quartal-quintal-septal mode on F (bases F, A, B♭, C, and E). Garbuzov observed the greatest variety of chords in Schoenberg's *Erwartung,* in which triple-based chords from the dominant group prevail, and in Stravinsky's *Rite of Spring.*

Garbuzov rejected the construction of chords by like intervals, such as by thirds, fourths, or fifths, since no stable acoustical basis for any such constructions exists: "All chords constructed on these principles in reality turn out to be multi-based chords, the acoustical bases of which have different intervallic relations."[184] He also rejected the idea of polytonality or atonality, considering polytonal or atonal chords to be multi-based chords. Even though he admitted that some chords exist that do not lend themselves to analysis by his theory, he saw no place for them:

Only the most universal recognition of the thought that, in music, as in living nature, organisms are formed thanks to the relationship of their elements (in nature—chemistry; in music—musical acoustics), may overcome the antinature principle of the purely mechanical construction of modes and chords, and banish them once and for all from musical art.[185]

Ex. 38   Igor Stravinsky, *Rite of Spring,* "Dance of the
Adolescents," bitonal chord

Ex. 39   Alexander Skryabin, a) Seventh Piano Sonata, beginning
chord; b) Eighth Piano Sonata, beginning chord

In the second volume of *The Theory of Multi-based Modes and Chords,* published four years after the first volume, Garbuzov tempered his approach, undoubtedly because of increasing political pressures. Describing the approach of volume 1 as too static, he reformulated certain aspects and added a new dynamic dimension to the theory of multi-based modes and chords. However, he did not alter the basic premises and analytical methods presented in volume 1.[186] He also included in his second volume more detailed analytical applications of his theory, written by his students Saul Grigorevich Korsunsky and Sergei Sergeevich Skrebkov.[187]

Undoubtedly the most fundamental alteration Garbuzov made concerns the natural pentachord. Although he retained it as a measure of acoustical relatedness between overtone series, for the purpose of practical analysis he reduced it to a major triad consisting of the partial tones 1, 3, and 5. He derived the remaining tones 9 and 15 of the pentachord from the partial tones 3 and 5, respectively. He thus reverted to a more acceptable acoustical interpretation. This more "classical," less "modern" emphasis permeates the entire volume. The reduction of the natural pentachord to a triad altered some of the details of analyses presented in volume 1, usually resulting in a greater number of acoustical bases for most of the modes and especially for the more complex chords. In volume 2, though, Garbuzov analyzed only the chords forming the harmonic language of the classical style, i.e., tertian structures up to and including the ninth chord, and modes containing from five to eleven pitches and from two to six bases.

The change from analysis in a static state to the analysis of a dynamic process led Garbuzov to discuss intervals, chords, and modes according to the manner of their generation, in addition to their static constitution as formed by multiple bases and the upper partials 3 and 5. He categorized these processes as "timbral," "timbral-harmonic," "harmonic," and "modal." These categories refer to the generation of individual tones (timbral), of intervals or chords through tones of coincidence (i.e., common tones between overtone series) or combination tones (timbral-harmonic), of tones, intervals, or chords through partial tones (harmonic), all of which are simultaneous occurrences, and of the generation of modes through the same processes and through the formation of cadences characteristic to the individual modes (modal), a consecutive occurrence. The bases are usually generated separately. For example, in both volumes Garbuzov analyzed the dominant-seventh chord in F as a duple-based chord with bases on C and B♭. In its dynamic state, though, it is a complex process of harmonic formation of the base C through the partial tones 3 and 5 from C (E and G), and a timbral-harmonic formation of the base B♭ through a tone of coincidence (D) between partial tone 5 of B♭ and partial tone 3 of the partial tone 3 of base C (originally partial tone 9 of C). The same process occurs in both high and low registers (ex. 40). He analyzed all the intervals and the chords of classical harmony and their inversions in a similar manner.

Concerning chords and tones analyzed individually, Garbuzov reached several conclusions. For instance, harmony but not timbre is affected by register. This constitutes, in Garbuzov's estimation, the main difference between harmony and timbre and reveals the role of equal-tempered tuning, which makes possible wide changes in register.[188] He also discovered that inverted positions of chords possess characteristics in addition to those of the

Ex. 40   Formation of dominant seventh chord on C

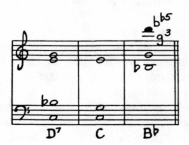

root positions of the same chords; this phenomenon is brought about by the different forms of generation of chords in different positions.

Garbuzov also discovered that the generation of mode constitutes only a higher form of sound generation. Therefore, no real difference in method exists between the simultaneous generation of sound and the consecutive generation of sound, "since the aural memory makes the process of modal formation of sounds occur as though it were simultaneous, and the realization of chords requiring some interval of time makes the process of harmonic and timbral-harmonic formation of sounds occur as though it were consecutive."[189] He defined mode, then, as "the formation of bases in consecutive time."[190] In this volume Garbuzov thus moved closer to the position of Yavorsky regarding the formation of mode as a dynamic process occurring in time.[191]

Of the twenty multi-based modes Garbuzov examined, eight of them do not contain a tonic. Each of these eight modes also lacks one or the other of two sonorities—the dominant or the subdominant. Based on his discoveries connected with the generation of sound, a base, for example C in the quartal-quintal mode, becomes tonic only when formed by the two opposing motions of subdominant (G to C) and dominant (F to C) (ex. 41a). Because of the high degree of acoustical relatedness between tones a fourth or fifth apart, and because the intensity of the timbral-harmonic formation of each pitch in these intervals is either the same (the fourth) or very close (the fifth), the modal formation of a fourth or fifth may take place either through the top tone of the interval or through the bottom tone, i.e., in two directions.[192] When the tone generated by the top tone of one fourth equals the tone generated by the bottom tone of another fourth, as in the minor seventh G-F to C, then the generated tone is doubly intensified. The resulting tonic thus contains characteristics of both base (in relation to the dominant) and overtone (in relation to the subdominant). This, then, is the modal formation of tonic, and is possible only with the presence of both the subdominant and the dominant. Garbuzov recognized the triad of resolution, a major triad in example 41b, as tonic because it meets these requirements: (1) the cadence progresses from the

Ex. 41   a) Tonal generation by fourths; b) modal formation of
         tonic

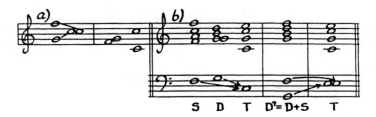

S   D   T   D⁷= D+S   T

smallest degree of relatedness (the minor seventh) to the greatest degree of
relatedness (the unison); (2) the quartal-quintal progressions in the cadence
exhibit the first degree of relatedness; and (3) the subdominant is raised to the
tonic as a fundamental tone to the overtone in the "dominant" direction, and
the dominant is lowered to the tonic as an overtone to the fundamental tone in
the "subdominant" direction, with tonic serving as a central point between the
two directions.

The same process, essentially, takes place in the minor mode. In this
volume in general minor maintains a more independent position relative to
major than it did in volume 1. Garbuzov no longer derived it from the third
tone of a corresponding major mode, but produced it autonomously. The
fullest minor mode, capable of forming all three types and containing the *S-D-
T* cadence (iv-V-i) is the minor tertial-quartal-quintal-sextal mode with bases
C, E♭, F, G, and A♭, shown in example 42.[193] Also, to construct the minor triad
Garbuzov had to include a major triad a minor third from the chord root; thus
the minor third itself becomes a duple-based chord, with bases on, for example,
C and E♭. In the minor triad, Garbuzov pointed out, the major element
produced acoustically by partial tone 5 from the root, in this case C and its
partial tone E, is overpowered by partial tones 2 and 4 from E♭ (two E♭'s) and by
the reinforcement of C and E♭ through G, a tone of coincidence occurring as
partial tone 6 (and 3) from C and partial tone 5 from E♭.[194] (See ex. 43.)

Ex. 42   Complete minor mode: minor tertial-quartal-quintal-sextal
         mode

Garbuzov's turning from a static, rigid interpretation of chords and modes
to a more fluid, dynamic one also affected his approach to analysis within a
musical context. Whereas he originally based the analysis of a chord primarily

Ex. 43   Formation of minor triad

on its structure, he later stipulated that, in a more dynamic analysis, the interpretation of a chord also depends on its context, particularly the chord to which it resolves. In the analysis of romantic and modern music, additional environmental factors influence the interpretation. For instance, in the opening two beats of Skryabin's Prelude op. 11 no. 9, shown in example 44a, the chord on beat two may be analyzed as a single-based chord on A, or as a duple-based chord with bases C♯ and A. However, the notes preceding the chord (C♯-B♯-C♯) led Korsunsky to accept the latter interpretation.[195] The analysis of the horizontal as well as the vertical aspect of the music also accounts for the modal presentation and development in the music, which Garbuzov had not examined closely in volume 1.

In another restriction involving analysis, Garbuzov stipulated choosing not the simplest analysis possible, which he earlier had advocated in cases where several possibilities existed, but the analysis most justifiable from the point of view of correct chord resolution by fourths or fifths, i.e., the highest degree of relatedness, as in the cadence *S-D-T*. In the same Skryabin Prelude, which fluctuates throughout between the tonality of E major and its relative minor C♯, the concluding cadence is in E major, but elements of C♯ minor are also present. The first chord of the cadence has two bases—F♯ and A—and the second chord also has two bases—G♯ and B. Following the pattern of the *S-D-T* cadence, the bases A and B resolve to the base E of the final chord; but the bases F♯ and G♯ do not resolve to the expected base C♯ (ex. 44b). The missing pitch C♯ is represented only by the tones most closely related to it—the tones F♯ and G♯—and by the tone E, which not only is part of the triad on C♯, but also is the other tonic base. The final chord, therefore, because of the missing C♯, renders the resolution incomplete.

Concerning the application of his theory to analysis, Garbuzov wrote:

At its present level of development the theory of multi-based modes and chords gives methods of analyzing musical works from the point of view of formal construction and harmonic and melodic "language." Of course, while the theory of multi-based modes and chords appears at times as *a theory of modes and chords* and may not provide methods of the detailed analysis of musical works with the full consideration of all their metric, rhythmic and other characteristics, even now it makes possible a very wide analysis and a sufficiently

Ex. 44   Alexander Skryabin, Prelude op. 11 no. 9: a) m. 1; b) mm.
           33-35

deep understanding of many musical phenomena. Therefore, I felt that this work should be
included both as a theory and also as practice, that is, both results of theoretical research and
also the application of them to the analysis of musical works.[196]

However, in general the analyses carried out by Korsunsky and Skrebkov in
the second half of volume 2 succeed more as general analyses than as special
analytical applications of Garbuzov's theory of multi-based modes and chords.
They did not maintain the level of detail in evidence in the analysis of the
Skryabin Prelude, for instance, but it is on this level that Garbuzov's theory
appears to be of use.[197]

In its entirety, volume 2 of *The Theory of Multi-based Modes and Chords*
fails to live up to the promise of volume 1. It constitutes a retreat from earlier
positions and may be said to contain merely an apologia for volume 1. It points
up the dilemma of Soviet theorists during the 1930s who faced a more
restrictive political climate and fewer opportunities for the expression of wide-
ranging views. Garbuzov evidently felt sufficient pressure regarding his earlier
theoretical views that he refined them to conform to prevailing political ideas.

The value of Garbuzov's theory of multi-based modes and chords lies not
in the theory *per se,* but in its acoustical verifications and explanations of
known phenomena. The idea that a mode or chord has two, three, or more
foundations was not readily accepted into Soviet music theory, but many of his
findings were subsequently applied, by Tiulin for instance. And Garbuzov's
explanation of the unfolding of mode and the definition of tonic through the
presence of both dominant and subdominant reinforced the already strong
emphasis in Soviet music theory on functional harmonic thought. In his
evaluation and analysis of Garbuzov's theory, Iosif Ryzhkin concluded that
Garbuzov, in developing his theory, had drawn closer and closer to positions
taken earlier by Rameau (the acoustical basis of the triad) and Riemann

(functional harmony), and had merely provided "a new argument for a previously given solution to an earlier presented problem."[198]

Ryzhkin also revealed striking similarities between conclusions reached by the differing applications of Garbuzov's theory of multi-based modes and chords and Yavorsky's theory of modal rhythm. Garbuzov, however, remained opposed to Yavorsky's theories and attempted to prove them false, stating, "The basic thesis of the theory of modal rhythm opposes the givens of acoustics."[199] He did not attach primary significance to the tritone, as did Yavorsky, but only secondary significance; and determined that the tritone is not "the carrier of instability in music in all possible conditions."[200] He believed that Yavorsky's double system, which he considered nonexistent and artificial, should be replaced with two single systems. He explained the resolution of the tritone to the major third as a progression of two tones with no acoustical relatedness to the closest interval with a stronger degree of acoustical relatedness. The constituent tones of the tritone themselves progress to tones with which they share the highest degree of relatedness: in the case of the tritone F-B, the F moves a fourth down to C, the dominant direction, and the B moves a fourth up to E, the subdominant direction. In its acoustical properties, therefore, this progression of the tritone to the major third resembles the classical cadence *S-D-T*. Ryzhkin viewed the main difference between the two theories in this light:

> The theory of multi-based modes and chords in contrast to the theory of modal rhythm takes the position that it examines functional relations of new modal-harmonic formations as acting on the model of classical major and minor, while the theory of modal rhythm examines classical major and minor, arising from new modal-harmonic formations.[201]

From this he concluded that as its main strength Garbuzov's theory "aspired to create a bridge from classical modes and harmonies to new modes and harmonies and to establish the continuity of the second relative to the first."[202]

Regardless of the fate of his individual theories, though, Garbuzov's legacy in Soviet music theory remains secure through his main contribution, the development of acoustics as a major aspect of Soviet music theory, and the development and application of strict research and laboratory procedures borrowed from scientific methods.

Garbuzov published a final work on his theory of the multi-based modes and chords in which he analyzed Russian folk song.[203] His later work reached even further into the area of acoustics. During the 1930s he developed his theory of "zone," on which he concentrated exclusively for the last decade of his life. Beginning in 1948 he devoted all his writings to the explication of this theory, which has since been accepted into Soviet acoustics more readily than his earlier work. In fact, for his centennial in 1980, only his works on this subject of zone were published in a commemorative volume.[204] Nevertheless, the importance of his earlier work and his influence and role in the development and growth of Soviet music theory during the 1920s and 1930s remain undisputed. His portrait, taken during that time, still hangs in a prominent position in the fourth-floor acoustical laboratory of the Moscow Conservatory, a testimony to his enduring influence in both theory and acoustics.

Lev Abramovich Mazel (1907-   )

For over fifty years, since 1930, Lev Abramovich Mazel has been a leading Soviet theorist. After receiving a degree in musicology from the Moscow Conservatory in 1930, he taught intermittently at the conservatory and other music schools in Moscow such as the Gnessin Institute until 1957. He received his doctorate from the Moscow Conservatory in 1941.[205] During the 1930s and 1940s, he devoted his research primarily to the topics of melody, musical analysis, and the history of music theory. His work in historical theory resulted initially in a series of articles on various musical theoretical systems, such as metrotechtonicism, multi-based modes and chords, analysis by the golden section, Kurth's theory of energetics, and functional harmony. Mazel eventually included much of this material in the two-volume work he coauthored with Iosif Ryzhkin, *Essays on the History of Theoretical Musicology.*[206]

Mazel's interest in theoretical systems, outside of their intrinsic historical value, lay in their application to musical analysis. His study resulted in his comprehensive analysis of Chopin's Fantasia op. 49, *The F minor Fantasy of Chopin. An Experiment in Analysis,* his major work from this period and a work highly regarded and suitably rewarded in the Soviet Union.[207] Stating that "the problems of the analysis of a musical work and of musical style constitute the central problems of our musicology," Mazel established two goals: to examine the Fantasia in detail, and to provide thereby a demonstration of analytical methods.[208] He approached the Fantasia on two levels. On one level he analyzed the technical and compositional aspects of the work—its formal structure, the thematic (melodic and rhythmic) interrelationships, and the tonal plan. On another level he approached the work from the aspect of style, investigating the content and significance of the Fantasia, Chopin's style in general, Chopin's place among the other romantic composers, and the evolution of the later instrumental forms of the romantic composers. Mazel saw a relationship between the technical and the stylistic aspects of analysis:

> The analysis of a concrete work is impossible without considering the regularities of a *given style,* which are generally historically formed; finding the content of the work is impossible without a clear idea about the expressive significance of the formal methods in this style. . . . The analysis of a concrete work and the study of the general characteristics and regularities of style represent two problems that are directly connected.[209]

Mazel did not attempt to impose a specific program on the Fantasia, a work that he chose largely because of its nonprogrammatic nature. However, he did analyze the general content of the work, discussing the functions of various segments according to their expressive content, and drawing analogies with literary and artistic ideas.

In general, Mazel considered it necessary not only to analyze separate elements such as form, harmony, rhythm, and melody, but also to examine the interaction of these elements and how they are joined together into an artistic whole that represents the general thought and content of the work.[210] He related this approach to the true meaning of "analysis" in music:

> Thus, the analysis of a musical work includes the factor of the synthetic scope of the whole. Expressions such as "analysis of form," "musical analysis," etc., arose only to distinguish the study of a musical work from its composition, that is, from musical creation, but not as the opposition of the analytical scientific method to the synthetic. In connection with this, musicologists sometimes use expressions that appear at first glance to be paradoxical (for example, "integral analysis").[211]

Mazel, therefore, approached analysis in a manner philosophically reminiscent of Conus, but where Mazel included in his examination all musical elements, Conus concentrated only on the temporal element. In addition, Mazel concerned himself less with adhering to a specific methodology; he used various methods only as means towards an end: the integrity and totality of a musical work, both by itself and in ever-widening contexts. Some methods he borrowed from other theorists; others he developed himself. From Yavorsky he borrowed the ideas of the anacrusis and the ictus (in a broad sense), variable mode, certain distinctions between the major and minor modes, intonation, monopartiteness, and turn.[212] From Ernst Kurth, he borrowed the theory of harmonic color, the idea of "energetics" and of the "general form of movement," specifically, the clarifying or obscuring alteration. From Catoire, he borrowed certain formal schemes and the application of metrics. Mazel applied these means, though not as used by their inventors in a "formalistic" and unilateral manner, but in a restrained way, taking only what he considered essential to illuminate the music:

> The use of ... different systems is allowable only so far as these positions reflect (though in hypertrophic form) different sides of objective reality, may be treated as unopposed to each other, and may be included in a single conception, methodologically opposed to *all* formalistic systems.[213]

Mazel approached style analysis in this manner:

> One must proceed above all by determining those historically formed regularities typical of a given style or styles, be they characteristic rhythmic, melodic, or harmonic turns, the principles of the development of musical thought, or the definite types of musical statement

(texture, etc.). Only then, in examining the particular manifestation of these typical regularities in a corresponding concrete case, can one draw conclusions about specific traits of the style of the composer and the work being examined.[214]

In order to do this, Mazel examined fragments of both classical and romantic compositions. Following the historical process, he traced within these works various compositional and stylistic devices through eras proximate to Chopin's, thereby placing Chopin within that process.

After examining the Fantasia in terms of the classical and romantic aspects of its structure, Mazel concluded that "the general scheme of the Fantasia, beginning with its exposition, displays the fullest expression of the confluence" of the classical forms of sonata and rondo-sonata, as interpreted by the romantic composers.[215] New characteristics in this amalgamated scheme preclude its being considered either a sonata or a sonata-rondo. For instance, the contrasting middle episode (C) in sonata-rondo form generally does not differ in either tempo or meter from the other sections; but in the Fantasia the middle episode changes both tempo and meter, thus acquiring "the function of the slow part of a cyclical form."[216] Also, the transitions, instead of being derived from the basic theme as in Beethoven, for example, result primarily from a triplet theme that originates in what Mazel termed the introduction (mm. 43-67), which connects the prologue (the opening "march" of the Fantasia) and the exposition (mm. 68-142). This triplet figure does not occur in the other themes, and "the completely special material 'derived from it'... very significantly... plays a great and independent role in the entire work."[217] The third special distinction between this structure and its classical predecessors is the special role and character of the prologue, which in the Fantasia consists of a greatly "independent and more or less complete part, the material of which is never repeated further."[218] This does not rule out the possibility, though, of particular thematic connections between the prologue and the main themes of the exposition. Considering these distinctions and peculiarities, Mazel allowed himself "to speak about the elements of cyclical form... anticipating the compression of a cyclical work into one movement in later composers."[219]

Mazel related the special role of the prologue and the introduction to the corresponding function of the introduction in literary poetic works, in particular ballads. The basic contrast developed in the exposition would be imperceptible if it and the general direction of the thematic and tonal development of the exposition were not contained in the prologue and the introduction: "Thus, the presence of the prologue and the introduction makes it possible to state the basic content of the exposition more directly and to concentrate its significant dramatic development in a comparatively brief time."[220] Specifically, the prologue states in embryo the thematic material used in the main theme (mm. 68-76), the concluding theme of the exposition (mm. 127-142), and the central episode of the development (mm. 199-222).[221] This thematic material consists of three main motives: the descending leap of a fourth (marked *a* in example 45), which usually occurs at the beginning of a theme and which may be expressed variously as an expansion or contraction of the original fourth, a two-note descending stepwise motive *(b)* that usually occurs between beats and frequently in conjunction with *a,* and a filled-in descending fourth *(c).*

Ex. 45   Fredrich Chopin, Fantasy op. 49: a) Prologue, mm. 1-4; b) main theme, F minor, mm. 68-70; c) main theme, A♭ major, mm. 73-75; d) main theme, A♭ major, mm. 77-78; e) concluding theme of exposition, mm. 124-29; f) central episode of development, mm. 199-206

Ex. 45 cont.

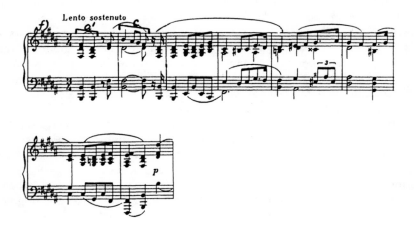

The introduction, of an entirely different character from the march-prologue, supplies harmonic material for the Fanatasia. It contains a "diatonic tertian chain," Mazel's term for a closed chain of tonalities consisting of two separately stated but adjacent diatonic chains. This tertian chain of tonalities anticipates the modulatory plan of the entire Fantasia (lower-case letters represent the minor mode):

Prologue
f———Ab—c———Eb—eb———Gb———————bb———Db—f———Ab
(Theme) 1   2   3   1   1   2   & coda
    Exposition ———Development——Recapitulation

Mazel observed that the minor mode usually appears alongside or in close proximity to its relative major. This occurrence resulted in a form of "variable mode," which here encompasses not major and minor modes simultaneously, its usual meaning as developed by Yavorsky, but consecutively, as movement from the minor to its relative major. Thus in the Fantasia appear five pairs of variable modes.

Mazel was also intrigued with the functional relations exhibited by the tonalities in the modulatory plan of the Fantasia. From the tonic (f-Ab), the Fantasia moves to the dominant (c-Eb), through the parallel minor of Eb to the subdominant sphere (Gb as II, bb-Db as IV of f), and back to tonic. Appropriately the Fantasia ends with a plagal cadence, db-Ab. In other words, the Fantasia displays a clearly functional plagal tonal direction: *T-D-S-T.* The plagal element in this plan, reinforced by the final cadence, may be related thematically to the fourths appearing prominently in two of the motives (*a* and *c*) from the prologue. Although Mazel referred to the tertian chain in the modulatory plan and its anticipatory role as "a completely new principle," he nonetheless pointed to the use by previous composers of separate elements of this principle, such as beginning the recapitulation in the subdominant, beginning the development in the parallel minor of the major tonality ending the exposition, and basing the modulatory plan of the exposition on a diatonic tertian chain, such as I-III-V. However, only Chopin initiated this new principle by combining these separate elements.

Throughout the analysis, Mazel referred to the "first element" and the "second element," two contrasting elements identifiable in the first few measures of the Fantasia. The first element usually is expressed as a deep register and a dark sound, a dotted rhythm, a disjointed thematic pattern, and unison or octaves—similar to the first two measures (ex. 45). The second element usually contains a smoother melodic line, higher register and brighter sound, and chordal harmonies, as in the third and fourth measures. These contrasting elements appear in different guises throughout the work and contribute to its overall expressive sound. Each may be represented by what Mazel termed the "character of sounding," the result of which makes it possible to speak about not only a "thematic reprise" or a "tonal reprise," but also a "registral reprise" or a "reprise by the character of sounding." In other words, Mazel connected many seemingly unrelated sections through elements not previously used in analysis. For example, he connected measures 93-94 with measures 109-110 through their "energetic movement by octaves in eighth notes," considering the "second idea to be a logical development of the first, in spite of the fact that the melodic figures of these ideas taken separately have almost nothing in common."[222] (ex. 46). Mazel commented further:

> Such a *concrete character of presentation* (register, "unison" or "chordal" statement, the presence or absence of chromaticism, in the melody or harmony, unity or great divisiveness of presentation, the general speed of sound progressions, "the general form of the movement," the character of the accompaniment, etc., etc.), that is, the concrete character of the very sounding, acquires here in a particular sense a more or less independent formative significance.[223]

Mazel also related material by the principle of "analogy in correlations," which is evident when

> the *correlation* between elements in one theme is analogous to the correlation of elements within another theme. So, frequently ... in a series of themes, a contrasting juxtaposition of the first element, in the majority of cases in the lower register, and the second [element] ("chordal"), usually in the higher register, is present. The *direct* relatedness of the corresponding elements of the different themes (the relatedness of basic forms of motion, even the registral relatedness) may *by itself* be *extremely insignificant*.... However, the character of the juxtaposition of the first element of the prologue with the second is

analogous to the juxtaposition of the F minor theme and the A♭ major theme of the exposition [the first and second elements of the main theme, shown in example 45].[224]

Ex. 46   Fredrich Chopin, Fantasy op. 49: a) mm. 93-94; b) mm. 109-110

According to Mazel, this principle of "analogy in correlations" has great significance for the romantic style:

> Owing to this principle, one motive or one theme may by its presentation in the work, its role and significance, functionally "substitute" for another, which it does not resemble at all.... This principle of "analogy in correlations" or "substitution of motives" is very characteristic... of Wagner.[225]

Mazel pointed out an example in the Fantasia:

> From the position taken and from some of their functions, the two concluding chords of the Fantasia [see ex. 49] "substitute" for the motive of the "octave exclamations" of measures 153-154 and 197-198 [also mm. 52-53 and 233-234, in ex. 47]..., in spite of the fact that the formal connection is very insignificant (two combinations instead of three; full-sounding chords instead of octaves, ascending movement instead of descending, presence of a change of harmony instead of octaves as such).[226]

Mazel had already pointed out the connective similarities between these same octave exclamations and the concluding chords. He also showed that the octave exclamations of measures 153-154 exemplify the "displacement of a thematic element in the repetition of a section."[227] These measures should have appeared during the second diatonic chain, approximately in measures 66-67, but were "displaced" until measures 153-154, where they appeared in their original context (as in mm. 52-53) (ex. 48).

Ex. 47   Fredrich Chopin, Fantasy op. 49: a) mm. 52-53; b) mm.
          153-54; c) mm. 197-98; d) mm. 233-234

An analogous situation occurs in the coda, where the octaves, which should have occurred approximately in measures 316-317, were displaced until the end. There, although they were preceded by material similar to an earlier occurrence (mm. 197-198), thus pointing to the correlative connection, they appear in a different guise which acts as a substitute, ending the work (ex. 49).

The various octave exclamations usually involve a diminished-seventh chord, occasionally a major-minor seventh chord that is interjected into the middle of what was to have been a full cadence, thereby thwarting the resolution, as in measures 142-143 (ex. 50). Mazel related this technique to the

Ex. 48   Fredrich Chopin, Fantasy op. 49: a) mm. 62-67; b) mm.
           150-157

influence of operatic, dramatic principles on Chopin's style. The interjected
chords themeselves, though, often exhibit a special bifunctionality; that is, they
can be interpreted functionally in two ways, depending on the surrounding
characteristics. For example, the beginning of the development section is
signalled by a broken cadence, in which the dominant of E follows the
dominant of E♭ (ex. 50). The question arises whether the second chord, the
dominant of E, is actually a diminished seventh chord on VII in B♭ (V of E♭)
with a lowered third (respelled: A-C♭-E♭-G♭), relating it to the following chord,
a diminished-seventh chord on VII in B♭ (A-C-E♭-G♭), or whether it is a
secondary dominant of the lowered second degree in E♭ major. Defending the
first interpretation, he pointed to the use of all the notes of the E-major scale,

Ex. 49   Fredrich Chopin, Fantasy op. 49: a) mm. 314-322; b) 327-
332

both in the chord (B-D♯-F♯-A) and in the surrounding thematic material (E♮, C♯, and G♯). Regarding the second interpretation, he observed that if this chord were a dominant of F♭ (C♭-E♭-G♭-B♭♭), the upper neighboring note to E♭ (D♯) would be F and not E.[228] Usually such a chord as this one with dual function signifies a modulation or deviation, but here none occurs. Mazel sensed only a resemblance to a deviation into D major. The harmony, unstable for twelve measures (mm. 143-154), finally settles back into the diatonic chain with e♭/G♭ variable mode, bringing with it a delayed resolution of the dominant seventh chord on B♭ from measure 142. Therefore the bifunctionality of this chord is exploited only as far as it effects a change from a stable tonality into an area of unstable harmonies. In other words, its bifunctionality is not fully realized. Nevertheless, the interpretation of this specific chord turns out to be less significant than the idea of dual function. As Mazel later pointed out, his concept is simply the idea of "variable function" introduced by Yury Tiulin.[229]

Ex. 50   Fredrich Chopin, Fantasy op. 49: mm. 142-146

Mazel derived the programmatic content of the Fantasia in large part from two of the seven segments within the development section. Of the other five segments, three consist of the three parts of the main theme from the exposition stated consecutively in C minor (mm. 155-163), E♭ minor (mm. 164-171), and G♭ minor (mm. 172-179). The remaining two segments, derived from material in the Introduction, demarcate the development section: the twelve-measure agitated unstable segment just discussed occurs at the beginning (mm. 143-154), and a slight variation of this segment an augmented second lower (mm. 223-234) occurs at the end of the development.[230] These segments make up the first, second, third, fourth, and seventh segments of the development section. The fifth and sixth segments contrast markedly. Mazel pointed out the pastoral, pentatonic nature of the fifth segment (mm. 180-198) and compared it to similar themes in early and late romanticists. The sixth segment, the "central episode" of a sonata-rondo form (mm. 199-202), is also characterized by a quiet, pastoral nature, presenting particularly in its tempo (Lento sostenuto) and rhythm (3/4) a decided contrast to the rest of the Fantasia. Mazel described it as a "metrically closed (8 + 8 + 8) independent part with its own inner structure, contrasting with the entire preceding development and presenting a completely different world, a different plane. . . . The chorale and organ character of the episode is combined with elements of recitative."[231] A summary of its harmonic content is given in example 51. Since this episode occurs after the fifth segment in e♭/G♭, Mazel viewed it as a deviation from G♭ into its subdominant, C♭, the enharmonic equivalent of its notated key of B major. Thematically, it is related to elements from the prologue and the main theme. Concerning its expressive content, Mazel commented:

> The "new plane" turns out to be in this sense something ephemeral, transient, deprived of a stable fundament; this is "a divine vision" or a conversion to the other, unreal world. In this [segment] is one of the "prayer" episodes from the many "organ" episodes of Liszt (for example, the first secondary part of the B minor sonata), having a more solemn, grandiose, and at the same time stable character.[232]

Ex. 51   Fredrich Chopin, Fantasy op. 49: harmonic content of B major episode from development, mm. 188-235

This central episode acquires even greater significance at the end of the coda, where its first two bars are stated in A♭ and developed subsequently into a type of cadence (mm. 320-332; ex. 49). Mazel derived the general content of the Fantasia largely from this episode:

> Through the entire development section, recapitulation, and coda, the basic content of the exposition never finds resolution. The development section gradually slows down, becomes still, and is transfigured onto a different plane: the B-major episode, the material of which turns out to be the central moment in the coda, is given. Unlike many codas (Beethoven's in particular) in which the material of a contrasting episode is introduced only so that it may be subsequently overcome by the final triumph of the basic thought, in the coda of the Fantasia neither the recitative, nor the subsequent triple figure, nor the concluding plagal cadence may be seen as overcoming or as a denial of the "episodic" choral phrase; they, rather, arise from this phrase, appear as its logical continuation and completion, and together with it present the final conclusion.[233]

Thus the transfigured material presented in the B-major episode of the development turns out to contain the ultimate resolution of the main themes of the Fantasia.[234]

> The resolution of some basic opposition... by its transfer onto a different plane, most frequently of all onto a plane religiously elevated and ideal, is very characteristic for many works of the romanticists. In these works the resolution of a question is impossible in the plane in which it is placed. The realization of the cherished dream is impossible on earth, but only in a different, better world and on a completely new plane.... A similar general idea of the opposition of the "human" and the "divine," the idea of the transfer of earth onto a heavenly plane is also present in the Fantasia of Chopin.[235]

However, Mazel stressed the differences in treatment between Chopin's romantic ideals and those of another romantic composer, Liszt:

> Chopin was not interested in general philosophical problems, and he did not consciously base his works on them. The idea of the Fantasia mentioned here does not penetrate the entire development of the work and does not envelop its artistic thought and content. It is not given in as pure and general a form as are the basic ideas in the works of Liszt, but is expressed through the totality of a great number of concrete and varied musical forms, that provide a unified line of aspiring sonata-ballade development. The principles of this development and the separate forms (for example, the march of the concluding part, connected with the national patriotic ideal of Chopin) are no less typical for Chopin and have no less significance for the content of this work, than the very general romantic ideas of the transfer of the "earthly" onto the "heavenly" plane.... The nonprogrammatic Fantasia of Chopin contains a great variety of concrete musical forms, joined to a richer "musical subject" or "musical plot," than many programmatic works of Liszt.[236]

Throughout his analysis, Mazel devoted much attention to the questions of form and thematic development, and to the relationships between the style of the Fantasia and Chopin's works in general and the styles of other romantic composers. He devoted the least amount of attention and was least successful, as he himself admitted, in discussing Chopin's melody and harmony. He gave two reasons for this:

> First ... the strength of the generalized romantic traits and, in particular, of the anticipation of characteristics of the melody and harmony of later composers is very great in this work; second ... individual traits of Chopin's creative style are manifested in this work in greater measure in the special combination and interaction of principles of construction, development, and contrast of musical thoughts, and in the form as a whole, than in the separate elements of the musical language. The characteristic peculiarities for Chopin of the latter are also expressed in the Fantasia, but to a somewhat lesser degree than in some of his other works.[237]

Mazel began his analysis with the goal of not dwelling on the separate elements but stressing their interaction and contribution to the whole; therefore, it is not too surprising that he should have chosen a work where this type of analysis was not only possible, but necessary.

Concerning Chopin's harmony, Mazel pointed out that the traits characteristic for Chopin's music are also characteristic for romantic composers in general—the variable modes, tertian chains, chains of cyclic modulations, the colorful role of chromaticism (contrasted in the Fantasia with "pure" diatonicism), and bifunctionality. Many of these traits anticipated the harmonic language of Wagner and even of the impressionists.

However, Mazel did distinguish two large groups of new, characteristic harmonic methods employed by Chopin: those connected with purely pianistic effects, and those connected "with the altered strengthening of the modal gravity, with the enrichment of function, and with sudden enharmonic modulations based on these enrichments."[238] To the first group belong the special arrangement of chords by the natural scale, the special use of registers, the coloristic use of the pedal point either as a single function or as a combination of two simple functions (tonic or dominant, for example), and also those colorful harmonic methods not connected with conditions attached to the second group, such as the juxtaposition of major and its parallel minor, and parallel seventh chords (which, incidentally, do not occur in the Fantasia). Examples from the second group occur more frequently in the Fantasia than examples from the first. Even so, they do not carry the static and schematic qualities and the loss of functional significance resulting from the process of enrichment and exacerbation of harmonic gravities that took place during the course of the nineteenth century. Harmony in Chopin's music had not yet taken a preeminent place, although some coloristic, "functionally simple" harmonic devices from the first group anticipated certain characteristic methods of impressionism, transferred through the music of the late romantics.

Mazel examined the cadence of the second theme (mm. 119-126), in which "the harmonic element 'subordinates' the other elements, as though 'absorbing' them"[239] (ex. 52). In this passage, a chain of cyclical deviations progressing by minor thirds ($E\flat$-C-A-f#[$g\flat$]-$E\flat$) is begun without warning and continues quite rapidly. However, the functional sense of the cadence (and of the entire period) remains completely clear. Moreover, it acquires a dynamic significance through its sudden, rapid, nonmelodic and repeated rhythmic motion, creating "the restrained pressure of a 'dam,' through which then 'break' the concluding chords of the $E\flat$ cadence."[240] This dynamic significance is so great that a further sixteen measures, containing the concluding part of the exposition (mm. 127-142), are needed to overcome the inertia created by the "exploding" cadence: "Here the colorful deviations within the expanded cadence and the special emphasis of the role of harmony at this moment (with the other elements subordinate to it) only *strengthen the functionally dynamic significance of this cadence* and do not oppose it."[241] From this and other examples, Mazel concluded:

> The harmonic methods of the "second group," if they also lead to the relatively independent role of harmonic complexes in short fragments, all the same they still do not lead to a weakening of the functional connections, and they also preserve the functional dynamic significance side by side with the coloristic [significance]. Only the methods of the second group, connected with moments of a static quality, may acquire a purely coloristic significance. This position, it seems to us, is a general characteristic of the harmony of Chopin as a whole.[242]

Mazel, then, showed the Fantasia to contain strictly applied formal principles and a unified integrity, more so than had been previously believed. He confirmed and strengthened the deeper, more progressive outlook towards Chopin's work that was just beginning to appear in the 1930s, and he succeeded

Ex. 52   Fredrich Chopin, Fantasy op. 49: mm. 115-129

in making a number of important contributions to the general knowledge about romanticism as a musical style and its role in the development of music. But whether he succeeded in fulfilling his goals of analysis is another question. He left many problems concerning the Fantasia unsolved. Some of the inadequacies of his analysis, such as the deficiencies in the harmonic and melodic analysis, and the disappointing analysis of the expressive content of the Fantasia resulted, according to Mazel, from the characteristics of the Fantasia itself. Other issues, such as a metrical analysis, he simply did not address.[243] In addition, his methods of stylistic analysis proved to be less than comprehensive. For example, he neither defined the term romanticism, nor explained which composers manifested this style (he concentrated almost exclusively on Beethoven, Liszt, and Wagner); nor did he verify his literary dramatic analogies or many of his musical analogies.

However, to accomplish what he actually set out to do would have involved a work of tremendous size; his analysis as it is takes up 135 pages. But given the apparent limits he imposed, the results do not lack merit. For Soviet music theory in the 1930s, Mazel's work, as a model for comprehensive analysis, provided an important step forward. Until that time, the study of separate elements was accepted in Soviet music theory almost as a given. Mazel, along with Boris Asafiev, was at the forefront of efforts to direct analysis on a more unified path. Part of this effort was due to the changed political climate: Mazel's requirement "to understand the work being analyzed as part of some general socially determined complex of ideological phenomena"[244] testifies to this. Mazel particularly was in a position to do this, for, as a result of his studies concerning different theoretical systems and his own inclination for analysis, he was well qualified to judge the efficacy of existing systems and to devise new methods where necessary. He remained unwilling to discard the legacy of Russian and Soviet music theory even though he did not wholeheartedly embrace all existing methods of analysis. For example, he made no use of Garbuzov's system nor did he develop in any way a rhythmic or metric analysis based on the theories of Catoire (and Riemann). His application of Conus's idea of metrotechtonicism to the prologue and exposition revealed little about those sections metrically or architecturally except to show a tendency towards proportion. Mazel was most successful in applying principles of form developed by Catoire, certain aspects of Yavorsky's theory of modal rhythm, and some ideas, mostly psychological in nature, from Kurth.

Mazel's contribution to Soviet music theory during this period thus lies in his synthesis of varied analytical elements into one cohesive whole, resulting in an approach that was at once practical and theoretically useful. His amalgamation of the technical aspects of analysis with stylistic questions joined two previously disparate elements into one aggregate, and provided a model for other similar works where before none had existed. His incorporation of historical and sociological elements into the analysis answered the requirements of a Marxist musicology, and his use of existing and newly invented theoretical methods demonstrated the enduring validity of those previous unilateral theories and the necessity for additional approaches not covered by those theories.

With his development of a comprehensive analytical approach, Mazel began his life-long contribution to the growth of Soviet music theory. His analysis of Chopin's F minor Fantasia therefore constituted only the first of his major theoretical works. He has continued to be interested in analysis, and has devoted several additional books, including his latest, to it.[245]

Yury Nikolaevich Tiulin (1893-1978)

From 1925, when he began teaching at the Leningrad Conservatory, Yury Nikolaevich Tiulin figured prominently in the development of Soviet music theory. His career spanned more than fifty years; he published his last work in 1977. In 1917 he graduated from the Petrograd Conservatory in composition and also received a degree in law from the Petrograd University. At the Leningrad Conservatory, he taught harmony, the analysis of form, and composition. From 1933 to 1948 he headed the theory faculty of the

Conservatory. He received his doctorate in 1939 for his dissertation, *A Study of Harmony*. It was published in 1937 and is his major work from the period.[246]

In his first work, *An Introduction to Harmonic Analysis Based on the Chorales of Bach*, a textbook written for an introductory course on harmonic analysis, Tiulin substituted Bach chorales for the usual written exercises in beginning harmony.[247] This new approach of using examples from the literature formed part of a new theoretical study of harmony, the basic principles of which Tiulin had developed beginning in 1925. Through his teachings at the Conservatory and lectures elsewhere (such as at the Moscow Conservatory in 1932), his ideas became better known; but full recognition came twelve years later when Tiulin published his *Study of Harmony*.

Tiulin had originally planned a three-volume series that would have encompassed chords and modulation as well as harmony, but he wrote only the first volume, subtitled "The Basic Problems of Harmony."[248] Tiulin based his theory of harmony on the ideas of mode as the primary foundation of musical thought and of the generation of the basic melodic and harmonic connections by their respective functions in that mode: "The study of harmony is above all the study of musical logic, manifested on a definite level of historical development as the modal functional harmonic system of musical thought."[249] According to his acknowledgments, Tiulin's theories of function were stimulated by those of Riemann, and his theories of mode by those of Yavorsky. In Tiulin's view, both theorists, while raising important questions, developed theories that were formalistic in nature and that reached incorrect conclusions. Nevertheless, Tiulin credited Yavorsky as the first "to raise musical theory from the sphere of pure empiricism to a scientific level and to create an integral and original theoretical conception, arising from a basic revision of existing theoretical conceptions."[250] Tiulin recognized the problem of mode as "the basic problem of theoretical musicology," and Yavorsky's raising of the question of mode as "the most significant achievement of the last decades."[251] Tiulin not only borrowed terminology from Yavorsky, but, more importantly, shared his views concerning the primacy of mode. Tiulin also drew on some of the theoretical ideas of Ernst Kurth.

Tiulin's prerequisites for a theoretical system require that it be logical, that it reflect and be verified by musical practice, that it represent phenomena of a sociological order, and that it be based on concrete material and not on abstract conceptions. These premises underlie *A Study of Harmony*. To begin, he discusses the various elements and processes that constitute the structure of music, or the sound fabric, as he refers to it. The warp and woof of the "fabric" are pitch, the vertical aspect, and duration, the horizontal aspect. These coordinates come together in a sort of "pitch-metric grid":

Music by itself contains neither spatial volume, nor spatial length, but possesses specific characteristics that we associate with spatial forms: a diapason of sounds is associated with the spatial volume (from this arises the idea of "aural space"), [and] through the visual representation of the sound fabric, temporal length is converted into spatial length—the horizontal of the sound stream.[252]

The vertical coordination of points (a minimum of two) of different pitch corresponds to the idea of harmony in a very broad sense, but is possible only in the consecutive movement of tones. The horizontal coordination arises as a result of the energy of tone connection (also a minimum of two tones), "which appears as a necessary prerequisite for the sensed side of melody."[253] The energy of tone connection—the phrase is derived from Kurth—denotes the intensity of the motion from one tone to another as it forms a melodic line. Two basic connections thus exist—a coordination of pitch, engendering harmony, and the energy of tone connection, engendering melody.

Melody and harmony therefore constitute the basic factors of the sound fabric. Melody contains two coordinated elements, dialectically opposed: "the song principle, which arises from durations in the sound line and aspires to overcome rhythmic boundaries" (melos) and "the motor principle, which arises from the alternation of supported moments of movement, and aspires to chain the melos into rhythmic limits."[254] Tiulin used rhythm here in the sense of "motor rhythm," which "is characterized by the accentuation of the supported moments of movement."[255] Harmony is perceived in two ways, either through the modal function of chords, or through "the very character of sound of the vertical [aspect], depending on the intervallic construction of the chord."[256] The perception of modal function depends on whether the purposeful direction of a chord to a modal center is confirmed or not. If it "is confirmed by a harmonic succession, then the motion closes in a cadence; if it is not confirmed, then there is cause for further motion. This is the essence of the modal function of chords."[257] The "character of sound" represents the "color function," the "phonic function," or simply, "phonism" or sonority. Color function acquires an active significance either when a break of melodic connections occurs or when modal functions contradict. Tiulin cited two moments when the color (phonic) and modal functions are correlated:

(1) The intensification of sonority owing to a break of natural modal connections, the contradiction of functional direction of a chord ... (2) the neutralization of sonority by the modal functions of chords: the more neutral the chord is in a modal functional relation, the more vividly its color function appears, and, in reverse, modal functional activeness neutralizes its harmonic function.[258]

To this he added: "In modal functional harmony the conflict of phonic and modal functions of chords is manifested in a dialectical unity: phonism and modal functionality may not exist separately."[259] Further, "Phonism and modal functionality are opposite sides of a single phenomenon."[260]

Tiulin summed up his idea of harmony in this definition:

> Harmony is above all the sphere of musical thought, coordinating the relation of tones in the vertical aspect, that is, in the plane of their combined quality.... This combined quality of tones inevitably arises in any simultaneous sound; consequently, each dissonant combination belongs to the sphere of harmony, whether it is subordinated to special harmonic regularities or not ("accidental" combinations). But the feeling of the combined quality of tones may arise also from their successive movement in such cases, when this succession is subordinated to special harmonic regularities.... Consequently, the idea of harmony belongs not only to the phenomenon of the simultaneous sound of tones, but also encompasses several phenomena of linear movement.... Harmony includes the entire sum of dynamic characteristics.... In sound movement harmonic regularities may not be uncovered without considering the elements arising in the process of movement—melody and rhythm.[261]

Tiulin summarized the interaction of the basic factors of sound fabric and their components in the diagram shown in figure 8.

Fig. 8   Basic factors of sound fabric

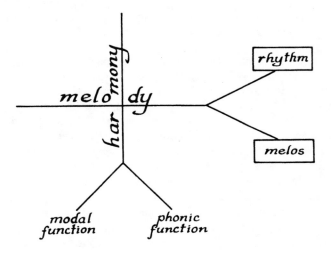

Texture results from "the totality of the methods of statement, and the general structure of the sound fabric, seen from the point of view of this interactivity of factors" shown in the diagram.[262] Form then becomes "the process of the development of the musical content as a whole."[263]

Tiulin considered acoustics to be significant to music only if examined in connection with artistic practice and confirmed by it. On this basis he acoustically confirmed certain elements such as the quartal-quintal foundation of diatonicism, the harmonic relatedness of tones based on the interval of a fifth, and the construction of triads, seventh chords, and ninth chords. He divided overtones into two groups, "constructive" overtones—those we hear—and "color" overtones—those we do not hear. Only the constructive overtones, those up to the tenth partial tone, take part in chord formation.[264] Chords are constructed by the "stratification of thirds," which, ultimately, when coupled with chromatic alternations, became one of the means of their destruction:

> The genetic approach to the origin of contemporary harmonic means reveals that the destruction of the tertian structure of chords went by three different paths, in some cases isolated, in others leading to complex, intricate results:
>
> a.   By the path of tertian layers (primarily dominant), in connection with altered complications. This path is very characteristic of Skryabin. The evolution of the ninth chord led to the "Promethean" chord.
> b.   By the path of consolidation (stabilization) in the chordal complex of "adjacent" melodic tones and the transformation of them into "secondary" chord tones. This melodic cluttering of a chord was caused by the complex color treatment of harmony of the romantic epoch. We notice the process of transferring elements from the horizontal into the vertical and their constant interaction in the course of the entire history of musical creation.
> c.   By way of the stratification of harmonic complexes—polyharmonic formations, having the root of origin in the stratification of the basic construction of the chord and in the polyphonic movement of harmonic layers.[265]

Tiulin found no basis for including upper partial tones in the structure of dissonant chords: "The aural adjustment of composers and listeners is directed towards tonal movement and least of all to the acoustical refinements of single sound groups."[266] Tiulin therefore agreed with Garbuzov on several points: the principle of acoustical relatedness, the formation of the triad, and the rejection of upper partial tones in chord construction. But, rather than considering acoustics as the only means of verifying musical science, as did Garbuzov, Tiulin relied in addition on psycho-physiological explanations.

Tiulin defined mode as "the gravitation or attraction of tones, [which] either overcome the energetics of melodic movement... or emphasize the energetics, closing the melody with a cadence."[267] Mode, "a semantic system," is "a logically differentiated system of joining tones on the basis of their functional interrelations."[268] Tiulin thus distinguished the idea of mode from any other linear or similar formations, such as scale, tonality, key, mood, or modal tonality. The last term, one of Yavorsky's, signifies "the tonality of tones peculiar to the mode of a given tonality."[269] Tonality alone is "the pitch level of a tone as the main supporting point of the mode, defining the functional significance of all remaining tones."[270]

Although modal thought developed along many different paths, Tiulin reduced these to three basic principles, which were not separate developments, but were freely intermixed: (1) the "melismatic accumulation of tones" by seconds, expanding the diapason from a single tone to a major third at the most, with the original generating tone as the main supporting point; (2) the "grouping for intonational possibilities through some intervallic space," usually a fourth, leading to the quartal-quintal frame of the scale, with a second supporting tone formed from this leap; and (3) a graduated melodic filling in of the intervals thus formed with seconds.[271] The melismatic accumulation of tones centered around the beginning tone, from which "arose the original functional connection—the dependence of tones, the original views of *modal gravity*.... Modal stability and instability in this case directly result from the rhythmic richness of tones."[272] In the second path, "modal stability arises from the intonational supporting points," from the fourth and the fifth.[273] The third path introduces unstable tones, filling in the gaps between the stable points. Tiulin thus opposed Yavorsky's idea of the origin of mode (see below).

This development of mode engendered melodic connections (seconds) and harmonic connections (quartal-quintal): "From secundal melodic connections arose the system of the melodic gravitation of tones on the basis of the harmonic framework of mode (triad). From the quartal-quintal connections arose the system of basic and variable functions of tones."[274]

Tiulin traced the historical development of modal thought from its premodal, nondifferentiated origins through the Greek modes, the church modes, the triadic framework, the period of the "centralization of mode," to the period of the "decentralization of mode" (the late romantics) and to Schoenberg's twelve-tone system, in which the mode completely disintegrated. Tendencies of Soviet music, though, have led in the opposite direction, "to the organization of new intonational possibilities in all capacities of modal connections on a stable, centralized diatonic basis."[275] Thus the main theoretical problem as Tiulin saw it was "to uncover the modal regularities of harmonic functional thought governing the musical legacy," specifically the Soviet musical legacy.[276]

Tiulin also investigated the relationship between diatonicism and chromaticism. Diatonicism is based on the Pythagorean system of successive fifths. Chromaticism, embodying the principle of the subdivision of tones, in turn, arises from diatonicism in three ways: (1) from changes of diatonic tones (the intensification of gravitational attraction, modal alterations); (2) from the "stratification of different diatonic systems, one on the other, in parallel tonalities (modal modulation)"; and (3) "in the capacity of a tonal superstructure over diatonicism, leading to the unification of diatonic systems of different tonalities and as a result—to the expansion of the tonal sphere (tonal modulation)."[277] Artificial scales, such as the semitone-tone scale, are neither diatonic nor chromatic, but comprise "a half-tonal system," in which chromaticism would lead to quarter-tones.[278]

In his discussions of melodic (modal) function, Tiulin was clearly influenced by both Yavorsky and Kurth. The idea of the stability and instability of tones of the major mode, and their gravitating tendencies, is basic to Yavorsky's theories, although Tiulin noted recognition of these tendencies by theorists even from the eighteenth century.[279] But Tiulin viewed the gravitational instability of certain tones of the mode as a consequence of formation and not, like Yavorsky, as a formative constituent of mode. The tones belonging to the tonic triad—the "harmonic tonic"—attract unstable tones, which tend to gravitate to the nearest stable tone. The term "linked tones" (derived from Yavorsky) describes the connection of stable and unstable tones on the strength of gravity. Only one tone of the mode has absolute stability—the tonic. Furthermore, stable tones play the leading role in modal organization. They form the essence of "modal centralization," while the unstable tones form the essence of "modal decentralization," as, for example, in the last works of Skryabin. Tiulin contrasted this view with Yavorsky's system of "modal gravity":

> The formation of stabilities in his theory turns out to be a *derived moment*, a consequence of gravity from the relationship of tones a tritone apart.... Such a system does not correspond either to the historical development of folk song ... or to the historical development of modal functional thought.[280]

Tiulin also contrasted the idea of modal attraction, or gravity, with Kurth's idea of energetics, which he considered useful as "an emotional factor in musical semantics":

> The tension of (melodic) movement depends on the conflict of energetics with modal gravity, in the process of which energetics in overcoming gravity engenders new phases of melodic movement. The conflict of energetics and gravity conditions the *semantic significance* of musical phenomena.... Melody as a sensed unity ... may arise only in the process of the conflict of feeling of a different order: the feeling of the tension of gravity and of the tension of energetics.[281]

Four factors influence the direction of motion: (1) the inertia of melodic motion, (2) motion by orbit, (3) occupied tone (hindering motion), and (4) intervals (resolution of the dissonance of the tritone, for instance). The second factor, motion by orbit, expands the idea of the linkage of tones developed by Yavorsky. It entails the motion around a stable center of both unstable tones adjacent to it; these tones are connected with each other and with the center tone, in the directions shown in example 53. An occupied tone, the third factor, involves the melodic motion from an interval of a second or a seventh to a unison or an octave, respectively, thereby hindering further movement because of a lack of tension.

Tiulin considered Riemann's theory of undertones and the origin of the minor mode to be groundless: it "does not correspond either to the physical nature of real sound, or to the regularities of our psychological perception."[282] Also contrary to Riemann and Rameau, Tiulin saw the minor triad as directly and not inversely analogous to the major triad, "since the modal indications (stability, the basic tone; the fifth to stability, embracing the harmonic function

Ex. 53   The movement of tones by orbit

of the dominant; the tertian tone) are arranged in them in the same order and are completely equal in their functional significance."[283] The two triads— major and minor—also exhibit equality in modal relation, position, and consonance. However, in its arrangement of intervals, the minor triad relates inversely to the major triad and does not equal it with regard to its phonic, or color, character, because of their respective positions in the overtone series. Tiulin concluded:

> Thus it becomes clear, that the attempt of theorists to prove the equal value of minor in an
> acoustical relation, by including it in the undertone or overtone series, is directed on a false
> path: namely, the unequal value in this relation serves as the only reason for its dependence
> on the major [mode] (with full equality in all other relations), which is an essential trait of our
> harmonic thought and runs through all musical literature.[284]

Tiulin identified three types of minor mode—natural, harmonic, and melodic; together they form the "full minor" mode. The melodic minor mode (ascending), though, does not have independent value, because the raised sixth degree (the "dorian sixth") arose from purely melodic motion: it constitutes a "melodic modal turn," not "a constructive harmonic turn," and forms therefore a "modal dissonance."[285] Essentially, then, the full minor mode consists of "two basic modal constructions," the harmonic, or the main minor mode, and the natural minor mode. Similarly, in major are three modes: natural, harmonic, and melodic. The latter two, which are similar to the comparable minor modes but with a major third degree, join to form the full major mode, in which the natural major mode dominates. The lowered seventh ("mixolydian seventh") of the melodic major mode, like the lowered sixth of the melodic minor mode, forms a "modal dissonance."

A "modal modulation" results from "a change of one mode to another within the limits of one tonality."[286] Many theorists, according to Tiulin, confuse this type of modulation with tonal modulation, which brings about a change of tonal center and corresponding functional changes of chords, while in a modal modulation the center and the functions remain unchanged. The use of modal modulation also results in the new, broader scale shown in example 54:

Ex. 54   The major-minor ten-tone scale

The unification of the parallel major and minor modes on the basis of modal modulation forms a major-minor ten-tone scale, whose interrelated tones form independent coordinated modal systems, firmly uniting the common quintal framework of the mode.[287]

Thus far only the melodic functional properties of mode have been discussed. Harmonic functional thought, in Tiulin's interpretation, is based on the quartal-quintal connection of tones. In each mode the primary acoustical dependence estabished between the tonic (producer) and dominant (derivative) creates a "functional tonic-dominant interrelation of tones *(T-D)*."[288] The same acoustical relationship occurs between tonic and subdominant, creating a "functional modal cell, consisting of three basic functional points of the mode and forming a sphere of the first degree of harmonic relatedness around the modal center[289] (ex. 55).

Ex. 55   The functional modal cell

The acoustical dependence from *T* to *D* is direct, from *D* to *T*—reverse; similarly, from *S* to *T*—direct, from *T* to *S*—reverse. The subdominant brings about a conflict resulting from its subordination to tonic within the logic of the mode, and the subordination of tonic to subdominant as a result of their acoustical relationship. The strength of the subdominant results from this conflict, in which the logical modal dependence of *S* on *T* eventually overcomes the acoustical dependence, and actually strengthens tonic as a tonal center, since the subdominant as a function exists only in its relation to tonic. The progression *T-S-D-T,* which Tiulin called a "cadential circuit," reveals and confirms the tonic of the mode.

But the acoustical significance of the subdominant, its position vis-à-vis tonic and its absence in the overtone series of the tonic, Tiulin explained, "compels it to attract the tonic function of the modal center. All our functional harmonic thought is based on this phenomenon."[290] If a change of function in conflict with the basic modal arrangement occurs, then Tiulin's "variable functions," which eventually are overcome by the basic functions in order to retain the basic modal arrangements also occur. Variable functions, though, are never destroyed by basic functions, since they always exist potentially in the mode. If the reverse situation occurs and the variable functions overcome the basic functions, then a "tonal modulation" takes place. The duality of tonic rests in its basic tonic function coupled with its variable dominant function (in relation to the subdominant); the duality of the subdominant rests in its basic subdominant function and its variable tonic function.[291]

This theory of variable functions defines the connections between the modal periphery and the modal center. Within the mode any two tones separated by a fifth can acquire a variable tonic or dominant function; these "peripheral tones" form a series of secondary modal support points, and in turn are directed towards the basic tonal center through intermediate secondary tonics and subdominants (ex. 56). Tiulin singled out the dominant of the dominant—*DD* or secondary dominant—as acquiring special significance, being drawn into the central modal cell by the first dominant. These secondary tonics and dominants, along with the secondary subdominants that inevitably arise, ultimately form a series of "secondary modal cells, similar to the basic cell of the mode"[292] (ex. 57). But not all the secondary tonics and dominants are equal: "The tonic functions of the sixth degree in major and the third degree in minor are significantly stronger than their dominant functions."[293] The full scheme of basic and variable functions of the tones of the mode, "the system of harmonic attractions," is shown in example 58.

Ex. 56   Variable tonics and dominants

Variable melodic functions also exist in two different categories. The first consists of the variable tonic accompanied by its upper and lower neighboring tones within the mode, creating a "cell of melodic attractions of tones"[294] (ex. 59). The second category exists within wider, more chromatic limits, and consists of the upper and lower leading tones to the basic and variable quintal frameworks. These leading tones serve as distinguishing signs of the variable functions (ex. 60). Special significance is accorded the lower leading tone of the dominant.

Ex. 57   Secondary modal cells, subordinated to the basic cell of
          the mode

Ex. 58   Scheme of all basic and variable functions of the tones of
          the mode

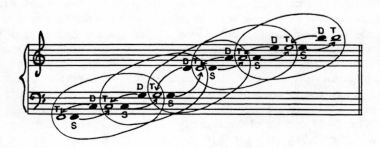

Ex. 59   Cells of melodic attractions of tones within mode

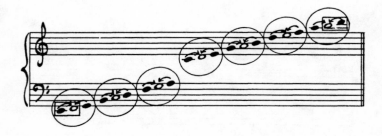

Ex. 60   Leading tones to quintal framework of each tonality

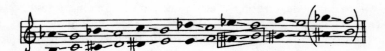

Tiulin provided a number of examples of this phenomenon, three of which will be illustrated here. In Bach's Prelude no. 8 in E♭ minor (from Book 1 of *The Well-Tempered Clavier*), the variable function appears attached to the "Neapolitan subdominant" (the Neapolitan sixth chord) (ex. 61). Here the B♭♭, "the attraction of a melodic turn from the subdominant modal sphere," clearly belongs to the Neapolitan subdominant chord on F♭ (m. 26):[295]

> The appearance of the B♭♭, alien to E♭ minor, is explained by the variable tonic function of this Neapolitan subdominant, which is tonic of the F♭ tonality and reveals the gravitation of the leading tone [B♭♭] to the third of its harmonic framework.[296]

Ex. 61   J.S. Bach, *The Well-tempered Clavier,* Book I, Prelude no. 8, mm. 25-27

In the case of Chopin's Etude op. 10 no. 6, also in E♭ minor, the Neapolitan subdominant attracts "not only a complex and completely independent melodic turn, but also a harmonic turn," which draws the tonal feeling away from E♭ minor, only to return to it after a measure and a half (ex. 62).[297]

The final example illustrates an instance of polyfunctionality, in Bach's Brandenburg Concerto no. 1, second movement (ex. 63):

> At the same time as the upper voices delineate the melodic movement in G minor, the bass voice changes its function to dominant and moves into the sphere of C minor. In this measure even the tonal unity is broken; each tonality temporarily acts by itself, disputing each other's functional predominance. Here occurs not a struggle of tonic with dominant... but a struggle of two independent tonic centers, an obvious case of polytonality. And only in the following measure is the dominance of a tonal center revealed, outlined by the melodic movement of the bass and compelling the upper voice to modulate. Because of this, tonal unity is established, but in the tonality of C minor.[298]

Ex. 62   Fredrich Chopin, Etude op. 10 no. 6, mm. 48-51

Ex. 63   J.S. Bach, *Brandenburg* Concerto no. 1, second
movement, Adagio, mm. 9-11

The development of the theory of variable functions carried great significance for Tiulin:

> This disclosure reveals the secret springs on which are based the logical interconnections of the elements of musical speech, the dynamics of structural formation, and . . . the dramaturgy

of the development of musical form. It is exceptionally important to understand the *principle* of the conflict of basic and variable functions, which the regularities of the connection of musical speech uncover.

The theory of variable functions has great significance in the study of chords, since it gives ... the key to revealing the functional connections of chords.

This theory adds new light to the process of modulation, reveals the genesis and regularities of polyfunctional and polytonal formations, and, through this, extends right up to the problem of contemporary musical thought.[299]

For Tiulin, variable functions were evident not only between tonic and dominant spheres, tonic and subdominant spheres, and subdominant and dominant spheres, but also between tonic and mediant spheres. He divided the triads of a mode into principal—I, IV, and V—and secondary triads—II, III, and VI. He related the diminished triad on VII to the dominant seventh chord, and therefore did not include it here. Separated by fifths and then correlated, the two groups form a tertian series creating two functional spheres, subdominant and dominant, revolving around the tonic sphere (ex. 64). The two mediant chords, M_N (VI) and M_V (III), contain the most functional ambivalence, belonging, in the case of M_N to T and S, and, in the case of M_V, to T and D. When accompanied by functional bass tones, they acquire a more definite functional significance as substitutes for the main degrees. Subsequently, the tonic group consists of I and VI[6]; the subdominant, IV and II[6]; and dominant, V and III[6].

Ex. 64   The tonic (T), dominant (D), and subdominant (S) spheres

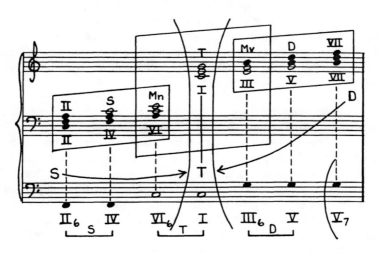

In acting as a substitute for I (as in interrupted cadences), VI acquires a "mediant function," introduced by Tiulin specifically for this degree. (In minor, both mediants play more essential roles—III as a variable tonic and VI as a

false tonic.) Thus the tertian connection T-M_N creates a prototype for all tertian correlations, "forming variable functions of tonic substitutes. A new series of variable functions arises: IV-II, VI-IV, I-VI, III-I, V-III."[300]

The theory of variable functions, like nearly all of Tiulin's ideas presented in *A Study of Harmony,* almost immediately won a permanent place in Soviet music theory. Indeed, his theories have become so generally accepted that very often they are used in Soviet theoretical works without acknowledgment, the ideas themselves having outstripped their author in importance. In this work Tiulin touched upon so many different areas that it is difficult to find a theoretical work written subsequently in the Soviet Union that does not include—acknowledged or not—some aspect of Tiulin's work.

Much of the success of Tiulin's theories may be attributed to their basis in musical practice. In addition, they form a logical conclusion for much of the work of previous theorists—Yavorsky, Catoire, Garbuzov, Riemann, and Kurth. Tiulin combined the most fruitful aspects of the work of these theorists in the areas of mode and harmonic function, and also melodic motion and function, with his own theories and refinements into a composite that, like Mazel's comparable work in analysis, carried both theoretical and practical application. Moreover, his analysis of the development of mode from historical and sociological viewpoints, and his investigation of the dialectical properties of function brought these theoretical concepts further into the sphere of Marxist-Leninist thought. His main contribution, though, lies in his definitive amalgamation of the theoretical topics of mode and function—two of the most important aspects of Soviet music theory. As a result, although he contributed a number of additional works to Soviet theoretical literature, *A Study of Harmony* remains his most significant work. In a similar vein, his article on the historical origins of modern harmony has nearly reached the status of a "classic" in Soviet musicology.[301] Of his later work, *The Natural and Alterable Modes* is of interest, for in it he delves more deeply into the question of modal formation and into the nature of Yavorsky's theory of modal rhythm.[302]

Each of these theorists contributed in an original manner to the legacy of Russian-Soviet theoretical musicology. Taneev, Catoire, and Conus were essentially prerevolutionary musicians; their works reflect a pure, nonideological approach, one devoted to revealing the mysteries of music in a systematic fashion. Taneev and Conus shared a preoccupation with classical proportions, and mathematical verification, but along two different paths. One resulted in infinite creative possibilities and the other in forced, consistently symmetrical interpretations. Taneev's combination of mathematics and music provided a universally applicable method for deriving more complex forms of counterpoint; however, Conus's attempts to prove the existence of universal architectural laws applicable to all music were unsuccessful because he failed to consider the psychological, auditory sphere of music, concentrating only on the spatial-temporal-visual aspects. Garbuzov and Catoire sought to provide a basis for the explanation of contemporary harmony: Garbuzov through acoustical phenomena, and Catoire through functionality and an expanded tonal system. Catoire and Conus both investigated metrical analysis, but, because of Conus's rigid adherence to beginning-accented meters, Catoire's approach proved more practical. The practical applicability of Catoire's theories in both harmony and form led to their widespread acceptance. Each theorist took an individual path in music theory, both in subject matter and in method.

Mazel and Tiulin, on the other hand, initiated more Marxist, comprehensive approaches to theory, including investigations of the technical means of music and also of its expressive content. The similarity of their philosophical bases—dialectics and the sociological and historical development of phenomena—led to a similarity of approach. Each took one basic idea, the Fantasy of Chopin in the case of Mazel, and the modal functional principle in music in the case of Tiulin, and examined it in its various manifestations. In the analysis of the Fantasy, this entailed the investigation of the formal, thematic, and harmonic elements as well as an examination of the social context and historical background of the Fantasy. In the analysis of mode and function, this involved the investigation of the historical, acoustical, psychological, and sociological aspects of these phenomena. The dichotomy that existed earlier between theories based on the physical nature of tones and on the measurement of time and proportion as a purely physical phenomenon, on the one side, and on the psychological perceptions of mode, function, consonance, and dissonance, on the other, was resolved somewhat in Tiulin's work (more so than in Garbuzov's work). Tiulin emphasized the dialectical nature in most of what he discussed, but this emphasis did not detract from the logic of his reasoning. In a similar resolution, Mazel combined purely technical analysis with style analysis.

It was the work of these six theorists, along with that of Yavorsky and Asafiev, that shaped Russian music theory during the period 1900 to 1950. The years from 1930 to 1950 witnessed the growing influence of political and sociological theory on musicology; and although this influence changed the direction of music theory in the Soviet Union, it did not diminish the achievements of Soviet theorists. They continued to produce notable works even within prescribed limitations, and continue to do so in the present time. The foundation for subsequent theoretical research, and for the entire discipline of theoretical musicology, was established mainly by these theorists. It is their legacy that must provide the background for any discussion of Soviet music theory.

Notes

1. Sergei Ivanovich Taneev's *Podvizhnoi kontrapunkt strogogo pis'ma* (Moscow, 1909) has been translated by G. Ackley Brower as *Convertible Counterpoint in the Strict Manner* (Boston, 1962). Quotations and citations will be from Brower's translation.

2. Thomas Hartmann, "S.I. Taneev," *Tempo*, no. 39 (1956), pp. 8-15; and Jacob Weinberg, "Sergei Ivanovich Taneev," *Musical Quarterly* 44 (1958): 19-31. Additional biographical sources in English include: Montagu Montagu-Nathan, *Contemporary Russian Composers* (New York, 1917); M.D. Calvocoressi and Gerald Abraham, *Master of Russian Music* (New York, 1936); and Leonid Sabaneev, *Modern Russian Composers*, trans. Judah A. Joffe (New York, 1927). The most thorough biographies are in Russian: Grigory Borisovich Bernandt, *S.I. Taneev* (Moscow, 1951); T.A. Khoprova, *S.I. Taneev* (Leningrad, 1968); and N. Bazhanov, *Taneev* (Moscow, 1971).

3. Taneev published his observations in an article: "Der Inhalt des Arbeitsheftes von W.A. Mozarts eigenhändig geschriebenen Uebungen mit den Unterweisungen durch seinen Vater im strengen Kontrapunkt und reinen Satz (41 Blätter Querquart gebunden)," *XXXIII Jahresbericht der "Internationalen Stiftung Mozarteum" für des Jahr 1913* (Salzburg, 1914). This article was first published in Russian in 1947: "Soderzhanie tetradi sobstvennoruchnykh uprazhnenii Motsarta v strogom kontrapunkte" [The contents of the notebook of Mozart's exercises in strict counterpoint done in his own hand], *Pamiati Sergeia Ivanovicha Taneeva, 1856-1946. Sbornik statei i materialov k 90-letiiu so dnia rozhdeniia* [In the memory of Sergei Ivanovich Taneev, 1856-1946. A collection of articles and materials for the 90-year anniversary of his birth], ed. Vladimir Protopopov (Moscow; Leningrad, 1947).

4. The correspondence between Taneev and Tchaikovsky has been published in two separate editions: Modeste Tchaikovsky, ed. *Pis'ma P.I. Chaikovskogo i S.I. Taneeva* [The letters of P.I. Tchaikovsky and S.I. Taneev] (Moscow, 1916); and Vasily Alexandrovich Zhdanov, ed., *P.I. Chaikovskii, S.I. Taneev: pis'ma* [P.I. Tchaikovsky, S.I. Taneev: letters] (Moscow, 1951).

5. Sergei Ivanovich Taneev, *Uchenie o kanone* [The doctrine of the canon], ed. Viktor Beliaev (Moscow, 1929). Beliaev's greatest difficulty in preparing this work for publication was the coordination of the musical examples with the text, since Taneev had left few indications. In all, Beliaev spent about two years on this project (p. VII).

6. In 1907 Taneev worked out a grandiose plan for future work, which he envisioned completing by 1913 and which included the following titles: *Tsvetistyi kontrapunkt strogogo pis'ma* [Florid counterpoint in the strict style], *Imitatsiia v prostom kontrapunkte* [Imitation in simple counterpoint], *Obratimyi kontrapunkt* [Invertible counterpoint], *Fuga v strogom pis'me* [The fugue in the strict style], *Fuga v svobodnom pis'me* [The fugue in the free style], and *Kanonicheskie formy na osnove podvizhnogo kontrapunkta* [Canonic forms on the basis of moveable counterpoint]. (Fedor Georgievich Arzamanov, "Zavety S. Taneeva" [Ordinances of S. Taneev], *Sovetskaia muzyka* [Soviet music], 1956, no. 11, p. 31.)

7. The main sources for Taneev's writings about form include: *Sergei Ivanovich Taneev. Lichnost', tvorchestvo i dokumenty ego zhizni. K 10-ti letiiu so dnia ego smerti 1915-1925* [Sergei Ivanonvich Taneev. Personality, creativity, and documents of his life. For the 10th anniversary of his death 1915-1925], ed. Konstantin Alekseevich Kuznetsov (Moscow, 1925); *Pamiati Sergeia Ivanovicha Taneeva, 1856-1946* (1947); *S.I. Taneev. Materialy i dokumenty: Perepiska i vospominaniia* [S.I. Taneev. Materials and documents: Correspondence and recollections], vol. 1, ed. V.A. Kiselev, T.N. Livanova, and V.V. Protopopov (Moscow,

1952); *S.I. Taneev; iz nauchno-pedagogicheskogo naslediia. Neopublikovannye materialy, vospominaniia uchenikov* [S.I. Taneev; From the scientific pedagogical legacy. Unpublished materials, recollections of students], ed. F.G. Arzamanov and L.Z. Korabelnikova (Moscow, 1967); Konstantin Alekseevich Kuznetsov, ed., *Russkaia kniga o Betkhovene* [The Russian book on Beethoven] (Moscow, 1927); Fedor Georgievich Arzamanov, "S. Taneev. Iz konservatorskikh lektsii" [S. Taneev. From conservatory lectures], *Sovetskaia muzyka*, 1953, no. 1, pp. 44-48; idem, "Zavety S. Taneeva," pp. 27-39; Liudmila Zinovevna Korabelnikova, "Novye materialy o S.I. Taneeve" [New materials on S.I. Taneev], *Sovetskaia muzyka*, 1959, no. 9, pp. 70-73. These sources also contain pertinent information: Fedor Georgievich Arzamanov, *Taneev—prepodavatel' kursa muzykal'nykh form* [Taneev—teacher of a course on musical forms] (Moscow, 1963); and Liudmila Zinovevna Korabelnikova, *S.I. Taneev v Moskovskoi konservatorii; iz istorii russkogo muzykal'nogo obrazovaniia* [S.I. Taneev in the Moscow conservatory; from the history of Russian musical education] (Moscow, 1974).

8. For a summary of Larosh's views, see my article, "Russian Music Theory: A Conspectus," in this volume.

9. Yuly Engel, "S.I. Taneev, kak uchitel'" [S.I. Taneev as a teacher], *Muzykal'nyi sovremennik* [The musical contemporary], 1916, no. 8, p. 52.

10. In a letter to Tchaikovsky dated August 18, 1880, Taneev wrote:

> Having finished study in the conservatory, I wanted to find out some things hitherto unknown to me. I began with double counterpoint in all intervals and wrote, it turns out, 140 small six-voiced exercises, using a Russian song for a cantus firmus. Then wanting to master the rules of the strict style, I wrote in the church mode 32 small fugues having no relation to Russian songs.
>
> For some time I studied the writing of exercises on melodies from church collections and wished in time to be able to write on these cantus firmi something sufficiently appropriate... not as a contrapuntal exercise but as a composition. This is my wish in this area—rather modest, as it turns out. Why do I do all this? Simply, because I want to make myself a composer.... In order to know something thoroughly, be it harmony, counterpoint, or instrumentation, some painstaking and dry work, which should precede artistic creation, is necessary. I am attracted to the elegance and well-roundedness of Mozart's forms, to the freedom and expediency of Bach's voice-leading; I try to penetrate, as far as I am able, into the secrets of their creation; I see that they knew much that I do not know. (*P.I. Chaikovskii. S.I. Taneev: pis'ma* [Moscow, 1951], p. 59.)

11. Viktor Beliaev, "*Podvizhnoi contrapunkt strogogo pis'ma* S.I. Taneeva" [Moveable counterpoint in the strict style of S.I. Taneev], *Muzykal'nyi sovremennik*, 1916, no. 8, p. 119. Tchaikovsky, for example, used this trial and error method in teaching how to harmonize a melody or how to write counterpoint. See my article, "Russian Music Theory: A Conspectus," in this volume.

12. Engel, p. 43.

13. Taneev wrote:

> Skill in the handling of counterpoint is of such advantage in composition that the beginner should devote part of his time to its study.... The result will be greater assurance and freedom in part-writing, skill in improving the musical content of the individual voices, the development (of special value in thematic work) of the ability to extract derivative combinations, the profit to be gained by acquaintance with an infinite variety of contrapuntal forms as means of artistic expression, and the subordination of

the whole realm of tonal material to the creative imagination. (*Convertible Counterpoint,* p. 300.)

14.   Ibid., pp. 18-19.

15.   Ibid., p. 299. Complex counterpoint is "counterpoint in which an original combination of melodies yields one or more derivatives" (p. 19). Of the three methods used in complex counterpoint, Taneev concerned himself mainly with shifting counterpoint, less with duplicated counterpoint, and not at all with metamorphosed counterpoint. In shifting counterpoint, a derivative is obtained by shifting the voices either vertically, horizontally, or a combination of the two. In duplicated counterpoint, "a derivative combination is obtained by duplicating one or more voices in imperfect consonances," thereby increasing the voices. "Each duplication is nothing but the vertical transference of a voice at an interval equal to an imperfect consonance" (p. 21). Metamorphosed counterpoint is also known as "mirror counterpoint."

16.   Ibid., p. 301.

17.   Ibid.

18.   Jacob Weinberg, "Sergei Ivanovich Taneev," p. 24.

19.   Taneev created a table that allowed him and his students to see at a glance the possible consonances and dissonances for a given combination and, via a moveable chain of numbers, to determine which combinations were possible. It is reproduced in *Muzykal'nyi sovremennik,* 1916, no. 8, opposite p. 60.

20.   *Convertible Counterpoint,* pp. 169-70.

21.   Taneev referred to the vertical index as *Iv,* for *Index verticalis,* but to avoid confusion with voice I, Brower substituted *Jv.*

22.   *Convertible Counterpoint,* pp. 37-40.

23.   Taneev identified two other types of shift: in a direct shift, the two voices retain their relative positions. A mixed shift indicates both direct and inverse shifts.

24.   *Convertible Counterpoint,* p. 207.

25.   In the last case, Taneev accompanied *Jv* and *Jh* with the Greek symbol for sigma, meaning sum. I have substituted the letter *S.* The index of the combination I + III is always equal to the sum of the first two indices: $Jv' + Jv'' = Jv\ S.$

26.   *Convertible Counterpoint,* p. 208.

27.   Beliaev, *"Moveable Counterpoint,"* p. 124.

28.   Taneev wrote, "The degree of technical maturity of a composer is verified best of all by the ability to have command of the sonata form." (Cited in F. Arzamanov, "Zavety S. Taneeva," p. 36.)

29.   *Convertible Counterpoint,* pp. 18-19.

30.   Ibid., p. 19.

31.   Ibid.

32.   Ibid.

33.   Ibid.

34.   Ibid.

35. Taneev to N.N. Amani, November 7, 1903, *Materialy i dokumenty*, 1:226.

36. Ibid., pp. 226-27. Taneev's idea of a unifying tonality is similar to Riemann's idea of a *Nebencentrum*, as discussed in *Systematische Modulationslehre*, pp. 202-03. But Riemann never connected this *Nebencentrum* with other tonalities or with the main tonality of a work, as Taneev did.

37. Viktor Beliaev, "'Analiz moduliatsii v sonatakh Betkhovena' S.I. Taneeva" ['The analysis of modulations in the sonatas of Beethoven' by S.I. Taneev]; *Russkaia kniga o Betkhovene*, pp. 191-204. Tannev choose segments from fifteen movements of ten of the first thirteen piano sonatas.

38. Taneev, cited in Arzamanov, "Zavety S. Taneeva," p. 36.

39. Cited in Beliaev, "'Analiz moduliatsii,'" p. 202.

40. Ibid.

41. Ibid. It is not difficult to see a similarity between Taneev's schemes of unifying tonalities and the structural harmonic outlines of Schenker. Taneev did not consider melodic motion or voice-leading as did Schenker, nor did he attempt to restrict the harmonic possibilities to a few set patterns. An outgrowth of Rimsky-Korsakov's idea of the modulatory plan, Taneev's theory of a unifying tonality has a practical application as a compositional tool; also, implicit in it is Taneev's plea for the preservation of tonality built on a diatonic foundation.

42. Although no writings by Taneev on this subject have appeared, he apparently discussed the rate and duration of harmonic change in his classes on form. Arzamanov refers to this occasionally in his work, *Taneev—prepodavatel' kursa muzykal'nykh form.*

43. Taneev to Amani, November 7, 1903, *Materialy i dokumenty*, 1: 227-28.

44. Ibid., p. 229.

45. Ibid., p. 230.

46. Taneev to Amani, November 8, 1903, *Materialy i dokumenty*, 1: 231. This view held by Fétis was pointed out to Taneev by his pupil Boleslav Leopoldovich Yavorsky, who later commented:

> The assertion of Fétis that modulation occurs only after the appearance of six half-steps to one of the tones of the tonic triad, was communicated to me in the '90s by the director of the Kiev musical school V.V. Pukhalsky. I in turn showed this to S.I. Taneev approximately in February 1900 in a statement written by me specially for him on my thoughts about internal auditory tuning and about the structure of modes. After this S.I. Taneev several times urgently asked me to find the corresponding place in the theoretical works of Fétis. (Boleslav Leopoldovich Yavorsky, "Pis'ma S.I. Taneeva k N.N. Amani" [The letters of S.I. Taneev to N.N. Amani], *Sovetskaia muzyka* [Soviet music], 1940, no. 7, p. 67.)

47. Ibid.

48. Ibid.

49. Taneev did not discuss this aspect any further; neither did the Soviet authority on Taneev's theories of form, Arzamanov. Rather, he concentrated on the contrast between the "authentic" character of a modulatory plan containing a tritone aspiring to a tonic and the "plagal" character of a modulatory plan lacking this tritone. A plagal modulatory plan is tranquil and placid whereas an authentic modulatory plan is dramatic, active, and in motion. (Arzamanov, *Taneev—prepodavatel'*, pp. 67-71.)

50. These schemes are reproduced in Arzamanov, *Taneev—prepodavatel'*, p. 85, example no. 30.

51. Taneev's notes on the development section are published in Arzamanov, "Zavety S. Taneeva," pp. 36-37.

52. S.I. Taneev, "Zametki o sonatnykh reprisakh Betkhovena"[Notes on sonata recapitulations of Beethoven], *S.I. Taneev. Iz nauchno-pedagogicheskogo naslediia* [S.I. Taneev. From the scientific-pedagogical legacy], pp. 150-54.

53. Beginning in 1897, those students at the Moscow Conservatory who completed three years of study, including Taneev's courses on strict counterpoint, fugue, and form, received the "diploma of a master of music theory. The more gifted students will be allowed to continue the course in the class of free composition." (Directions from the Artistic Council of the Conservatory, cited in Arzamanov, "Zavety S. Taneeva," p. 33.

54. Georgy Lvovich Catoire, *Teoreticheskii kurs garmonii* [The theoretical course of harmony], 2 vols. (Moscow, 1924-26); *Muzykal'naia forma* [Musical form], 2 vols., ed. L.A. Mazel, D.B. Kabalevsky, and L.A. Polovinkin (Moscow, 1934-36).

55. Sergei Vasilevich Yevseev, "Georgii L'vovich Katuar," *Sovetskaia muzyka*, 1941, no. 5, p. 48. Biographical information is also included in Montagu-Nathan's *Contemporary Russian Composers* (London, 1917). For additional sources in Russian, see: Viktor Beliaev, *G. Katuar* (Moscow, 1926) and Vladimir Georgievich Fere, "Georgii L'vovich Katuar (1861-1926)," *Vydaiushchiesia deiateli teoretiko-kompozitorskogo fakul'teta Moskovskoi konservatorii* [Prominent figures of the theoretical compositional faculty of the Moscow Conservatory] (Moscow, 1966).

56. Catoire's development of functional principles has gone unnoticed by Western theorists who have studied in detail the adoption and dissemination of Riemann's theories. Renate Imig and William C. Mickelsen both mention Gevaert, whose book on harmony influenced Catoire, but do not acknowledge Catoire or the important role of functionalism in Soviet harmonic theory. (Renate Imig, *Systeme der Funktionsbezeichnung in den Harmonielehren seit Hugo Riemann* [Düsseldorf, 1970]; William C. Mickelsen, *Hugo Riemann's Theory of Harmony* and *History of Music Theory*, Book III by Riemann, trans. and ed. W.C. Mickelsen [Lincoln, Nebraska, 1977].)

57. François Auguste Gevaert, *Traité d'harmonie théorique et pratique*, 2 vols. (Paris, 1905-07).

58. Catoire took most of his examples from the music of Beethoven (16 examples) and Wagner (16), followed by Skryabin and Chopin (6 each). The remaining 20 or so examples come from the music of European romantic and Russian composers. Gevaert had concentrated in his examples not only on the music of Wagner and Beethoven but also on music from French and Italian opera. Catoire used few of Gevaert's examples.

59. *The Theoretical Course of Harmony*, 1: 4.

60. The frequency of occurrence is determined by the number of tones in a given system minus the number of fifths between the tones of the interval. For example, the tones of the interval F-F♯, an augmented unison, are separated by seven fifths on the circle of fifths. Assuming ten tones within the system beginning with F (calculated along the circle of fifths), the number of tones in the diatonic major-minor system, the interval of the augmented prime occurs three times within that system.

61. *The Theoretical Course of Harmony*, 1: 5.

62. Ibid., p. 15.

63. In all groups the *1* superscript indicates a major ninth. The brackets around a letter indicate that a tone of the group other than the root is the bass tone: one pair of brackets for the second tone of the column, two pairs for the third tone, etc. The dominant group contains the dominant triad *d*, the dominant seventh chord *D*, the dominant ninth chord D^1, and the half-diminished seventh chord $[D^1]$.

64. *The Theoretical Course of Harmony*, 1: 38.

65. In all groups the *2* superscript indicates a minor ninth. The letter *Z* in the subdominant group indicates a diminished fifth, from II to ♭VI. In the tonic group the flat attached to both *T* and *Q* refers to ♭VI and ♭VII; the letter *Q* refers to ♭III.

66. However, partial intertonal deviations into tonalities not completely within the system—♭VI, V, and minor IV, V, II, VI, and III—are possible.

67. The five enharmonic duplications: ♯IV/♭V, ♯I/♭II, ♯V/♭VI, ♯II/♭III, ♯VI/♭VII. No tones in the chromatic system duplicate enharmonically the seven central diatonic tones. Catoire excluded ♯III, ♭IV, ♯VII, and ♭I for this very reason.

68. The three minor triads of secondary significance—♯I, ♯V, and ♯II—do not enter into the construction of diatonic systems.

69. *The Theoretical Course of Harmony*, 1: 78.

70. Catoire also investigated the occurrence of the augmented fifth and the diminished seventh, mainly in augmented triads and diminished seventh chords. The diminished second, he pointed out, does not enter into the construction of chords, and the augmented third is equivalent to the perfect fourth, which occurs only in accidental combinations. He did not mention the augmented unison or, of the ultrachromatic intervals, the doubly diminished fourth (doubly augmented fifth).

71. Catoire added these ultrachromatic chords to Gevaert's basic designations of *U*, *O* (*D*, in Catoire's version) and *I* (*J* in Catoire's version). Catoire also added varieties to *U* and *J* chords and designated their occurrence on II as a subdominant function (secondary dominant). The *UJ* chord is the same chord used as the basis for Skryabin's harmonic system as analyzed by Varvara Dernova. See Roy J. Guenther, "Varvara Dernova's System of Analysis of the Music of Skryabin," in this volume.

72. It also, Catoire pointed out, is known as a French augmented sixth chord. The $[U^2]_{11}$ in first inversion equals a German augmented sixth chord.

73. *The Theoretical Course of Harmony*, 1: 101.

74. Ibid.

75. The major seventh chord with a lowered fifth, from the *U* chord, equals the leading-tone seventh chord with a raised third, a $[J^1]$ chord. The diminished seventh chord with lowered third, a $[U^2]$ chord, equals the minor seventh chord of II with a raised basic tone, a ♯*S* chord. All four chords are from the chromatic system.

76. (Moscow, 1897). See my article, "Russian Music Theory: A Conspectus," in this volume.

77. For example: Nikolai Nikolaevich Sokolovsky, *Rukovodstvo k prakticheskomu izucheniiu garmonii* [A guide to the practical study of harmony], 3 vols. (Moscow, 1906-11).

78. The harmony textbook by Teodor Fridrikhovich Miuller, *Garmoniia* [Harmony] (Moscow, 1976), is based on the diatonic-chromatic hierarchy. An example of a recent article utilizing the functional theory of harmony is: Yury Kholopov, "Funktsional'nyi metod analiza

sovremennoi garmonii" [The functional method of analyzing contemporary harmony], *Teoreticheskie problemy muzyka XX veka* [Theoretical problems of music of the twentieth century], vol. 2, ed. Yury Tiulin (Moscow, 1978), pp. 169-99.

79. See "A Conspectus," in this volume.

80. Kabalevsky completed chapters 6, "Simple two- and three-part form" (which Catoire himself had begun), and 7, "Complex three-part form"—continuing in number from the first five chapters of volume 1. Mazel completed chapter 8, "Sonata form," and 9, "Form of the rondo and the rondo-sonata."

81. *Musical Form,* 1: 12.

82. Ludwig Bussler, *Musikalischen Formenlehre* (Berlin, 1978); Hugo Riemann, *System der musikalischen Rhythmik und Metrik* (Leipzig, 1903); Ebenezer Prout, *Musical Form* (London, 1893) and *Applied Forms* (London, 1895).

83. *Musical Form,* 1: 11.

84. Ibid., p. 14. Catoire distinguished the study of metrics from the study of rhythmics, which he defined as "the study of the interrelation of tones by their comparative length."

85. Ibid., p. 13.

86. Ibid.

87. Ibid., p. 14.

88. Ibid., p. 28.

89. Ibid., p. 35.

90. As illustrations, Catoire cited well-known examples from Beethoven, the Piano Sonata op. 13, first movement (bars 19-27), a large structural unit of eight measures, and Mozart, the Overture to *The Marriage of Figaro,* first seven measures, in which the small three-part structural unit consists of seven bars, the last intruding into the next structural unit with new musical content.

91. In Grosvenor Cooper and Leonard B. Meyer, *The Rhythmic Structure of Music* (Chicago, 1960), the Mozart passage is analyzed as an anapest.

92. *Musical Form,* 1: 35.

93. Ibid., pp. 68-69.

94. Ibid., p. 68.

95. The Scherzo of Beethoven's Fifth Symphony is a compound three-part period containing three sentences, each between 40 and 50 measures and each consisting of two large structural units with various extensions and an addition. However, the metrical unit equals not one measure but two, thereby making the period only 70 units long, and each of the sentences between 20 and 25 units long. Catoire's analysis: Sentence 1 (mm. 1-44): two large extended structural units (mm. 1-18 and 19-38) and one expanded supplement (mm. 38-45). Sentence 2 (mm. 45-97): one large structural unit (mm. 45-60), one small structural unit (mm. 60-70); one large structural unit (mm. 71-90); and supplement (mm. 90-97). Sentence 3: two extended large structural units (mm. 97-115; 116-132) and supplement (mm. 133-140).

96. I have retained the transliterated letters *f, b, m,* and *d,* which represent the Russian words *fraza* [phrase], *bol'shoi* [large], *malyi* [small], and *dopolnenie* [supplement]. But I translated the longer terms, such as *exp* for expansion, which in Russian is *ras* for *rashirenie,* and *abb* for abbreviation, which in Russian is *sok* for *sokrashchenie.*

97. Donald Francis Tovey, in *A Companion to Beethoven's Pianoforte Sonatas* (London, 1931), described this movement as "a sonata form with archaic (or melodic) exposition, but considerable development and expanded recapitulation" (p. 53).

98. For instance, in one type of romantic rondo described by Catoire, the main part does not always occur in the main tonality of the rondo, but in different tonalities in succeeding statements. In another type, while its outward appearances resembles rondo form, short development sections that work out the main material in a manner similar to the middle sections of simple three-part forms occur in the place of episodes with new material.

99. Lev Abramovich Mazel, "Predislovie" [Preface], in Catoire, *Musical Form*, 1: 8. Mazel also referred to Catoire's method of statement as being "frequently revealingly formalistic" (p. 9).

100. Catoire wrote in the Introduction, "Any musical work ... is undoubtedly always embodied in a definite 'form.' This form is created together with content, [and is] closely connected with it. For each artistic work, essentially a *new form* is created" (p. 12).

101. Georgy Eduardovich Conus, "Metrotektonicheskoe razreshenie problemy muzykal'noi formy (Konspekt muzykal'no-nauchnogo issledovaniia)" [The metrotechtonic solution to the problem of musical form (A summary of musical scientific research)], *Muzykal'naia kul'tura* [Musical culture], 1924, no. 1, pp. 36-41, rpt. in *G.E. Konius: Stat'i, materialy, vospominaniia* [G.E. Conus: Articles, materials, reminiscences], ed. G.G. Golovinsky (Moscow, 1965), pp. 87-96.

102. Georgy Eduardovich Conus, "O metrotektonicheskom razreshenii problemy muzykal'noi formy (Moi otvet L. Sabaneevu)" [On the metrotechtonic solution to the problem of musical form (My answer to L. Sabaneev)], *Muzykal'naia kul'tura* [Musical culture], 1924, no. 3, pp. 216-28; "K notnomu metrotektonicheskomu planu Adagio sostenuto sonaty Betkhovena op. 27 no. 2" [On the metrotechtonic plan of the Adagio sostenuto of Beethoven's Sonata op. 27 no. 2], *Muzykal'noe obrazovanie*, 1927, no. 1, pp. 92-114, rpt. in *G.E. Konius: Stat'i, materialy, vospominaniia*, pp. 97-110; "Sintaksis muzykal'noi rechi" [The syntax of musical speech], *Proletarskii muzykant* [Proletarian musician], 1930, no. 4, pp. 22-30; *Kritika traditsionnoi teorii v oblasti muzykal'noi formy* [A criticism of traditional theory in the area of musical form] (Moscow, 1932); *Metro-tektonicheskoe issledovanie muzykal'noi formy* [The metrotechtonic investigation of musical form] (Moscow, 1933) (presented in double columns with a French translation: *Diagnose métrotectonique de la forme des organismes musicaux*).
       These works were published posthumously: *Nauchnoe obosnovanie muzykal'nogo sintaksisa; k izucheniiu voprosa* [The scientific basis of musical syntax; toward study of the question] (Moscow, 1935) (also in French); "Analiz Adagio Pateticheskoi sonaty Betkhovena" [The analysis of the Adagio of Beethoven's Sonata Pathetique], *G.E. Konius: Stat'i, materialy, vospominaniia*, pp. 76-86; and "Kratkoe izlozhenie osnovnykh printsipov teorii metrotektonizma" [A short presentation of the basic principles of the theory of metrotechtonicism], *Voprosy muzykovedeniia* [Questions of musicology], vol. 1 (Moscow, 1972), pp. 219-46.
       Other theoretical works: *Sbornik zadach, uprazhnenii i voprosov (1001) dlia prakticheskogo izucheniia elementarnoi teorii muzyki* [A collection of problems, exercises, and questions (1001) for the practical study of the elementary theory of music] (Moscow, 1892); *Sinopticheskaia tablitsa elementarnoi teorii muzyki* [A synoptical table of the elementary theory of music] (Moscow, 1893); *Posobie k prakticheskomu izucheniiu garmonii* [A textbook for the practical study of harmony] (Moscow, 1894); *Dopolnenie k sborniku zadach, uprazhnenii i voprosov (1001) dlia prakticheskogo izucheniia elementarnoi teorii muzyki* [A supplement to the collection of problems, exercises, and questions (1001) for the practical study of elementary theory of music] (Moscow, 1896); *Zadachnik po instrumentovke* [A book of problems on instrumentation], 3 vol. (Moscow, 1906-09); and *Kurs kontrapunkta*

strogogo pis'ma v ladakh [A course of counterpoint in the strict style in modes] (Moscow, 1930).

For biographical information, see Pavel Dmitrievich Krylov, *G.E. Konius* (Moscow, 1932); Valentin Eduardovich Ferman, "Pamiati G.E. Konius" [In memory of G.E. Conus], *Sovetskaia Muzyka*, 1933, no. 9, p. 110; and *G.E. Konius: Stat'i, materialy, vospominaniia.*

103.   Conus, "O metrotektonicheskom razreshenii," p. 226.

104.   Conus explained his theory to Taneev in a letter dated December 11, 1902. The portion analyzing Beethoven's Piano Sonata op. 13 has been published as "Analiz Adagio Paticheskoi sonaty Betkhovena." The correspondence between Taneev and Arensky, published in *S.I. Taneev. Materialy i dokumenty: Perepiska i vospominaniia* (vol. 1, pp. 67-197), includes letters from 1902 in which Conus's analyses of their works are discussed.

105.   G.E. Conus, "Muzykal'naia forma i ee analiz" [Musical form and its analysis], reviewed in *Russkaia muzykal'naia gazeta* [The Russian musical newspaper], 1904, no. 16, p. 429; P.A. Karasev, "Lektsiia G.E. Koniusa o muzykal'noi forme (v Moskovskom literaturno-khudozhestvennom kruzhke)" [The lecture of G.E. Conus about musical form (in the Moscow literary artistic society)], *Russkaia muzykal'naia gazeta*, 1908, no. 10, pp. 233-36.

106.   Conus, "Metrotektonichskoe razreshenie," p. 36.

107.   Conus, "K notnomu metrotektonicheskomu planu," p. 96.

108.   Conus, *Metro-tektonicheskoe issledovanie*, p. 11.

109.   Ibid., p. 10.

110.   Conus, "K notnomu metrotektonicheskomu planu," p. 93.

111.   Conus, *Metro-tektonicheskoe issledovanie*, p. 11.

112.   Ibid., p. 10.

113.   Conus, *Nauchnoe obosnovanie*, p. 16.

114.   Ibid.

115.   Conus, *Metro-tektonicheskoe issledovanie*, p. 13.

116.   Conus, "Kratkoe izlozhenie," p. 240. This article, published by A.I. Kondratev, was compiled from lectures given by Conus at the Moscow Conservatory during the academic year 1932-33. It would appear that Conus was working on a more difficult theory concerning the criteria for grouping cells together; unfortunately, his death in 1933 precluded the work's completion.

117.   Ibid., p. 241.

118.   Conus, "Analiz Adagio Paticheskoi sonaty Betkhovena."

119.   Conus, *Metro-tektonicheskoe isslodovanie*, p. 22.

120.   Ibid., p. 23.

121.   Ibid., p. 22.

122.   Conus, "K notnomu metrotektonicheskomu planu," p. 94.

123.   Conus, "Metrotektonicheskoe razreshenie," p. 37.

124.   The earlier version is from "Analiz Adagio Paticheskoi sonaty Betkhovena," p. 76. The later version is from *Nauchnoe obosnovanie*, p. 34.

125.   Conus, "Analiz Adagio," p. 86.

126.   Ibid., p. 79.

127. Ibid., pp. 79-80.

128. Conus, "K notnomu metrotektonicheskomu planu," p. 95.

129. Conus, "Metrotektonicheskoe razreshenie," p. 38.

130. Cf. Cooper and Meyer, *The Rhythmic Structure of Music.*

131. Conus, *Metro-tektonicheskoe issledovanie,* p. 26.

132. Ibid.

133. Conus, *Nauchnoe obosnovanie,* p. 13.

134. Conus, *Metro-tektonicheskoe issledovanie,* p. 27.

135. Conus, "Metrotektonicheskoe razreshnie," p. 39.

136. Ibid., p. 40.

137. Conus, *Nauchnoe obosnovanie,* pp. 12-14.

138. Ibid., p. 19.

139. Ibid., p. 13.

140. Ibid., p. 31.

141. Ibid., p. 13.

142. Tovey, *A Companion to Beethoven's Pianoforte Sonatas,* pp. 198-202. Conus, *Nauchnoe obosnovanie,* p. 31 and Supplement.

143. Not to be confused with Iosif Ryzhkin's definition of the traditional school, which includes theorists of the nineteenth century up to Riemann and the functional school (Ryzhkin, "Traditsionnai shkola" [The traditional school], in Iosif Ryzhkin and Lev Mazel, *Ocherki po istorii teoreticheskogo muzykoznaniia* [Essays on the history of theoretical musicology], vol. I [Moscow, 1934], pp. 79-121).

144. Conus, *Kritika traditsionnoi teorii v oblasti muzykal'noi formy.*

145. Hugo Riemann, "Metrika" [Metrics], *Muzykal'nyi slovar'* [Musical dictionary], ed. Y. Engel, trans. from 5th German ed. (Moscow, 1901-04), p. 850.

146. Ibid.

147. Catoire wrote in the introduction to *Musical Form:*

> A further problem [of musical form] is the study of the laws by which musical works are combined to create one artistic whole. To establish regularities in the structure of an artistic work is a problem of higher order; this regularity undoubtedly exists, but it is very complex and in any case may not be reduced to a simple measurement of time, to a purely arithmetic calculation of measures (p. 12).

And from the text:

> One ought, of course, strictly to differentiate such *symmetry in time* from *spatial symmetry,* which we see in the fine arts, mainly in architecture. Schopenhauer, in carrying out a detailed parallel between time and space in the beginning of the second volume of his book *The World as Will and Idea,* says: "Rhythm (meter) exists *only in time;* symmetry exists *only in space.*"
> Whereas symmetry in space represents the correspondence at *any distance of identically constructed* parts of a building, symmetry in time ... is the juxtaposition of

two absolutely adjacent, but not always identically constructed parts, answering each other as thesis to arsis (p. 13).

148. Taneev, cited in F. Arzamanov, "Zavety S.I. Taneeva," p. 32.

149. A.S. Arensky to S.I. Taneev, March 15, 1902, *S.I. Taneev. Materialy i dokumenty,* 1: 177-78. Conus analyzed Arensky's First Symphony in C minor.

150. S.I. Taneev to A.S. Arensky, March 22, 1902, ibid., p. 180.

151. Ibid.

152. Leonid Sabaneev, "Neskol'ko slov o metro-tektonicheskom analize prof. G. Koniusa"[A few words about the metrotechtonic analysis of professor G. Conus], *Muzykal'naia kul'tura,* 1924, no. 2, pp. 137-46.

153. Ibid., pp. 145-46.

154. Boleslav Yavorsky, cited in Conus, "O metrotektonicheskom razreshenii," p. 227. Yavorsky did not actually approve of Conus's system; no source for this quotation is given.

155. Valentin Ferman, "O printsipe metrotektonizma" [On the principle of metrotechtonicism], *Muzykal'noe obrazovanie* [Musical education], 1928, no. 2, pp. 24-31.

156. The term *factur* may best be defined as texture.

157. Ferman, "O printsipe metrotektonizma," p. 25.

158. Ibid., p. 27.

159. Ibid., p. 30.

160. Ibid., pp. 30-31.

161. Ibid., p. 31.

162. Ibid. Apparently Conus was not offended by Ferman's remarks, for in 1930 Ferman began graduate study at the Conservatory with both Conus and Mikhail Ivanov-Boretsky. Conus may have accepted Ferman's article as a political necessity; he himself was unwilling to make any gesture in this direction.

163. Lev Mazel, "O metrotektonizme"[On metrotechtonicism], *Proletarskii muzykant,* 1929, nos. 7-8, p. 54.

164. Ibid., p. 55.

165. Ibid.

166. Ibid., p. 56.

167. Lev Mazel, "Obshchii obzor teoreticheskogo muzykoznaniia posle Rimana" [A general survey of theoretical musicology after Riemann], *Ocherki po istorii teoreticheskogo muzykoznaniia,* vol. 2 (1939), pp. 15-16.

168. "Iz redaktora" [From the editor], *Nauchnoe obosnovanie muzykal'nogo sintaksisa,* p. 3. By 1952 Conus's theory was being described in this manner:

> The theory of metrotechtonicism of Conus is openly formalistic, ignoring the necessity of analyzing the ideological artistic content of music and is devoted to investigating only the temporal relations of the parts of musical form. . . . The theory of Conus, which arose as the result of modern Western influence, sharply breaks with all traditions of Russian classical musicology. (V.A. Kiselev, T.N. Livanova, and V.V. Protopopov, in *S.I. Taneev. Materialy i dokumenty,* 1: 178.)

Harsh assessments such as this one, attributable to the political mood of the time, have since been mollified.

169.   Conus, *Metro-tektonicheskoe issledovanie*, p. 7.

170.   Conus, *Nauchnoe obosnovanie*, p. 14.

171.   Yury Kholopov, "Georgy Eduardovich Konius," *Muzykal'naia entsiklopediia* [Musical encyclopedia], vol. 2 (Moscow, 1974), col. 934.

172.   Nikolai Alexandrovich Garbuzov, *Teoriia mnogoosnovnosti ladov i sozvuchii* [The theory of multi-based modes and chords], 2 vols. (Moscow, 1928-32). The first volume was also published in a German translation: *Vielfalt akustischer Grundlagen der Tonarten und Zusammenklänge: Theorie der Polybasiertheit* (Moscow, 1929). For biographical information on Garbuzov, see: S.S. Skrebkov, "Nikolai Aleksandrovich Garbuzov (1880-1955)," *Vydaiushchiesia deiateli teoretiko-kompozitorskogo fakul'teta Moskovskoi konservatorii*, pp. 115-20.

173.   Among them: "Natural'nye prizvuki i ikh garmonicheskoe znachenie" [Natural overtones and their harmonic significance], *Sbornik rabot po muzykal'noi akustike* [A collection of works on musical acoustics], vol. 1 (Moscow, 1925), pp. 7-15; "Akusticheskaia priroda mazhora i minora" [The acoustical nature of major and minor], ibid., pp. 16-19; "Novye techeniia v muzykal'noi nauke v period revoliutsii" [New tendencies in musical science in the period of the revolution], *Muzyka i revoliutsiia* [Music and revolution], 1926, no. 1, pp. 31-33; "Akustika i teoriia muzyki" [Acoustics and the theory of music], *Muzyka i revoliutsiia*, 1926, no. 3, pp. 18-21; "Nekotorye voprosy psikhologicheskoi akustiki" [Some questions of psychological acoustics], *Muzyka i oktiabr'* [Music and October], 1926, nos. 4-5; "Slyshim li my intervaly i akkordy tak, kak oni napisany?" [Do we hear intervals and chords as they are written?], *Muzyka i revoliutsiia*, 1927, no. 2, pp. 21-26; "Garmonicheskoe vidoizmenenie akkordov natural'nymi prizvukami" [The harmonic variety of chords through the natural overtones], *Sbornik rabot Sektsii po muzykal'noi akustike* [A collection of works of the Section on musical acoustics], vol. 2 (Moscow, 1929); "Sovremennaia muzykal'naia sistema i pravopisanie natural'nogo zvukoriada" [The contemporary musical system and the spelling of the overtone series], ibid.; "K voprosu ob edinichnoi i dvoinoi sistemakh B. Iavorskogo" [On the question of the single and double systems of B. Yavorsky]. *Muzykal'noe obrazovanie*, 1930, no. 1, pp. 18-22; "Zavisit li garmonicheskoe dvizhenie v muzyke ot neustoichivosti tritona" [Does harmonic motion in music depend on the instability of the tritone], *Muzykal'noe obrazovanie*, 1930, no. 3, pp. 16-21; "O konsoniruiushchikh i dissoniruiushchikh intervalakh" [On consonant and dissonant intervals], *Muzykal'noe obrazovanie*, 1930, nos. 4-5, pp. 11-14; "Priroda minornykh ladov" [The nature of minor modes], *Muzykal'noe obrazovanie*, 1930, no. 6, pp. 19-21.

174.   Such a view had been promoted by Leonid Sabaneev and Arseny Avraamov during the previous decade. See my article, "Russian Music Theory: A Conspectus," in this volume.

175.   Garbuzov, *Theory of Multi-based Modes*, 1: 14.

176.   Garbuzov defined mode in this manner: "Modes I call scales, which are created by man according to the laws of psychological acoustics not yet established, and on the basis of which both folk and serious music were and are being constructed" (*The Theory of Multi-based Modes*, 1: 15).

177.   Ibid., p. 19.

178.   Garbuzov did not include in this calculation the relationship between C and B♭. He always looked for the closest acoustical relationships, in this case the fourth and the fifth.

179.   Even though the pentachords from C and B♭ appear to share two common tones, the two C's in pure tuning turn out to be separated by a comma. Thus only the D is common to both pentachords.

180.   *The Theory of Multi-based Modes*, 1:30. The major or minor in the name of the mode refers to the quality of the second, third, sixth, and seventh intervals above the basic or tonic note.

181.   Ibid., p. 44.

182.   Catoire, *The Theoretical Course of Harmony*, 1: 96, 101.

183.   *The Theory of Multi-based Modes*, 1: 182.

184.   Ibid., p. 183.

185.   Ibid., p. 186.

186.   Garbuzov wrote this in the preface to the second volume:

> Though both works [volumes] concern multi-based modes and chords, between them there exists a very essential difference: in the first work modes and chords are examined irrespective of the processes occurring in them, that is, in their *static state;* in the second modes and chords are examined as more or less complex processes, that is in their *dynamic state.* The understanding of modes and chords as processes led to a series of essential changes in those views that I established after my first experiments; in spite of this, I consider that the path taken by the theory of multi-based modes and chords was completely correct. The novelty and complexity of the material with which I was concerned in the first period of my research, the series of working hypotheses, which I needed to construct for the explanation of many phenomena, compelled me in this period to be limited to studying the collected material in the *static state* and only then, after several years, to get down to studying this material in the dynamic state. But the change in views on several musical phenomena, which took place in me owing to a change of *conditions,* causing me again to study the material I had collected, did not destroy such basic principles on which my theory operated. (*The Theory of Multi-based Modes*, 2: 3.)

The "change of conditions" mentioned by Garbuzov does not refer to his move to different research institutes after the disbanding of GIMN in 1931, for, as he stated, he had by this time completed some of the research that he had not yet presented. The sense of Garbuzov's statements leads me to believe that he resuscitated this material out of political necessity. Yet he refused to recant his previous views.

187.   Sergei Sergeevich Skrebkov, "Ladovaia struktura sonaty v svete teorii mnogoosnovnosti" [The modal structure of the sonata in light of the theory of multiple foundations], *The Theory of Multi-based Modes*, 2: 79-129; and Saul Grigorevich Korsunsky, "Analiz garmonicheskogo iazyka muzykal'nykh proizvedenii s tochki zreniia teorii mnogoosnovnosti" [The analysis of the harmonic language of musical works from the point of view of the theory of multiple foundations], *The Theory of Multi-based Modes*, 2: 130-68.

188.   Garbuzov reached similar conclusions in his article, "Slyshim li my intervaly i akkordy tak, kak oni napisany?", in which he investigated the impact of register on the character of the sound of a chord.

189.   *The Theory of Multi-based Modes*, 2: 75.

190.   Ibid., p. 62.

191.   Of course, the nature of this process remained different for each theorist. See Gordon McQuere, "The Theories of Boleslav Yavorsky," in this volume.

192. The higher the number of common tones between overtone series, the greater the degree of their acoustical relatedness. A series a perfect fourth or perfect fifth apart (four or five common tones) thus forms the first degree of relatedness. Series major and minor thirds and sixths apart (two or three common tones) form the second degree of relatedness; and series at the distance of major and minor seconds and sevenths (one common tone) form the third degree of relatedness. Series at the distance of a tritone (no common tones) form the fourth degree of relatedness, or more accurately stated, are unrelated.

193. He also constructed incomplete minor modes, the minor tertial-quintal mode (bases C, E♭, G), and the minor tertial-quintal-septal mode (based C, E♭, G, B♭), both of which lack the subdominant; and the minor quartal-sextal mode (bases C, F, and A♭), and the minor tertial-quartal-sextal mode (bases C, E♭, F, A♭), both of which lack the dominant. The most complete major mode is ideally the major tertial-quartal-quintal-sextal mode (C, E, F, G, A), in which the inner triads, here E and A, are also strongly related. So, for example, the other modes constructed all contain secondary triads in the relationship of a perfect fourth or fifth. Only the last mode, a minor secundal-quartal-quintal-sextal-septal mode, contains secondary triads in the relationship of a major sixth, which is the second degree of relatedness.

194. Garbuzov reached similar conclusions in two articles mentioned above: "Akusticheskaia priroda mazhora i minora" and "Priroda minornykh ladov."

195. These analyses, as mentioned, were not done by Garbuzov, but by his students Skrebkov and Korsunsky under Garbuzov's supervision. Skrebkov analyzed the Haydn Piano Sonata in C major; Beethoven's Sonata op. 57; Chopin's B♭ minor Sonata, the first movement; Liszt's B minor Sonata; Skryabin's Sixth Sonata op. 62; Prokofiev's Second Sonata op. 14, the first movement; and Aleksei Stanchinsky's Allegro in F major op. 2. Korsunsky analyzed Skryabin Preludes op. 11 no. 9, op. 34 no. 4, and op. 74 no. 1; a Beethoven bagatelle; Schumann's "Valse Allemande" from *Carnival;* Chopin's Mazurka op. 29 no. 3; Grieg's "Erotic"; Debussy's Prelude no. 5; Prokofiev's "Mimoletnost" no. 16; and Miaskovsky's "Prichuda" no. 1.

196. *The Theory of Multi-based Modes,* 2: 4. Garbuzov's emphasis on the practical application of his theory and his concession that his theory did not provide a comprehensive analytical approach are consistent with developments in Soviet music theory during the 1930s.

197. Korsunsky and Skrebkov also wrote a pamphlet, edited by Garbuzov, in which they applied his theory to melody harmonization and modulation: *Nekotorye problemy kursa garmonii v svete teorii mnogoosnovnosti* [A few problems of a harmony course in light of the theory of multiple foundations] (Moscow, 1934).

198. Iosif Ryzhkin, "Teoriia mnogoosnovnosti (N. Garbuzov)" [The theory of multiple foundations (N. Garbuzov)], *Ocherki po istorii teoreticheskogo muzykoznaniia,* 2: 232.

199. Garbuzov, "K voprosu ob edinichnoi i dvoinoi sistemakh B. Iavorskogo," p. 21.

200. Garbuzov, "Zavisit li garmonicheskoe dvizhenie v muzyke ot neustoichivosti tritona," p. 18.

201. Ryzhkin, "Teoriia mnogoosnovnosti," p. 227.

202. Ibid.

203. Garbuzov, *O mnogogolosii russkoi narodnoi pesni* [On the polyphony of Russian folk song] (Moscow, 1939). He followed three principles of his theory: the acoustical relatedness of tones (he assigned nonrelated status to the intervals of the second and seventh as well as the tritone); tonal subordination, in which tones corresponding to the overtones are subordinate to those corresponding to the bases; and tonal retention, in which musical tones are kept in the memory for a certain length of time and therefore will influence subsequent ones. This last principle is also found in the works of Boris Asafiev.

204.   *N.A. Garbuzov. Muzykant, issledovatel', pedagog* [N.A. Garbuzov. Musician, researcher, pedagogue], comp. O.E. Sakhaltueva and O.T. Sokosova (Moscow, 1980).

205.   Mazel also received a degree in mathematics from Moscow State University in 1930. Earlier he graduated from the Skryabin Musical Technical School in Moscow in 1926, where he studied with Catoire. The title of his dissertation was *Osnovoi printsip melodicheskoi struktury gomofonnoi temy* [The basic principle of the melodic structure of the homophonic theme]. Mazel never published this work, but in 1952 published *O melodii* [On melody].

206.   Lev Abramovich Mazel and Iosif Yakovlevich Ryzhkin, *Ocherki po istorii teoreticheskogo muzykoznaniia,* 2 vols. (Moscow, 1934-39). Between 1929 and 1934 Mazel published five articles: "O metrotektonizme" [On metrotectonicism], *Proletarskii muzykant,* 1929, nos. 7-8, pp. 52-56; "Opyt issledovaniia zolotogo secheniia v muzykal'nykh postroeniiakh v svete obshchego analiza formy" [Experimental research on the golden section in musical works in light of a general analysis of form], *Muzykal'noe obrazovanie,* 1930, no. 2, pp. 24-33; "Preliudiia A-dur Shopena v svete teorii mnogoosnovnosti ladov i sozvuchii" [The A major Prelude of Chopin in light of the theory of multi-based modes and chords], *Muzykal'noe obrazovanie,* 1930, no. 3, pp. 28-32; "O muzykal'no-teoreticheskoi kontseptsii Kurta" [On the musical theoretical concepts of Kurth], *Muzykal'nyi al'manakh* [The musical almanac], ed. N.I. Cheliapov (Moscow, 1932), pp. 31-60; and "Funktsional'naia shkola v oblasti teoreticheskogo muzykoznaniia" [The functional school of theoretical musicology], *Sovetskaia muzyka,* 1934, no. 4, pp. 76-90.

207.   Lev Abramovich Mazel, *Fantaziia f-moll Shopena. Opyt analiza* [The F minor Fantasy of Chopin. An experiment in analysis] (Moscow, 1937), written in 1934. He received two prizes for it, one at a competition for young scientific workers organized in 1937 by the Academy of Sciences and Komsomol, and one at the All-Congress Competition of Musicological Works in 1937-38. Mazel reprinted this work, along with three more recent articles also on Chopin, in *Issledovaniia o Shopena* [Research on Chopin] (Moscow, 1971), pp. 7-142. All quotations are taken from this later edition.

208.   *Fantaziia,* p. 7.

209.   Ibid., pp. 9-10.

210.   Mazel singled out melody as the most ignored element in theoretical research. He attempted to remedy this situation by devoting his next two works (1941 and 1952) to the topic.

211.   *Fantaziia,* pp. 7-8.

212.   Yavorsky's term for the anacrusis, the "pred'ikt," may also refer to the dominant preparation in the development for the return of the main theme in the recapitulation. The word "turn" is a translation of the Russian word "oborot." See Gordon D. McQuere, "The Theories of Boleslav Yavorsky," in this volume.

213.   *Fantaziia,* p. 14. That Mazel used parts of various systems successfully is significant, for in the 1930s it had to be demonstrated that their use was practicable and consistent with Marxist philosophy. This Mazel did by combining rather strictly formal ideas with purely dynamic ideas into a new, more dualistic, dialectical (using the language of the time) unity, which was more acceptable.

214.   Ibid., p. 13.

215.   Ibid., p. 26.

216.   Ibid., p. 27.

217.   Ibid., p. 28.

218. Ibid.

219. Ibid., p. 29.

220. Ibid., p. 112.

221. Mazel does not mention that these three themes are the only extended melodies in the Fantasia, and represent a progressive softening and redirection of tension through each successive statement. The tonalities move from F minor to A_b major to B major, interspersed with E minor and B_b minor, and finally A_b in the coda.

222. *Fantaziia*, p. 120.

223. Ibid.

224. Ibid., pp. 122-23.

225. Ibid., p. 124.

226. Ibid.

227. Ibid., p. 54.

228. Another interpretation that Mazel did not mention is a German augmented sixth chord in E_b. While not spelled correctly, in relation to the previous harmonies ($E_b{}^6$-A_b-$F_b{}^7$-$B_b{}^7$), it could be a "reverse" German augmented sixth chord, which, instead of resolving to a B_b chord, is preceded by it. A smoother resolution would involve E_b in second inversion. Mazel did note, at a different point in the analysis, the importance of the augmented-sixth chord. He pointed to its occurrence preceding the exposition (mm. 64-66), where it is neither spelled correctly nor resolved properly. It receives a delayed resolution to the proper tonality, but not in the right register or to the right notes.

229. *Fantaziia*, p. 89. This aspect of bifunctionality also appears in Catoire's *Theoretical Course of Harmony*, in his discussions of common chord modulation. Mazel and particularly Tiulin expanded this idea beyond its original conception and use in modulation.

230. The material in these two segments derived from the introduction consists of continuous triplet figures, sharply accented and rhythmic harmonies, and the octave exclamations. Until its appearance in the coda, this material always precedes the main theme of the exposition.

231. *Fantaziia*, p. 96.

232. Ibid.

233. Ibid., p. 115.

234. The feeling of resolution is heightened by the occurrence in the preceding measures of most of the twelve-measure agitated unstable section which heretofore always preceded the main theme. Here, the main theme is expected, but instead the theme from the B major episode is substituted, indicating the close thematic connection between the two segments. Thus the harmonic, melodic, and rhythmic conflicts in the Fantasia are resolved and the piece is concluded.

235. *Fantaziia*, pp. 115-16.

236. Ibid., pp. 116-17.

237. Ibid., p. 119.

238. Ibid., p. 137.

239. Ibid., p. 139.

240. Ibid., p. 140.

241. Ibid. According to Mazel, cyclical modulations in Liszt and Wagner, on the other hand, are connected with strengthening the coloristic element at the expense of the functional dynamic element.

242. Ibid., p. 141.

243. Mazel apparently was unwilling here to delve into the problem of a metrical analysis. Elsewhere he stated, "A really critical mastery and study of Riemann's concept [of metrical analysis] remains one of the problems of our Soviet theoretical musicology." ("Predislovie," in Catoire, *Muzykal'naia forma*, p. 10.)

244. *Fantaziia*, p. 11.

245. *Analiz muzykal'nykh proizvedenii* [The analysis of musical works] (Moscow, 1959); *Stroenie muzykal'nykh proizvedenii* [The structure of musical works] (Moscow, 1960); and *Analiz muzykal'nykh proizvedenii* [The analysis of musical works] (Moscow, 1967), written together with V.A. Zuckermann. His latest two books are *Problemy klassicheskoi garmonii* [The problems of classical harmony] (Moscow, 1972) and *Voprosy analiza muzyki* [Questions of the analysis of music] (Moscow, 1978). This last work approaches the question of analysis from the point of view of aesthetics.

246. Yury Nikolaevich Tiulin, *Uchenie o garmonii* [Study of harmony] (Leningrad, 1937). This work was awarded the first prize at the All-Union Competition for Musicological Works in 1939. It contains two parts: "The Basic Premises of Musical Thought" (Part 1) and "The Modal Functional Bases of Musical Thought" (Part 2). For additional information on Tiulin, see Nikolai Georgievich Privano, ed., *IU. N. Tiulin: Uchenyi. Pedagog. Kompozitor. Sbornik statei* [Y.N. Tiulin. Scholar. Teacher. Composer. A collection of articles] (Leningrad; Moscow, 1973).

247. Tiulin, *Vvedenie v garmonicheskii analiz na osnove khoralov Bakha* (Leningrad, 1927).

248. *Uchenie o garmonii*, p. 13. Volume 2 was to have been titled *Uchenie ob akkordakh* [Study of chords] and Volume 3, *Uchenie o moduliatsiakh* [Study of modulations].

249. Ibid., p. 14.

250. Ibid., p. 16. Yavorsky had said much the same about Taneev in 1909; see "Russian Music Theory: A Conspectus," in this volume.

251. *Uchenie o garmonii*, pp. 16-17.

252. Ibid., p. 22.

253. Ibid., p. 23.

254. Ibid., p. 24.

255. Ibid.

256. Ibid., p. 25.

257. Ibid., pp. 25-26.

258. Ibid., p. 27.

259. Ibid.

260. Ibid., p. 28.

261. Ibid., p. 29.

262. Ibid., p. 31.

263. Ibid.

264. "The *normal limit* of audibility of overtones extends to the eighth partial tone and includes the four different tones of the seventh chord. The *extreme limit* extends to the tenth partial tone and includes the five-tone ninth chord." (Ibid., p. 53).

265. Ibid., p. 57. Tiulin referred in point *a* to Volume 2, which never appeared. However, his pupil V. Dernova developed this idea along with ideas of Yavorsky's. See Roy J. Guenther, "Varvara Dernova's System of Analysis of the Music of Skryabin," in this volume.

266. *Uchenie o garmonii*, p. 56.

267. Ibid., p. 59.

268. Ibid., p. 60.

269. Ibid. Yavorsky defined modal tonality as a mode at a given pitch level. See Gordon D. McQuere, "The Theories of Boleslav Yavorsky," in this volume.

270. *Uchenie o garmonii*, p. 60.

271. Ibid., pp. 64–66.

272. Ibid., p. 65. The idea of modal gravity is also borrowed from Yavorsky.

273. Ibid., p. 66.

274. Ibid., p. 69.

275. Ibid., p. 71.

276. Ibid.

277. Ibid., p. 82.

278. Again he referred to Soviet music: "A firm diatonic basis, undoubtedly, should be a condition of the creation of Soviet musical style, in connection with an aspiration to solid modal organization. This must by no means be understood as a self-limitation to the diatonic sphere, but as the organization of chromatic and altered possibilities on a modal diatonic basis." (Ibid., p. 83).

279. He referred in this capacity specifically to the treatise of Anton Bemetzrieder, *Leçons de clavecin et traité de musique* (Paris, 1776). He also referred to Ryzhkin's article on the traditional school in *Ocherki po istorii teoreticheskogo muzykoznaniia*, pp. 110–13.

280. *Uchenie o garmonii*, p. 97.

281. Ibid., p. 98.

282. Ibid., p. 103.

283. Ibid., p. 105.

284. Ibid., pp. 107-108.

285. Ibid., p. 107.

286. Ibid., p. 103.

287. Ibid., p. 117. Tiulin's combination is identical to Catoire's ten-tone major-minor system.

288. Ibid., p. 118.

289. Ibid.

290. Ibid., p. 121.

291. Tiulin pointed out how close Riemann came to this idea:

> Riemann in his work *Musikalische Logik* (pp. 51-53), analyzing the functional interrelations of chords in the cadence, at one point comes close to the idea of variable function: he correctly observes in the interrelation of *T* and *S* their contention for tonic significance.
>
> Unfortunately, Riemann dwells on this phenomenon only as a particular case, and does not draw general conclusions. The variable functional relations that arise in any progression of chords remained outside his perspective, owing to which his functional theory suffers from one-sidedness and from essential gaps in explanations of musical phenomena." (Ibid., p. 122.)

In this regard, Tiulin also made reference to Simon Sechter (*Die Grundsätze der Muziklischen Komposition*, 1853), Gevaert, and Heinrich Schenker (*Harmonielehre*, 1906). Schenker's theory of tonicalization is similar to Tiulin's theory of variable function:

> Not only at the beginning of a composition but also in the midst of it, each scale-step manifests an irresistible urge to attain the value of the tonic for itself as that of the strongest scale-step. If the composer yields to this urge of the scale-step within the diatonic system of which this scale-step forms part, I call this process *tonicalization* and the phenomenon itself *chromatic*. (Heinrich Schenker, *Harmony*, trans. Elizabeth Mann Borgese, ed. Oswald Jones [Chicago, 1954], p. 256.)

292. *Uchenie o garmonii*, p. 124.

293. Ibid., p. 125.

294. Ibid., p. 127.

295. Ibid., p. 129.

296. Ibid., p. 130. This same example is found in Schenker, *Harmony*, p. 258: "The major triad [F♭-A♭-C♭] ... confers upon itself, without further ceremony, the rank of a tonic."

297. *Uchenie o garmonii*, p. 133.

298. Ibid., p. 135.

299. Ibid., p. 136.

300. Ibid., p. 143.

301. Yury Tiulin, "Sovremennaia garmoniia i ee istoricheskoe proiskhozhdenie" [Contemporary harmony and its historical origin], *Teoreticheskie problemy muzyki XX veka* [Theoretical problems of music of the 20th century], vol. 1 (Moscow, 1967), pp. 129-82.

302. Yury Tiulin, *Natural'nye i al'teratsionnye lady* [The natural and alterable modes] (Leningrad, 1971). Tiulin's textbooks on harmony include: *Teoreticheskie osnovy garmonii* [The theoretical foundations of harmony], coauthor Nikolai Georgievich Privano (Leningrad, 1956); *Uchebnik garmonii* [A textbook of harmony], coauthor Privano (Moscow, 1957-59); *Kratkii teoreticheskii kurs garmonii* [A short theoretical course of harmony] (Leningrad, 1960); and *Stroenie muzykal'noi rechi* [The structure of musical speech] (Leningrad, 1962). His last work was *Uchenie o muzykal'noi fakture i melodicheskoi figuratsii* [The study of musical texture and melodic figuration], 2 vol. (Moscow, 1976-77).

Glossary

Sources of Russian Chant Theory

azbuka. An elementary grammar; a treatise on the chant.

demestvenny chant. A branch of the Russian chant using a notation different from the znamenny type.

diastematic. Showing the relative height of musical pitch. Cf. *neumatic.*

fitnik. A collection of fity. See *fity.*

fity. The traditionally unnotated melismas used at points in the melodies designated with the Greek letter theta (θ). See *fitnik.*

gorovoskhodny kholm. See *kholm.*

hirmologion. One of the important collections of hymns sung at matins in the Eastern Orthodox Church.

kholm (pl. *kholmy*). The representation of a knoll to depict the ascending and descending musical scale of the chant. Sometimes also called *gorovoskhodny kholm* [ascending knoll].

khomovoe singing. Old Believer chant with an obsolete linguistic recension. The usage retains music over the Old Church Slavonic mute vowels and often results in a distorted meaning of the text.

kokiznik. A collection of popevki. See *popevki.*

krug. A comprehensive collection of hymn texts.

litsa. Melismatic passages in the Russian chant.

neumatic. Pertaining to the usage of neumes or unheightened musical signs. Cf. *diastematic.*

obikhod. A collection of frequently used hymn texts.

obikhodny chant. The harmonized chant developed in Russia during the eighteenth and nineteenth centuries.

oktoechos. The collection of hymns for each of the eight liturgical modes of the Eastern Orthodox Church.

pomety. The red letters added to the Russian neumes to indicate the relative height of musical pitch.

popevki. Characteristic melodic formulas.

priznaki. Slight alterations of the original Russian neumes to indicate the relative height of musical pitch.

razvod (pl. *razvody*). An expansion of a traditionally abbreviated neumatic musical notation.

znamenny. Pertaining to the usage of the Russian neumes.

The Theories of Boleslav Yavorsky

dvazhdy-lad [duplex mode]. Occurs when both possible resolutions of the tritones of a simple mode are employed in the same mode. The result amounts to two simple modes a tritone apart. See *lad.*

dvazhdy-sistema [duplex system (either single or double)]. System employing both possible resolutions for its tritone(s); for example, the tritone B-F resolves to C-E, and its enharmonic equivalent, B-E♯ resolves to A♯-F♯. See *dvazhdy-lad*.

gran' [boundary]. Separates the two parts of a symmetrical system or intonation.

intonatsiia [intonation]. The smallest melodic unit that, when combined with others either vertically or horizontally, creates all musical textures. An intonation is the musical manifestation of man's natural need for expression, and has an analogy in the flow of speech. Yavorsky's intonations also reflect his division of musical structures into categories of stable and unstable; each intonation must exhibit the process of instability resolving to stability.

lad [mode]. An interrelated complex of auditory gravitations (unstable to stable pitch connections) made up of tritones and their resolutions. Yavorsky's modes are transposable, possess a hierarchy among the pitches, and have functional categories of dominant, subdominant, tonic, and subtonic.

ladovyi ritm [modal rhythm]. Defined by Yavorsky as the "unfolding of modes in time." Since modes are comprised of tritones and their resolutions, there is motion in musical space and in musical time, thus showing a connection between pitch and rhythm.

moment [moment]. One part of a systemic or modal gravitation, a "moment." The term also appears as "modal moment" [ladovyi moment], in which sense it means something very similar to "function," that is, the role a tone or sonority plays in relation to the mode. The "collective moment" [soedinennyi moment] is the combination of all the unstable tones of a mode.

nesopriazhenie [disjunction]. The motion of an unstable tone to a stable tone by skip, but in the direction of its natural gravitation. See *sopriazhenie*.

oborot [turn]. The combination of two or more intonations vertically resulting in a succession of sonorities having a true bipartite intonation in at least one voice. The term *turn* is roughly equivalent to *cadence*, but without the latter's sense of ending a phrase. Turns make up the fabric of harmonic successions.

obratno-sopriazhennyi ton [inversely conjunctive tone]. An unstable tone that resolves to a stable tone that has another gravitation directed towards it. In C major, F and D-D♯ are inversely conjunctive tones because they both resolve to E.

simmetrichnaia sistema [symmetrical system]. A tritone and its resolution. It is called "symmetrical" because of the equal and opposite movement of the two tones toward resolution. A single symmetrical system has one tritone; a double symmetrical system has two tritones a semitone apart. These structures are basic to Yavorsky's theories of mode, since the tritone is the only unstable interval, that is, the only interval that evokes motion.

slukhovoe tiagotenie [auditory gravitation]. That property innate in man that perceives the tritone as unstable, requiring resolution. It is the auditory equivalent of the gravity of the physical world.

soedinennyi moment [collective moment]. See *moment*.

soedinitel'naia intonatsiia [connective intonation]. An intonation whose second moment, its resolution, is delayed until after some intervening intonations.

sopostavlenie s rezul'tatom [comparison and result]. The principle that comparison is the source of all perception. The tritone compares two tones, and the result is its resolution. Other kinds of comparisons involve durations and tonalities.

sopriazhenie [conjunction]. The step-wise connection of an unstable tone with its tone of resolution. See *nesopriazhenie*.

vvodnyi ton [leading tone]. An unstable tone that resolves to a stable tone that has no other gravitations directed towards it.

Varvara Dernova's System of Analysis of the Music of Skryabin

bol'shaia engarmonicheskaia sekventsiia [major enharmonic sequence]. A sequence of three tritone-linked chord pairs, the roots of the first chord of each pair ascending or descending the whole-tone scale. Because of the tritone root relationship of chord pairs and because of the whole-tone limitation of root movement, the sequence cannot contain more than three chord pairs without repeating itself. This sequence is one means of explaining chord progressions in Skryabin's music (see *malaia sekventsiia* and *funktsional'naia sekventsiia*).

dvazhdyi lad [duplex mode]. One of several modes in Yavorsky's general theory of the horizontal and vertical organization of pitch in relation to time in music, the theory of modal rhythm. The central factor in the duplex mode is the tritone, whose inherent instability implies two different resolutions to points of greater stability. Both of these resolutions are considered part of the duplex mode, thus uniting the divergent implications into a single organizational system.

funktsional'naia sekventsiia [functional sequence]. A progression in which a chord of dominant structure (i.e., having at least a major third and a minor seventh) resolves by root movement of a fifth to another chord of similar structure. Either of the two chords may be a member of a tritone nucleus. This sequence can be extended, theoretically, and is also used to explain chord progressions (see *bol'shaia engarmonicheskaia sekventsiia* and *malaia sekventsiia*).

iskhodnoi dominant [initial dominant]. Labeled in Dernova's system as DA, the first of the two chords in a tritone nucleus.

lad (*ladovyi*, etc.) [mode (modal, etc.)]. A complex of stable and unstable tones, the unstable ones having tendencies to resolve to certain stable ones in both melodic and harmonic contexts. In contrast to traditional Western concepts of "mode," in which a specific intervallic character or organization around a tonal center is implicit, the Russian *lad* concept is much more general in dealing with functional relationships, such that many learned and folk styles can be accommodated by it. Thus, in translation, in addition to *modal*, it is often necessary to use *tonal, gravitational, polar*, and other related terms to convey the proper sense of the Russian usage to non-Russian musicians.

malaia sekventsiia (tsepnaia sekventsiia, tsepnaia posledovatel'nost') [minor sequence (linked sequence, linked progression)]. The symmetrical overlapping or linking of two tritone-related chord pairs whose roots do not fit in the same whole-tone scale. The result is four chords whose roots are successively a minor third apart; thus, this sequence explains root progressions involving that interval (see *bol'shaia engarmonicheskaia sekventsiia* and *funktsional'naia sekventsiia*).

proizvodnoi dominant [derived dominant]. Labeled in Dernova's system as DB, the second of the two chords in a tritone nucleus.

slozhnyi bas [compound bass]. The lowest two notes (i.e., the bass notes) of a chord which, judging from the musical context, clearly results from the combination of one chord of a tritone nucleus with the root (and perhaps other members) of the other chord of the nucleus. A structure unique to such situations often results: tritone, minor seventh, tritone, in ascending order from the lowest chord tone.

tritonovoe zveno [tritone nucleus]. A pair of dominant-like chords whose roots are a tritone apart (and which, in Dernova's structural model only, are understood to be enharmonically equivalent in pitch content). For each of Skryabin's late works, Dernova assigns a reference tritone nucleus which displays that work's predominant chord structure and fundamental transposition level. The two chords are linked by a bracket in analysis, and are considered equal to each other, based both on their equivalent pitch content and on the tritone characteristics of the duplex mode concept. The term *nucleus* has been used instead of the literal *link* to emphasize the generative nature of the reference chord pair: it is usually the initial and closing pair of chords for a work, and all progressions within the work are explained by using structural models derived from that pair.

v. The symbol used to refer to the thirteenth of a chord, which Dernova consistently calls the added sixth.

w. The symbol used to refer to the minor third above the root of a chord. Generally this note appears in the second chord of a tritone nucleus, the same pitch having appeared as *v* in the first chord of that nucleus.

Boris Asafiev and *Musical Form as a Process*

forma [form]. A shape, operating in time, that is unique to one musical work. Form and content are seen as related manifestations of intonations.

intonatsiia [intonation]. Broadly, any kind of human communication by means of sound. Intonation in music is distinguished from intonation in speech by the use of intervals. *Rhythmic intonation* [ritmo-intonatsiia], as in chant, closely allies pitches and words. True musical intonation, potentially or actually independent of words, is the communicative essence of some musical structure, linking composer and listener through the medium of performance. In a narrow sense it may be an identifiable fragment that coincides with a motive, but it is not a structural unit. It may also be an entire section of a work. An intonation reflects the environment and era that created it, and may also have some value as an image.

intonatsionnaia arka [intonational arch]. Sometimes "sound arch," the answering of intonations at a distance. If an intonation requires additional intonational material to resolve some contrast that has been set up, it can happen after some intervening material, especially in development. Resembles Yavorsky's *connective intonation* [soedinitel'naia intonatsiia].

kant [kant]. A typically Russian genre of choral song that flourished in the eighteenth century. Originally religious, the subject matter expanded to include patriotic and eulogistic texts. Musical materials are direct, with a slow processional rhythm and simple diatonic harmonies.

krizis intonatsii [crisis of intonations]. An era during which the existing body of intonations no longer is perceived as adequately communicative, and a new body enters the musical language. Such a crisis is often related to contemporaneous social or political currents.

melos [melos]. The linear aspect of music. Melody is an instance of *melos*, which includes the "quality and function of melodic formation" (*Musical Form*, Supplement 2).

ritmo-intonatsiia [rhythmic intonation]. See *intonatsiia*.

simfonizm [symphonism]. The symphonic principle of development applied to all music, not just symphonies; the dramatic developmental potential of music.

ton [tone]. "The tension or effort required to express an affect" (*Intonation*, Epilogue). May also be roughly synonymous with tone quality or tonality.

tonnost' [tonation]. The manifestation of tone in some continuity, governed by rhythm and timbre.

The Contributions of Taneev, Catoire, Conus, Garbuzov, Mazel, and Tiulin

diatonicheskaia tertsovaia tsep [diatonic tertian chain]. As used by Mazel, it signifies a movement, either of chords or of tonalities, by diatonic (major or minor) thirds. Mazel used it in reference to the tonal plan of Chopin's Fantasy.

faktur [musical texture]. Tiulin applied this term to the musical sound fabric, analyzed from the viewpoint of melodic and harmonic interactions.

fonizm. Literally, phonism, or, the effect of a chord's sound, depending on its intervallic constitution. A German equivalent would probably be *klang*.

glas. In Odoevsky's usage this term means church mode. However, its meaning is actually more complex. Applied in reference to Russian chant, it means the sum of the diatonic melodic formulas (*popevki*) of small range which together may form a linear series of notes similar to a scale or mode. It is derived from the Old Slavonic word for voice, *golos.*

kharakter samogo zvuchaniia [character of sounding]. Through the use of this concept, Mazel connected elements or themes that were usually considered unrelated, for example, by means of the register, texture, or general thematic motion.

muzykal'no-tvorcheskii volevyi akt [musical creative volitional act]. Conus developed this term, which he used in reference to the formations brought about by the grouping of cells or pulsating waves. It therefore occurs on the lower levels of Conus's hierarchic organization. However, Conus also used this term to refer to the next higher levels, since he lacked sufficient terms for those levels.

naklonenie [mood, or tendency]. Most frequently, this term implies mood—major or minor.

ob'ediniaiushchaia tonal'nost' [unifying tonality]. In Taneev's usage, this term designates the tonality towards which other tonalities aspire or around which other tonalities cluster as chords in a key in their relationship to tonic.

osmoglasie. The system of eight *glasy.*

osobaia funktsional'naia dvuznachnost' [special bifunctional significance]. Used by Mazel in reference to a chord with bifunctionality, it resembles Tiulin's idea of variable function (*peremennaia funktsiia*).

pokrovnyi [integumentary, or covering]. Conus's term for the iambic, thematic material that "covers" the trochaic, skeletal foundation.

pul'sovaia volna [pulsating wave]. Conus formed the term from a combination of the idea of the human pulse with the idea of a wave in physics. Essentially, it is the musical pulse, the steady "beat" of time. Also called the structural (*stroitel'naia*) pulsating wave.

takti vysshego poriadka [measures of higher order]. Conus's term for the higher levels in his hierarchic organization of groupings. "Musical creative volitional acts" may be grouped into "measures of higher order."

Index

Abramsky, Alexander Savvatevich, 153
Academy of Arts (St. Petersburg), 3
Academy of Sciences of the USSR, 221
Acoustics, studies related to: and Garbuzov, 45-46, 51, 52, 314-29; at GIII, 47, 48; at GIMN, 43-44, 45-46; and Odoevsky, 16-17; and Skryabin, music of, 39-40, 41, 314; and Tiulin, 347-48, 352-53
Aesthetics of music, 6, 43, 44, 57, 76 n. 172
Akimov, P.V., 78 n. 188
AK MUZO (Academic subdivision of the musical division of Narkompros): Moscow, 42-43; Leningrad, 42, 73 n. 147
Albrechtsberger, Johann Georg, 7
Aliabev, Alexander Alexandrovich, 5
All-Night Vigil: Old Believer, 92; of Rachmaninoff (op. 37), 97
All-Soviet Scientific Session on Musicology, 58
All-Union Conference on the Theory of Modal Rhythm (1930), 149, 152
Amani, Nikolai Nikolaevich, 269
Amphilokhy, Archimandrite, 106 n. 39
Analogy in correlations (Mazel), 334-35
Anna Ivanovna, Empress, 2
Araja, Francesco, 2
Aranovsky, Mark Genrikhovich, 147
Arapov, Boris Alexandrovich, 53
Arensky, Anton Stepanovich, 15, 27; and Conus, 309; *A Guide to the Study of the Forms of Instrumental and Vocal Music,* 28; *A Short Guide to the Practical Study of Harmony,* 27, 29
Aristov, G., 68 n. 81
Aristoxenus, 242
Arnold, Karl, 5, 6, 61 n. 13
Arnold, Yury Karlovich, 5, 8, 61 n. 13
Arzamanov, Fedor Georgievich, 71 n. 119, 361 n. 7, 363 n. 42
Asafiev, Boris Vladimirovich (pseud. Igor Glebov) 170, 343, 373 n. 203
   compositions, 221: *Altynchech* (opera), 220; *The Flames of Paris* (ballet), 220; *The Fountain of Bakhchisarai* (ballet), 220; *A Prisoner of the Caucasus* (ballet), 220; *Snezhnaia koroleva* [Snow queen] (children's opera), 219; *Zolushka* (children's opera), 222
   contribution to Soviet music theory, 33, 55, 59, 359
   as dean of OTIM, 47, 48
   life of, 218
   literary works, 221: *A Book about Stravinsky,* 219, 222, 224, 247; *Eugene Onegin, Lyric Scenes of Tchaikovsky: An Attempt at Intonational Analysis of Its Style and Dramaturgy,* 220; *Glinka,* 220, 249; *Grieg (1843-1907): Research,* 220; *Ideas and Thoughts,* 221; *Intonation,* 58, 218-23, 225, 247, 248; *Melos* (essays edited by Asafiev and P.P. Suvchinsky), 219; *Musical Form as a Process,* 48, 49, 218-20, 222-25, 235, 247-49; *Symphonic Etudes,* 219, 249
Asioli, Bonifacio, 61 n. 12
Association for Contemporary Music (Moscow), 50
Athos, Mount, 96
Atonality, 46, 76 n. 170, 77 n. 179
Auditory gravitation. *See* Gravitation, auditory
Auditory horizon, 126, 128
Augmented-sixth chord, 9, 10, 11, 20-21, 26, 27, 66 n. 73, 365 n. 72, 375 n. 228
Averbukh, Liya Abramovna, 148, 160
Avraamov, Arseny Mikhailovich, 170, 188; and atonal music, 77 n. 179; and omnitonality in Skryabin's music, 40-41, 314, 371 n. 174; and "Universal System of Tones," 45
Azanchevsky, Mikhail Pavlovich, 15, 63 n. 40
Azbuka, 83, 90, 93, 104 n. 25; of Diletsky, 90; of Metallov, 87, 95-96; of Mezenets, 87, 90; Old Believer, 92. *See* Demestvenny; Znamenny